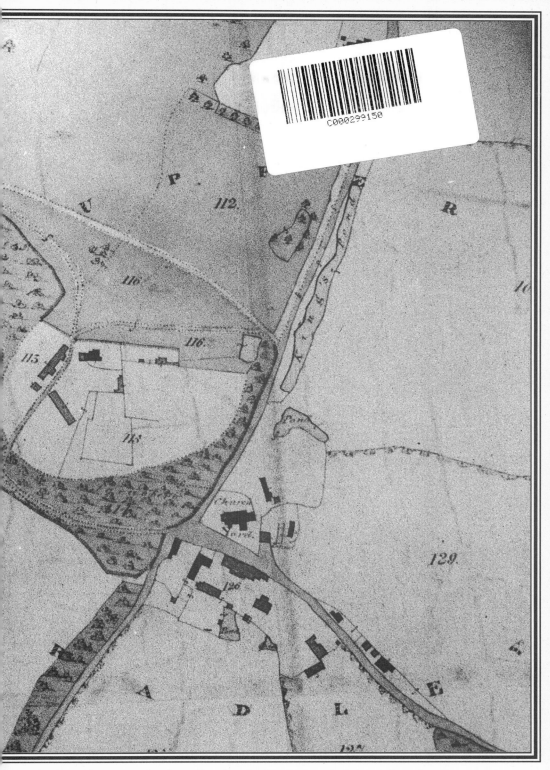

a ha-ha to keep out the deer. Another ha-ha surrounded the park to keep them within its bounds. Lancelot 'Capability' Brown planted the woodlands to conceal the village buildings and the Park Farm (110) from the House.

No Ordinary Place

BY THE SAME AUTHOR

No Ordinary Place

Radley College and the Public School System

CHRISTOPHER
HIBBERT

Christopher Hibbert.

JOHN MURRAY
Albemarle Street, London

Front endpaper: A tithe map of the Radley estate in 1843. The building which was to be used as School is shown to the right of number 113. It was moved to the outbuildings below 117. The house and its grounds were surrounded by a ha-ha to keep out the deer. Another ha-ha surrounded the park to keep them within its bounds. Lancelot 'Capability' Brown planted the woodlands to conceal the village buildings and the Park Farm (110) from the House.

Rear endpaper: Radley College, 1997, by Jeremy Bays.

First published in 1997
by John Murray (Publishers) Ltd.,
50 Albemarle Street, London W1X 4BD

A catalogue record for this book is available from the British Library

ISBN 0-7195-5176-5

Typeset in 11/13 pt Stempel Garamond by
Servis Filmsetting Ltd, Manchester

Printed and bound in Great Britain by
The University Press, Cambridge

Contents

Contents

Illustrations

Illustrations

The author and publishers would like to thank the following for permission
to reproduce illustrations: *colour plates* 1, Tate Gallery, London; 7, David
Rae-Smith (past Chairman of the Council); 8 and 10, Christopher Andrews;
9, Grosvenor Studios; 12, Chris Honeywell; 13, Folio Bookshelving,
Kingston Bagpuize (responsible for the joinery and shelving installation of
the new Library); *black-and-white plates* 37, W.M.M. Milligan; 74 and 76,
Daily Mail; 96, Ian Ellis; 102, Christopher Andrews; *rear endpaper*, Jeremy
Bays.

Acknowledgements

IN 1948 A.K. BOYD, an Old Radleian and a don at Radley for over thirty years, published his centenary history of the school. Authoritative and perceptive, it is one of the best histories of a public school ever written. No book could pretend to take its place and my debt to it is incalculable. This book covers the first hundred years of Radley's history in far less detail than its predecessor, but it has at least had the benefit of various sources which were not available when Boyd's book was written, or which were used discreetly or not at all for fear lest they caused distress or embarrassment to persons then living. It carries the story forward a further fifty years, covering a century and a half from the time of Radley's foundation by that eccentric visionary, William Sewell, and tracing its development from a sparsely populated institution which was not expected to survive to the thriving and respected place it is today.

I was first asked to consider writing the book by my friend, Sir Patrick Nairne, with whom I had been at school here in the 1930s. Throughout the time I have been at work on it he has given me constant help and encouragement as has our mutual friend, Peter Way, who has known Radley intimately as boy, don and Social Tutor under four Wardens. Both he and Pat Nairne have read the book chapter by chapter as it has progressed and have given me much useful advice for its improvement while being in no sense responsible for such views as I have expressed. I am deeply grateful to them both, as I am to Radley's Council who have given me their support throughout.

Several others, Old Radleians, present Radleians, dons, former dons, dons' sons, wives and daughters have read the whole or parts of the book in draft and have likewise made valuable comments, corrections and suggestions. Among these are two Old Radleian friends, Leo Cooper and Tim Rix, both with wide experience in publishing; four members of Radley's Council, David Rae Smith, John Pattisson, Michael Martin and Michael Melluish; six former dons at Radley, Peter Stuart, Simon Langdale, Paul Crowson, James Batten, Christopher Hirst and the late Canon Ronald Lunt, and two present-day dons, Hamish Aird and David Hardy.

I have also greatly profited from lengthy, instructive and revealing conversations with Radley's three most recent Wardens, Wyndham Milligan, Dennis Silk and Richard Morgan, with the widow of their predecessor, Joan Wilkes, and with the widow of John Wilkes's Sub-Warden, Sheila Morgan. Peter Wilkes, Warden Wilkes's son, now Headmaster of Cheltenham, has been good enough to read the chapter dealing with his father's time at Radley.

I have also had useful and interesting conversations with the late Micky Jones, Dennis Silk's Bursar; Anne Raby, daughter of the don, G.T. Hellard, and her husband, Ralph Raby; Dr A.G.S. Bailey; Jeremy Ward; John Scott; Leonard Cooper; Gordon Fergusson; Bill Stretch; Hamish Francis; Sam Phillips; and Maurits Sillem.

I am most grateful, too, in a variety of ways to the Lord Craig of Radley; Jock Mullard, Honorary Secretary of the Radleian Society; Richard Beauchamp, Radley's Bursar; Mary Hutchinson, the Warden's Secretary; E.G. Nugee, QC; Sarah Drummond of the Good Schools Guide Advisory Service; Barry Eastick; Patrick Mullins; Oliver Stutchbury; J.P. Rudman; Barry Webb; David Walden; Richard Hylton-Smith; Richard Blencowe; John Ashby Rolls; David Carr; Liz Arkell; Dr John Rae; Roland Wilcock; Robin Miller; Paula Willcox of the Independent Schools Information Service, and Martin Blake. Hamish Francis has kindly read the proofs.

For supplying me with information about their respective schools and, in several cases, with histories of them I am most grateful to the following archivists: J.B. Lawson, Shrewsbury; A.G. Macpherson, Haileybury; Paul Pollak, the King's School, Canterbury; David Byatt, Gordonstoun; M.A. Clark, Rossall; Alasdair Hawkyard, Harrow; T.H.C. Noon, Blundell's; Ms Karen Garvey, St Edward's; D.R. Young, Christ's Hospital; Ronald Symons, Monkton Combe; Norman Rosser, Malvern; R.L. Bland, Clifton; Peter King, Hurstpierpoint; Christopher Dean, St Paul's; G.C. Houghton, The Leys; D.H. Ford, Oundle; Alan Scadding, Epsom; the Revd F.J. Turner, Stonyhurst; Nicholas Hinde, Felsted; John Plowright, Repton; Mrs M.E. Griffiths,

Sedbergh; M.D.W. Jones, Brighton; D.W.R. Whicker, Canford; R.G. Miller, Bedford; Mrs H.M.H. Given, Glenalmond; Alan Shrimpton, Bryanston; Anselm Cramer OSB, Ampleforth; R. Nigel Argent, Ardingly; R. Custance, Winchester; F.H.G. Percy, Whitgift; Dom Philip Jebb, Downside; J.P. Rudman, Uppingham; Mrs Penelope Hatfield, Eton; Bijan Omrani, Wellington College; M.J. Barrett, Gresham's; and R. MacLean, Rugby.

For help in the same way I am also most grateful to Anthony Hudson, Headmaster of Pangbourne; John A. Chapman, Headmaster of Leighton Park; R.G. Silk, Bursar of Denstone; J.A. Harvey, Assistant Bursar of Ellesmere; Major Shaw McCloghry, Secretary of the Old Bloxhamist Society; R.H. Philp, Director of Studies at Fettes; T.C. Cobb, Registrar of the Old Tonbridgian Society; Mrs H. Murray, Librarian of Dauntsey's; C.G. Wakeham, Membership Secretary of the Bootham Old Scholars' Association; Peter Fielder, Registrar of the Bromsgrovian Club; Mrs A.C. Wheeler, Librarian, Charterhouse; Robert Smith, Marlburian Club Secretary; Mrs Alison Sparks, Librarian, Loretto; Robin Harrison, Secretary, Old Eastbournian Association; Antony Collieu, Director of Studies, Bradfield; Peter Holmes, Westminster; Barbara Gent, Giggleswick; and Anne Archer, Librarian, Bedales.

Friends who have kindly supplied me with information based on their experiences at schools other than Radley include Charles Wentworth-Stanley, R.H. Owen and Robert Clerke (Eton), Roger Bygott and Sir David Spedding (Sherborne), John Gelder (Gresham's), Eric Battersby (Marlborough), Desmond Seward (Ampleforth), Tim Pearce and Ian Mitchell (Uppingham), Francis Sheppard and A.J. Salmon (Bradfield), John Guest (Fettes), Godfrey Whitelock (Sedbergh), Sir Campbell Adamson and Colonel Michael Wilcox (Rugby), Commander G. McC. Rutherford (Oundle) and Desmond Flower (Lancing).

I owe particular debts of gratitude to Charles Wrinch who, since a most illuminating and amusing conversation about Radley in London at the outset of my work, has sent me from his house in Guernsey a series of letters full of interesting, arcane and diverting information; to Sue Brown of the Radleian Society; and to Tony Money, Radley's Archivist and President of the Radleian Society, whose long experience as a don, unrivalled knowledge of the Archives and generous response to my every request have been of inestimable help to me during the five years I have spent upon the book.

Wardens of Radley

R.C. Singleton	1847–1851
W.B. Heathcote	1851–1852
William Sewell	1853–1861
R.W. Norman	1861–1866
William Wood	1866–1870
Charles Martin	1871–1879
R.J. Wilson	1880–1888
H.L. Thompson	1889–1896
Thomas Field	1897–1913
E.G. Selwyn	1913–1918
Adam Fox	1918–1924
W.H. Ferguson	1925–1937
J.C. Vaughan Wilkes	1937–1954
W.M.M. Milligan	1954–1968
D.R.W. Silk	1968–1991
R.M. Morgan	1991–

Part I

Prologue

WHEN THOMAS ARNOLD applied for the headmastership of Rugby in 1827, one of his sponsors, the Provost of Oriel, declared his belief that he would 'change the face of education all through the Public Schools of England'. There could have been no doubt that changes were sorely needed.

Rugby had been founded in 1567 by a rich London grocer as a free school in his native town; but like other schools of similar foundation, its original character had been transformed and, by Arnold's time, its fee-paying pupils came from quite a different background from that of the sons of the Rugby tradesmen whom the philanthropic grocer had intended his grammar school to serve. This was true not only of schools founded by other wealthy merchants, by rich prelates and local worthies, such as Harrow, which was created by a yeoman farmer, John Lyon, in 1571; Winchester, established in 1382 by William of Wykeham, Bishop of Winchester; Repton, founded ten years before Rugby by Sir John Port, grandson of a wealthy Mayor of Chester; Blundell's, the foundation of a clothier of that name in 1604; and Tonbridge, endowed by Sir Andrew Judd, Lord Mayor of London, in 1553. It was true also of those schools endowed by the royal exchequer, among them Eton (1440), Sherborne (1550) and Westminster (1560), and of those schools which were established by, or came under the jurisdiction of, City livery companies, for example Gresham's (the Fishmongers' Company, 1555) and Oundle (the Grocers' Company, 1556).

Instead of opening their doors to poor scholars, mostly from families living nearby, all these schools, and many others like them in the early nineteenth century, were offering a more or less expensive education to boys from upper-class families all over the country and from

3

the families of a rapidly growing and increasingly prosperous middle class whose traditions and mores they enshrined and perpetuated.

In many ways these public schools – so called to distinguish them from schools which were privately owned – had changed little since the seventeenth century. The curriculum was still largely confined to the classics. There were certain schools, among them Christ's Hospital (founded in 1553) and Uppingham (1584), which from an early date instructed boys in a wider variety of subjects, including arithmetic, geometry and even modern languages; but most offered little other than Greek and Latin. This was true even of Shrewsbury, despite the reputation it acquired under its reforming headmaster, Dr Samuel Butler, who at the age of twenty-four inherited a school of less than 20 boys in 1798, increased its numbers to 230 by the time he became Bishop of Lichfield in 1836, and so greatly enhanced its standing that, under his no less remarkable successor, Benjamin Hall Kennedy – the 'greatest classical scholar of the century' – Shrewsbury was to be deemed by the Clarendon Commission, which was set up in 1861 to enquire into the 'great public schools', to be one of them, alongside Eton, Harrow, Westminster, Winchester, Charterhouse, Rugby, Merchant Taylors' and St Paul's.

> Nothing could have been worse for the development of my mind than Dr Butler's school, as it was strictly classical, nothing else being taught except a little ancient geography and history [wrote Charles Darwin] . . . Much attention was paid to knowing by heart the lessons of the previous day; this I could effect with great facility, learning forty or fifty lines of Virgil or Homer whilst I was in morning chapel; but this exercise was utterly useless, for every verse was forgotten in forty-eight hours . . . In my spare time I studied chemistry and as it was an unprecedented fact, I was nicknamed 'Gas'. I was once publicly rebuked by the head-master for thus wasting my time on such useless subjects.

John Sleath, High Master of St Paul's, told a parent in 1837, 'At St Paul's we teach nothing but the classics. If you want your son to learn anything else you must have him taught at home.'

Nor had these schools much changed in their punishments of boys who failed to meet the standards required of them in their classical studies. To be sure, corporal punishment in most of them was not administered as routinely and as brutally as it had been in the days of the Revd John Keate, the small and formidable Headmaster of Eton from 1809 to 1834, who was said to have flogged up to forty boys a day, except on Sunday, and one peculiarly recalcitrant pupil almost every day and on one day twice. A predecessor of Keate's at Eton, John Foster, who was even more severe and far more widely disliked, once 'called up several boys to repeat their Homer . . . and if they missed a word . . . he whipped them . . . He cut one of the boys, who had got his lessons as well as he could, until he was quite raw.' At Rugby, at a rather later date, boys were regularly flogged four or more times a week for 'failing to perform what was beyond their capacity'. And, as late as 1837, life at Repton was 'a reign of terror', in the words of a parson who had been there as a boy of ten at that time.

> Winter and summer we had to be in school by seven o'clock. In the winter the mornings and evenings were dark, and we each had to carry our own bit of candle, which was stuck on the desk in a dab of grease. If we were late it was either a hundred lines or a caning, sometimes a flogging . . . There was hardly a day without some lad being birched, and the system brutalized the school . . . I have seen thirteen boys publicly flogged in one morning.

These savage beatings were far from effective: 'The noise from Keate's classes was continuous and deafening, so that passers-by would stop and listen in wonder,' Jonathan Gathorne-Hardy wrote in *The Public School Phenomenon*. 'Not four months after he had birched the entire lower fifth for loitering on the way into chapel, they had taken instead to yelling at the tops of their voices as they sat down.' Yet beatings were defended as being central to the public school ethos. 'To touch a single twig of the hallowed birch is regarded as a kind of sacrilege,' commented Sir Leslie Stephen, who was at Eton in the 1840s. 'From the moment the accolade has been laid – not across your shoulders – you are a member of a strange order of Chivalry.' It was, indeed, a kind of disgrace not to be beaten.

It was possible, of course, for a backward boy to evade the birch by getting a cleverer one to do his work for him. Many boys progressed up their schools in this way, contriving to escape the attention of over-worked and underpaid masters, some of them extracting work from younger, brighter boys by bullying them into submission. In 1844 Robert Cecil, one day to become Prime Minister as the Marquess of Salisbury, wrote to his father, 'I have been kicked most mercilessly since I saw you last for refusing to do a fellow's theme for him . . . He kicked me and pulled my hair as hard as ever he could for twenty minutes and now I am aching in every joint and hardly able to write this.'

In all public schools bullying, varying in degrees from year to year, from house to house and dormitory to dormitory, was more or less endemic. It was possible to escape bullying by having an exceptional charm of manner, by being amusing or precociously good at games; but it was rarely that a new boy was spared such initiation ceremonies as were handed down in most schools from one generation to the next. At Harrow, for instance, new boys were subjected to the customary tossing in a blanket until they were satisfactorily bruised by knocks against the ceiling; at Rugby they were forced to drink a foul substance which often made them ill for days; at Winchester they were put through the ordeal of 'tin gloves' in which their hands were seared with burning brands of wood, an agonizing experience intended, so it was said, to harden the fingers of fags so that they could grasp the hot handles of frying-pans and coffee-pots when preparing meals for their masters.

Fagging was also endemic. Small boys could be seen constantly running errands and performing menial tasks, acting as hairdressers, barbers, cooks and boot boys for prefects or for any older boys entitled by tradition to call upon, or shout for, their services. At Westminster, a school renowned for the great store it set by scholarship, fags were sent scurrying about even at those times when they were meant to be studying. At Winchester, so it was said, fags fought each other for places round the fire where they could make toast for their masters who sat behind them holding whips. Samuel Rogers related the plight of Lord Holland who was required to make toast with his bare hands: his mother sent him a toasting fork; the fagmaster broke it over his head; and this accounted for Holland's permanently misshapen fingers. There were few schools in which fags were not occasionally to be seen on illicit errands, creeping out to buy liquor and risking a thrashing if caught.

The amount of drinking in public schools was astonishing. Beer was served at meals because water was so impure; but forbidden wines and spirits were consumed in studies and dormitories by the gallon. A Wykehamist recorded in his journal in a far from unusual entry: 'Sat up all night with three other fellows swigging wine ... At four o'clock [we drank] a great bowl of punch.' This was towards the beginning of the century; but T.H. Green, the philosopher, who went to Rugby in 1850, believed he was the only boy in the whole school who did not drink alcohol.

Together with wine and spirits, a large amount of food was consumed in dormitories and elsewhere, since the meals to be had in the dining-halls of nearly all early nineteenth-century public schools were as sparse as they were unpalatable; and boys who plucked up courage to ask for more might well be caned for impertinence. To make up for this lack of proper sustenance, boys gorged themselves on whatever they could buy, or poach, or get their parents to send them from home. All in all, so the *Quarterly Journal of Education* declared in 1837, 'Before an Eton boy is ready for University he may have acquired a confirmed taste for gluttony and drunkenness [as well as] an appetite for brutal sports.'

If the food at public schools in the first half of the nineteenth century was such as might be served in a parish orphanage, the accommodation was little better. A report in 1837 stated that 'the inmates of a workhouse or a gaol are better fed and lodged than the scholars of Eton.' The next year, E.C. Hawtrey, Eton's Headmaster, answered a deputation asking for hot water to be laid on in college with the words, 'You will be wanting gas and turkey carpets next.' Twenty years later two cartloads of rats' bones were excavated from beneath the floorboards of the notorious Long Chamber where over fifty Etonians were shut up for the night and left to their own devices and to such comfort and pleasure as they could find in each others' beds.

In the earlier years of the century there had been occasional riots in which masters had feared for their lives. In 1808 there were violent disturbances at Harrow where senior boys had paraded about with banners declaring 'Liberty and Rebellion' in protest against curtailment of their rights to flog their juniors. Ten years later there had been riots at Winchester which had to be quelled by soldiers with bayonets. At Shrewsbury, the Headmaster, locking himself in his study and bolting the shutters, had felt obliged to request armed protection from the Mayor. After these disturbances at Shrewsbury had subsided, Dr Butler wrote to certain parents asking them not to allow their sons to return to the school in possession of loaded firearms. It was not surprising that William Gladstone, who was sent to Eton at the age of eleven in 1821, later expressed the opinion that to send a boy who was not strong to a public school was 'madness'.*

---

*A similar opinion was expressed earlier by another Old Etonian, Lord Chatham, who had 'scarce observed a boy who was not cowed for life at Eton . . . A public school might suit a boy of turbulent, forward disposition, but would not do where there was any gentleness.'

Yet parents in the 1820s continued to send their sons, weak as well as strong, to public schools. It was pointed out that these schools, despite the limitation of their teaching methods, did produce scholars: Shrewsbury, said Butler, produced more prizemen at Cambridge, in proportion to its numbers, than any other school in England. It was not, however, to turn them into scholars that most parents sent their sons to a public school. It was at least partly so that he could make influential friends, who would be of use to him in his later career, that Gladstone's father, a Liverpool merchant, sent his son to Eton. Also, it was felt that a public school education would transform uncouth boys into gentlemen, instil into them both manners and manliness, and inspire them with those particular virtues which Tom Brown's father hopes will be inspired in Tom: 'Shall I tell him he's sent to [Rugby] to make himself a good scholar?' Mr Brown asks himself. 'Well, but he isn't . . . I don't care a straw for Greek particles or for the digamma, no more than does his mother . . . If he'll only turn out to be a brave, helpful, truth-telling Englishman, and a gentleman, and a Christian, that's all I want.'

And that was all that men like Mr Brown and Thomas Hughes, his creator, a barrister who was himself at Rugby in the 1830s, wanted for their sons. Parents who had been to a public school themselves warmly commended what they perceived as the benefits that such an education provided. Beating had done them no harm. Games were rough, of course, but they trained a boy to withstand the knocks of later life and taught him to value team spirit. Admittedly there was a bit of bullying, but boys had to learn to fend for themselves sooner or later, and a boy who gamely resisted bullying would have learned a valuable lesson. As for fagging, such fathers as these tended to agree with Gladstone that it was 'one of the most salutary parts of the whole system; a fag who was appointed to some upper boy of the same house, from that moment acquires a friend interested in his well-being, willing to guide him in his difficulties and protect him from the aggression of others'. A fag, in short, would learn to gaze in 'manly confidence and fresh fearless self-respect . . . with bold but untrembling look upon men of every rank and condition'. The whole public school system, in fact, was designed to develop the character of boys who were to take their place as gentlemen and leaders of men in the wider world.

Yet as the nineteenth century progressed the critics of the system were becoming ever more vocal and ever more persuasive. As stories of the inadequacies and cruelties of public school life spread about the middle-class world – 'the worst educated middle class in Europe', as they were later to be described – parents were increasingly coming to believe that Fielding, an Old Etonian, had been right to make one of his characters in *The Adventures of Joseph Andrews* declare, 'Public Schools are the nurseries of all vice and immorality.' Perhaps Sydney Smith, a Wykehamist, had not exaggerated unduly when he had said, 'The public school system is an intense system of tyranny of which the English are very fond. They think it fits a boy for the world; but the world, bad as it is, has nothing half so bad.' No doubt Mary Wollstonecraft, who knew some public school masters at first hand, was not far off the mark when she expressed the opinion that there was not perhaps 'in all the Kingdom a more dogmatical or luxurious set of men than the pedantic tyrants who reside in colleges and preside at public schools'.

These and later criticisms of the merits of existing public schools had led to a sharp drop in the numbers attending them, a sharp rise in the numbers of parents who, while they could well afford to do so, did not choose to submit their sons to the rigours of a boarding education. The 2nd Earl Grey, who had himself been to Eton, did not send his son to a public school; nor did Disraeli's father. Ruskin was educated by his mother; Sir Richard Burton was given no formal education at all. Tennyson did not go to a public school; nor did Lord Macaulay; nor the poet, Coventry Patmore, nor the scientist, Lord Armstrong. In Gladstone's fourth Cabinet of seventeen members, only eight were educated at public schools – four at Eton, two at Harrow, one at Cheltenham and one at Rugby. Four were educated privately at home and five went to day schools.

While public schools were shrinking, day schools were prospering and new ones being founded. In London, King's College School opened in 1829, University College School in 1830, and the City of London School was established on new principles in 1837. Liverpool College was founded in 1840; and in Cheltenham – a flourishing spa whose population had risen to 36,000 – a 'Proprietary Grammar School' was established with shares allotted to those 'moving in the circles of gentlemen, no retail trader being under any circumstances admitted'. When this school opened in 1841 there were 120 pupils, a large proportion of them day boys.

While new day schools were opened, boarding schools continued to decline. The numbers at Charterhouse, where there had been 480 boys in 1825, had fallen to scarcely more than a hundred in 1833; Harrow's numbers had dwindled from 350 towards the end of the eighteenth century to 69 in 1844, Eton's from 627 in 1833 to 444 in 1835. The fall at Westminster was even sharper, from a peak of 440 in the eighteenth century to 67 in 1841. At Rugby there had been 381 boys in the earlier days of John Wooll, Thomas Arnold's predecessor. By 1837 there were 123. To this decline, and much else besides, Dr Arnold was expected to turn his attention.

*

At the time of his appointment as Headmaster of Rugby, Arnold was forty-two years old. The son of a collector of customs who had died when he was a child, he had been educated at Winchester and at the age of sixteen had won a scholarship to Corpus Christi College, Oxford. After taking a first-class degree, he had obtained a fellowship at Oriel, and, having taken Holy Orders and married a parson's daughter, he had settled down at Laleham where he had continued his studies and taken private pupils preparing for university entrance. Spare and shortish in stature, with eyes deeply set beneath emphatic eyebrows, his countenance when at rest, according to one of his biographers, had a 'somewhat stern expression, which became formidable when moved to anger, but the effect was all the greater when, in his playful or tender moods, which were frequent with him, his eyes gleamed and his whole face lighted up'.

His decision to become a schoolmaster surprised many of those who knew him, for he made no secret of the fact that he did not like young boys. 'Riotous, insolent and annoying to others', they presented a 'spectacle almost more morally distressing than the shouts and gambols of a set of lunatics'. Moreover, Arnold was not wholly convinced that a public school education was best suited to remove the 'evil' he detected in the very nature of boyhood, though he did believe that 'the trials' of a public school might be 'useful to a boy's character'. At Rugby he did not attempt to lessen these trials: the system of fagging was continued and corporal punishment still administered, sometimes with great severity and once by himself in the heat of fury upon a sickly boy who was believed, mistakenly, to have been lying and who, to repeated cries of 'liar', received eighteen strokes of the rod, incapacitating him for two days. At the same time classics remained supreme in the curriculum, science being regarded as 'only fit for earning a livelihood' and 'of no educational significance as a preparative for power'. Games were still played roughly and with enthusiasm, though the Headmaster evinced no interest in them; while the older boys continued to hold sway over the younger as a separate and privileged élite.

Indeed, it was through his chosen sixth form that Dr Arnold endeavoured to spread his gospel throughout the school, to infect it with his own moral fervour, to elevate it to a sense of what he termed 'moral thoughtfulness'. This sixth form emerged through a system of purging: immoral, incorrigibly lazy or backward boys were required to leave the school, and all boys were watched for symptoms of incipient decay.

Only those boys who came up to the Headmaster's high standards – only those, it might be said, who subscribed to his own views and sense of morality – were permitted to enter the circle of his trust. Those admitted regarded him with an admiration verging on worship: one of them, the poet A.H. Clough, 'would look up into his face with an almost feminine expression of trust and idolatry'. Two others, Arthur Penrhyn Stanley, who was to become Dean of Westminster, and Charles Vaughan, a future headmaster of Harrow, used to nudge each other excitedly when Arnold rose to deliver one of his memorable sermons in the school chapel. Stanley loved Arnold 'to the very verge of all love and admiration'; and it was his *Life and Correspondence of Dr Arnold* that did more than any other work, apart from *Tom Brown's Schooldays*, to perpetuate that admiration in future generations.

Less gifted boys at Rugby, those who could not share their Headmaster's high ideals and strict religious scruples, were less influenced by his fervent spell, less inclined to listen to his sermons with rapt attention. Wary of his evident determination to save their souls as well as to mould their characters, they rebelled against his disconcerting watchfulness. Copies of prayers especially written to be said in Rugby chapel were kicked to pieces about the school's corridors. When funds were solicited for the chapel, buttons and facetious cheques were placed in the offertory. The emotional Headmaster wept with disappointment.

Some of his pupils' parents and several Old Rugbeians shared the feelings of his more rebellious boys. At a Founder's Day dinner in 1835 only ten people turned up when the Headmaster announced his intention of attending it. 'More than a hundred would have attended if it had pleased the autocrat to have remained at home.' It was contended by such critics of Arnold's endeavours that the Rugby of his day was producing far more prigs than the 'Christian gentlemen' of his ideal.

Yet Arnold did succeed in offering an acceptable education for middle-class parents who wanted to give their sons the advantages of a public school education without sending them to a place where the vices of eighteenth-century schools lingered on more persistently than they did at Rugby. They recognized in Arnold a man of vision and probity, a Christian moralist who was in sympathy with the revivalist spirit of the Anglican Church and with their own hopes for the future of nineteenth-century society, a man who shared their fears of social upheaval. He never achieved at Rugby all that his admiring champions have claimed for him, but his greatness lay 'not in what he achieved but in the directions he pointed'.

Certainly from the Rugby over which he presided – and from that of his successors, A.C. Tait, Edward Goulburn and Frederick Temple – Old Rugbeians and assistant masters went forth to other schools to spread, with varying degrees of success and conviction – and with some deviations from the prescribed course – the ideals of their original mentor. They went to Monkton Combe and Felsted; Henry Hart went to Sedbergh; and Henry Walford – who liked it to be supposed that he was 'the Slogger' in *Tom Brown's Schooldays* – went to Lancing. C.J. Vaughan went to Harrow where his highly successful career – during which he raised numbers from 60 to 469 – was suddenly cut short when it came to light that he was having an affair with a boy to whom he had written passionate love letters. G.E.L. Cotton, appointed at Rugby by Arnold at the age of twenty-three, was brought to Marlborough to restore order to the school after a violent rebellion, and did so with the help of various dedicated young masters, several of them, like himself, from Rugby.

Not long after Cotton left Rugby, J.S. Phillpotts, yet another Rugby master, became Headmaster of Bedford where, a notable success, he remained for twenty-eight years.

The tall and domineering John Percival, recommended by Temple as a man in the Arnold tradition, became the first Headmaster of Clifton, a school whose high reputation he established within ten years, though his good work there has been overshadowed by his notoriety as a headmaster who – encouraged to do so, it is said, by his wife – put all the boys in his football teams into trousers, tightened at the calf, lest the sight of their fellow players' knees should arouse impure thoughts.

A.G. Butler, also recommended by Temple, left Rugby to be the first Headmaster of a reconstituted Haileybury which, within five years, had been turned into a first-rate school, its numbers raised from 54 to 360.

Before any of these men had left Rugby – indeed, while Arnold was still Headmaster there – a man who had never been a schoolmaster himself had turned his thoughts to the creation of a school founded on quite different principles from all others.

I

William Sewell
1804–1847

'It seemed as if those eloquent lips could only open to emit godlike sentiments and assert uncompromising principles. In truth they were not often closed.'

WILLIAM SEWELL CAME from a family of some distinction. His father, the son of a Fellow of The Queen's College, Oxford, was a solicitor on the Isle of Wight, Recorder of the Borough of Newport, twice its Mayor and, for a time, Deputy Governor of the island. He and his wife, a parson's daughter, had twelve children, six sons and six daughters, all but one of whom survived into adulthood, three of them into their nineties. No fewer than four of the six brothers and one of the daughters were considered worthy of record in the *Dictionary of National Biography*. The eldest, Richard Clarke Sewell, a Fellow of Magdalen College, Oxford, was a gifted poet and a prolific writer on legal subjects; the youngest, James Edwards, was Warden of New College from 1860 to 1903. The fourth son, Henry, after serving as a partner in his father's firm, sailed for New Zealand where, in 1856, he became its first Premier. Their sister, Elizabeth, was a well-known writer on all manner of subjects, author of devotional and historical works, children's books, novels and short stories, all of an improving nature as became the founder of the Ventnor St Boniface School for girls. William was the second son, born at Newport on 23 January 1804.

He was sent to Winchester where he appears to have been completely happy, although evidently something of a pious outsider, refusing on one occasion to fight another boy who bullied him, declining even to return the bully's first blow. He refused also to take part in a school riot in which other boys hurled paving stones on the masters from the top of the tower, nearly killing one of them. His virtues and talents were eventually rewarded by his being appointed Senior Prefect.

Having gained a postmastership at Merton in 1827, he obtained a first in Literae Humaniores, was elected to a Petreian Fellowship at Exeter* and soon won both the Chancellor's English Essay and Latin Essay Prizes. He was ordained in 1830.

By the time he was thirty, Sewell had become one of the best known and most effective lecturers in Oxford, despite tendencies towards loquacity, excessive discursiveness and personal reminiscence. With his back to the fire, his ancient gown gathered up with his left hand, he would talk with remarkable fluency, though in a 'querulous, invalid voice', rarely glancing at a note. 'In fluency of speech, fertility of mind, fascination of manner, he had no contemporary rival,' wrote the Revd William Tuckwell in his *Oxford Reminiscences*. 'His public teaching like his private talk was ever rousing, persuasive and lofty. It seemed as if those eloquent lips could only open to emit godlike sentiments and assert uncompromising principles. In truth they were not often closed.'

Another of those who attended Sewell's lectures observed that they were nearly always 'very interesting, partly because he wove in whatever he was thinking about, with little regard to the subject of the lecture. Once, when he ought to have been construing the *Georgics*, he spent nearly the whole hour in discussing Newman's "Theory of Development".' Why, yet another of his fascinated if exasperated auditors felt constrained to ask, 'does he call it lectures on Plato, or Butler, and so on, when it is all lectures on Sewell?'

Busy though he was in Oxford, as lecturer, tutor, Examiner in Greats, Librarian of his College in 1837, Sub-Rector in 1835, Dean in 1839, and from 1836 as Whyte's Professor of Moral Philosophy, Sewell found time to write works on Christian morals and Christian politics, on Platonism and the structure of the Greek language, to compose poetry, sermons, commentaries and translations, to write long letters to a succession of correspondents including Gladstone, and to contribute numerous articles to the *Quarterly Review* on subjects as diverse

---

*The name of the Fellowship was derived not from the College's patron saint, St Peter, but from Sir William Petre, Queen Elizabeth I's rich and trusted counsellor, and Exeter's munificent benefactor, whose arms, impaled with those of the College's founder, are above the College gate.

as Gothic architecture and Thomas Carlyle, Irish peasants and seven-teenth-century divines. He also found time to make frequent visits to the Isle of Wight to see his family and to attend to such duties as were incumbent upon his tenure of the curacy of St Nicholas in Carisbrooke Castle.

While on these visits he often stayed with the hospitable architect, John Nash, at his country house, East Cowes Castle, where he met Nash's niece, to whom he became engaged. The engagement was, however, broken off, the reason, according to his sister Elizabeth, being that his parents disapproved of the match on the grounds that it would put a stop to his university career, since Fellows of Colleges had to be bachelors. In his unpublished 'Reminiscences', however, Sewell himself gave a different and highly ambiguous reason:

> Circumstances which I am bound not to reveal made me acquainted sub-sequently with facts which left not a shadow of doubt on my mind then, nor on my mind now after so many years have passed, that it was a clear indisputable duty to break off the engagement, were it only for the sake of that person whose happiness I was bound to consult, and to break it off without leaving any opening for a renewal of the idea . . . The breaking off of that engagement broke off, or rather prohibited, all future ones.

A young scholar of Exeter College, who was to become Professor of Modern History at King's College, London, wrote of Sewell at this time that, although he was a man of 'genuine religious feeling, a man respected as one who fasted and prayed and whose fortune and intel-lect were unreservedly at the service of religion', although he was pos-sessed of 'real rhetorical and dialectical talent', he had 'never really mastered any single branch of learning'. This scholar went on to say that 'there was also a certain taint of insincerity about him [Tuckwell refers to his 'taint of superficiality'] . . . His manner, which was intended to be winning, was too effusive and caressing for the average undergraduate.' Moreover, Sewell was tiresomely possessed of 'a supreme belief in himself'. He was known as 'Suillus' (swine) which 'although a play on his name', as George Orwell observed in a review of his biography in the *Observer*, 'hardly suggests esteem or affection'. It was added that he had no sense of humour, a comment, it must be said, belied by some of his private letters, which, allowing for their facetiousness, are often genuinely funny and pleasantly playful.

Yet whatever reservations were expressed about his character and manners, no one doubted the depth of Sewell's religious feeling, the sincerity of his interest in the Oxford Movement, that influential body of opinion which rejected the Protestant element in Anglicanism in favour of the Catholic as it existed before the Reformation and which denied the right of Parliament to oversee the affairs of the Church. These views were being formulated in the University in these years by the so-called Tractarians, among them John Keble, E.B. Pusey, J.H. Newman and R.H. Froude, with all of whom Sewell was on terms of friendship, despite occasional disagreements which led Newman to describe him as 'very unreal' and to comment that he had 'a word ready for anything'. Although he himself would never have denied his High Anglicanism and always insisted upon the virtues of abstinence and fasting, he condemned the use of vestments and the practice of confession, had an obsessive mistrust of Jesuits and deeply deplored Newman's conversion to Rome. His novel *Hawkstone* was to contain a bitter attack on Roman Catholicism. In the end he felt obliged to sever his connection with the Tractarians, though not his friendships with them.

Devoted as he was to the Anglican Church, concerned as he was for its revival, and conscious of how religious guidance had been wholly lacking at Winchester, it was not long before Sewell turned his thoughts to the foundation of a school in which the Prayer Book and the Chapel would be the supreme inspirations. The longer he considered the idea, the clearer his view became of the kind of school he had in mind. Most public schools, he believed, were too big, too ugly, too detached from the outside world, too bound to the exigencies of a narrow curriculum. Ideally boys should be brought up in the atmosphere of a pleasant country house, surrounded by beautiful things; they should be taught by masters who were not merely concerned with their schooling, but deeply interested in their welfare as though in a family. They should be allowed the privacy of cubicles, not thrown into the rowdiness, roughness and vice of dormitories.* He

---

*By the end of the century cubicles had become quite common in public schools. Eton had long had them. After seeing them on a visit to Edward Thring's Uppingham, John Mitchinson had them installed in the dormitories at the King's School, Canterbury; and at the suggestion of the Prince Consort dormitories at Wellington were from the beginning divided into cubicles. So were they at Charterhouse – known there as 'cubes' – when the school moved to Godalming. In the building known as Gownboys at the London Charterhouse boys had been obliged to sleep two in a bed up till 1805.

wished, he said, to make them 'Christian gentlemen and Christian scholars, not by an artificial hothouse system of superintendence . . . but by the tone and atmosphere in which they lived, as in the bosom of one large Christian family, surrounded by the best society and provided with all that is needed to strengthen and enlarge and purify their minds'.

Although he believed he could achieve these aims only by founding a new school rather than attempting to reform an old one, he applied for the Headmastership of Winchester in 1835. Beaten by Dr Moberly by one vote, he claimed afterwards to have been thankful when he failed: he could now concentrate on founding a new school untrammelled by ancient traditions and the sitting tenants of a hidebound common room.

*

His first attempt to establish such a school was made in Ireland. At the invitation of Lord Adare, son of the Earl of Dunraven and Member of Parliament for Glamorganshire, Sewell made a tour all over the island in the summer of 1840 and returned to Oxford fired with enthusiasm for the founding of a school there, 'a Winchester and Eton, and something more than Winchester or Eton', which would save Ireland from the domination of Roman Catholicism and put new life into the decaying Irish Church.

He was encouraged in his endeavours not only by Lord Adare but also by two other Irishmen both, like Adare, concerned about the state of the Irish Church and sympathetic to the ideas of the Tractarians. These two men were William Monsell, later Lord Emly, Adare's brother-in-law, and Dr J.H. Todd, a Fellow of Trinity College, Dublin, soon to become Regius Professor of Hebrew. The rich Archbishop of Armagh, Lord George de la Poer Beresford, agreed to be Governor of the proposed school, and the Revd Nugent Wade, Rector of St Anne's, Westminster, took it upon himself to join the London committee and later to serve as a member of the governing council. The headmaster of the school was to be an Irish clergyman, Robert Corbet Singleton, a bachelor in his early thirties who had been at school in Dublin and had taken his degree at Trinity College. A teacher of mathematics, who combined a love of music with a sound knowledge of Latin, Singleton was a quietly imposing figure whose pleasant features were given a somewhat inquisitorial cast by the strong lenses of a pair of small pince-nez. He and Sewell, who recognized his qualities and knew him to be a man of substantial private means, were at this time on the best of terms.

Sewell himself was indefatigable in his efforts to make his proposed venture a reality, writing innumerable letters soliciting funds, using his left hand when his right ached so much he could no longer use it, travelling about Ireland with Monsell and Todd in search of a suitable property. In the end he found Stackallan, a country house in County Meath which was rented from Lord Boyne.

All the while on his travels he was planning the constitution of the school. It was to be a college rather than an ordinary school with a Warden and Fellows who were to act *in loco parentis*, undertaking their duties as fathers or elder brothers would in a family, for love of the undertaking rather than for financial gain. They were to share the same modest fare as the boys, whose table manners and neat, clean appearance they were to ensure were those of young gentlemen. They were not be indulged with wine. The whole life of the College was to revolve around its Chapel where, in accordance with the Book of Common Prayer, the full choral services of Matins and Evensong were to be celebrated daily. The feasts of the Church were to be observed by the whole school and fasts by Warden and Fellows. Religious teaching was to be given a special importance in the curriculum; so was music which was to be under the direction of Edwin George Monk, a kind and sensitive man in his early twenties who had been organist in his home town of Frome.

Classics were to be taught, of course, but not to the exclusion of other subjects. Modern languages and modern history as well as mathematics were to be found places in the curriculum; so were science, drawing, including architecture, and the Irish language. When the school's numbers reached a reasonable size, then games would doubtless be played; but at the start there would be fencing lessons, rowing on the nearby River Boyne, and garden plots in the grounds. There would be expeditions into the surrounding countryside and picnics and boating parties.

The school, the College of St Columba, named in honour of the sixth-century Irish saint, opened on 1 August 1843; and at first all seemed to go as well as Sewell had hoped, even though by the end of the first term there were no more than seven boys. The numbers slowly rose, however; seven Fellows were appointed; so was a Dame, Mrs Burky, 'a stout, comely, good-natured, open-handed, open-hearted Irishwoman'; so were 'five little naked Irish boys', who were provided with 'little dresses of coarse dark grey cloth' and employed as servitors.*

Yet, although Sewell provided an almost idyllic account of the school in his *Journal of a Residence at the College of St Columba* published in 1847, there were difficulties from the beginning: debts mounted, eventually reaching £25,000, despite generous donations from the Visitor and the Warden who did all he could to keep expenses down and spent all his private income of about £500 a year on the College. Before long all the Governors resigned; and both Lord Adare and William Monsell were received into the Roman Catholic Church. Most critical of all, there were irreconcilable differences of opinion as to the College's strict rules of fasting. Some of the Fellows wished to be allowed to use their own discretion in the matter. They were supported in this by the Visitor. But Singleton, encouraged by Sewell, stood firm: there could be no relaxation of the rules. In the end, in May 1846, Singleton, 'always obstinate in small matters', felt compelled to resign as Warden.

*

Sewell, however, refused to consider the experiment a failure. Indeed, he protested that it had shown him that his educational theories could be put successfully into practice, and had encouraged him in his long-held belief that schools established on St Columba's principles could and should be founded in England. And so, on 5 March 1847, he and Singleton, Nugent Wade and Monk – who had resigned from St Columba's with Singleton – met in a room in Turl Street, Oxford, to discuss the foundation of the first of these proposed schools.

They were agreed as to the essential elements of this English St Columba's. Like that College it was to have

a Chapel, an Organ, a Bell, a Library, a Common Room, a Warden and six or seven Fellows . . . Fasts and Feasts were to be visibly observed – the

---

*Among the pupils at St Columba's were the two sons of the novelist, Anthony Trollope, who was then working in Ireland in the Post Office. Trollope himself had been at Harrow, then at Winchester, then at Harrow again. He had been unhappy and bullied at both schools, and had no wish to send his sons to either; and, when they left St Columba's under a cloud, he chose to send them to Bradfield, a school for 'the careful education of boys as loving children of the Church of England', rather than to Radley which was appreciably more expensive.

whole College was to wear a proper academical dress – the Fellows to dine in Hall, and to take their meals also at the same time as the students. The diet of the whole body was to be gentlemanly but not luxurious – the furniture of the table to be dignified but the fare simple.

Also as at Stackallan the Warden and Fellows were to be content with the most modest remuneration, £200 for the one, £100 for the others. Fees for the boys were to be set at £100 a year,* but every tenth boy was to be accepted free of charge.

One of the principal faults in existing public schools was the inadequacy of the number of masters in relation to the numbers of boys: at Charterhouse in the time of John Russell, Headmaster from 1811 to 1832, there were only eight masters for 430 boys; at Eton in 1833 the ratio in the Upper School was nine to 570; and at Rugby, as late as 1848, there were twelve assistant masters for 490 boys. At Radley, Sewell insisted, the proportion of masters to boys must be considerably higher than this.

Harshly as Sewell criticized the existing public school system, he acknowledged its success: 'It has sent out into the Legislature, into the Army, into the Professions, into the House of Commons, into political life, into the magistracy, into society generally, English boys with English minds, toned and trained to work with the machinery of the British Empire . . . Our best men have been Public School men.' Believing this, he was anxious to perpetuate in his new school what was best in the older foundations. He insisted for instance that, while the school was to be 'a handsome place', it was not to be an indulgent one. There was educational value in the endurance of hardship. His boys would have to get accustomed to cold baths; they must learn to bear pain, for without the endurance of pain they could not expect to become men.

His school, Sewell also insisted, would not adopt the almost universal system of division into houses which would break up its unity. Instead seven boys would come under the care of a particular Fellow

---

*These fees were higher than those charged at most other public schools at this time. Cheltenham's fees were only £35 a year, Lancing's £40, Marlborough's 50 guineas rising to £70 in 1860, Bradfield's 60 guineas. Bedales charged no more than £90 a year when it opened, years later, in 1893. Stonyhurst was still charging only £65 in 1918, Uppingham no more than £110 in the 1880s, Rugby £118 in 1901 and Shrewsbury £117 in 1916. Radley's fees were raised to £117 in the 1860s.

in a way which was later to develop into the system of Socials. The school would, however, adopt the traditional practice of appointing Prefects, since 'governing the school through the school [was] everything. It was one of Arnold's strong points.' Sewell's 'first principle', then, was to be very careful in choosing Prefects, in selecting boys 'most fit to exert a good influence': not necessarily good athletes or good scholars but boys of good character, the office of Senior Prefect in particular requiring 'a thorough gentleman'.

But this was to look far into the future. There were other more immediate requirements than a Senior Prefect. The most pressing of these was a building to house the boys over whom the Senior Prefect was to preside.

2

Radley Hall
1847

'It stands in a park surrounded by trees, some of which are quite magnificent.'

I N HIS JOURNAL Singleton set out their requirements: the house was to be near a main line railway, not too far from London and convenient for a market town, yet thoroughly in the country and in 'interesting country'. It was to be a 'handsome place', if possible with fine trees and near a river. For months past Sewell had been looking for such a place without success. 'One place was too much out of the way, another too expensive, a third not large enough, a fourth not interesting enough; – here, a house that would only be let for a short term, – there, one that would be sold but in too dilapidated a condition to make purchase more than a foolish venture.'

Numerous houses were considered by him and by Singleton before they heard of Radley Hall, a property '4 or 5 miles from Oxford, and 2 from Abingdon'. The manor had formerly belonged to Abingdon Abbey and, after the Dissolution of the Monasteries, had been granted to Thomas, Lord Seymour of Sudeley by King Henry VIII. It had later come into the hands of the Stonhouse family, and it was in the 1720s that Sir John Stonhouse built Radley Hall, and in the 1770s that the eighth baronet, Sir William Stonhouse, employed Lancelot 'Capability' Brown to lay out the grounds whose enduring beauty has contributed so much to the atmosphere and ethos of the College. Sir John's daughter married Sir William Bowyer, whose son, Admiral Sir

George Bowyer, inherited the estate in 1794 five years after the Hall had been sketched by the fourteen-year-old J.M.W. Turner.

The Admiral's son, having dissipated the family's fortune on misguided business ventures, went to live abroad, leaving the house, by then bereft of its contents, in the care of his eldest son, George. For a time the building had been used as a private school, the Radley House Seminary, the fees at which for 'Parlour Boarders' were 60 guineas per annum, 'single beds being provided for all without additional charge'. This school had not long survived; and when Radley Hall was brought to Sewell's notice it had been empty for some time and the garden was a wilderness. It had been considered and rejected by the Duke of Wellington during his long search for a country estate which had resulted in his purchase of Stratfield Saye.

Sewell and Singleton, accompanied by Monk, first went to see the property on 8 March 1847, and, despite the state of the garden, were most favourably impressed:

> It is a very large, well-proportioned structure [Singleton recorded in his journal] with a great deal of cutstones about it . . . It stands in a park, surrounded by trees, some of which are quite magnificent . . . The Thames is within a mile of it . . . The accommodation in the house is very considerable, presenting abundant room for Warden, Fellows, servants and 30 boys . . . We are particularly struck by . . . a fine expanse of level sward in the front of the house where boys could play cricket or anything else they fancied to great advantage . . . [Radley itself] is a pretty, modest, little village with a rural and retired air [and] a very picturesque Parish Church, partly mantled with ivy.

Unfortunately, there was 'nothing which could be made available for School room, Hall or Chapel'. Nor were there any outhouses, apart from some 'very dilapidated buildings, and a ruinous Barn at some distance'. Moreover, there was another problem to consider: the 'very grave question' of being so near Oxford and the consequent danger that the proposed collegiate form of the school, and the titles of Warden and Fellows, would arouse jealousy and hostility in certain senior common rooms of the University. There was also the likelihood that the school would be oppressed by curious and disruptive visitors.

Sewell, with characteristic optimism, insisted that these were trivial objections. On the contrary, so he asserted, 'there was a very important body of persons within the University who would hail the effort with joy, and would be delighted to be furnished with a visible proof that persons could be got to live together under rule, without luxury or more than very moderate remuneration for labour – and yet be happy'. As to their being besieged by visitors, Sewell said there was no need to 'apprehend any serious embarrassment in that way, for that the distance of Radley from Oxford was beyond an ordinary walk'. Indeed, it was 'of great consequence that we *should* be visited,' he said,

> in order that we might be known . . . There was no place in England where we should be more likely to get boys than in this neighbourhood. Numbers of persons, who are constantly consulted by parents about a desirable school for their children, would be within reach of us, – and the undergraduates, hearing of our fame, would be sure to take home the most flattering accounts, and thus we should soon be stocked with students . . . Moreover no position could be more favourable for our getting suitable persons for Fellows – in fact, we had only to choose instead of to search.

Infected by Sewell's enthusiasm, the three men returned to Oxford in excited mood, Singleton going so far as to say that if Sewell could raise £4,000 or £5,000, and guarantee boys enough to pay the first year's expenses, he himself was willing to risk 'a few thousands' of his own money. Nothing was said about the collapse of the previous school at Radley. Nor, apparently, was reference made to the story that the house was haunted by the ghost of the one-legged Admiral Sir George Bowyer which could be heard on occasions clumping up the stairs, nor to the legend that the place had been cursed by the man who had given it to the monks of Abingdon Abbey from whom it had been sequestrated.* There was, however, a more tangible difficulty which had to be faced: the terms upon which Radley Hall might be secured.

Sewell had originally been led to believe that Mr Bowyer was unwilling to lease it for more than a very short period. Their hopes of

---

*The Revd Thomas Stevens, the excessively superstitious founder of Bradfield College, was to attribute Radley's early difficulties to this curse. Radley would have to move, he asserted, because it occupied 'land of robbery from the Abbey of Abingdon'. When the Revd Stephen Poyntz Denning applied for the headmastership of Bradfield, Stevens opened his letter before those of the other applicants and was said to have announced, 'This is an omen. Stephen Poyntz Denning. Stevens appoints Denning.' He then threw the rest of the letters away unread. 'This is doubtless apocryphal,' wrote Bradfield's historian, John Blackie, 'but it is not entirely out of character.'

obtaining a longer lease had, however, been raised by Bowyer's brother – 'oddly enough' encountered at the house peering through one of the windows – who suggested that a 21-year lease might be entertained. Encouraged by this, Sewell wrote to the elder Bowyer proposing such a lease 'with power of renewal'. To this Bowyer would not agree; it was 'out of the question'; it was tantamount to 'an entire alienation of the house'. On the other hand, he would not charge much rent; 'he thought more about a good tenant than emolument'. So Sewell consented to a 21-year lease without option of renewal in the sanguine expectation of 'realizing such profits in the meantime as would suffice to build a college from the ground on another, more permanent site'.

Over the next few weeks, Singleton and Sewell set to work with a will, talking to architects and builders, making enquiries about the cost of temporary wooden buildings, of terracotta roofs and mullioned windows, and of a chapel to be built of brick. On one occasion when the two men went over to Radley, they found that the man at the gate had gone to Abingdon market, taking the keys of the house with him; and they had to make use of a ladder and 'other burglarious expedients' to effect an entry. It was a nasty, blustery day in early April: the wind was strong and cold, the windows rattled in their frames, the doors banged on their hinges and gusts of cold air swept down the corridors. Singleton could only hope that the house and the elements were expressing a desire for a tenancy and not a hatred of it. He noticed there were numerous crows; but, since they appeared on all sides, he trusted the omens were not bad.

3

Bills of Account

1847

'All these things will tell wonderfully . . . in giving dignity to the College.'

SEWELL SEEMED TO entertain no forebodings, brushing aside all difficulties, all counsels of caution. 'He has the happy habit of annihilating time, space & distance,' Singleton said of him. 'He turns difficulty into facility, and disappointments into certain assurance of what one wants.' Casting one man, a partner in Gosling's Bank well known for his interest in church causes, in the role of benefactor, he already saw £3,000 in the College purse; approaching another he had every hope of a munificent bequest. He felt confident of the generosity of Mrs Sheppard, the rich sister of the old President of Magdalen College, Martin Routh, who was to die in office with his mental capacities unimpaired in his hundredth year. He felt sure, too, that he would get help from that great philanthropist, Angela Burdett-Coutts, who had promptly answered a request for a contribution to St Columba's with a cheque for £500 and an invitation to a party.

Sewell already had some experience in begging. In his 'Reminiscences' he recorded how he and Singleton had driven up the Strand one day in a cab, calling at banks and bearding Henry Hoare, whose wife, Lady Mary, he had had to dine with him at Exeter College. He walked in boldly, 'told Hoare at once that he might send if he liked for a policeman, for we were come to beg; but he received us very kindly and gave us ten pounds'.

*

Despite his boldness, Sewell was never as successful in raising money as his contemporary, the Revd Nathaniel Woodard, whose pamphlet, 'Public Schools for the Middle Classes', set out his plans for educating these classes in new public schools offering Church of England teaching at a comparatively modest cost. These schools were to be of three grades, 'the first for the sons of clergymen and other gentlemen; the second for the sons of substantial tradesmen, farmers, clerks and others of similar situation; and the third for sons of petty shopkeepers, skilled mechanics, and other persons of very small means . . . The charges in all the schools shall be on as modest a scale as the means of the Woodard Society will allow.'

Although his High Church tendencies and his advocacy of the confessional aroused strong opposition in some quarters, Woodard was remarkably successful and resolutely determined. When he planned to have an exceptionally large and fine Gothic Revival chapel at Lancing, the first of his schools, his architect objected to the size on the grounds that the subsoil would not stand it. 'I did not ask you if you *could* build a chapel there,' Woodard answered sharply, 'I told you to build it.' An objection by the Chancellor of the diocese that the altar in the chapel's crypt was not 'moveable', met with the retort, 'Twelve horses brought it in, and twelve horses could take it out.' 'Everybody thinks that it is no use opposing me,' wrote Woodard. 'Even the Earl of Chichester, a Whig and an inveterate Low Churchman, told me that I must succeed.'

He succeeded triumphantly. Indefatigable in raising money for these foundations, he solicited funds at luncheons and dinners, at garden parties and public meetings all over the country. At a luncheon and garden party held to celebrate the opening of Denstone he came away with gifts to the value of over £5,000; another luncheon, given in Manchester for 200 people, raised £20,000. After yet another luncheon he informed the wealthy guests that they would not be allowed to leave the room until they had subscribed £10,000 between them. It was all done with a combination of outrageous importunity, sly persuasion and appealing charm. Lord Halifax once told him, 'It is a privilege to receive a begging letter from you.'

*

As a money raiser Sewell could not pretend to be in Woodard's class. It was some time before he received his first cheque specifically for Radley. This was for £20 from a Captain Beaufort. It was Radley's 'first visible, tangible property' and as such Singleton begged leave to set his eyes on it. Sewell readily obliged and 'to say the truth [Singleton] did not detect any reluctance in Sewell to pull it out of his pocket'. But of the much larger sums which Sewell predicted were on their way, there was as yet no sign. Miss Burdett-Coutts wrote 'very kindly' to say how glad she was to hear of 'any scheme for the good of the Church', 'that the design laid before her seemed a most important one'; but because of her other commitments, 'she could not speak about the money part of it' just for the moment. Mr Sharpe of Gosling's Bank eventually agreed to make a contribution to the proposed school; but the sum offered was £300 rather than the £3,000 which Sewell had been so blithely expecting.

Clearly inspired by the apparently unfailing confidence of Sewell – who 'had no doubts that funds would come' – Singleton recorded on 14 April 1847: 'Upon the whole, I felt a stronger feeling than ever this evening that we shall have a College.' He wrote to his brother in Ireland to warn him that he would be sending for money to further his plans; and, although the brother advised caution and he himself recognized it as 'a bold step', he was 'determined to spend' £1,000 on 'a magnificent Organ'. A month later, without any strong reason for such peace of mind, he professed that he had 'ceased to be uneasy about funds, having several openings through which, please God, money will come in'.

Sewell in the meantime was laying out far more than Singleton's £1,000 for an organ. He was buying and ordering all kinds of expensive objects and furniture, though he had as yet no means of covering the cost. One day at Exeter College, Singleton was shown a fine specimen of carved oak cornice which, Sewell had decided, would look very well in the dining-hall, 'tho' not rich enough for the Canopies in the chapel'. Another day, on a visit to London, Sewell was sorely tempted by a fifteenth-century manuscript which had 'belonged to Bishop Heber who gave £200 for it'. Stained glass was bought in Wardour Street, seven 'magnificent old chairs' in Bristol; from Gloucester came 'several bosses & corbels, and other things of that kind, obtained from old churches which had been furnished with new fittings'; from Stoke-on-Trent came 'delft and china made for us, with our own device' by Minton.

Enquiries were made about surplus oak fittings at Merton College; lengths of serge of 'an excellent make' and 'somewhat expensive' were acquired at Herbert's, the upholsterers. Carpets were ordered as well as beds and bed coverings and bedroom furniture, though a line was drawn against 'a Turret Clock' by Vulliamy at £235; but even so it was decided to build the turret anyway so that the clock could be 'admitted hereafter if funds come'. Chairs, which had once graced the Prince Regent's rooms at Carlton House, came to Radley with two bronze doors from Florence, a Turkey carpet, sixty yards of magnificent brocade from the Queen of Portugal's chapel at Belém, a cashmere carpet from Tibet, stained glass from Cologne, 'a fine painting of Ignatius Loyola which had been purchased at Cardinal Fisch's [Fesch's] sale'. These were followed by 'sixteen old panels, exquisitely carved with Scripture devices' (price £140), 'a magnificent Grace-cup, beautiful in shape and chasing . . . and an excellent Salver for the Grand Inkstand'.

For his own part, Singleton was very pleased when he purchased for £10 'a very large assortment of prints and drawings from Walter's little print shop in Oriel Lane'. 'Some of them appeared very valuable,' he wrote, 'including a few of Paranese's [Piranesi's] views of Roman remains, and a great many etchings and coloured drawings by the Old Masters, very fine indeed.' 'Knowing it to be of great consequence that the boys should have access to sterling works of art, either for copies, or simply as objects to look at', he 'felt no difficulty in laying out this sum'.

> We are going to get portraits of great and good men . . . to hang up in our hall [Singleton added in his journal]. This would not only give it a character, but teach by the eye the value of high principles. Sewell also says he will get casts to place about the room which is to be the prefects' study. He has also got prints of the twelve Caesars which are neatly framed and glazed, and these are to hang around the walls.

A few days earlier Singleton had bought a 'magnificent proof of Chalon's picture of the Queen in her robes . . . Also Strange's print of Charles 1st . . . and its match, Henrietta Maria and her children . . . Also another print of Charles . . . All these will give a loyal air to my sitting room, & help to teach the boys to honour the crown, and to pay especial reverence to it when worn by a martyr.' He intended that, while his bedroom should be very simple with a bedstead of iron, 'no curtains, bed furniture, no carpets', his sitting-room should be 'very handsome', and so, in addition to carpets and other furnishings, he purchased for it 'a very finely carved cabinet'.

Sewell was still equally busy, buying 'some quaint old plate including a beautiful wine cup'. To this were added four stands for holding candelabra made of old oak, 'very well carved and costing £5 apiece',

> seven portraits of Edward 6th, the two Marys, etc., a beautiful sketch of the Duke of Marlborough on a prancing horse . . . also four magnificent Crayon drawings of Bassano, Rembrandt, Van Dyck, & Guido . . . seven historical pictures & four very fine portraits of great masters – together with silvered sconces, a very fine wrought-iron chest . . . and a magnificent piece of carved work, representing passages in the life of our Lord. This [altarpiece] was very costly, the sum asked being £140 but put into perfect repair £190.

Singleton comforted himself with the thought that 'all these things will tell wonderfully, not only in giving dignity to the College, but also in exciting the tastes of its members and Alumni'.

4

The First Radleians

1847

'Every day they were to sit down to dinner as if they were at their father's table.'

UNFORTUNATELY RADLEY'S FUTURE alumni were being extremely slow in presenting themselves. Several people had expressed interest in the school, but no parents had come forward with a definite proposal to place a son there, although a letter had been received from Lord Charles Thynne to say that he had been told about Radley by Lady John Thynne and wanted to know more about the project, since he had 'a boy of 9 years old, for whom he was anxious to find a suitable school'. Sewell was naturally delighted by this, for not only was Lady John Thynne's husband the third son of the Marquess of Bath, he was also Canon and Sub-Dean of Westminster. What better recommendation could there be? And how fortunate would it be if Radley's first boy was a scion of so distinguished a family? Singleton, too, had high hopes of this connection, noting in his journal, 'The prestige of our first boy coming of titled people is not to be despised.'

Three weeks after this encouraging letter from Lord Charles Thynne was received, however, Sewell called at Singleton's lodgings in New College Lane, produced a letter from his pocket and told him to be 'prepared for the worst blow we have had yet'. After due consideration Miss Burdett-Coutts had come to the conclusion that 'her duty to the Bank' prevented her from advancing any money for the establishment of the college at Radley.

Hard as this blow was, both Sewell and Singleton were soon pro-
fessing themselves not at all cast down. Admittedly they might, *'for the
present'*, have to delay building the proposed hall, schoolroom and
dormitory, but the chapel could go ahead as planned though without
the projected apse; and by degrees, Singleton wrote, 'as students come
in, we hope, please God, to proceed with the other buildings. Next
year Miss Coutts may be more at liberty. It really is rather a comfort
to meet with checks. If all went smoothly, we might become alarmed
for the cause, as it seems to be a law that great works are never accomplished without great difficulties.'

As soon as they had £6,000, Sewell said, they could open the school,
although he had more sensibly aimed to raise £20,000 for St
Columba's, and Gladstone, in 1840, had considered £25,000 as a
minimum sum for the establishment of the 'college for Scotch
Episcopalians' which was opened as Glenalmond in 1846.*

In 1853 a far larger sum than this was considered necessary for the
establishment of Wellington, a school originally intended as a charitable institution for the orphans of army officers. The Governors, of
whom Prince Albert was President, announced that over £100,000 had
been raised by subscription but decided that a further £50,000 for a
building fund would have to be sought from the Government.

While waiting for their extraordinarily modest £6,000 to come in, the
two would-be founders of Radley continued with their preparations to
receive boys at the school. Singleton and Monk began choosing young
boys as both servitors and choristers. These boys were to be given a
religious as well as a choral training, taught to be servants, and to do
housemaid's work so as 'to diminish the number of female inmates as
much as possible'. They were at first to be given nothing but lodging,
food and a uniform of a 'coat of coarse Oxford grey cloth, extending
nearly to the knees and confined to the waist by a leather strap'. They

---

*Gladstone had intended Glenalmond 'partly for training the clergy, partly for
affording an education to the children of the gentry and others who now go to
presbyterian schools or who are tended at home by presbyterian tutors'. Sir Ninian
Comper, the church architect, was sent there by his father, the Revd John Comper,
one of the leaders of the Anglo-Catholic revival in Scotland. By the time Sir Ninian's
sons had come of public school age, Glenalmond had become a school of social
cachet. Sir Ninian's observation to the Headmaster, Anthony Barnes, 'We've always
called Glenalmond the Eton of the North', was met with the response, 'Yes – and
we've always called Eton the Glenalmond of the South.'

were, Singleton hoped, to be turned into 'nice boys and afterwards valuable members of a class which sadly requires improvement'.

While Singleton was choosing six boys as servitors, Sewell went to Exeter College to copy out such of the College's statutes as he thought would be suitable for Radley. He then approached the energetic and ingratiating Samuel Wilberforce who had been appointed Bishop of Oxford in October 1845 and who was to prove a good friend to Radley. Wilberforce agreed to become Visitor provided he approved of the Statutes; and, when he saw them, he did approve of them, though he raised some objections to the rules about fasting, and objected also to the name St Columba's, which, he thought, in view of its association with the school in Ireland, might 'create enemies' and cause confusion. Sewell and Singleton agreed that the name might not suit; and, 'on looking about for another', they felt inclined, so Singleton recorded, 'to dedicate the College to St Peter, he being the patron saint of Exeter Coll. – but chiefly for our Lord's injunction to him: – "Feed my Lambs".'

Wilberforce, gratified that his advice had been so readily followed and sufficiently impressed by the religious and educational ideas to be put into practice at Radley, decided to send two of his three sons there.

*

On the afternoon of 10 May 1847 Sewell, Singleton and Monk went to Radley to take possession of the house. They celebrated Evening Prayer in the room which was to be the Warden's, 'surrounded by bare walls, solitude and silence'. They still had very little money and were shortly to be shocked by an estimate of over £1,600 for the construction of the chapel, a figure far higher than they had expected. 'What are we to do?' Singleton asked. 'We must have a chapel and something good too, otherwise we should fail at once.' So they decided to go ahead and accept the builder's price. And, as though in confirmation of the rightness of their decision, two days later they heard at last from Mrs Sheppard with a cheque for £1,000.

More shopping quickly ensued. Paintings were bought, heads and full-length portraits of Christ and the Virgin, King James I, Newton and Boyle, Shakespeare, Handel and Samuel Johnson. On no good authority one of these pictures was supposed to be by Hogarth, another by Reynolds, a third by Rembrandt. 'Why go to this expense in pictures?' Singleton asked himself and replied with the by now familiar justification:

Because we wish to surround the boys with an atmosphere breathing greatness and goodness . . . Religion and morality, history & truth, wisdom &
learning are best taught by example, & pictures are a sort of example . . . I
far prefer a landscape. Yet so far as education is affected, a few portraits of
celebrated men would be much more useful. For this purpose I would
rather have a dozen respectable paintings of historical characters than a fine
Claude; – I mean, of course, if we could not have both. At the same time, if
we flourish, I hope we shall have a fine picture gallery, a fine museum,
sculptures, engravings, gardens, busts, – in fact, a little world of art all pros-
trate at the feet of Religion & Holiness. We are to educate gentlemen; a
gentleman is a Christian refined, and man cannot be refined without the
arts. Sewell and I wholly accord on this point.

Indeed, Sewell expressed very similar views in his 'Reminiscences'.
In justifying the expense he incurred in buying for the school some
bronze candlesticks 'which were really ornamental, modelled from old
candelabra of a classical character', he wrote:

Well, you will say they were expensive. They were . . . [but] remember the
idea of Radley was a family in which noblemen's sons might live as in their
own father's house; at least surrounded with something above the ordinary
level of schools, and every day they were to sit down to dinner as if they
were at their father's table . . . People fancied I was fond of ornamentation,
that I had the bronze candelabra to indulge my own ideas of magnificence.
I had them to form the boys to good manners . . . the little courtesies of the
gentleman; and this lesson was to be taught by the style in which they found
themselves.

Not everyone found these arguments persuasive. There was much
talk of Radley being organized upon absurdly luxurious lines, of
Sewell's anxiety to attract the sons of the noble and the rich at the
expense of the sound and the scholarly. There was much talk, too, of
the school being founded on the most questionable religious principles. The Archbishop of Canterbury, William Howley, an unimaginative man, an opponent of both the Reform Bill and the Roman
Catholic Relief Bill, to whom Sewell wrote as a fellow Wykehamist,
was rather more friendly than had been expected but was far from
enthusiastic about his proposals for the school. So was the Archbishop
of York, the eighty-nine-year-old patrician, Edward Harcourt, an Old
Westminster who had been Archbishop for forty years and wrote to
say he declined to be associated with the project. So were other
bishops, in particular, the Bishop of Winchester, the evangelical Old

Etonian, C.R. Sumner. 'The fact is,' commented Singleton, 'that the Bishops are all afraid, not of Sewell for many of them have expressed their cordial appreciation of the line he has taken in the theological movement of the day – but of the Puritan and more Protestant party.'

The Vicar of Radley, Dr Radcliffe, an elderly man who lived in Oxford, was downright hostile, declining to visit the Hall and behaving most dismissively when either Sewell or Singleton called upon him. Towards the end of May the *Oxford Chronicle*, quoting an article which had appeared in the *Church and State Gazette*, carried a 'damaging and misleading' report, headed 'Semi-Popery in Oxfordshire', which warned its readers that an 'institution was to be created, *within four miles of the University of Oxford'*, where 'choral services were to be substituted for the simple performance of divine worship' and 'compulsory fasting' was to be 'part of the discipline of the Romanizing establishment'. The Bishop of Oxford was urged to 'see to this without delay' or he would have more work on his hands than he would find convenient.

Not long after the appearance of this article, four Irishmen, who were working on a farm in the district, came to the Hall to ask when Mass was to be celebrated. Mrs Burky, who had come over from Stackallan to act as Dame at Radley, reported that the general talk in Abingdon was of the founders of the school being 'absolute Papists'; and a partner in one of Oxford's largest banks had been heard to state categorically in a railway carriage that 'Radley had fallen into the hands of the Roman Catholics.'

5

The First Warden
1847–1848

'It is curious to see how every one is affected by the place.'

MAKING AS LIGHT as he could of the reports of Radley's
Romanizing influences, Sewell installed Singleton as first
Warden of St Peter's College, Radley, on St Columba's Day,
9 June 1847, in a room in the Hall they proposed to use as the Music
School. Twenty-four people were present, including Mrs Burky and
her daughter and the first two of the six servants to have arrived. Most
of the rest were Fellows of Oxford colleges, friends of Sewell. Also
there were three ladies – it being Sewell's wish that the presence of lady
visitors should always be one of Radley's notable features – two of
them sisters of the Rector of Exeter College, the third Sarah Acland,
wife of Henry Wentworth Acland, the Old Harrovian Fellow of All
Souls and Aldrichian Professor of Clinical Medicine.

After the ceremony the party proceeded to the Common Room for
dinner, Mrs Burky in tears, protesting that she had never been so
happy in all her life. In the Common Room, Singleton noted, 'several
bowls of flowers were spread about, & gave a gay and finished look to
the repast, while our plate added a quiet handsomeness, exactly suited
to the sort of college that we want to have'.

When he went to bed, perfectly satisfied with the day's proceedings,
Singleton was pleased to be able to say that his own quarters gave the
same impression of gentlemanly comfort without ostentation as the
Common Room. His bedroom, indeed, was rather more comfortable

than he had originally intended, with carpets on the floor, engravings of Charles I and Queen Victoria on the walls, and either side of the bed 'an old patterned chair with seven crowns'.

Singleton would have been more completely content, however, had more boys been entered for the school. The Statutes limited the numbers to 200, but it seemed doubtful at first that a fraction of that number would be reached. There were still enquiries enough: he was particularly pleased to record that Lady Catherine Clarke was 'desirous to get her boy admitted if we would take them as early as 7 years old'. But when the school officially opened on 17 August there were only two boys to place upon the books, neither of them from titled families. The first was George Melhuish,'the son of a gentleman in the neighbourhood of London', as the Warden described him; the other was Samuel Harvey Reynolds, 'the son of a gentleman [a surgeon] from Stoke Newington'. Three days later 'the Revd Henry Clutterbuck brought his nephew, Alexander Clutterbuck'.*

To care for these boys, in addition to the Warden, Mrs Burky and the two servitors, there were three Fellows. These were Monk, who became Precentor; Edward Irvine Howard, a scholar of Lincoln College and son of the painter, Frank Howard;† and a white-haired, retired naval officer fifty-five years old, Captain William Haskoll, a man of kindly and modest disposition who could not be persuaded to talk much of the naval battles in which he had fought, though there were prints of some of them hanging on the walls of his room. Appointed Sub-Warden, he was to teach Latin and French; and so that he could play a decent part in the Chapel services, he took singing lessons, never having previously 'sung a note in his life'.

Despite the precarious state of the school's finances it was decided that Haskoll and the other assistant masters should be paid £130 a year instead of the £100 originally proposed, the Warden receiving £250.

---

*Both Melhuish and Reynolds were to take first-class degrees at Oxford and become parsons, Melhuish dying young and Reynolds enjoying a moderately distinguished career as hereinafter described. Clutterbuck married the daughter of a baronet and became a brewer in Suffolk.

†Howard brought with him one of his father's pictures, 'Thetis Dipping Achilles in the Styx', which hung in Common Room until it was sold in the 1970s. Soon after he arrived Singleton asked Howard to design the College seal. The Device of St Peter and the Keys, surrounded by the legend, *Collegium Sancti Petri Radleiense A.D. MDCCCXLVII*, is also Howard's work.

Since their three pupils were of different ages, ranging from sixteen in the case of Reynolds to nine in Clutterbuck's, they had to be placed in three forms which, as Singleton said, was 'rather vexatious'. All boys were to have curtained cubicles which they were allowed to decorate in accordance with their own fancies. 'In some the hunting picture, in some the Japanese fan style predominated,' a boy who came to Radley some time later recorded of the school's cubicles, 'and in the majority might be seen pictures of the owner's home or members of his family . . . A candle on a stand placed on every alternate partition lighted two cubicles at once, and at night, nightlights in large perforated cylinders at intervals on the floor of the central passage threw great shadows and circles of light on the ceiling.'

Each boy, Singleton noted in the summer of 1849,

> has music *every* day and spends ¼ of an hour every evening on Latin or Greek composition.* We have also arranged to give them more time *together*, so that they can play a good game of cricket . . . However, it is hard to say how things will answer till they are tried. Tomorrow we shall put the plan into practice. Clutterbuck is likely to give us great trouble; he is evidently the first candidate for the cane: indeed, Sewell says he will be whipped before the end of the week.

The time-table for the first of the year's two terms† (or halves as the terms are still known at Eton) was as follows:

6 o'clock	Rise
6.30–8	School
8	Breakfast
9	Chapel
10.15–12	School
12–2	Play
2	Dinner
3.30–6	School
6	Chapel followed by tea
7.15–9	Music and Composition
9	Bed

---

*As well as music and the classics, the curriculum, now as later, included French and history, mathematics, geography and English. The first half-hour every day was devoted to divinity.

†As in other schools the year's first term ran from January to the end of June, the second from August to just before Christmas.

About thirty-three hours a week were spent in School (where all boys were taught simultaneously) compared with twenty-six today. Saturdays were half-holidays, and one and a half hours were free on Wednesday afternoons.

During their free hours the boys played cricket, or a kind of free-for-all football, or they occasionally went boating on the river until this, like swimming, was forbidden. Games of fives were played against the walls of school buildings; gymnastic exercises were supervised by a former army sergeant; and prizes were awarded for the best kept garden plots.

*

One of the advantages of Radley's time-table, so Singleton said, was that it 'got rid of luncheons which cause trouble and stuffing'. He had excessively strong views on this.

> We should teach [boys] that we are not allowed by Religion to eat & drink for the sake of enjoyment [he had written in his journal in April that year]; and, consequently, that when they are furnished with an ample supply of the best food, all feasting upon supplemental delicacies was plainly self-indulgence, in fact, a form of gluttony . . . A perfect system must exclude all these costly, sickening, selfish – I had almost added dirty – indulgences . . .
> Why boys at school are to be visited with the severest penalties if introducing fermented or distilled drinks, and at the same time permitted every liberty to overload their stomachs with all sorts of luscious, stimulating, & unwholesome solids, seems unintelligible at least.

The trouble was that boys who were at Radley in its early years were not 'furnished with an ample supply of the best food' and had little opportunity of overloading their stomachs, it being forbidden for boys to bring in supplies from outside the school.

> Our food was coarse and unpalatable [one Radleian remembered]. Nothing in the way of sweets or fruits was ever allowed. Parents coming to see their boys were only allowed to inspect them on the premises, they were not permitted to take them into Abingdon or Oxford. Of course, the ingenuity of the boys was taxed to the utmost to mitigate the severity of our diet. Servitors were bribed to put apples in our beds. All kinds of bulbs were dug up in the park and the gardens, and eagerly devoured. Cowslip-roots were a delicacy, nasturtium, crocuses and hyacinths did not long

remain in the gardens . . . Acorns were collected in great numbers and stored away in holes dug in the park. These were secretly cooked in the flames of candles.

Complaints about food were common enough in most public schools at this time. At Westminster, if anything were to be left at dinner, it would be served up cold for supper. At Marlborough, one boy complained that he suffered from 'almost constant hunger',while another wrote, 'The carving was done by the two biggest fellows at the head of the table. Think what the mangled meat was like when our turn came . . . Though that was the only meal of the day at which we had anything beyond bread and butter, it was often impossible to eat it. It was a rare event to go to bed without feeling a positive craving for food.' Moreover the beer was sour, as it was at Bradfield, where it was noted for its 'consummate nastiness', and at Rugby, where it was described as 'frightful'.

Indifferent and scanty as the food was at Radley, the Warden was strict in his insistence that the rules about fasting should be observed, that the boys should have no puddings in Lent, that on Fridays no dinner be served for the Warden and Fellows 'but that a lunch of bread and butter be provided in the Bursary at 2 o'clock for all to partake of who may be so disposed'. On certain specified days there was no butter at tea.*

These provisions about fasting, and the references in the Statutes to confession, provided those who railed against Radley's supposed Romanist tendencies with ammunition to use in their renewed attacks. There were absurd rumours going about, so Singleton complained: 'We are a monastery, a mystery, only remarkable for austerity.' An Oxford man, seeing the Fellows coming out of Chapel in their gowns, observed that he had 'never seen such an idolatrous place in his life'. The whole place was rumoured to be 'so thoroughly Romish that even the locks were got from the Inquisition'. So annoyed did Singleton become by these attacks that when it was proposed that Lord Portman's nephews should be sent to the school, he declined at first to have them, despite his regard for the aristocracy, because their mother was said to have 'expressed scruples on religious grounds at letting

---

*Masters at Radley were required to observe some, though far less stringent, rules about fasting until as late as the early 1930s.

them attend a place with which she had been pressed by friends to have nothing to do'.*

Singleton , however, comforted himself with the thought that, whatever its detractors might say about it, Radley was a happy place. Indeed, he reflected that, unless some exercise in self-denial were imposed, 'the College would be almost too agreeable a place'. He himself rose early every morning at half-past five, half an hour before Captain Haskoll roused the entire school by the beating of a gong. This was 'a labour of love with the Captain', according to one of the boys, 'and he performed it punctually to the moment. It was often his way to wait in the passage at the top of the House, gong in hand, for a good five minutes until the appointed hour came. He then struck with a will.' By that time the Warden would have knocked on Monk's and Howard's doors. At half-past six he appeared in the School Room for the prayers with which the day began.† 'The place is one of discipline,' he wrote; 'real but not oppressive; and we are all very happy, I do believe in consequence of it. The house is, thank God, a "House of Peace".'

Radley was certainly a place of discipline. 'Conduct and character were closely watched,' Reynolds recalled.

> Faults were observed and checked not only as against the college rules, but as inconsistent with the high standard to which we were expected to conform. Nothing however trivial was allowed to pass without notice. Our dress, our behaviour at meals and during play-hours, and at all times, was under constant scrutiny and control . . . Life at the place was for many of us a cramped and artificial life. It would have been better if we had been left a little more to ourselves.

---

*In the event, one of these boys, Henry Fitzhardinge Berkeley Portman, 'a little boy nine years old', did go to Radley; and, after an undistinguished career there, took Holy Orders. A kinsman, Francis John Portman, later Professor of History at Lahore Government College, grandson of the 1st Viscount Portman, was at Radley in 1892–6.

†The School Room had been created from the tumbledown barn which had been moved from its original site and re-erected with panelled walls, the panelling having come – so Sewell improbably claimed – from the Houses of Parliament where it had survived the fire of 1834. It is more likely that it was intended by Barry and Pugin for panelling the new House of Lords but not used for that purpose. The stained glass is by Thomas Willement (1786–1871), the heraldic writer and artist in stained glass to Queen Victoria, whose work can be seen in the Temple Church and St George's, Hanover Square.

Throughout the day, which began at six o'clock on Sundays as well as on weekdays, the boys were required to perform their tasks at exactly specified times and to appear in School and Chapel at the precise moment laid down. School rules, which imposed silence upon them in the dormitory and prohibited running on entering or leaving it, demanded, for instance, the ringing of the first prayer bell as soon as all the boys had closed the curtains of their cubicles. The servitors had to 'put out the candles 7 minutes after the 2nd bell on ordinary nights'. Washing was carried out in little tin baths known as 'tumbies' into which the servitors poured water of variable quantity and temperature.

Boys who were not properly washed, or who failed in any other way to meet the high standards expected of them, were punished in a variety of ways, by lectures or the writing of lines and translations, solitary confinement or banning from Chapel, by the imposition of diets even more meagre than those commonly served, by extra drill by the former sergeant, a cavalryman who ordered boys about as though they were horses, or by beatings carried out by Warden and Fellows alike.

Closely as they were all watched, it appears that new boys at Radley were as liable to be bullied as they would have been at other schools. In later life one of them recalled:

All discipline was exclusively in the hands of the Warden and Fellows, who kept school by turns, and 'tunded' delinquents at 12 o'clock every day to their hearts' content.* Of course under these circumstances it was no wonder that bullying in every conceivable form was rampant. The only check upon this was a form-licking administered by the form on some tyrannical monster who had made the life of the small boys a burden to them. One favourite plan of bullying frequently resorted to on wet half-holidays, when there was nothing *better* to do, was for the bigger boys to gather all the small boys together for a 'squash' in Lower Recess, where they were huddled together in the corner and charged with might and main by the big tyrants, till there was scarcely any breath in their bodies.

---

*'Tunding' was a slang word for beating, imported from Winchester, and obsolete at Radley long before beating itself was abandoned there. More common words and phrases once in use at Radley were 'swishing' for a beating by the Warden; 'bummer', to beat with a fives bat; and 'study licking', a beating in the Prefects' Study (Pups' Study). To 'ratten' was to kick a new boy's (a new bug's) shins.

Whether or not the boys were over-regimented or more than commonly bullied, the many visitors to Radley seem to have been much struck by the school's generally contented atmosphere in the 1850s. One of these visitors was Dr W.E. Jelf, the classical scholar and Christ Church tutor, who rode out from Oxford soon after the beginning of the first term. Jelf, who had been at Eton in the 1820s, was, according to Singleton, 'perfectly amazed and rejoiced to find what we had done, and how we had done it. "When I came out I expected to see you in a half-finished, hugger-mugger state, – but really your plans are so advanced and your arrangements on such a scale of dignity that it is ludicrously wonderful."' He shook Singleton warmly by the hand, saying, 'Mr Warden, I congratulate you.'

Following a visit by two other dons, Singleton commented contentedly, 'It is curious to see how every one is affected by the place, – even Fellows of Oxford Colleges recognize a college in it instantaneously and are as reverent & respectful as possible. Would this have been the case, had we been niggardly in furniture and appointments generally?'

The Rector of Exeter College paid a visit and was 'greatly struck with the happy and gentlemanly appearance of the boys'. Even the bishops began to come round. 'Dr Blomfield, the Bishop of London, although in dispute with some of the more ardent Tractarians in his own diocese, appeared quite satisfied and promised £100.' Headmasters and would-be founders of other schools arrived to make inspections. The first of these was Dr Woolley whom Singleton described as 'the head of a large School at Rossyl near Fleetwood, where he is very anxious to introduce as much of our system as possible but is embarrassed by a Council, or some such drag who fetter him effectually as they hold the purse-strings'.

Rossall had been founded in 1844 at the instigation of the Revd George Bowers, Rector of St Paul's, Covent Garden, and author of an influential pamphlet, 'A Scheme for the Foundation of Schools for the Sons of Clergymen and others' (1842). John Woolley, who had been a scholar of Exeter College when Sewell was Sub-Rector and a Fellow of the College from 1840 to 1841, was its first Headmaster. He was an intimate friend of Arnold's disciple, Arthur Penrhyn Stanley, and hoped that Rossall would develop upon Arnoldian lines. He did not, however, last long at Rossall, where he showed himself more of a scholar than a disciplinarian; and his attempts to introduce 'as much of [Radley's] system as possible' into the school were not successful.

Rossall did become a school mainly for the sons of clergy but it had a pronounced Low Church bias.

Two months after Woolley's visit to Radley, Nathaniel Woodard came to Radley. Singleton had never heard of him, describing him rather dismissively as 'a Mr Woodard who is trying to establish a school for the middle classes on the Church System at New Shoreham. He seems to have a good deal of energy and boldness, which essential qualities are not likely to be much embarrassed by over-refinement. I dare say he is just the man for the work.'

Indeed, he was. After founding Lancing as one of his 'upper schools' for the 'sons of clergymen and gentlemen of limited means' in 1848, he supervised the foundation of Hurstpierpoint, a 'middle school', the following year. These were followed by a 'lower school', which later became Ardingly in 1858. Before he died in 1891, eight other Woodard Schools had opened, among them Bloxham (1860), Denstone (1873) and Ellesmere (1884). Worksop was to follow them in 1885.

Radley's growth was not so impressive. At the beginning of the new term in January 1848, there had been only ten new boys to add to the three of the previous year, though nine others came later in the term. At least Singleton was able to say that all the new boys were 'gentle-manlike' and 'promising-looking' except two named Hill, 'vulgar and ill-countenanced' boys who had formerly been at Marlborough and showed 'what a low place Marlborough must be'. But few of the parents of Radley's new boys were people of any distinction and none was from a titled family as both Singleton and Sewell would have so much preferred. Singleton reassured himself with the reflection that not all titled people were as desirable as might be hoped. One day a Lady Churmside came with her daughters. 'I did not know who they were,' Singleton confessed. 'But hearing a title mentioned was very civil. It turned out that they were the family of some physician . . . and, to say the truth, I did not think they were the style quite up to that of Lords and Ladies.'

Far more to Singleton's taste was the 'very religious, tender-hearted' General W.H. Sewell, a distant relative of William Sewell, who had spent the last twenty years in India and had come home to settle his son at school in England. 'When he sat down to breakfast & saw all the boys looking so gentleman-like and happy, the tears came into his eyes, & he could not eat.' He told Singleton that he had been at two public schools himself, Eton and Westminster, and had 'a horror of them'. He wanted, he said, a place where his son would be cared for, and hoped that Singleton would take him. Singleton, of course, did.*

Although the school expanded slowly, the Warden resisted the temptation to enlarge the numbers by being too easy-going in the choice of whom he should admit, by refusing to take any more ill-looking boys like the Hill brothers and an undesirable youth named Robert Crawley Gibbs who was to leave Radley for Eton in 1850. All the other boys were 'really nice', 'gentlemanly and docile' and 'with very few exceptions, very lovable'. Even the Hill boys, so Singleton decided in September 1848, were 'turning out nice, gentlemanly, orderly boys – & therefore very happy, being much attached to their College'; while Gibbs, originally a dirty boy, 'full of odious tricks, sucking his fingers at meals and other horrors', had become tolerably clean and begun to 'assume the appearance of a gentleman'. Indeed, the influence of Radley was 'telling most wonderfully on all the boys'.

They delight in their music lessons, their great ambition being to sing in Chapel. They are getting on well with their band [which the Warden had given Monk permission to form 'provided it did not interfere with cricket, & other manly & muscular diversions'] and are fulfilling their engagement to be industrious & steady. Scholarship is on the advance & behaviour vastly improved . . . In fact they are a fine, manly, distinguished set of fellows, very obedient and respectful, very cheerful, full of animation & spirits, brought to quiet in School and decorum in Chapel.

---

*W.R.D. Sewell, the General's son, did not go into the Church as his father had hoped and he himself had at that time intended. Instead he followed his father into the Indian Army, fought in the Mutiny and died on the voyage home in 1859. Of the thirty-six boys who came to Radley in 1847 and 1848, a quarter took Holy Orders. Of the remainder, seven went into the Army, one into the Navy, five went abroad and five, living in the country, became either Justices of the Peace or Deputy Lieutenants. One became an insurance broker, one a Russia broker in Eastcheap, one a brewer, one a solicitor, one joined the Royal Irish Constabulary and one the Civil Service. Of the remaining three, one died as an undergraduate at Oxford, another also died young and of one nothing is known.

6

Growing Pains
1848–1851

'What a dreadful state of lawlessness that school must be in.'

BOTH SEWELL AND Singleton took obvious and natural pleasure in observing and recording the failings of other schools, particularly of Marlborough which Sewell went to see in October.

Marlborough had been founded in 1843 by the Revd Charles Plater, an obscure parson's son, who had himself been to the King's School, Canterbury. Unlike Sewell, Plater had no influential friends; but he had been able to interest the 'ever active' Rector of St Paul's, George Bowers, and the Archbishop of Canterbury in his scheme for an 'Institute for the Sons of the Clergy', the need for which 'being apparent to all who consider that the average net professional Income of the Clergy is not more than £200 per annum, while the known average expense of Education for a Boy does not fall below £60 per annum'. It was announced that the school was at first to be limited to 200 boys, two thirds of them the sons of clergymen, who were to pay no more than 30 guineas a year; the remainder, the sons of lay gentlemen, would be charged 50 guineas a year. Mathematics and modern languages would be taught as well as classics and there would be 'sound theological teaching'. The project was an immediate success. At the beginning of the first term 199 boys presented themselves at Marlborough Collegiate School which had been established in the former Castle Hotel just outside the town. Two years later there were 250 boys, by Christmas 1846 four hundred.

Marlborough was, said Singleton, 'a fair example of a School of the age' and, although Sewell found it 'better than he expected', it was 'sadly deficient in tone'. It had lost sight of the fact that 'to make a boy a scholar with the positive view of making him a Christian' was 'the secret of education'. The boys were 'not clean-looking in their persons'; and, while the dormitories seemed neat enough, there was 'scarcely room to pass between the beds so that there must be want of decency'. The masters, whose rooms, incidentally, were 'like vulgar bedrooms', did not have their meals with the boys; also there were too few of them for the large number of boys. Further criticism came from the Hills' elder brother who was curate of Bradfield: 'Marlborough was a horrid place, – all sorts of vice prevailed.' The boys were allowed to go into town by themselves, the mother of two Marlburians told Singleton when asking if he would accept them at Radley. One of her sons 'had made but little progress, & the other none at all . . . they were compelled to join in bolstering matches & so on'. A nice chapel was being built, so Sewell added in his report to Singleton;* but they were going to curtail the services, and what was far worse, according to the Bradfield curate, the boys 'took *novels* into the services with them.

At Radley, on the contrary, so Singleton persuaded himself, the boys did not find the chapel services irksome, though they had to attend full Matins and Evensong every day, each lasting three quarters of an hour. 'I certainly have not heard the slightest thing to make me think they did find the services tedious,' he wrote in his journal. But in fact the boys grew far more restless in these long services than Singleton supposed. 'In the Warden's opinion,' wrote S.H. Reynolds, 'he was helping to form a habit of prayer. The habit he did form was rather of inattention to prayer. Perhaps if the Warden, at the end of one of his long Saint's Day services, when he had been performing as the prominent figure and singing away to his heart's content, had heard, as I have heard, the exclamations from some of the boys, he would have been less sure of the habit of prayer, and how it was to be formed in boys.'

When the numbers in the school made it impossible for them all to go for Holy Communion to the village church – in which the aisle leading to their pew 'was lined with Sunday School boys & girls whose

---

*This neo-Gothic chapel, designed by Edward Blore, was completed in 1848. In the 1880s, when school numbers had much increased, it was demolished and replaced by the present chapel by G.F. Bodley and Thomas Garner.

odour was most offensive' – the boys were 'infinitely delighted', the Warden supposed, to have 'the full Cathedral service' in their own chapel and thus be freed from 'Mr Ratcliffe's irreverence' in the parish church, from 'the scandalous singing' there, and from the 'women, both inside and outside the church, staring at them'.

While finding fault with the chapel services and much else at Marlborough, Singleton was to make no reference to the riot which broke out there in 1851 after an order had been issued for the closing of the school gates at dusk every evening. The lodge of the unpopular college porter, who had reported boys for dancing in the moonlight on the roof of the mansion, was attacked with bricks; fireworks were let off all over the school; classroom windows were smashed; masters' desks were broken open and thrown into bonfires; chairs and desks were shattered and textbooks scattered about the floors. The more the boys were flogged, the worse the pandemonium grew. By the time order had been restored much damage had been done to the school's reputation: at the beginning of the next term numerous boys expected at the school did not arrive.

While he made no note of this riot, Sewell did, however, record 'an *émeute* which took place at Winchester among the gentlemen commoners, owing to Moberly, the headmaster, having forbidden the customary display of fireworks on the evening previous to the holidays'. He cut out a report of this disturbance which appeared in the *Globe*:

> The young gentlemen, however, were determined to have their fireworks, and obtained the usual supply, which was thrown over the wall into the playground during the time of divine service on Saturday. No sooner was the service over than the commoners made to their playground, and speedily kindled a large bonfire, and commenced kicking about fireballs. Dr Moberly, being informed of what was going on, hastened to the spot, when a number of serpents were directed against him, and he was obliged to retire. On Sunday, the Doctor having intimated his intention of severely punishing the ringleaders, the youths refused to attend chapel, and on Monday morning declined making their appearance, and, for protection, barred their master out, who, in his turn, barred them in. The besieged stood out several hours, but before eventide they were starved into a surrender, when some of the most forward were flogged, and one of them, who had rendered himself particularly obnoxious, was expelled.

Singleton also heard – and made a note in his journal – of two other scandals at Winchester, one of a boy there being forced to fag at cricket and, having been tried beyond his strength, dying as a consequence; the other of a boy 'being thrown into the water, and taken out nearly lifeless. He was then thrown in again and drowned. There is something quite shocking in this. What a dreadful state of lawlessness that school must be in.'

How different, the Warden congratulated himself, was the atmosphere at Radley. It was

> all the result of self control, & this brought about by the *'genius loci'*, – the refinement of the Society of Gentlemen, of music, and above all – of the daily prayer. Bold, manly, vigorous at their games . . . the boys are evidently very proud of their College . . . A word of reproof brings tears down their cheeks, even from the oldest and biggest. Altogether, we have quite succeeded in creating a domestic system . . . only to be got in a good school . . . No wonder that the poor fellows are so happy under such a system.

*

But when the school broke up for Christmas on 19 December 1848 there were still only thirty-six boys, though twenty-five more were to arrive in January, of whom no fewer than sixteen were the sons of clergymen, two of these the sons of the Revd Lord John Thynne and two others the sons of Bishop Wilberforce. The financial position of the school was thus beginning to look rather safer, all the more so since Mrs Sheppard had presented it with two gifts of £500 each, in addition to the £1,000 she had already given.

More boys, however, entailed the employment of more masters, and those of a satisfactory sort proved difficult to find. The Warden was perfectly happy with Captain Haskoll, the Sub-Warden, and Monk, the Precentor, while as to Howard, he was 'getting quite to love him', he was 'so obliging & good-tempered'. But when it came to the selection of further Fellows there was difficulty in finding men as agreeable and gentlemanly as these three.

'To be a successful teacher,' Singleton explained, 'he must be something of a gentleman, must be a member of our Common Room, & dine at our Table – and so on. It would never do for his position amongst us to be such as would induce the boys to look down upon him.' And, when Monk needed an assistant, he felt constrained to add, 'But how difficult to get among musicians a person competent in his duty, and yet, combining with skill in his art, modesty and gentlemanlike manners.'

1. Radley Hall in 1789: a watercolour by J.M.W. Turner painted when, aged fourteen, he was staying with an uncle at Sunningwell. The original is in the Tate Gallery

2. George Pyne's depiction of the school in 1859, showing boys playing cricket in their ordinary clothes. The Clock Tower and Dormitory Clump, now cut down, can be seen on the left, the House on the right, with Dormitory and the Octagon between them

3. A view of Radley in 1913 painted by the Revd J.H. Kirkby, Social Tutor (E Social) 1879–1914 and Sub-Warden 1909–14. Dormitory is on the left, Covered Passage on the right and, between them, the Octagon and Markets which, originally a covered brick arcade, later became studies and masters' rooms

4. An autumn day at Radley in the 1890s. The old Chapel which can be seen behind the boy on the bicycle was demolished in 1895. This watercolour was given to Sister Boddy who bequeathed it to the school

5. Haymaking in the 1870s. A watercolour of the House with, to the right, the spire, which used to stand on the top of Pups' Study

6. The Clock Tower, formerly known as the Bell Tower, was designed by the don, Edward Howard. Shop in the background was opened in 1894. The semi-circular slab over the door was put up to commemorate the Senior Prefectship of R.W. Risley who rowed in the Oxford University Eight for four years from 1857 to 1860, a record at that time

7. Looking across the Pond to the House, a watercolour by Sir Patrick Nairne presented to David Rae Smith on his retirement as Chairman of the Council

8. Boys walking to a lesson past Memorial Arch, Sir Thomas Jackson's last work for Radley

9. A don, Simon Barlass, taking a French lesson

10. Looking towards the golf-course across the Pond in which many balls are lost. Trout are fished in the Pond and it is also used for teaching new boys how to scull

11. Radley's golf-course, opened in 1871, was one of the earliest courses in England. It was ploughed up in the First World War; its successor was ploughed up in the Second. The present course was opened in 1985

12. Chapel, originally designed for a school of 250 boys, can now, after skilful alterations, accommodate over 600. A service was held here in June 1995, a hundred years after it was consecrated by Dr William Stubbs. At an earlier service a lesson was read by the Old Radleian great-grandson of Bishop Stubbs, Stephen Stubbs

13. Radley's new Library, installed in the old School, was opened in 1996 by Field Marshal Lord Bramall, a member of Radley's Council. The shelving can accommodate 40,000 books. This corner of the Library takes the place of those classrooms off School which Radleians formerly knew as 'the Slums'

Certainly Singleton did not think J.S. Boucher, who was considered for a Fellowship in 1848, would be a suitable choice: he was 'too vulgar'. However, Howard assured the Warden that he had been so accustomed to 'well-bred people' he was expecting too much. So Boucher was elected. So was the Warden's brother, Samuel Singleton, though the Warden himself had strong reservations about him, too, on 'two or three [unspecified] accounts', and gave way to his election only under pressure. None of the other Fellows appointed by Singleton stayed long; and it was doubtful that three of them had been officially appointed at all, for when the time came for them to read the text of their promises before the Warden in Chapel they were all quite unable to decipher Sewell's atrocious hand in which the Latin formula had been written. They showed it to the Warden who could not make it out either and at last 'in an agony said, "Oh, say anything."'

If the appointment of suitable new Fellows was a serious problem, the choice of domestic staff was an even worse one. The Warden admitted to being 'sadly annoyed by candidates for the office of [butler] who, one after another, [had] turned out quite incompetent'. One, who said that he was left-handed at his interview, turned out to have a withered right arm and could not lift heavy dishes. 'Of course I gave him notice,' Singleton commented, 'warning him against a suppression of truth on so important a point.' His successor proved to be a drunk who nearly burnt the house down. In all, five butlers came and went within fourteen months.

The young servitors were quite as tiresome, 'exceedingly careless for a very long time', as the Warden described them. 'They need smart discipline. Mrs Burky has repeatedly punished them, but it is not enough.' He himself gave them a 'tremendous scolding' after they had been caught going into one another's beds to eat apples. 'They shed floods of tears'; but he decided that, if their conduct did not improve, he would have to beat them. And beat them he did. So did Monk and Howard, in his presence. 'The expressions of pain drawn forth from one of them assumed the form of sympathy for his person – "Oh my poor back" was his repeated exclamation.' Singleton had to admit that had 'the occasion not been so grave, it would have been highly amusing'.

His pupils were, of course, beaten too, since, despite all that he wrote in his journal about the happiness of the school and the gentlemanly demeanour of his charges, instances of misbehaviour were far from infrequent. As in all schools, there were fights and there were bullies. As Sewell had predicted, the first boy to suffer was Clutterbuck who more than once climbed back into bed of a morning after he had got up at the sound of the gong and was consequently late for prayers.

> So I got a good hazel switch [Singleton recorded], & laid it about him pretty soundly. He spun like a cockchafer, and shrieked like a sea-bird, and, as punishment was inflicted in a large empty room, the sound was magnified & prolonged ... Reynolds, I hear, was in fits laughing at his screams.

This punishment not having the desired effect, Clutterbuck was again punished for the same offence by 'a sound caning on the back' and told that, if he dared to lie in bed again, the Warden would not 'fiddle with the cane again but would administer a flogging of some moment'. The troublesome boy did offend again and on this occasion the Sub-Warden, on the Warden's instructions, 'carried him off to the shoe-room. Reynolds & Hill held 2 arms, & after five strokes he gathered his legs under the chair, which the Sub-Warden with some difficulty succeeded in finding and capturing – and then, holding them both, he became an easy victim to a baker's dozen.' 'It will be some little time,' Singleton hoped, 'before he courts his bed again at improper periods.' There is no record of Clutterbuck's having repeated this particular offence; but it was not long before the wretched boy was again in trouble, this time for having taken part with one of the Hill brothers in a fight to which he was apparently urged by 'nearly all the boys in the School'.

These fights – which generally took place at Radley in the area known as the Fifth Form Recess in School – had long been a recognized part of public school culture; and in many schools the authorities turned a blind eye to them. At Marlborough 'fights might take place anywhere, the field, the schoolroom, the dormitory ... unless the principals were leading fellows in the school. In that case the Upper Fifth was sometimes selected. All arrangements would have been made beforehand.' At Shrewsbury fights were frequent, 'amounting, it is said, to as many as seventy in one term'. In one of these the future Archbishop of York, William Thomson, landed a fierce blow that 'set his opponent's nose bleeding so badly that the boy feared he might almost bleed to death'. 'It was always said that Butler [the Headmaster] watched the fights from his window; at any rate, if this be untrue, he certainly turned a blind eye to them.' At Radley later in the century, recalled Hugh Burdett Money-Coutts, later the 6th Lord Latymer, fights could not last more than five minutes, as they were not allowed (by custom) to begin till the bell began to ring and had to stop as soon [as the Chapel procession began to be formed] . . . There were generally two or three fights every term . . . both combatants had to come into chapel, unless they were so gory the Prefect was obliged to send them to the infirmary. In chapel they were, of course, the target for the eyes of the whole school, searching for signs of conflict. If they missed chapel they were punished for missing chapel, not for fighting. Rather brutal? Perhaps.

As at Shrewsbury, masters at Radley usually turned a blind eye to these organized fights. When one of them noticed a boy's badly bruised face, he asked him how it had come about. The boy confessed and was told to report to the master later. In the meantime the boy's opponent was discovered with an even more bruised and swollen face. 'My own bruises were a mere nothing in comparison,' the victor of the fight recalled sixty years later. 'I was sent for again – and commended – or shall I say forgiven. [Mr Orlebar] was quite impressed.'

Warden Singleton's attitude to these fights was ambiguous. He recognized that they must 'clearly be inhibited', but was not at all clear how to set about putting down so well-established a custom: 'The whole question of fighting is an embarrassing one – but must be dealt with.' The Warden's method of dealing with it in the case of Clutterbuck and Hill does not sound very promising: 'I made them both promise, not to abstain from fighting, but when they were provoked to repeat the passage – "Little children love one another."'

Singleton accepted that bullying, 'the vulgar, unmanly, ungodly practice of bullying', must be dealt with and dealt with more severely than fighting, but he was forced to conclude that some boys seemed even to invite it. Clutterbuck, for example, was 'a terrible baby & a very provoking baby too, so his face is almost always like Joseph's coat. He is vexatious, & then everybody torments him, & even little Howard is said to have given him a drubbing – he is such a coward.' However, when a boy named Richards – 'an odd boy, made rather a butt of', who was to die at Oxford before he was twenty – was persistently tormented by a notorious bully of whom nothing more was heard after his departure from Radley, the culprit was conducted to a room, separated from the Schoolroom by an oak partition, where he could not be seen but his cries could be heard. 'There, with a stout rod of elm twigs,' Singleton wrote, 'I gave him severe chastisement. Very miserable at having to do it, for I have lately got fond of the boy, and to raise red weals upon fair flesh is not exactly to my taste. He once turned round and said to me; – "Oh Mr Warden, you don't know how you hurt." I was sad but inexorable. This case and the way it had been treated, will settle forever any doubts that might be entertained of the opinion of the College on such matters.'

With the older boys, Singleton, who prided himself upon being feared as well as loved, chose to correct faults and punish misbehaviour by threats of expulsion or fearsome lectures which, he was pleased to recall, often resulted in the culprits breaking down in tears. In more serious cases a boy might be flogged, then placed in solitary confinement and on a very spare diet with written work to perform. In one case a boy named Willis, the son of a parson, was flogged by Singleton at the specific request of his father, for 'idleness and untruth'. This boy – a boy 'physically far from strong who never cared to join in our school games' – had already been 'severely whipped' for telling a lie to one of the Fellows. When his father wrote again, repeating his demand that his son should be flogged for disobedience, evidently unaware that the boy had already been whipped, another severe beating was accordingly administered. Caught lying yet again, he was separated by Singleton from the other boys, kept away from Chapel and placed on a very meagre diet. It was intended that he should be whipped again 'when his back should be recovered'. Before this punishment was carried out, however, the father protested at his son having been so severely beaten twice and he castigated the College for 'wreaking its vengeance upon a lad who was only bringing forth the natural fruits of the neglect of the College'.*

---

*Willis became a parson like his father, married twice, and lived to be ninety.

7

A Riotous Mood

1851

'I am sure [this affair] will establish once and for all the discipline of the school.'

O N ONLY ONE occasion in Singleton's time did discipline at Radley come close to breaking down altogether as it had done at Marlborough. The trouble began when a small boy named Elliot stood up at tea-time 'and coolly went to the bell and rang it'. On enquiring the 'meaning of this extraordinary movement', the boy calmly replied that the school 'wanted more butter'. Few requests could have been calculated to annoy Singleton more. He was 'perfectly astounded by this impudence', telling Elliot that he must never presume to behave like that again. But, realizing that 'the little boy would never have dared do such a thing without encouragement', he summoned his elder brother to the bursary together with Samuel Reynolds, who, as the oldest boy in the school, was frequently called upon to account for the misbehaviour of his juniors.

The Warden discovered that some boys had been given twice as much butter as others and those who had not been thus favoured, 'considering this to be a grievance, consulted at table about the remedy & hit upon what appeared to be a sovereign one'. He found that Reynolds had not discouraged the proceeding and that the boy's older brother had rather forwarded it, so he gave them 'first a good rowing, then a good lecture'.

After this several of the boys, in riotous mood, smashed the windows of the granary of a nearby farm, clambered through the frames and threw out everything they could carry.

The whole school was summoned before the Warden who roundly condemned the 'wantonness of the outrage', denouncing it as 'utterly unbecoming Christian gentlemen' and questioning every boy as to the part he had played in it. Discovering that every boy without exception was more or less guilty, he once more singled out Reynolds for 'sanctioning such bold and vulgar mischief' and, when Reynolds explained that he had not 'joined in the act', the Warden asked the 'great goose' if he did not realize that 'a man who was voluntarily present at a murder, without doing anything to prevent the deed, was, in the eye of the law, no less guilty than the principal, and, if discovered, would be hanged along with him.' The Warden went on to say that the whole school would be punished.

The next day he announced what this punishment should be: they must pay for the damage; and, with the exception of the youngest boys, they would all be confined within bounds, deprived of their half-holiday, and congregate in the Schoolroom to write out impositions. The boy who appeared to be the principal ringleader would be flogged; while Reynolds, as bigger and older than the rest, would suffer a 'punishment still heavier than that dealt to any of the others': the Warden and Fellows would teach him nothing nor have anything to do with him until the following Saturday night, 'in which interval during school hours he should be deployed in a perpetual writing of Latin and Greek translation'. Then the Sub-Warden carried the ringleader, one of the Hill brothers, to the Shoe Room, and there the Warden 'birched him soundly'. 'He roared as much as I could have wished,' Singleton commented, 'protesting "that he should faint", information which produced no change of purpose.'

As for Reynolds, the Warden held him largely responsible not only for the misbehaviour of his juniors on this occasion, but also for the subsequent hissing of a much disliked master who, in the Warden's absence, had beaten a boy with what was described as 'downright brutality' for 'making a mistake in his algebra', giving him, so another boy counted, '42 or 43 cuts with a stick – an outrageous punishment'.

Years later, long after Singleton's death and shortly before his own, Reynolds angrily responded to the comments about these episodes in the Warden's journal he had discovered in the Radley College archives. He had had a distinguished career which gained him an entry in the *Dictionary of National Biography*. Awarded a scholarship to Exeter

College, he had won both the Newdigate Prize and the Chancellor's English Essay Prize, gained a first-class degree and then been appointed a Fellow of Brasenose College. He had edited Bacon's essays and written *Notes on the Iliad*. For over twenty years he had been on the staff of *The Times* and for twenty-two had been Vicar of East Ham. But the years and his achievements had not softened his resentment at Singleton's observations about his conduct at Radley. His refutation of them was written as though in a white heat of right-eous anger.

He wrote of the 'pain and indignation' with which he had read Singleton's journal, of the shameful injustice with which he had been treated at the school, of the Warden, in his 'self-complacent egotism', never listening to a boy's defence of his conduct but brushing all excuses 'petulantly or impatiently' aside. Reynolds wrote also of the Warden's inaccurate descriptions of boys he did not like as, for instance, the 'vulgar and ill-countenanced' Hill brothers, one of whom, while admittedly ugly, was, in Reynolds' opinion, a 'bright, good-tempered, active, energetic fellow, well-liked in the school', while of the other the 'worst that could be said against him was that he was very deaf'. As for Singleton's character:

> The fact I believe to be that Mr Singleton's training and disposition had not fitted him to be head of an English public school. He was an Irishman; he had never been at a public school and I am not sure that he had ever been at school at all; and during his stay at Trinity College, Dublin, he had kept himself practically aloof from the society and amusements of the place . . . I do not say that he was ever intentionally unjust in his treatment of his boys; but he was overbearing, rash, impulsive, impatient of opposition, and when he had once formed an opinion he was simply incapable of owning himself or thinking himself in the wrong.

As to his own conduct in the school, Reynolds was anxious to make it clear that he had no delegated duty as a Prefect; he was simply 'a little bigger and a little older than any of the others'. Yet there were 'very numerous instances' in which his and Elliot's influence was 'exerted to check evil, and to maintain a sound and healthy moral tone in the school', of which, incidentally, Singleton knew 'much less than he fancied he did'. 'In all these instances' they never received 'the least help or encouragement from Mr Singleton'.

*

The Warden remedied one of the faults of which Reynolds complained in March 1851. Before the whole College gathered together in the Schoolroom he appointed eight Prefects, handed them their caps of office, the Senior Prefect's being decorated with a silver tassel, the others with a white tassel. Care was taken to ensure that the ceremony was an appropriately solemn one; it lasted for an hour and twenty-five minutes, beginning with a prayer, followed by a long address delivered by the Warden who, when his oration was over, raised his own cap in acknowledgement of the bow with which the Prefects received theirs. The Warden then addressed the Prefects as to their duties in the presence of the rest of the school: they were 'by every possible means to enforce the College discipline in *all* parts', 'put down all bad language and mean ways. Irreverence, indecency, low slang and whatever is un-Christian and ungentlemanly in expression must be the object of unceasing and exterminating war.' 'Dishonourable behaviour at games, and anything like trickery, cheating, or pilfering must be visited heavily.' They must protect 'the whole School in their privacy. Every desk [was] to be accounted a sacred spot.' They must 'maintain the discipline of the dormitory'. In other schools the dormitory was 'only a second playground'; at Radley it was to be 'a sort of second Chapel, sacred to devotion and holy rest'. The Prefects were also to preserve 'decorum and gentlemanly behaviour at table in Hall'.

They were vested with powers of punishing boys by ordering offenders 'to write out, or commit to memory, extracts from English, Latin or Greek authors', or by imposing extra drill. At the same time they were to have certain privileges, including their own study, which was to be out of bounds to all other boys and in which they could remain after the other boys had gone to bed, on condition that they themselves were in the dormitory by a quarter to ten. They would be allowed to go into Chapel whenever they liked and into the dormitory 'after a certain hour of the day', provided they did so 'for the purpose of retirement, meditation and devotion'. They would be permitted to leave the precincts of the College on the understanding that they did so in threes, did not go into any town or village, 'unless simply to pass through it', did not repair to shops or houses of entertainment, simply using the privileges of their liberty to 'cheer and brace both body and mind'.

After imparting some sensible advice about being suitably strict while sometimes passing over minor delinquencies 'if the offender is not aware that you know of them', the Warden ended his oration –

parts of which must have been quite incomprehensible to the younger members of his audience – in his most grandiloquent vein:

> Well is it that novelty is tricked in gaudy trim and hope is spangled with attraction. Were it otherwise the stoutest heart might quail before the threatening hosts of doubts and dangers, of mortifications and failures with which the future is pregnant . . . If you act on the suggestions which have now been thrown out, we may have good reason to expect that your inferiors in rank throughout the School will look up to you with confidence and regard, and render that cheerful obedience which, when not extorted by violence or fear, will promote a spirit of manly respectfulness, the grace of the Christian gentleman.

8

The Fellows' Revolt
1851–1852

'I must regard the Institution as my own property.'

IF THE BOYS at Radley did look up to their new Prefects with confidence and regard, a similar report could not be given of the Fellows, who were constantly at odds with the Warden and the Founder and, indeed, with each other. By the time of the Prefects' institution, the three original Fellows and four others who had been elected in 1849 – Samuel Singleton, the Revd John Boucher from St John's College, Cambridge, Edmund Savory from Oriel College, Oxford, and Joseph Cox from Lincoln – had been joined by three more.

One of these was James Baker, a young man of twenty-four who had been at University College and, having taken Holy Orders, was later to become Chaplain at Winchester where he had been at school. He was a man of principle and charm but highly contentious and out-spoken. He made no secret of his profound disagreement with the Warden's declared belief that boys should be ruled by fear before they could be guided by affection; and argued strongly against the pre-vailing use of harsh corporal punishment as a means of keeping them in order. He had handed in his resignation when the brutal thrashing of the boy who could not do his algebra properly had not met with the general condemnation of the other Fellows, though he had been per-suaded to withdraw it when it was agreed at a College Meeting that, in future, beatings should be limited to eighteen strokes.

But it was not only the harshness of the discipline at Radley that concerned Baker; he was also at odds with the Warden and some of his colleagues over the introduction of new subjects into the curriculum at the expense of the classics. He spoke about this to Singleton in so heated a manner that the Warden was outraged and made up his mind that he must get rid of him.

By this time several other Fellows were considering leaving Radley of their own accord. One of their principal grievances was their salaries of £130, a parsimonious remuneration which must surely have been at least a contributory reason why so many Fellows left after two or three terms and why their replacements were not men who had shone at university. 'The assistant masters,' wrote a contemporary observer of the Radley scene, 'were gentlemen, but not scholars, for the salaries were very low.'*

The Warden supported the Fellows in their complaints, despite what he had earlier written about the need to command the services of gentlemen willing 'to submit to labour and discipline simply for the sake of doing good'. Sewell, however, still clung to this ideal. He would 'rather see Radley sunk in the Thames' than agree to an increase in the Fellows' salaries. He was eventually persuaded to agree to an increase of £30 a year but even this modest sum was denied them when the school's liabilities – well over £20,000 – became known.

The trouble was that Sewell, as Founder of the school, treated it almost as though it were his private property. Income due to it, including the boys' fees, was paid into his private account at Coutts's Bank and expenses were incurred at his whim. The reckless purchase of works of art and other objects for the school had by no means ceased, though Singleton who had in the past conceded they were necessary for the sort of school they had in mind – and had spent a good deal of

---

*Although their board and lodging had to be taken into account, their salaries of £130 a year were rather less than they might have earned as clerks, the most numerous class of salaried men in early to mid-Victorian England. Junior clerks in the Civil Service, who were slightly better paid than their contemporaries in solicitors' offices and the like, had about £125 to £300 a year; assistant clerks £300 to £600; senior clerks up to £900; while chief clerks started at about £1,000. By the 1890s starting salaries for Radley masters had risen by no more than £30 to £160 a year. By this time fifteen senior masters at Rugby were being paid £500 a year (£600 a year if they did not have a house) plus a capitation fee of £1 for every boy over a total of 300 to a maximum of 500. Other masters were paid £450 a year.

his own money upon them – did his best to curb the extravagances. One day Sewell 'brought out an exquisite 15th century chest . . . of wood stamped with gilded leather'. Another day there appeared a silver gilt pastoral staff which Bishop Wilberforce, fearing accusations of papistry, thought 'ought not to be borne in procession nor exhibited just at present'. Then came a 'costly group of carvings' – the present altarpiece – which, however, was temporarily removed as two of Sewell's brothers, who happened to be at Radley at the time, considered it bore 'a very Popish air', while Singleton's own 'personal repugnance was great'.

Eventually Sewell was prevailed upon to agree to hand over the boys' fees when the numbers in the school reached forty; but by the time they were more than twice that number they were still, as before, going into his own account. They would have to do so, Sewell said, until the school's income covered its expenditure. The Fellows threatened to write to all parents asking them to send their fees direct to the College rather than to Dr Sewell; Sewell ignored this threat and the Fellows did not carry it into effect. When pressed upon some other point and shown what the Statutes, which he had himself approved, had to say upon the matter, he threw them to the floor, declaring them to be nothing but waste paper. He did not attend another College Meeting while Singleton was Warden.

It was not only in the matter of its finances that Sewell treated the school as though he owned it personally; he frequently came over from Oxford to take friends or acquaintances round the buildings and grounds, or sent them to Radley on their own with assurances that they would be welcome. When complaints were made to him about this all too common practice, which often disrupted the school's lessons and other activities, Sewell asked that rules should be drawn up so that he could tell intending visitors when to go and what entertainment they might expect when they got there. But the rules were broken whenever it suited Sewell to break them, and he and his visitors continued to turn up at Radley much as they had always done.

Singleton responded by allowing a new Fellow to occupy rooms in Radley Hall which Sewell had kept for his own use. Sewell had agreed to give the rooms up; but the Warden allowed the new Fellow to move into them two months before the agreed date. This Sewell said was yet another instance of the Warden's determination to 'exclude the Founder from the College', a complaint calculated to annoy Singleton who persistently maintained that he, too, was entitled to be recognized as a Founder of Radley, a title which Sewell had bestowed upon him in a letter to Bishop Wilberforce in 1847 when the relations between the two men were perfectly cordial but which he repudiated later when they had deteriorated beyond repair.

One of the main causes of dissent at Radley, not only between Sewell and Singleton but also between Singleton and the Fellows, arose from the collegiate establishment of the school which – according to the letter of its Statutes – allowed the Fellows as much say in its organization and routine as the Warden himself. Singleton pressed for a change in the constitution, pointing to the efficacy of the system in force at Eton and Winchester and pressing for the transmogrification of the Fellows into tutors and for the establishment of a new governing body of Fellows, non-resident and unpaid. The existing Fellows naturally opposed this suggestion. So did Sewell, appealing to the authority of the Statutes which had previously been dismissed as so much waste paper.

Argumentative as ever, James Baker asked why the Statutes were not read out each term as one of their clauses required. Singleton replied that the simple reason was that the College's one copy had been transcribed by Sewell and no one could read his writing. Undeterred, Baker undertook to make a copy in his more legible hand, a task that must surely – if completed – have taken longer than the single night he claimed it did, since the Statutes run, line after Latin line, rule after Latin rule, for over eighty pages.

Although the duties and responsibilities of the Fellows were carefully laid down in the Statutes, it was soon evident that they did not intend to submit to them. The Warden referred to their 'gross neglect of duty', 'their unkindliness, worldliness and rebellion'. He was obliged to send them a message expressing a wish not to receive, and declining to answer, 'any more impertinent letters'.

By July 1851, having accepted defeat over the question of the collegiate system, Singleton decided to resign. But after informing the Fellows of this decision, he changed his mind. His departure, however, could not now be delayed for long.

A few days after the beginning of term on 20 August, the Warden and Fellows, having learnt that Sewell was looking for a new Warden without consulting them, temporarily composed their differences to formulate a resolution which they sent on to him: 'The Revd William Sewell, having taken upon himself to enter into negotiation with different persons with a view to filling an expected vacancy in the

Wardenship, the Warden and Fellows at present resident unanimously request that he will henceforth avoid any interference in matters the management of which the Statutes confine to other parties.'

The alliance of Warden and Fellows against the unauthorized encroachments of the Founder was predictably short-lived; and, within a few weeks of this resolution being passed, over half the Fellows, strongly urged by Baker, had made up their minds that the Warden must abide by his earlier decision to resign. When they heard of this, the boys, almost unanimous in their dislike of the rebellious Fellows, entered the battle on the Warden's side, issuing a memorandum signed by all but five of the dwindling number of boys at that time in the school, testifying their 'sincere and unqualified submission and attachment to the Warden'.

It was not so much that they had all outgrown that fear of him which he had endeavoured at first to instil and had come in the end to love him as he hoped they would, as that, in the age-old manner of schoolboys, they disliked the idea of change and would rather be ruled by a man they knew than a devil they might have reason to hate. Besides, they had come to recognize the Warden's qualities. To be sure, he was long-winded and pompous on occasions; he could be unduly, impatiently severe; he was of cramped sympathies and hasty in forming ideas that soon became prejudices, yet even Samuel Reynolds conceded that he was sincere and unselfish, that he had the good of the school at heart, that he was a 'warm-hearted impulsive Irishman of very deep and sincere religious feeling'. While 'he did not succeed in impressing himself upon us as a permanent force', Reynolds concluded, 'we respected and looked up to him as long as he was Warden and we were schoolboys'.

As schoolboys, Reynolds' contemporaries would have agreed with the Revd William Tuckwell, who knew him well, that Singleton was 'self-sacrificing', 'generous and high-principled'. What they had no means of knowing was whether or not, as Tuckwell maintained, 'his manners told unfavourably on Oxford men. Over a pipe or on board his yacht he was a genial Irish gentleman, but at the Radley high table, exalting not his person but his office, his stern elevation of manner was repellent.'

He certainly felt most strongly that the behaviour of the Fellows was insulting both to him personally and to his status as Warden. He reacted by abrogating the Statute which required the boys to raise their caps to the Fellows on encountering them, a highly provocative step which encouraged the boys to suppose that they might with impunity be rude to the Fellows, and to demonstrate their disapproval of those few boys who continued to show them respect. On meeting two Fellows on their way out of school an entire form, with a single exception, ostentatiously ignored them, while the one who did touch his cap was 'threatened with a thrashing by one of his companions'.

When they discovered the disgraceful way in which the school was now being run, several parents voiced their alarm. One, a doctor of divinity, condemned the Warden's behaviour as being wrong and 'wrong in a very odd way'; he considered it 'outrageous and preposterous that boys should know anything of the disagreements of their superiors'. Another parent wrote to express amazement that the conduct of certain boys had not resulted in their expulsion. Both Bishop Wilberforce and Lord John Thynne removed their boys from the school. Reginald Wilberforce, who was to go into the Army, before becoming a barrister, went on to Rugby; Ernest, who was to become Bishop of Chichester, went to Harrow; one of the Thynne boys went into the Army, the other, by now eighteen, to Balliol College, Oxford. Other boys were removed to Haileybury, Winchester, Eton, Cheltenham and Bradfield. One boy had already been removed the year before and sent to Harrow; another had gone to Lancing, two others to Winchester. It was feared that Radley College was on the verge of dissolution.

The troubles were exacerbated by the excitable James Baker who preached an inflammatory sermon in Chapel, concluding with a scarcely veiled attack upon the Warden against whom he had already expostulated violently in 'a manner unbecoming to a Fellow'. For this offence he subsequently apologized before resigning with two other Fellows in October.

By then there was little doubt that the Warden would himself have to resign. The finances of the school had fallen into such a sorry state, the debt grown to such a figure, and income fallen so low that the manager of the Oxford branch of the London and County Bank, who had been appointed College Treasurer, warned the Warden that, unless drastic steps were taken, the school would have to be declared insolvent. Yet, hoping that he might be able to make some arrangement about the £3,000 he had lent to Sewell, the £1,000 he had advanced towards the cost of the organ and the additional sums he had laid out on other things for the good of the College, the Warden delayed handing in his resignation as long as he possibly could. By 7 October, however, he felt he could wait no longer and that night he left, severing himself from a position for which he felt that he was 'better fitted than any [he had] ever occupied before or since'.*

*

At eight o'clock the next morning the election of Singleton's successor was announced. He was the thirty-nine-year-old Revd William Beadon Heathcote, Fellow and Bursar of New College. A fellow Wykehamist, he was a friend of Sewell who described him as 'earnest, religious-minded and able'. But whether or not he was able enough to save Radley from dissolution he was not given sufficient time to show. He was not told the full details of its financial position; nor was he informed that the College as yet had no lease from the owners of the freehold. He did know that the numbers of boys in the school had fallen by almost half in the past year, from 84 to 45, and were likely to fall even further before the coming year was over. He also knew that there were only two Fellows left apart from the Precentor, Monk, and the amenable Captain Haskoll who was asked to resign his place as Sub-Warden to a clergyman, the Revd William Smith, sometime scholar of Lincoln College.

Heathcote set to work, however, as though determined to revive the spirits of the school. He divided it into an Upper and Lower School, a division that might well have been made before since the oldest boy in the school was eighteen and the youngest not yet eight. He placed the younger boys in their own dormitory with their own matron; he had both dormitories heated by pipes instead of the open fire which had formerly been lit on the rarest of occasions and then with the risk of burning the whole place down. He instituted an Easter holiday; he reopened the boathouse which Singleton had closed down and instituted swimming classes, appointing a properly qualified instructor and

---

*In fact, although only forty-one, Singleton did little after leaving Radley and going to live with his mother in Ireland. Despite the money he had spent on Radley, he was still comfortably off; and after his mother's death was able to buy Minster Court at York where he collaborated with his friend, Dr Monk – who had been appointed the organist of the Minster on leaving Radley – in producing the *Anglican Hymnbook* for which he wrote nearly thirty of the hymns, and translated numerous others from German and Latin. His English version of *The Works of Virgil* was published in 1855. He died on 7 February 1881, having been almost blind for some years. He was buried in his family's vault in St Patrick's Cathedral, Dublin.

allowing all who could pass a swimming test to take out a boat. 'We like Mr Heathcote,' one boy wrote home, expressing what was apparently a general opinion, 'because he allows us to climb and have mustard.' The Fellows were also content to have their salaries raised to a modest £160 a year, the Warden's being £500.

But the finances of the school remained a problem that was proving intolerable; and, as Heathcote began to realize the full extent of the crisis, he accepted the fact that he would have to resign as Singleton had done.

The only solution seemed to be for Sewell to take over as Warden himself and 'to reunite in the same hands the responsibilities, the income, and the labour'. 'Practically, therefore,' he added, 'I must regard the Institution as my own property, and its collegiate conditions . . . suspended.' He did not take this decision lightly. The school was more likely to fail than to survive; he was nearly fifty years old and had no experience of teaching boys nor any particular wish to teach them; he had no desire to leave Oxford, his comfortable rooms at Exeter, his friends in the University and the pleasant life that he led there. He felt, however, that he had no choice: Radley, he believed, was his mission in life, a mission he was called upon by divine will to perform.

Heathcote announced his resignation on 13 November 1852.* All but three of the Fellows went with him. Five days later the boys were told. One of the departing Fellows said that they 'seemed to feel it most deeply . . . Some burst into tears.'

---

*Heathcote became Vicar of Sturminster Marshall, then of Compton Bassett, Wiltshire. He was Prebendary and Precentor of Salisbury Cathedral until his death in 1862. The Heathcote Prize, a scholarship for classics and later for classics and mathematics, was founded in his honour in 1863. In 1928 it was won by L.G. Scarman, later Lord Scarman, Lord of Appeal in Ordinary.

9

The Founder as Warden
1853–1861

'O what mischief have I known in schools from not foreseeing all contingencies.'

'WHEN I CAME here, sorely against my will, and with the deepest conviction on the part of all who knew me of my own utter incompetency for the office,' Sewell told the mother of one of his Prefects some years after first taking up his duties as Warden, 'there were [several] things which I dreaded. 1st. The boys getting up trees and tumbling down and breaking themselves. 2. Having to whip them. 3. Having to speak in Chapel. 4. Having to get up at 5 in the morning. 5. Having to govern men. 6. Their being very ill.'

Despite the light-hearted tone of this letter, there can be no doubt of Sewell's reluctance to embark upon a new career. He was warned to expect a rebellion; and when he first entered the Schoolroom, he found that the legs of his chair 'had been sawn away so that when the Warden sat down he was to fall upon his back'. He avoided this fate by not sitting down; but what he termed 'the bad spirit in the school, quarrelling, discontent and fighting', made him extremely wary of other affronts to his dignity.

The restoration of discipline in the school was, therefore, his first essential duty. He set about this in a variety of ways, often by ridiculing culprits in front of the assembled school. In his 'Reminiscences' he described an example of this:

I was very anxious at Radley to stop the shamming system which is so common in schools – the lying in bed in the morning and having a little headache . . . I used to go round the dormitory in the morning and see the patients . . . Curiously enough we found at Radley the lineal descendants of Sir Godfrey Kneller, Horace Walpole and Sir Walter Raleigh* – and Walter Raleigh was a very unfavourable specimen of his kind . . . notorious for his shirkings and snufflings.

I found him in bed one morning with a headache and, expressing my deep sympathy and compassion, I explained to him that the illness required careful treatment and that the warmth of the bed was likely to be prejudicial . . . I called the attention of the whole school to the alarming nature of his disposition, which showed itself in general sleepiness and unwillingness to face the morning air on mathematical mornings, but which went about 12 o'clock . . . The boys were in a roar of laughter . . . A dose [prepared by the Dame] was brought in – it was very black and unutterably nasty. But I begged him to drink it slowly, and as he hesitated to drain it to the bottom I pressed on him a second cup – while the boys were convulsed . . . We had no more shamming.

And when I think of the 'going continent' [on the sick list, a phrase still used] at Winchester . . . I am very proud of my success. I doubt if any serious treatment could so have enlisted the whole school on the right side.

In maintaining discipline Sewell relied, as Arnold had done, to a great extent upon his Prefects who, he considered, were far more useful in governing the school than the Fellows were. He took great care to choose the most suitable boys, those 'with good physique, good practical administrative powers and thorough *gentlemen*', and he gave them wide powers. They were not allowed to carry canes about with them as they were at Harrow, but it was tacitly accepted that they were permitted to use them. As well as wide powers they were granted many privileges – far too many, complained the Fellows who, Sewell thought, were jealous of them.

Sewell also relied for the maintenance of discipline upon the Black Book, a record of perfidy also known as such at Charterhouse. 'I hear the black book is much worse than I thought,' one boy, the nine-year-old John Godley, the future Lord Kilbracken, wrote home to his mother at the beginning of his first term. 'I very nearly got down in it today.' A boy whose name appeared in it for some misdemeanour was liable to be kept in the Schoolroom for the half-hour of freedom which

---

*G.T.C. St J. Kneller subsequently joined the Army; so did one of the Walpole brothers; the other became Librarian to the House of Commons. *The Radley Register* records nothing of E.W. Raleigh other than his death in 1897.

the boys had before going to bed at half-past eight, or he might be required to fag at the ball-courts which entailed running fast to fetch the balls which went out of play. If his name appeared three times in the Black Book – and it could be so entered for a single offence – the boy was beaten, and often severely beaten, eighteen strokes still being the official maximum but twelve being more frequent than six, as the extant Books testify. In later years, a man who had been at Radley in Sewell's time, although a Prefect and good at games, confessed, 'Radley cruelty has spoilt my life.'

To the matter of flogging Sewell devoted more pages in his 'Reminiscences' than to any other aspect of his Wardenship. It was a question that clearly concerned him deeply and he was intent upon explaining to his nieces, for whom his 'Reminiscences' were written, why he considered that 'giving it up altogether was ridiculous'.

> It was sure of giving pain, whereas other punishments to some minds might be painless [he explained in elaborating its advantages and justifying its use]. It could be measured out in some kind of proportion. It took no time. When over it was all over. A long rankling punishment is always an evil with boys; it nurses a spirit of rebellion and revenge. It was better than impositions because it took no time from their exercise.

Before detailing his procedure at Radley, he looked back to the 'whipping scenes at Winchester' and confessed himself 'amazed and ashamed that in the 19th century the Mother of all our great Public Schools could have persevered in such a caricature of punishment'. Every morning before prayers, as the boys were arranged in two lines, the Headmaster called out the names of those to be punished.

> The poor victims knelt down successively; two boys undid their braces and exposed an interval of bare back ... Gabell [the Revd Henry Dison Gabell, Headmaster from 1810 to 1823] armed himself with an instrument consisting of a handle on which divergent apple twigs were artistically fastened, and then delivered four or five or more strokes upon the loins, in which I imagine he generally contrived that the apple twigs should fall not on the bare back but on the coat and trousers. It was a mere play ... the whole thing was a farce.

Far from a farce, however, was a public scourging at Winchester which was performed before the whole school, a birch rod being used and 'applied where it usually is applied without reserve or delicacy before the public eye'.

For more serious offences at Radley Sewell imposed 'a flogging with a regular birch', on one occasion at least administering twenty strokes. These birchings took place in private, though once – he thought 'once only' – in an 'ante-room where the boys could hear, not see'.

Sewell went on to describe how, when he became Warden, the boys had a notion that he was 'a frightful flogger'; and he let them know, on the day after his arrival, that he would not hesitate to prove himself to be so were it required of him. In his first address to them in Chapel he suspended the weekly communion, telling the boys that he knew that things were going on in the school which were wrong and they must be punished for them. He spoke of the affection he had for them, of the confidence which he wanted to repose in them; but if that confidence were to be misplaced and that affection unmerited he would not hesitate to 'scourge them with a rod of iron'.

Although, as he said, he was represented in the press and 'in some popular trashy book' as 'a specimen of a tyrannical pedagogue', he did not hesitate to carry out his threat whenever he considered it necessary. He gave examples of this. There was, for instance, the case of Edward Nunes Phillips who was in the First Eight, the First Eleven and the First Twelve. Together with 'another giant', S.E. Illingworth, also seventeen years old, Phillips handed in some unsatisfactory exercise; and, since 'anything like the shuffling, the copying, the lying, the imposture, which at ordinary schools [ceased] to be regarded as a sin, was denounced and punished with the utmost severity' at Radley, both boys were berated before the entire school and then told they were to be flogged.

> I sent them down the school amidst a dead silence while I followed them into the flogging room [Sewell recorded] . . . The two giants knelt down one after the other, divested themselves of their integuments and I gave them a severe caning . . . And I do assure you I am not in the slightest degree exaggerating when I say that both of them (though they were considerably hurt) when they got up from their knees came to me and burst into tears and put their arms around my neck and kissed me as a child would its father. They knew that I had a great affection for them and what I did was done for them . . . To this hour, some of the most delightful, touching blessed associations I have are connected with the whipping room at Radley.

One of these delightful associations concerned a boy, 'a fine, athletic, manly, handsome boy', 'full of will and spirit, but a gentleman'.

This was Robert Wells Risley, the son of a parson and one day, like so many Radleians of his generation, to become a parson himself. Having 'a high regard and affection' for the boy, Sewell appointed him Senior Prefect and was consequently warned by the Fellows that he was spoiling him. Determined to show that he was not, Sewell one day blamed him for some boys being late for dinner, disregarding Risley's justified excuses with the words, 'You are responsible. You know the importance of punctuality and that I never allow excuses. It is right that punishment should fall upon you, and the punishment which will do you most good is caning you.'

Remember that if the Prefects were sacrosanct, if it was profanation to touch them with a cane, to cane the Senior Prefect was like caning the King. Such a thing had never been seen or heard of . . . I observed Risley's face flush violently and his lips work. 'Risley,' I said, 'take off your gown.' And without the slightest hesitation, after one perceptible struggle, he took off his gown. 'Go into the passage,' I said. And Risley went, only saying, 'Would you rather cane me, Sir, as I stand, or shall I kneel down?' (I am giving the exact words, for I have never forgotten that moment). 'Kneel down, Risley,' I said. And he did kneel down. And then I flung away the cane, telling him what was perfectly true, that not for worlds would I touch him but I was told that I was spoiling him . . . I think when I made that boy get up from his knees and he put his arms around my neck was the most exquisite moment of enjoyment that I ever had.

'Will you have another of my flogging experiences,' Sewell asked his nieces. 'They soothe me more than I can express.' Without waiting for an answer, Sewell then related his dealings with another boy, Edmund Downes, who, having gone on to the Royal Military Academy at Woolwich, abandoned a promising career in the Royal Artillery to qualify as a physician and become a medical missionary in India. Downes was a 'fine fellow, physically speaking', and became a Prefect; but he did not do so well academically, and once told a lie to avoid a lesson. Sewell gave long consideration as to how best to punish him. Whenever he had such a case to consider he used to take the Chapel key, lock himself in and lie down with his face on the altar steps to consider the problem. In this case he decided to tear off the white tassel of Downes's cap, the insignia of the Prefect, before the assembled school and to send the victim to the flogging room, taking the precaution of instructing the butler to have three strong workmen at hand, as well as the usual Fellows and Prefects, in case of resistance.

But Downes made no resistance and I gave him a severe flogging. And when it was over I sent everyone out of the room but him and made him come and sit down by my side and (foolishly weak as I was in such cases) I burst into tears . . . The boy's heart was touched. He wrung my hand earnestly . . . I took him back into the school – the boys in a dead silence – and I told them . . . he had behaved as a boy should do under such circumstances, that I was satisfied there was good in him and the good would henceforth be everything. I gave him his tassel again and rehabilitated him in full power.*

'Do you observe in this case one advantage which there is in corporal punishment?' Sewell asked his nieces. 'There are cases in which complete and immediate rehabilitation (as in the Prodigal Son) is the best if not the only way to save, and the punishment once administered you are at liberty to do this without violating justice . . . I am ashamed to linger round these memories . . . and yet is not education made up of them? And no one can understand Radley without such details. I did in fact possess enormous power over the boys.'

---

*Weeping and kissing a boy after beating him would not then have been considered so sexually dubious as it would today. Tears flowed readily and unashamedly down many manly early Victorian cheeks, as they had earlier flowed down those of the Duke of Wellington when he read the casualty list after the Battle of Waterloo. In a letter to the father of a boy who had come to him in distress about 'a decrease of religious views', Singleton had written: 'He came to me in an agony of repentance . . . After holding out for some time, I took him to my arms, where he kissed me all over, crying most bitterly; and I need not say that I kissed him as tenderly.' A later Warden (the Revd William Wood) kissed a boy of eighteen who had fallen downstairs; and William Sewell kissed a boy who had won a scholarship to Oxford.

10

Sewell's Radley
1853–1861

'A sort of Scholastic Utopia realized.'

OWER AS WARDEN, Sewell certainly had: he once rolled a boy up in a carpet to demonstrate forcibly how he could wield it over him. But the influence he exercised over the majority of the boys is more difficult to gauge. In his letters home John Godley mentions him often enough, but very rarely is there more than a passing reference: 'I do hate School now (more than I ever did before) most awfully,' he wrote miserably one winter's day, having decided at the beginning of his first term that he liked it very much. 'The Warden is a great deal more strict. I don't know what it is and I don't care, but I do hate it fearfully.' William Oliver, a parson's son, two years younger than Godley, who had come to Radley from Eton, also had little to say about Sewell in his reminiscences of school life, describing him briefly as a 'rough old bear' who told a pack of lies about his boys, 'his Radley boys who never did anything wrong'. In his later distinguished life Godley concluded that in Sewell's character there was 'a strong tinge of humbug'.

It may have been true, as Dean Stanley said, that Radley 'turned out lads that went unscathed through all the temptations of an Oxford life', that these Old Radleians, as an Oxford undergraduate observed of them, were 'nice fellows but so jolly innocent', and that, as another undergraduate said, 'You Radley men never talk smut.' It may even have been the case, as Sewell's nephew, the Revd Arthur Sewell,

74

recalled in old age of his time at Radley in the 1850s, that 'in the one long Dormitory, without the supervision of a Master, were seventy lively and healthy boys, only cubicles with light curtains separating them. Instead of the rowdy scenes that might have been antici-pated . . . not a word was spoken, not a boy left his cubicle. When the prayer bell rang every boy was on his knees communing with God.' It is, however, difficult to imagine the Dormitory, as Warden Sewell once described it, being 'holy ground', a 'restful haven from the day's labours', in which a 'cloud of prayers floats silently upward' and 'bended knees have worn the floor-boards smooth'.

Certainly this description does not rest easily with Sewell's frequent assertion that his charges were naturally ill-disposed. 'I hate little boys,' he once told a parent, not altogether jocularly; he had no taste for their society, he said on another occasion; he had always disliked them. He was 'never surprised to hear of any folly or any wickedness among schoolboys'. When they were thrown together, ill-disciplined, to 'ferment in a mass', they generated a 'frightful corruption'. Nor was Sewell very successful in his dealings with them. In his misguided attempts to gain their favour he would give them sixpenny pieces when they played well at fives, or throw apples to them out of his window, presenting an extra one to the boy who caught them with one hand. He would place his palm on a nervous boy's head when speaking to him, and, with his other hand, feel the beating of his heart. 'Again and again,' he said in one of his sermons, 'when you little ones have come to me, and I have put my hands to your hearts, I have found them beating so violently, and seen tears before I spoke a word, starting into your eyes, that, before I could tell you what I wanted, I have been obliged to put my arms round you, and tell you not to be frightened.' To read such sermons – in another of which he protested to the school: 'I love you all very dearly; every day since I have been surrounded by you, that love has increased' – is to be persuaded that Lord Kilbracken's charge of humbuggery is not altogether unjustified.

To be sure, he grew very fond of some of the older boys, as they grew fond of him. He kept in touch with them after they had left the school, and allowed them as much freedom and pleasure as he deemed appropriate while they were there. Indeed, the number of holidays and half-holidays and the parties he organized during term astonished other headmasters. As well as the regular holidays on various Saints' Days, extra holidays were given for all kinds of reasons – when dis-tinguished visitors requested them, when Fellows left, when games were won, when awards were gained at Oxford or Cambridge, when boys passed into military academies, when Old Radleians distinguished themselves, when there were national triumphs to celebrate. There were school feasts and picnics; there were form dinners and Scots dinners and Irish dinners, cricket dinners and Prefects' dinners and Confirmation dinners; there were outings to Exeter College where the boys sang to entertain the Warden's guests in the College hall, and to Oxford prison where they could witness the wages of sin. There were special celebrations on All Saints' Day and Whitsun and Trinity Monday and, most notably, on St Peter's Day when there were concerts and dinners and speeches and chapel services, when lamps were placed on the lawn and in the trees and Chinese lanterns and fairy lights lit both Hall and Schoolroom, and the boys paraded with torches and the choir sang the Hallelujah chorus.

On one occasion at least, when a big dinner was given to celebrate a Fellow's wedding, the carpet was rolled back and there was dancing and 'how amusing it was to see how the good resolutions of the grave dons not to dance melted away at the sound of the harp and the violin'.

Commenting upon his introduction of ladies to Radley, Sewell wrote:

> The boldest, the most important thing I ventured to risque at Radley, the feature in the system which I am sure had there, and will have, if followed, the most important of all influences on the Christian education of Public Schools in England, was the introduction of Ladies. I tremble at the audacity of the idea . . . Radley was imperilled more than once by the dislike which Singleton had to seeing ladies there.

*

While Radley was celebrated for its parties, outings and junketings, the rigour of its ordinary working days was quite as severe as that of other public schools. These days began at 5.45, even earlier than in Singleton's time. There were still eight and a half hours of lessons, including one and three quarter hours devoted to music and composition; and the boys still had to spend long hours in Chapel. Sewell confessed himself concerned by this.

> The time [he wrote] – at least ¾ of an hour and usually more, twice a day – was a considerable space taken from the school work, and it placed our boys in a very unequal position in regard to other schools; and as our range of work embraced more subjects, we could less afford to lose it . . . Other

schools were springing up on something more or less of the Radley system and they felt the same difficulty; satisfied that the Chapel was to be made the foundation and centre of the whole, but still perplexed with the length of our service. Even from Cheltenham College I had letters from the Chaplain expressing his conviction that ours was the right system and asking for guidance in setting up choral services.

Eventually Sewell reduced the time of both morning and evening services to half an hour each on weekdays. On Sundays, however, in addition to half an hour spent in learning the Gospel and Collect in the morning and another half an hour repeating their Catechism in the afternoon, the full services were continued with early Holy Communion at 7.0, Matins at 9, Holy Communion and Sermon at 12.0 and full evening service at 6.0. 'We all attended regularly,' Sewell wrote. 'There were no exceptions and all took interest in the music, were proud of their Chapel and recognized it as the foundation of the whole system.'

Boys at Radley had good reason to enjoy the music in their Chapel, which became of 'real Cathedral status' under the capable and enthusiastic direction of Dr Monk; but the Warden's celebrated sermons were another matter. In them, as A.K. Boyd observed, Sewell

> so enlarges the boundaries of sin that one feels everything to be embraced which is contrary to his own rather fastidious sense of propriety. To talk in school, to play anything like tricks, to lie on wet grass, not to open your mouth when you speak, to use nicknames, to borrow small sums of money, to keep on wet shoes, to draw caricatures 'of those who are labouring for your souls' – these are but a few of the vices against which Sewell thunders.

Ridiculed though they were by William Conybeare in the *Quarterly Review*, the sermons were, nevertheless, effective when Sewell alluded to current events or addressed a particular group of boys, calling attention to them by name either in praise or censure, keeping them alert or apprehensive in case their own names were mentioned. Yet Sewell himself admitted that, when he moved from particular cases to generalizations, the boys, who had been listening intently, 'threw themselves back and composed themselves to inattention'. On the whole, he concluded, he 'effected far more good, instilled more of Christian principle in the Schoolroom at Radley than in sermons in Chapel'.

Among the great number of sermons he preached, there are those that are fluent, lucid, instructive, even inspiring; there are others, dealing powerfully – apocalyptically – with such specific subjects as dormitory rules that must have put the fear of God into the minds of the boys; and there are those which even a critical Fellow could admire. One such Fellow was the Revd William Wood, Sub-Warden since 1855, a Fellow also of Trinity College, Oxford, who had come to Radley in 1853. Wood praised one of Sewell's sermons as 'most graphic'. But just as often he had cause to complain of a *'very, very* painful' sermon, 'most exaggerated and calculated to do much harm', or 'a frantic sermon' such as Wood had never heard. There was one on the 'degrading' and 'disgusting' habit of smoking which another clerical Fellow, Henry West, found so embarrassing he felt obliged to 'bury his face' all the time in his surplice. Wood thought that 'even from W.S.' he had never heard 'so mad a discourse'.*

The most distressing of Sewell's sermons, however, were those in which he referred dismissively to 'ordinary schools', comparing the products of a typical 'coarse, vulgar, ordinary school' to the 'manly, bold, vigorous, chivalrous, gracious . . . simple, natural . . . gentle, refined, courteous, kind, considerate, ever tender and affectionate' paragon produced by the 'Radley tone'. This tone, so he claimed in a sermon which became known notoriously as the 'Blood Sermon', was characterized by a due respect for rank, a respect, he said, which was to be demonstrated that very night when the Senior Prefect was to give a dinner in Middle Hall to all the boys of noble blood: 'No boy is to feel jealous of the good dinner these little bloods are to have. We are all to look up to them as possessing something we could never attain to ourselves, and honour them accordingly.'

> Be assured, my boys [he told them], that this little act and sign, petty as it is, asserts and establishes among us a grand principle for our own welfare here, as a great place of education for our future conduct in the world . . . Look on the boys who will dine together today – many of them very young – many of them with no personal claim to any particular respect, not with jealousy and contempt, but with manly, honourable, elevating respect for rank. And that feeling carried out into the world will save you alike from the vulgarity, and degradation of the tuft-hunter; and from the sullen malignant meanness of the democrat and the republican.

---

*Smoking by masters was a matter of contention in many schools. At Wellington in E.W. Benson's time, for example, it was virtually a condition of employment that a master should not smoke. In consequence, one master 'had a pit dug at the bottom of his garden where he and like-minded colleagues could smoke undisturbed'.

On listening to these words, West was even more embarrassed and offended than he had been when warned against the vicious habit of smoking. He 'groaned and took to reading the Marriage Service'. Wood, who afterwards described the sermon in his journal – and 'What a sermon!' – contemplated leaving the Chapel. Monk in the organ loft was able to creep away.

Having published a volume of sermons, Sewell was suspected of having another volume in mind. Wood and two other Fellows plucked up courage to warn him against a second publication. The Warden was angered by their interference, and told them sharply that he had no intention of publishing another volume. This was strictly true but disingenuous: a new volume did appear in 1859; it was identical in appearance to the first but a note informed the reader that it was printed for private circulation.

Sewell's relationship with the Fellows was ambiguous. Contented enough now among themselves, they were often at odds with the Warden – over his sermons, over the inconsistency of his punishments, the extravagance of his parties when their own meagre salaries and the wages of the servitors were not always regularly paid, over the interruption of school work for what Wood called 'a constant round of amusement', over the Warden's refusal to allow the Fellows 'a stronger brew of College beer', over their right to be consulted as Fellows of the College on important matters relating to it, such as the choice of Prefects which had originally been settled at College Meetings but was gradually taken over by the Warden himself who then decided that it should rest with the boys themselves, a solution condemned and already twice rejected by the Fellows.

On occasions the Warden took decisions first then told the Fellows about them afterwards. Without consulting them he instituted a new office in the school, that of Senior Inferior, a kind of Sub-Prefect, who was to enjoy certain privileges, including the right to take younger boys to Oxford. The Warden was 'pretty sure' the Fellows would not agree with him about this innovation, he told the Sub-Warden, so, in order to spare them 'the pain of going against him', he had not troubled to consult them.

From time to time the Fellows stood up to the Warden, invoking the College Statutes, and sometimes they gained the day. For instance, when the Warden endeavoured to assume sole responsibility for the election of new Fellows, the existing Fellows united in opposition against him. But generally, by a combination of deviousness, obstinacy and evasiveness, Sewell contrived to get his own way; and such differences as arose were likely to be ended by a display of emotion, genuine or contrived, which sometimes touched the Fellows but more often embarrassed or irritated them. On one occasion the Warden knelt submissively before Wood in his study, on another he laid his head on his shoulder, and on a third, laid it on Wood's chest and sobbed aloud. He solemnly shook hands with all of them to signal the end of a disagreement about the unequal punishments he had inflicted upon two Prefects for the same offence.

The Fellows undoubtedly had good grounds for their complaints. Their salaries, still modest enough, continued to be irregularly paid, yet money could always be found, it seemed, not only for all kinds of jollities, but for a succession of new buildings and the purchase of works of art.

Soon after Sewell had taken over as Warden there appeared in Chapel the splendid early sixteenth-century reredos which had already been seen at Radley in Singleton's time, but had then been removed, being considered, with its polychrome and gilding, to have 'a very Popish air'. There also appeared a fine chandelier at the east end of Chapel as well as a magnificent ormolu chandelier in the Schoolroom. New buildings went up apace: a covered way with a gallery above it was constructed between the House, Chapel and the Schoolroom; a building subsequently known as the Octagon was erected to house studies and a library; quarters were built for the servitors; and in 1859 a huge and extraordinary corrugated-iron structure, rumoured to have once served as a cathedral in some newly developed Australian town, came into use as a gymnasium at a cost of £1,800.* Nearby there appeared a shop, while the College's first completed building, the Bell Tower – later Clock Tower – which had been designed by Edward Howard, was transformed by the addition of buttresses to provide four new courts for playing fives. The clock was added in 1864.

Unlike Thomas Arnold, Sewell set great store by the playing of games. Indeed, he said that the playing fields and the river were of scarcely less importance at Radley than Chapel itself: they were 'a

---

*The structure, although evidently designed for export, seems never to have left the docks at Tilbury. It was said to be the first gymnasium to have been erected at a public school. But Uppingham had a gymnasium a few weeks earlier. This, however, was built 'on a shoe-string purse' and by 1902, being 'very out-of-date', was replaced by a new building at a cost of £5,000.

second Chapel in fact'. In the summer the boys played cricket, not very successfully at first: in their first recorded match in 1853 the school team was easily beaten by Bradfield, a school of about the same size. They also played their own special version of football and went down to the river to swim and to row.

All kinds of other games were played apart from cricket, fives and football. In their letters home and in their subsequent reminiscences of these years, Radleians refer to hockey and ice-hockey, quoits and rounders, archery and athletics, as well as such activities as paper-chases, coursing and gymnastics, games of prisoners' base, rook shoot-ing, climbing trees and clambering up the outside of the House, sliding down its banisters and undertaking the kind of improbable feat recorded by W.B. Woodgate, a future hero of the rowing world and founder of Vincent's Club at Oxford, who, for a bet at Radley, raced up and down Covered Passage between School and Chapel a hundred times, a distance of four and a half miles, within an hour, eating two pots of jam on the way.

> I might say a word as to games [wrote Woodgate who was at Radley in the 1850s]. Scientific strategists of modern football or hockey would deride the rough and ready style in which such games were played ... Each school had its own local code, and there were no standard numbers for a side, nor offi-cial placing of a field ... There was no flannelizing for games; we rolled in the mud in our everyday linen shirts and cloth trousers, ignored rain, and then sat at school hours after play in our sodden attire. Yet I never knew of any pneumonia resulting; we were used to it, like eels to skinning, – the fittest survived.

Inured as they might have become to sitting in form in cold, wet clothes, it cannot be said that public schools of the time produced boys of imposing physique. Woodgate, who was to row in the Oxford Eight and to win great distinction at Henley, was 'undeniably stunted in growth': when he went to Oxford he was well under 10 stone. So were many of his contemporaries: the average weight of the Second Eight at Radley in 1856 was 7 stone 12 pounds. Woodgate attributed his poor physique to the 'limited sleep hours' which he, like most public schoolboys of his time, were allotted by the time-table, and to the food which was still quite inadequate.

'I sometimes look back with wonder,' he wrote, 'at what we boys used to accomplish on the short commons of our day. On whole and half-holidays we dined at 4 p.m. Bread-and-butter breakfast with a chunk of dry bread for lunch, had to last us from 8 to 4 p.m.' Nor was the food served at dinner either plentiful or appetizing. Usually there was meat, but pudding was supplied on only three days a week; and no boy was allowed more than two glasses of beer. When tea was served on a Sunday between seven and half-past in the evening, jam was not allowed. As in other ways, the Prefects were indulged, however, by being allowed a decent meal, with beer, at night after the less privileged had gone to bed.

Boys who were not Prefects were expected to rely for any extra provisions on hampers sent from home. John Godley's letters are replete with references to his hampers and to those of other boys, to parcels containing honey and 'glycerine and elder-flower', biscuits and ham. The ham he was particularly pleased to have because 'otherwise it would have been cold junk'. It was always a problem, though, to protect the food from mice. 'There are a great many mice in my cupboard,' he told his mother one winter's day. 'I hear them as I lie in bed going gnaw, gnaw, gnaw at my biscuits . . . I wish when you send me that parcel you spoke of you would send me that double mouse trap of mine.' Godley's contemporary, Charles Talbot, whose parents were in India, where his father, the Hon. Gerald Talbot, was serving as Private Secretary to the Governor-General, also reported problems with mice which ate great holes in his waistcoat and jacket to get at the crumbs of biscuits in the pockets.

Some boys supplemented the school's food by poaching expeditions. One of those who snared rabbits in Radley wood was Woodgate.

> I secured my plunder and sneaked down to waylay the carrier's cart [he wrote]. I consigned my game to him, labelled to myself as if a present from some patron or parents. Thus I had it for dinner next day.

Yet, despite the hampers and parcels that came from home, and the game brought back to school from poaching expeditions, the boys were as often hungry as not. 'I hope you will not think me very extravagant when I tell you that I generally eat 2 concentrateds a day,' Godley wrote to his mother. 'However, I am really very hungry.' He therefore took all the more pleasure in outings to Oxford where one of the Fellows, Richard Norman, who had private means, sometimes took his form – or at least those members of it whose names were not in the Black Book – and where they all had a decent meal together. Norman also allowed them to go in their spare time to his room where Godley was 'very fond of toasting [his] biscuits over the fire'.

1. William Sewell at Exeter College,
Oxford, *c.* 1835

2. Sewell lecturing in the Moral
Philosophy Lecture Room at Oxford, 1841

3. Sewell, Radley's founder,
and Warden 1853–61

4. A Spy cartoon of Sir George Bowyer,
3rd baronet (d. 1883) who in 1855, after
eight years' negotiation, agreed to a
50-year lease of Radley Hall and 140 acres

5. The Revd Robert Corbet Singleton, co-founder and first Warden of Radley, 1847–51

6. The earliest portrait of Radley boys, by John Gilbert, RA, 1849. Thomas Spyers, (*right*) entered the school in January 1849. The son of a clergyman, he became a surgeon. His younger brother, Henry Spyers, became Senior Prefect. He followed his father into the Church and was appointed Headmaster of Weybridge School in 1880

7. A group of boys in the 1850s standing outside the Cloister, now Covered Passage, with Ante-School on the left

8. The Revd William Beadon Heathcote, a friend of the Sewell family and Sub-Warden of New College, who became Warden for a brief period in 1851

9. The old Sixth Form Classroom, formerly Ante-School

10. The Upper, or Long, Dormitory was built in 1849. There were 70 cubicles with curtains rather than doors

11. Dormitory, Octagon and House in the 1850s

12. Fives players at the Bell Tower courts in the 1850s. On the left is the Revd William Wood who was to return to the school as Warden in 1866. Second from the right is the Revd William Macrorie who became a don at Radley in 1855, and was appointed Bishop of Maritzburg in 1869. Between Wood and Macrorie stands the Hon. H.C.G. Forbes, afterwards 19th Lord Forbes, a don at Radley 1855–61. The fourth player is a boy at the school. The players are wearing gloves; an alternative form of the game was played with bats. William Wood's wife captioned this photograph 'The Convicts'

13. Warden Sewell with Fellows of the College outside the old Chapel in 1858. Standing (*from left to right*) are the Hon. H.C.G. Forbes, the Revd R.W. Norman (future Warden), the Revd William Macrorie and Robert Sewell. Captain William Haskoll is seated between Norman and Macrorie on the Warden's left. William Barber, who later became a successful Queen's Counsel, is sitting on the ground with his head resting on his chin

14. The old Chapel, built just north of the present Chapel, was begun before the school opened. It remained in use until the end of the Easter Term, 1895. The interior was dismantled in the Easter holidays and the structure was demolished the following term

15. The Radley Eight in 1859. The average weight of the crew was only 10 st. 1 lb. Three of the oarsmen took Holy Orders, one became an Irish land commissioner, one a coffee planter, one entered the Consular Service, one emigrated to New Zealand, one had an estate in Wales and one (the Hon. H.G.L. Crichton, son of the Earl of Erne) joined the Army. This crew challenged Eton but were refused, being told that 'Eton did not intend to row any more such matches with Radley'. They had been beaten at Henley by Eton by three-quarters of a length the previous year

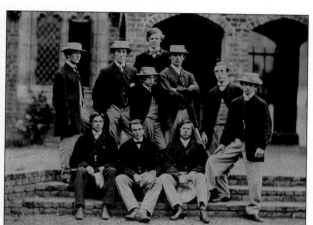

16. The Radley Cricket XI, 1860. Of the ten members of the XI whose future careers are known, one joined the Army, one became a farmer in South America, one was appointed Librarian to the House of Commons, all the remaining seven took Holy Orders. The captain in the middle is Arthur Sewell, nephew of William Sewell and son of R.B. Sewell. He died at Cambridge in 1947 aged 106

17. A group of boys, ten and eleven years old, in 1860

18. A group of senior boys in 1860. The three boys standing at the back on the left are C.A.P. Talbot, the Senior Prefect (1860), the Hon. H.G.L. Crichton (Senior Prefect, 1862) and W.T. Monsell

19. Edward Handley. He took Holy Orders on coming down from Magdalen College, Oxford

20. Robert Taunton Raikes, the earliest of many members of his family to attend Radley. He rowed in the Oxford Eight in 1865 and 1866, became a solicitor and succeeded to the Treberfydd property in 1901

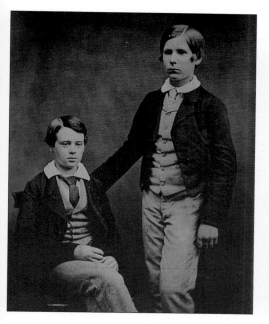

21. Stuart Le Blanc Smith (*left*), having won several events at Henley in the 1860s and 1870s, became a stock-jobber in the family firm; Henry Edward Burney, a future lieutenant-colonel in the Oxfordshire Light Infantry

22. Percy William Charrington (*left*) went to the United States, becoming a farmer in Virginia; Edward Aveling Green achieved some distinction as a sculptor, painter, carver and ecclesiastical decorator

23. The Pond in the 1860s with the House in the background and Dormitory to the left. The man holding the punt pole is the Revd William Wood, Sub-Warden 1854–63 and fifth Warden 1866–70. The man in the top hat with the children is Thomas Haycroft, Sewell's butler. Mrs Haycroft was the College Matron. Also in the punt are two Fellows, the Revd Thomas Stebbing, under the umbrella, and the Revd Septimus Andrews

24. The Old Gym which was built in 1860. Radley was the first public school, after Uppingham, to have a gymnasium. The roof was painted with multi-coloured stripes to prevent dizziness in rope-climbers

In the coldest weather this room was the only place where Godley and the rest of the form could keep warm, so they were much distressed when the room was closed to them because they had been unable to resist a plate of Mr Norman's oranges.

*

'I am sorry to say that our weather is still very cold' is a characteristic complaint in one of Godley's letters. 'I can hardly hold that jolly pen you sent me.' 'I wish you would send me a warm black waistcoat,' he wrote in another typical letter, 'mine is so cold I haven't been able to wear it . . . It is bitterly cold.' He was plagued with colds and chilblains: 'One of my hands is so chilblained that I can't touch the palm of it with my fingers; and the other is so chapped that I can't play at fives because I bloody the ball.'

The Talbot brothers were similarly afflicted with colds and chilblains as well as boils:

> This is a very cold day indeed. I asked Mrs Haycroft [the Matron, wife of the College butler] to give me some camphorball which she did . . . I did not play football because the chilblains on my feet hurt when I walk . . . A good many of the boys have gone home [in March 1857] for coughs and colds which a great many of us have had lately . . . Two of the boys got inflammation of the lungs and one of [them] very dangerously, and two of them had the fever.

It was considered useless consulting the school doctor. His first question, so Godley alleged, was '*invariably*, "What do you generally take for this?", and if one was to say castor oil for a sprain he would order it immediately to a certainty. The boys generally answer "port wine."'

Sixty or so years later, Godley remembered the hardships of Radley well enough; but he decided that he had on the whole been 'very happy there'. He 'thoroughly enjoyed the cricket, boating and bathing', though not the football, while there were many things which made a lasting impression upon him, notably the music and ritual of Chapel and the beautiful surroundings of the school which gave him 'that love of out-of-door nature' which had proved 'one of the strongest feelings' of his life.

He was forced to conclude, however, that the teaching in his day was 'not very good', though he made exceptions in the cases of Richard Norman and of William Barber, who later became a Queen's Counsel and County Court judge and was, in Gerald Talbot's opinion, 'a very nice person indeed'. Godley also excepted from his general condemnation R.F. Clarke, a former Fellow of St John's College, Oxford, and W.W. Jackson, later Rector of Exeter College. The Warden himself, while an amusing talker and entertaining anecdotalist, was by general consent not a good teacher. He might have been better had he concentrated upon a few of the boys as, mistakenly, he thought Thomas Arnold had done at Rugby; but, swooping down as he did upon one form then another, he had little influence upon any of them. 'As a teacher he fails,' Norman wrote of him. 'He is too full of theories and crotchets to pass knowledge to boys.'

Yet he was sincerely concerned to turn them into scholars; he urged them constantly to work hard even in the holidays when they were advised to study or write for three or four hours every day after breakfast; he opened a *Liber Argenteus* in which he recorded the successes and worthy endeavours of meritorious pupils. He was constantly interrupting school work for some kind of social event, regularly annoying the Fellows by adding yet another to the long list of extracurricular activities which their pupils were free to take up and often urged by the Warden to do so. There was a Debating Society as well as a Discussion Society, a Shakespeare Society and a Petreian Club whose members read papers on a variety of subjects. The brass band was followed by a string band. There were concerts and declamations, lectures, charades and plays. A performance of *Henry IV, Part I* lasted for three and a half hours. There was also a Rifle Corps which Sewell would have liked to put into uniform; but the Fellows derided the idea and this was one of the few occasions on which the Warden was unable to get his own way by persuasion or guile.

Visitors to Radley were still most welcome, ladies invariably, lecturers frequently – one day a Belgian chef came to talk about cooking – and interesting celebrities as often as they could be enticed to a meal. The young Algernon Charles Swinburne came several times, both before and during his time at Balliol. Sewell had tried hard to induce Swinburne's parents, Admiral and Lady Jane Swinburne, both of them very High Church, to send Algernon to Radley. But they were not to be persuaded: he was sent to Eton and, although as 'a queer little elf' it was feared he would be bullied there, 'something a little formidable about him' kept tormentors at bay. On his visits to Radley his behaviour inclined Sewell to be grateful that he had not had him as a pupil. He once came screaming out of a meeting of the Debating Society declaring Radleians were 'a lot of Philistines' for casting a vote against the poetical qualities of Tennyson's *Maud*; and at a dinner party given especially for him by the Warden he appeared wearing dirty shoes and an extremely old morning coat.

*

Although he failed to persuade Admiral Swinburne that Radley was more suitable than Eton as a school for his son, Sewell did manage to persuade several other well-to-do parents to entrust their children to him. Numbers in the school rose steadily. From 55 in 1853 they grew to 122 in 1855 and 152 two years later.* Ranging from nineteen years old to as young as eight, they were not all as prepossessing as Sewell would have liked. 'A fair proportion of them were as good a lot as could be found at any public school,' Lord Kilbracken wrote; 'but at the other end of the scale was a baddish set . . . I have been told that some of them had been accepted on easy terms in order to keep the school full.'

The good did preponderate, however. Visitors were struck by the 'gentlemanliness' of the boys, those polite manners which the Warden was so anxious to instil in them, and by a general atmosphere of contentment. Charles Dodgson, the mathematical lecturer from Christ Church better known as Lewis Carroll, who visited Radley at this time, considered it 'a very well arranged establishment', much more so than Rugby where he had spent three unhappy years in the late 1840s and where, so he complained, he had been obliged to waste 'incalculable time in writing impositions'. He was 'particularly struck by the healthy, happy look of the boys at Radley and their gentlemanly appearance'.

> The dormitory is the most unique feature of the whole: in two large rooms, by a very trifling expense in woodwork, every boy has a snug little bedroom secured to himself, where he is free from interruption & annoyance. This, to little boys must be a very great addition to their happiness, as being a kind of counterbalance to any bullying they may suffer during the day. From my own experience of school life at Rugby I can say that if I could have been secure from annoyance at night, the hardships of the daily life would have been comparative trifles to bear.

---

*Radley was still a comparatively small school. In the 1850s there were over 400 boys at Marlborough and Rugby, and over 600 at Cheltenham.

There was, so Kilbracken said, 'some bullying at Radley but not much' – a statement later confirmed by Lord Latymer – while fagging, which made life almost unbearable for young boys in some other schools, was not oppressive. Godley himself actually claimed to enjoy it.

An Oxford undergraduate who had himself been at Shrewsbury – where also fagging was not too burdensome – came over to Radley quite often in 1854 and was most favourably impressed by the place. 'Altogether it struck [him] as a sort of Scholastic Utopia realized.' Certainly when the time came for John Godley to leave for another school he was unwilling to do so, unhappy as he had been from time to time in the past. When he had arrived at the age of nine, his father – who had himself been miserable at his preparatory school and was determined to spare his son similar experiences – had intended that when he was thirteen or fourteen, he should go to Harrow, his own old school. When the time came, however, the lists at Harrow were full except in the cases of two houses with poor reputations. So, having 'a strong opinion against Eton' and, having become convinced that 'the standard of attainment at Radley was not a high one', he turned his thoughts to Rugby. He had been a great admirer of Dr Arnold and entertained a scarcely less high opinion of Dr Temple, the then Headmaster. So when an unexpected vacancy occurred in one of the best houses in the school, Jex-Blake's, he did not hesitate.

Godley 'received the news of his father's intention with grief and dismay' and by return of post wrote him a letter, 'over which [he] shed many tears, begging him to reconsider it'. His father declined to do so. His son went to Rugby where he found the food much better than it had been at Radley and the school much warmer. At Rugby he won an exhibition to Balliol where he had the reputation of being a brilliant classical scholar. He sent his sons to Eton.

Had Godley stayed at Radley, he might well have added another to the rather modest total of ten scholarships and exhibitions which the school won in the eight years of Sewell's Wardenship.

Yet, while Sewell's Radley did not produce many scholars, it had no reason to be ashamed of the subsequent careers of its alumni. Many went into the Army and served with distinction; and several went into the Church; one became a bishop and another, Henry Bazeley, a well-known revivalist preacher. J.X. Merriman distinguished himself as a statesman in South Africa where he was Prime Minister of Cape Colony in 1908–10; Woodgate was one of England's finest oarsmen, and W.E.W. Collins a celebrated cricketer, renowned for his unique achievement in dismissing three batsmen with one ball: one was hit on the thumb, dripping blood onto the field; the second fainted in horror at the sight of it; the third refused to go in.

I I

Financial Collapse
1860–1861

'So long as the child is saved do not care for the parent.'

'A VAST ASSEMBLY CAME,' wrote William Tuckwell in his *Reminiscences of Oxford*, describing the opening of Radley's gymnasium on the Gaudy of 15 July 1860. 'Sewell, in full doctor's dress of scarlet and black velvet, welcomed us – as usual, a perfect host. We sat down to a splendid banquet [described elsewhere as a 'Belshazzar feast']; Dan Godfrey's band discoursed sweet music; 600 lbs. of strawberries, we were told, covered the tables at dessert.' The dinner was followed by a concert. Before it there had been a splendid picnic at Nuneham. The whole affair, Tuckwell was told, 'cost *somebody* £1,600'. All went off very well, William Wood, the Sub-Warden, commented, ' – *mais*'.

The qualification was only too apt: the College was on the verge of financial collapse. In order to bring some order into its chaotic accounts the Warden had called in his brother, Robert Burleigh Sewell, a solicitor, in whom he reposed a quite unjustified trust as an expert in financial affairs. Robert Sewell's appointment as Treasurer had not proved a success. The school had sunk ever deeper into debt, the exact amount of which was impossible to fathom but was believed to be approaching £50,000. There was talk of amalgamating the school with Westminster which was said to be looking for premises in the country; there were rumours, too, that the Warden had had a letter from Archdeacon Augustus Saunders, who had been Schoolmaster of

Charterhouse, enquiring as to the possibility of acquiring Radley as a site for Charterhouse which was then considering a move to the country.* At the same time there was renewed speculation that Miss Burdett-Coutts would come to Radley's rescue.

Meanwhile the College survived from week to week under the threat of imminent dissolution. At last, after years of negotiation, the terms of a 50-year lease of the house and 140 acres of the park were agreed; but it seemed doubtful that the school would survive for five months, let alone for fifty years. At the end of the Christmas term 1860, the Fellows would have departed unpaid and the boys would have had no money for their journeys home had not the College been lent £1,000 by Richard Norman, who came to its rescue again at the beginning of the following term with a further loan of £1,800.

Enduring salvation came at last in the comforting shape of the kindly-looking and heavily bewhiskered John Gellibrand Hubbard, whose son had entered the school in the Lent term of 1856. Hubbard had been educated by a tutor in England and at school in France; and in 1821 had entered the counting-house of his father, a successful Russia merchant. Seven years later he had been elected a Director of the Bank of England, and soon afterwards had entered Parliament as Conservative Member for Buckingham. A Privy Councillor, he was to be raised to the peerage as Baron Addington. An acknowledged expert on financial matters, possessed of an ample fortune, and of High Church beliefs, he might well have been chosen as the ideal man to save Radley even had he had no connection with the school already. When approached by Robert Sewell, he readily agreed to provide the money immediately needed to keep the College afloat for the time being, on condition that its finances were placed under his direct control. He was to be assisted in his endeavours by two other parents of Radley boys, neither of them rich but both models of social respectability and financial probity. One of these Trustees was Lieutenant-Colonel Robert Moorsom of the Scots Fusilier Guards who had had to retire from the Army on grounds of ill health after serving in the

---

*The position of Charterhouse, situated in a slum area close to Smithfield Market, had become critical. In 1825 there had been 480 boys in the school; ten years later there were less than a hundred. In 1872 the school moved to Godalming to an estate found for it by the then Schoolmaster, William Haig Brown, who increased its numbers to over 500 and re-established its reputation.

Crimea. The other was the Hon. Gerald Talbot, the father of Charles Talbot who had survived his boils and chilblains to become Senior Prefect.

The transparent honesty of these two men and the financial resources of the equally straightforward Hubbard succeeded in salvaging the endangered reputation of the school and in rescuing it from the bankruptcy which an importunate tradesman might well have forced upon it. The operation, however, entailed the departure of William Sewell to whose financial irresponsibility the crisis had largely been due. His departure had been accepted for some time as a natural consequence of the school's predicament. In October 1856 Wood had reported that the Fellows had altogether lost confidence in the Warden; and, in a conversation with Sewell that month, the Sub-Warden had warned him of the Fellows' feelings, of their deep concern over the extravagant expenditure on entertainment and building. The Warden had assured him that there was really no cause for concern: his brother had told him 'only the other day that all was well'. Sewell had not looked untroubled, though. He had been very pale and 'leant back in his chair with his eyes shut'.

Since then the strain had increasingly told upon him; and when he was at last persuaded by Colonel Moorsom and Gerald Talbot that the only solution was for him to go, and for Hubbard to take the place entirely into his own hands, he seemed on the verge of collapse. His letters at this time, redolent of self-pity, make painful reading: 'I am in your hands to do what you like, to go and black shoes if necessary tomorrow . . . Do not mind me . . . So long as the child is saved do not care for the parent . . . Save the child.'

Concerned 'to save the child', Sewell was at the same time anxious to save himself, turning to the Trustees to support him after his retirement from the scene. He would require at least £200 a year, he told them, hinting that unless provision were to be made for him, he would have to reconsider his resignation and have second thoughts about handing the school over to Hubbard and the Trustees. After all, so he 'distinctly' told the Fellows, 'Radley was intended to be the treasury which was to pay his father's debts, his own whims and private extravagances – a very complete family nest-egg.'

Colonel Moorsom, usually so restrained, lost his patience with Sewell's demands, procrastinations and evasions. The idea of Radley working 'not for the good of the Church, but to pay off the debts of the Sewell family [was] quite preposterous'. Norman, who had himself lent more money to the school than he could well afford, thought the behaviour of the Warden was 'beyond all endurance'.

Even after Sewell had agreed to the Trustees' terms and, at a meeting in London, had signed an agreement with them, he continued to maintain that he had been hard done by, hinting that Hubbard had acted dishonestly both towards himself and the College's creditors. In fact, Hubbard, who was not able to reimburse himself fully for twenty years, supported the Trustees in their initiation of a 'Liberation Fund' so that Sewell should not spend the rest of his life plagued by debt.

*

After spending an uncertain period in England in broken health, Sewell removed himself from the reach of his creditors by going to live in Germany, subsisting, it seems, on the remains of this 'Liberation Fund', on small sums from Exeter College, where his Fellowship had been sequestrated, and on an allowance paid to him by his sister Elizabeth, the novelist. Between translations of Homer and work on a book published posthumously, *The Microscope of the New Testament*, he wrote his 'Reminiscences' which were sent in instalments to his nieces and which – interspersed with chunks of indifferent verse and together with amusing and acute character sketches of men he had known in the past – contained recollections of Radley and his days there as Warden.

On the outbreak of the Franco-Prussian War, he returned to England. One day he 'summoned up courage to drive through the Park at Radley. Boys were playing cricket as usual,' he recalled, 'and I was glad to see the trees and shrubs I planted were all thriving, especially a screen which I had planted to keep the north wind from the playground. I did not, of course, go in.'

He did, however, attend an Old Radleians' Dinner on 24 June 1872 in Willis's Rooms where one of his former pupils, the Hon. Augustus Erskine, by now the 12th Earl of Kellie, was in the chair. He was sixty-eight years old by then, in poor health, leaning on a stick; but he spoke for almost an hour and would have spoken about five times as long had he actually delivered the text later published as *The Founder's Speech, 1872* which runs to 115 pages.

Despite the length of his oration, his words were well received by the forty guests who were, no doubt, well satisfied to hear their old school praised so highly by its Founder. Lyrically as he commended Radley as it had been under his own Wardenship, however, Sewell was not so complimentary about his colleagues: in dealing with the foundation of the College he did not even mention Singleton; and, in describing his own time as Warden, he was patronizing about the Sub-Warden, reserving his fulsome comments for a Fellow of higher birth, the Hon. Horace Courtenay Gammell Forbes, afterwards the 19th Lord Forbes. But perhaps those parts of the speech dealing with the Fellows were omitted from the text as delivered at the dinner.

Sewell's lengthy and characteristic eulogy of aristocracy seems not to have been omitted, however:

> The aristocracy of England I cherish, and always wished you to cherish with a profound veneration . . .
>
> I endeavoured to bring to Radley and into habitual contact with you the first and best society in England . . . I liked you to feel that they came there as to no ordinary place, that not only men but ladies of high rank liked to stay there . . . How was it, an Eton master asked, that such an aspect of dignity was given to Radley? And as he little knew the how he probably guessed as little the why this dignity was given to it. And now I will confess it. It was mainly with the thought of Eton . . .
>
> You were proud of having at your head a boy of noble name [Charles Talbot]. You know, as I have told you before, that in my heart of hearts I planned and constructed Radley as a school for the aristocracy of England, an aristocracy of which the pride and the power lies deep in its heritage of blood.

His audience, his 'own dear boys', he was proud to remember, listened to his words with attention and evident approval. He had been in 'a great state of nervousness' beforehand, since he was 'very weak both in mind and body'; and he feared that tears might 'come very soon'. Yet, in the event, he felt quite at home with them, and believed that 'no Head Master of a Public School, or of any school, ever met his old boys with such entire openness, ease, freedom from reserve, and entire sympathy.'

Although he had declined invitations to previous Old Radleian Dinners, Sewell was sufficiently encouraged by his reception at Willis's Rooms to attend the next dinner which was held at the Freemason's Tavern where Charles Talbot, who had joined the 14th Hussars on leaving Radley and was to become British Consul at Boston, was in the chair.

But the next year the invitation was again declined. Sewell, by then living in the Isle of Wight near to his birthplace, was, by his own account, 'very weak'. He died on 14 November 1874 while on a visit to his nephew, headmaster of a preparatory school near Manchester. A memorial service was held at Radley in a Chapel draped in black. The address was given by the Revd John William Burgon, the High Church Vicar of the University Church of St Mary the Virgin and soon to become Dean of Chichester, who spoke movingly of Sewell's character and attainments as Founder and Warden of the College.* 'What chiefly roused all his Christian chivalry,' Burgon declared,

> what so completely stirred up what was manly and energetic in him, as to cause him to descend into the arena of life (so to speak) as a combatant . . . was the terrible theory, which certainly has prevailed in connection with public school life [Burgon himself had been educated at a private school in Blackheath] – a theory already, thank God, in a great degree exploded – that a schoolboy must needs go through a career of carelessness, irreligion, acquaintance – familiarity rather – with sin and defilement, in order to the formation of a manly character.

In lapidary inscriptions a man is not upon oath. But for all his faults, his deviousness, his self-regard and self-delusion, his financial irresponsibility and obsessive class-consciousness, Sewell deserved this epitaph. He had succeeded in making Radley a more tolerant public school than most. The idyllic surroundings chosen by him and Singleton did seem to have some of the desired effect upon the aesthetic sensibilities of the boys; and most of these boys did become, as Lord Kilbracken had become, more aware of the beauties of nature than they might otherwise have been.

There was undeniably at Radley an understanding and sympathetic relationship between master and pupil unusual at other schools in those days. The wider curriculum, including scientific subjects as well as the humanities, the music, the College's collection of paintings and works of art served to give the boys a deeper understanding of what education should be. The cubicles gave them that privacy and sense of security denied to most boys at public schools; and, while William Tuckwell was putting it too strongly when he said that 'the moral

---

*J.W. Burgon won the Newdigate Prize in 1845 with *Petra* which contains the line 'A rose-red city – "half as old as time"' – the only line which anyone now remembers from that poem. The Newdigate has since been won by three Old Radleians, S.H. Reynolds, *The Ruins of Egyptian Thebes* (1853), Peter Way, *Caesarion* (1948) and Andrew Motion, *The Tides* (1975).

tone of the boys under Singleton's rule was perfect', there was no doubt that parents had less cause to complain of bullying than they would have had elsewhere. Moreover, the services in Chapel, with what John Godley called 'such jolly singing' and 'such an awfully jolly organ', did encourage a large proportion of boys to take Holy Orders after leaving school.*

Sewell's ideas as an educationist have had their influence on his suc-

---

*Of the 269 boys who entered Radley in Sewell's time from 1853 to 1861 49 took Holy Orders, 59 joined the Army (only two the Royal Navy), 30 went abroad, more to become planters, farmers or merchants than to join the Colonial Service or to serve the Empire in other ways. For most of the rest no future occupation is recorded in the College archives, although several seem to have retired into the country, some of them to inherit family estates. Eleven became barristers or solicitors, six doctors or physicians, five became stockbrokers or stock-jobbers, five Members of Parliament (three Conservative, two Liberal), four schoolmasters (one, W.M. Furneaux, Headmaster of Repton), four civil engineers, one a sculptor and painter, and one a naturalist.

This record may be compared with that of Marlborough where 792 boys – almost three times as many as at Radley – were entered on the school books in the same period. Over three quarters of the Marlborough boys (599) were the sons of clergymen as compared with scarcely more than a third of Radley boys (99). Yet almost exactly the same proportion from each school became clergymen themselves, 148 at Marlborough as against Radley's 49. A considerably lower proportion of Marlburians joined the Army (141 as against 59). But far more Marlburians joined the Royal Navy (34 as against 2).

Proportionately more Marlburians went abroad than Radleians: 47 became servants of the Crown in the Empire, mostly in India. In addition, 28 went to Australia, and three became missionaries, having converted to Rome. A further 30 became civil servants at home. The most common other occupations were lawyers (48), merchants and businessmen (48, eleven of them abroad), engineers (39, 23 of them abroad), surgeons and physicians (36), coffee, tea and sugar planters (19). Seventeen went into banks, twelve became schoolmasters, seven became academics, six land agents, five stockbrokers, four wine merchants, three journalists and two actors. There were two Members of Parliament; one founded the Church Lads' Brigade, another was appointed Garter King of Arms. Unlike the Radleians, only one or two of them seem not to have been gainfully employed.

A rather smaller proportion of boys from the older public schools took Holy Orders or joined the Army. Of the 348 boys who entered Winchester, for example, between 1853 and 1860, no more than 59 became clergymen; 52 joined the Army and 37 the Navy.

As was to be expected, a much higher proportion of Wellingtonians joined the Army. By 1879 out of 1,849 men who had been at Wellington, over half (992) were the sons of army officers and well over a third (755) became officers themselves.

cessors at Radley to this day; and the ethos of the school he founded, for all its changes of direction in subsequent years, has never been lost. As George Orwell observed in his review of Sewell's biography, *A Forgotten Genius* by Lionel James, 'If he is now forgotten, this book, which is mostly a mass of ill-digested documentation, is not likely to make him less so, but the author does show good reason for thinking that Sewell, as much as, or even more than Arnold, was responsible for giving the public schools their present character.'

In reviewing Thomas Hughes's preface to the sixth edition of his *Tom Brown's Schooldays*, the *Gentleman's Magazine* in 1858 compared the 'new system established at Radley' favourably with the regimes established at some older schools from which emerge 'sad stories, some of which we know to be true, of most barbarous, savage cruelty being tolerated, and of boys, well-disposed but of timid and sensitive temperament, being worried and bullied even to death'.

The new system established at Radley [the *Gentleman's Magazine* continued] has, perhaps, hardly yet had a fair trial. It has many obvious advantages, and seems in many respects better suited for the sons of gentlemen who are wished to be brought up as gentlemen, than the coarse, vulgar slang, the roughness and brutality of Westminster or Winchester. Those who have been brought up under the old system will of course abuse the new one, and be honestly prejudiced against it, on the ground that it is calculated to make the boys *milk-sops*; but this remains to be proved; hitherto we have not observed any symptoms of it.

12

Mr Norman's Interregnum
1861–1866

'Every tie on Earth seems to be wrenched asunder.'

O N THE EVENING of the day upon which he had resigned the Wardenship, Sewell had installed his successor in Radley College Chapel. The new Warden was the Revd Richard Whitmore Norman. The Senior Fellow, he had been one of the first appointments made by Sewell, to whom he had often shown a loyalty withheld by his colleagues. A graduate of Exeter College, he was now thirty-two years old, a capable schoolmaster, respected and liked by his pupils, one of whom, the young Charles Talbot, had mentioned him often in his letters to his parents:

> This afternoon we had Grecian History and I happened not to answer 4 questions so Mr Norman got very angry and told me that he should put me down in the Black Book and that he should put me down twice if I did not know my Latin grammar afterwards . . . This morning we went up with our Roman history to Mr Norman and he stopped me after it to tell me to cheer up as I was doing better since he had spoken to me yesterday.
> This morning we went up with Xenophon and I had to construe and I said it quite quick and Mr Norman said I had done it very well indeed, of which praise I was extremely glad.

The Fellows of the College were generally agreed that Norman was a decent fellow, yet there was a reserve in his manner, a certain petulance which sometimes found expression in the droop of the clean-shaven skin around his unsmiling mouth that men found repugnant. There was doubt, too, that he had the strength of character and physique for the demands of his new post. William Wood, who would, no doubt, have been appointed Warden himself had he not been granted a term's sabbatical to accompany Sir Arthur Gordon on a tour of the Near East, liked him well enough but decided that he was 'not first-rate' and expressed the hope that he would be able to find 'first-rate Classics to join him'.

There were several vacancies to fill. There were also several impending vacancies: most of the existing Fellows had not been at Radley for more than a term or two and of these several were soon to depart. The salaries offered to new Fellows were not enticing. The Warden was adequately paid, his salary being increased by Hubbard from £500 to £600 a year. At the same time £400 a year was allotted to the Sub-Warden, an office temporarily resumed by Wood – after he had returned from his tour of the Near East and married Colonel Moorsom's daughter – until he left Radley for a parish in Buckinghamshire. But, apart from the drawing master (£200 a year), Monk's successor as Precentor (£230), a science master (£300), and those men who had been at the College for several years (£250 and £200), no Fellow received more than £160 a year.

Fees – in addition to an entrance charge of £10 10s. – were £117 2s. a year, including compulsory extras for the gymnasium, medical attendance, laundry and 'instruction in Experimental Science'. During the uncertain times of Sewell's later Wardenship, numbers had fallen as boys had been taken away to other schools. So, in Norman's first term, there were only 136 boys in the school – one more than there were in his last – and in attempting to balance his books, Hubbard not only had the salaries of the Warden and Fellows to find (£3,180 a year) but also the wages of a large staff, whose remuneration ranged from 9s. a week paid to an antiquated gardener who had worked for the Bowyers in the eighteenth century to over £400 a year paid to Archibald MacLaren – founder of the Oxford preparatory school, Summer Fields – who was in charge of Radley's gymnasium. In addition to the butler and storekeeper (who also managed Shop) there were fourteen servitors, seven maids, six gardeners, a cook (assisted by an under-cook and a baker), a mason, a carpenter and carpenter's apprentice, a nightwatchman, a lamp-cleaner, two shoe blacks, who also acted as knife cleaners and sharpeners, and two grooms. There was also a matron (£96 a year), a sick nurse (£35 a year) and a bursar (£96 a year).

Hubbard was naturally anxious to get his money back, but he was determined also that Radley should remain true to the faith in which it had been founded. He invited four distinguished men to join Moorsom and Talbot as Trustees, the 6th Duke of Marlborough, Lord Richard Cavendish, younger brother of the 7th Duke of Devonshire, Sir Richard Phillimore, the jurist, and the Revd F.K. Leighton, Warden of All Souls. The Duke of Marlborough, Lord Richard Cavendish and Phillimore visited Radley rarely and never stayed long; but Leighton and Talbot came down more often, while Hubbard and Moorsom were both assiduous in their visits and attendance at Trustees' meetings.

At one of these meetings it was agreed that various objects bought for the school by Sewell, some of them still unpacked and stored in the coach house, should be sold. It is not known how much was sold, but Hubbard himself bought various articles at valuation and gave one of the College's pastoral staffs to Bishop Wilberforce, the other to Walter Kerr Hamilton, the Old Etonian Bishop of Salisbury.

The new Warden was not sorry to see the relics of Sewell's extravagance leave the premises; but he was too much of a Sewellite to change the essential atmosphere of the College. Visits to Oxford were curtailed; and, although lessons began at 8 o'clock instead of 6.30, a stricter regard was had to the demands of the curriculum, while the brighter boys were strongly encouraged to enter for one or other of the three scholarships, the James, Gibbs and Heathcote, all founded in Norman's time and carrying with them the right to wear a scholar's gown, a particular distinction at Radley then, since there were no entrance scholarships.

Yet there were still more holidays than at most other schools; Lenten fasts and observances were continued; extra-curricular activities continued as before; plays – or at least scenes from plays – were still performed and, when these died out, there were Recitations, delivered by boys in evening dress. Feast days and Gaudies were celebrated, if not as lavishly as in the past, at least with a generous spirit. One parent, the Hon. Henry Sugden, son of Lord St Leonards, a former Lord Chancellor, complained that the school holidays, fourteen weeks in the year, were too long. But, when enquiries were made at other public schools, it was found that at most the holidays were quite as long and at Winchester, Charterhouse, Rugby and Shrewsbury even longer, only Cheltenham with just over ten weeks and Wellington with thirteen and a half being shorter.

Henry Sugden's belief that the holidays were too long was not likely to be shared by his sons or other boys at the school; though an article in an early issue of the school magazine, *The Radleian*, which was founded in 1864, suggests that there was a feeling at Radley that there was too much 'lounging about', too much inclination to watch games, or even ignore them, than to play them.

Since there was no school uniform, clothes were a major interest for loungers and sportsmen alike, as, indeed, they were at other schools, few of which had hard and fast rules about uniform. At Bradfield, for example, the variety of trousers was legion; at Shrewsbury, in Samuel Butler's day, a boy described one of his shirts as having 'pink sprigs' and another 'with cerulean frogs on a check ground'; at Oundle there was little uniformity of clothes apart from straw hats in summer as late as 1880; and it was not until the 1920s that boys at Rugby were all required to wear stiff collars.

From an early date Eton chose to dress in black as the school had done during the long mourning for King George III; at Marlborough, C.G. Bradley, who became Master in 1858, 'made a determined effort' to introduce black peaked caps, black jackets with five buttons and grey striped trousers; and at Wellington from the beginning boys had been required to wear a quasi-military uniform of a dark green coat with brass buttons, plaid trousers and a cap with a gilt crown set in front. But these were exceptions. There was a general feeling that uniforms were strongly to be resisted as the mark of charity boys such as the poor fellows at Christ's Hospital in their blue cassocks and yellow stockings. When new caps in house colours were introduced at Tonbridge in the 1890s they were ridiculed as making Tonbridgians 'look like errand boys'.

John Godley's letters home from Radley had been full of references to clothes, to his gown, the non-arrival of which was a source of much anxiety during his first days at school, to trousers and waistcoats, to 'peg-tops' which were 'not laughed at because a good many chaps' had them, to the new, high-crowned College cap in the new school colours of red and white which in September 1858 replaced the former colours of red and black check. Boys in mourning wore black caps which were also preferred by those of quiet taste to whom the school colours seemed rather vulgar.

For everyday wear most of the senior boys sported tail coats under the gowns which all boys had to wear, and trousers of various colours, usually pale brown or pale grey, usually striped or checked. They were allowed to carry walking sticks and some of them affected monocles.

Junior boys wore short coats, or Eton jackets with turnover collars, and ties of their own choosing, usually in the brightest colours. Outside the school grounds all boys were required to wear top hats. Those older boys who could grow them, wore whiskers. According to additional Statutes, which came into effect after Sewell's time, moustaches could be worn by boys during their last term, provided permission had been obtained from the Warden. Beards might also be worn by any captain of a major school game if the Warden permitted.*

Sewell would certainly not have granted such permission. He hated beards and occasionally despatched jocular remonstrances in Latin verse to Fellows whose side-whiskers threatened to become too luxuriant or to cover too much of the face. In a photograph of Sewell and the College Fellows in 1857, all the Fellows appear to have side-whiskers but only Norman has a beard and this is a far from emphatic one. William Wood's dense black beard is evidently of post-Sewell growth. Only one Fellow, the Hon. Horace Forbes, as an indulged aristocrat, had presumed to sport a moustache. By contrast, a photograph of 1878 shows a majority of Fellows with moustaches.

*

In Sewell's time all boys had been required to play football unless they could show some reason for not doing so; but this rule now lapsed and a suggestion that cricket should be made compulsory was sharply attacked in *The Radleian*. As it was, it was difficult to get a decent cricket team together in the 1860s without recourse to wet-bobs who were always liable to be called upon for the more important matches such as those played against Old Radleians and those few Oxford colleges which raised scratch elevens to play against the school. Indeed, cricket was considered so inferior a sport when compared with rowing that 'one man's sole qualification to be captain of the XI was that he had got too fat to row in the Eight.'

It could not be said, however, that Radley rowing was as yet of any distinction. The school certainly produced one or two first-class oarsmen. Philip Gurdon and R.W. Risley both won Blues before becoming parsons; R.T. Raikes, father of four Radleians and the pro-

---

*These same Statutes decreed that only the Senior Prefect could bring his wife back to College. A note in the Prefects' Book against this rule qualifies the privilege by stating that the Warden's permission was required and that 'this permission is unlikely to be obtained'.

genitor of many more, also rowed in the Oxford Eight, while W.B. Woodgate won the Diamond Sculls at Henley and was five times victorious in the Silver Goblets. But the Radley Eight, proudly as they turned themselves out in their cerise flannel jerseys trimmed with white, their blazers with the Maltese cross on the pocket, and their straw hats with red and white ribbons, were never a successful crew. In 1858 Radley accepted a challenge to row against the Eton Eight at Henley; but Eton, having won that race, declined a challenge the next year, with the dismissive comment that they 'did not intend to row any more such matches with Radley'. Accordingly, Radley rowed that year and the next on their home stretch of the river against Old Radleians or Oxford colleges. They were granted permission to enter for the Ladies' Plate* at Henley in 1861 but were defeated by 3¾ lengths, the cox, a future Bishop of Kingston upon Thames, having been responsible for some mishap at the start.

Radley's football teams were rather more successful in their games against Oxford colleges, but since they played to Radley rules which, while similar to Harrow's, were unique to the school, their opponents were at a disadvantage. A school match was played against Bradfield in 1864; but this engagement was not repeated the following year because of the ill-feeling generated by failure to agree upon common rules.

The younger boys in the school still wore no special clothes for playing their games: indeed when in 1862 one young boy turned up for a cricket match against another form wearing flannels he was told that it was 'beastly cheek' to do such a thing, having been in the school for only a year. The boys in the First Football XII, however, permitted themselves the brightest plumage, including red velvet caps with silver stripes and blue or silver tassels. A photograph of the formidable-looking team of 1866 shows them in skull-caps, striped short-sleeved shirts and white flannels. Soon afterwards white knickerbockers were introduced and were worn with magenta stockings. Two Prefects photographed wearing this uniform are shown exercising their privilege to grow moustaches.

With the help of such authoritative-looking Prefects, Warden

---

*A trophy in the form of a ewer presented by the 'Ladies of Henley'. It was first awarded in 1846; the winners the previous year were given medals instead, the ewer being not then ready. The Princess Elizabeth Cup, now the principal race for schools, was inaugurated in 1946.

Norman seems to have been able to maintain discipline in the school without such regular recourse to corporal punishment as was found necessary in Sewell's day, although there was one occasion when, after a 'gross breach of Dormitory discipline', six malefactors were summoned for a beating before the entire school one morning at half-past eight. Three of the culprits submitted; but the others refused to do so. Whereupon three labourers were summoned to the school. They marched in, so Wood said, 'spitting on their hands'. Two of the three victims then submitted to a caning. It was announced that the third should be expelled. He left Radley within the hour, although, after a petition had been presented by the boys and a College Meeting had been called, his punishment was remitted to one of 'removal', so that his chances of going to university would not be affected. He did not choose to go to university, however: he joined the Army as a volunteer, was sent out to New Zealand and was soon killed fighting the Maori.

After this episode Norman had little trouble with the boys; but he found the Fellows more difficult. Indeed, the problems presented by the collegiate system, and the Fellows' insistence that their status and privileges must be defined by a 'constitution', became so burdensome to the Warden that he appeared often to be almost distraught. On one occasion, in Wood's words, he 'quite gave way and burst into tears'.

When the Fellows formally expressed an entire 'lack of confidence in the Warden' the Trustees began to consider that yet another Warden would have to be replaced. They were helped in coming to this decision by the fact that the present incumbent had never been officially installed. Moreover, he was clearly not in good health and, so they thought, might even welcome the opportunity of making way for a successor. In this they were mistaken and, to their evident surprise, when notice of their intentions was served upon the Fellows, five of them – no doubt concerned that the Trustees might take it into their heads to appoint new Fellows as well as a new Warden – threatened to resign if the Warden were deprived of his office. Encouraged by this, Norman asked the Trustees to confirm him officially as Warden, a request granted by the Trustees who had in the meantime received a refusal of an offer of the appointment to the Wardenship which they had made to the Revd H.P. Liddon, the entertaining and companionable Vice-Principal of St Edmund Hall and a notable University speaker and lecturer.

At the start of the next term, however, it was obvious that the

Warden's health had deteriorated even further, while his *rapproche-ment* with the Fellows had not survived the holidays. The protagonists struggled through the term for week after uneasy week, the Warden on one occasion being observed after a College Meeting to be 'nearly in hysterics'. By March 1866 he could face no more; and one day he suddenly left Radley without warning. Soon after his departure he sailed for Canada where he became a Fellow of McGill College, Vicar of Quebec and Dean of the Cathedral of All Saints, before dying in Toronto.

13

Trouble in Common Room
1866–1870

'The great schools with rich foundations absorb the cleverest boys.'

WITHIN A WEEK or two of Norman's disappearance, the Trustees agreed to invite William Wood to leave his Buckinghamshire parish and to take over as Warden for three months until a permanent headmaster could be appointed. Wood discussed the offer with his wife, then sent his reply by telegram: 'I accept.'

There were to be many occasions during the next three years when Wood and his wife both had cause to regret that this telegram had ever been despatched, for the difficulties that he had with the Fellows were far more unpleasant than even Norman had known. Only one of them welcomed his return to Radley with any show of warmth. This was George Wharton, a small, enthusiastic, friendly, talkative young man whose eccentricities were to be ever more pronounced as year followed year. He was to become known as 'Kitty', partly because of his whiskery resemblance to a cat, partly because of a certain cattiness in his nature, noticed by Samuel Butler on a visit to Radley in the 1890s: 'He looked like an Italian sacristan. He was superficially polite but very spiteful – this is why the boys called him "Kitty".'

By then Wharton had developed into an indulged and often troublesome institution in a school which he was to know under nine Wardens, to some of whom, as well as to some of his colleagues, he was to be maliciously disloyal. The son of a country parson who hinted that he was connected with the Dukes of Wharton – and whose wife liked it to be known that she was descended from the long and ancient line of the Wharburtons of Cheshire – George Wharton had been educated at home before winning a choral scholarship at Queens' College, Cambridge. He was not in the least intellectual; he took his degree by an *aegrotat* and, having failed in his examination for deacon's orders at the end of his first term at Radley, for many years he could not face the ordeal of a further examination and it was not until 1874 that he was ordained. He had once been in love with a young lady; but her refusal of his offer of marriage had led to a vow never to marry anyone else, and, in the words of his biographer, he thereafter 'lived happily wedded to his organ'.

He had come as Precentor to Radley after a time spent at Bradfield, and at first was most unhappy here, 'longing so very much' for his 'dear old Willy', his beloved friend William Knox Little, for whom he had conceived a profound devotion, a deep attachment later also to be felt for a Radley boy, the Hon. Charles Horatio Nelson, son of the 3rd Earl Nelson and grandson of the great Admiral's nephew. Wharton was unhappy, too, about the standard of the music and singing in Radley Chapel, which had deteriorated sadly since the departure of Monk for York. His diary entries for these early days at Radley make sad reading: the first Chapel service was 'not at all satisfactory'; he felt 'rather miserable', he prayed that he would soon 'get more comfortable'.

The atmosphere in Common Room did nothing to comfort him. The other Fellows were quarrelsome, dissatisfied, touchy and generally morose, bickering about the manner in which the Chapel services were conducted, complaining about their salaries, their status, their food. Several of them declined to take their meals in Hall, having dinners served in their rooms. They smoked in front of the boys in defiance of the Statutes. Lazy or incompetent in the discharge of their duties, they protested against such steps as Wood felt able to take in cutting down expenses; they remonstrated with particular animosity when the Trustees decided to strengthen Wood's hand by abolishing the bogus collegiate system and transmogrifying the Fellows into schoolmasters or – as they were to be more generally known at Radley – dons. Most of them considered leaving the school and those who could find other employment did leave: very few of those appointed between 1862 and 1872 stayed more than three years. When Wood was officially confirmed as Warden on 14 June 1866, after a number of other men had either been rejected or had declined to be considered, Common Room received the news in silence.

Mrs Wood, who had been unable to accompany her husband to Radley from Prestwood because she had just given birth to their third child, heard of the confirmation of his appointment with 'the greatest pleasure'. She 'had always loved Radley,' she wrote. 'My eldest brother [Colonel Henry Manvers Moorsom] went there as a student in 1849 & from that time forward it had always been a place of happy associations to me.' She was soon to be sadly disillusioned.

On the night of her arrival she had dinner alone in the drawing-room while her husband dined in Hall, as he was always to do. After dinner, she recorded, 'when the Gentlemen came up to the Drawing Room I gave them Tea ... and on this first occasion we began to find troubles. The first act of the Trustees on appointing the new W[arden] was to do away with the title of "Fellow", which proceeding, though highly necessary was extremely unpopular. It was not my Husband's act, though he quite approved of it, but the masters attributed it to him & visited their dissatisfaction on him.'

> The dissatisfaction [Emma Wood continued] showed itself in vexatious opposition to whatever Dr Wood did ... (I call him by his present title but he was then Mr Wood) ... & all his endeavours after a more cordial feeling appeared to be considered either as insincere or as a sign of weakness. On this first night some very unpleasant remarks were made about some changes he had made in the Chapel, though it was simply in the way of windows in the roof. It was commented on and criticized in a way so painful that I early said good night & retired to bed, & how many tears have I shed in that bed ... I did not of course come forward in any way, my business was to keep out of the way.

It was, however, difficult for Mrs Wood to keep out of the way. She was not the retiring personality which her account of her husband's Wardenship is inclined to suggest. Although small in stature, she was a formidable lady with a very loud voice which carried all over the house. She was 'a devoted Churchwoman', in the words of her daughter, and had been brought up in the Oxford Movement, her parents being friends of the Kebles. Her grandfather was General H.J. Campbell, a veteran of the Peninsular War; and she herself had been drilled by a sergeant in the Guards who had shouted at her and her sisters, 'Bellies in, young ladies! Bellies in!' Proud of her ancestress, Lady Mary Wortley Montagu, and of having known George III's daughter, Princess Sophia, whom her grandfather had taught to ride, she had at first refused the hand of William Wood, knowing that her adored father would have preferred a son-in-law from his own Scots Fusilier Guards. It was at least understandable that in Oxford the story went about that Radley no longer had a Warden but a Wardeness.

The first disagreeable term ended with three of the more trouble-some masters having left; and the Woods could but hope, as the Warden put it, that the next 'would be a pleasanter term than the last'. It was not. One misfortune followed another: the Warden went down with influenza; one of his sons fell seriously ill; his much loved father-in-law, Robert Moorsom, died; two more masters left; another made a fuss about fasting in Lent and was asked to leave; a fourth was the subject of investigations required by the Bishop of Oxford into 'a most distressing charge'; a fifth, George Wharton, was rudely interrupted by a boy whilst saying grace in Hall and was severely criticized by the other masters for not dealing properly with the impertinence. 'A case of cruelty' involving five boys resulted in severe floggings.

The New Year, 1868, brought further troubles, including the death of a boy from pneumonia. Colonel Moorsom's death was followed by the resignation of Gerald Talbot as a Trustee; and neither of the two men appointed to fill the vacancies – the Old Etonian the Hon. Charles Lindley Wood, later 2nd Viscount Halifax, and Henry Barnett, MP, whose son was at the school – were very regular in their attendance at Trustees' meetings. The Warden was consequently obliged to do more business than he would have chosen with the now often brusque J.G. Hubbard, who held him responsible for the falling numbers of boys in the school and who endeavoured to compensate for this by reducing salaries, which had been increased towards the end of Norman's Wardenship – the Sub-Warden's to £300 a year, the Precentor's to £200 and those of the other masters, much to their indignation, to £150 with a capitation fee of £1 a boy after one year's employment.

The falling number of boys – due as much to the troubles of Sewell's and Norman's time as to his own perceived shortcomings – was a con-stant source of anxiety to the Warden, as were the number of boys taken away from Radley to be sent to other schools. 'He was ever anxious to raise the numbers,' his wife wrote, 'yet to retain the power of refusing to take very backward and delicate boys, of which there had always been a large proportion at R[adley], too large for the good of the place . . . The great schools with rich foundations absorb the cleverest boys.' By the time Wood became Warden, there were more-over many good preparatory schools in existence, whereas when Mrs Wood's brother had gone to Radley there were 'several little fellows there of under 10 years old (he himself was nine) but latterly there [had] been scarcely any [there] under 13'.

The number of boys in the school – which had fallen to 133 by the time of Wood's first term in 1866 – slumped to 79 at the end of the last in 1870. Between these dates two entrance scholarships were founded but the first winners of both of them left after two years in the school.

Yet the academic record of Wood's Radley was not as unsatisfactory as might have been expected. At a school from which a large number of boys went into the Army (twice as many by now as went into the Church) and almost as many went abroad on leaving school, five uni-versity scholarships were won as well as a demyship at Magdalen College and an exhibition at Keble. It was generally agreed by outside examiners that, despite the disagreements in Common Room, Radley boys were adequately taught, and that the curriculum was not nearly as narrow as it was in some other public schools, history and English literature being given due attention – too much attention in the view of certain disgruntled classical dons on the staff.

The disgruntlement of the dons, somewhat abated in the early months of 1868, became more marked than ever in the summer term. One particularly intransigent don was dismissed, only to intrigue against Wood from the King's Arms at Sandford; two other masters were also asked to leave; yet another, S.J. Owen, whom Wood had con-sidered a friend and who had been appointed by Sewell at the same time as himself, left after having sided with the rebels. Then came an even greater problem: Hubbard's insistence that the Bursar should be answerable in all matters to him rather than to the Warden. The Bursar, so Mrs Wood maintained, 'claimed an independent authority . . . No one who had not experienced it could believe the amount of annoy-ance we underwent from this cause.' Her husband explained his own views in his journal:

> I tried in vain to make Mr Hubbard and the other Trustees (who of course deferred to him) understand that although the finance was properly in their hands and the Bursar responsible to *them*, he must also in matters touch-ing on discipline be under my orders as Warden.
>
> Exactly the same questions arose (as I afterwards heard) at Wellington College where the Bursar, an Army man, maintained that he was exempt

from Dr Benson's authority. Benson threatened to resign, and the Governors were wise enough to settle it as he desired.*

The annoyance became insupportable when, after a servitor was discovered to be guilty of a series of thefts, the Warden was not informed. Wood complained to Hubbard that it was quite intolerable to have a member of Common Room who took such an independent line. The Bursar left soon afterwards; but a successor was appointed by Hubbard on the understanding that he would be responsible only to himself. Wood offered his own resignation. Hubbard accepted it with the comment, 'You have been hardly tried more than once, but all the trials have been more or less an evidence of a want of suitability between the Warden and his work.'

A man of good sense and the utmost sincerity, a devoted husband and father, deeply attached to his many friends, Wood had done his best at Radley. In face of severe tribulations, he had achieved some modest success in providing its pupils with a sound education without losing sight of Sewell's ideals of 'gentlemanliness' and 'aristocratic pre-eminence'. Those who thought as Sewell did could take pride now in such alumni as the Hon. Harold Gathorne-Hardy who was not only a son of the Earl of Cranbrook but was also to become a Fellow of All Souls; Lord Charles Douglas-Hamilton, a son of the 11th Duke of Hamilton and the author of several distinguished legal and historical works, and the Hon. Hamilton John Agmondesham Cuffe, afterwards 5th Earl of Desart, who married a daughter of the 4th Earl of Harewood and became Director of Public Prosecutions.

---

*At Wellington the administration of the school was divided between the Headmaster, Edward White Benson, who was responsible for the staff, discipline and the curriculum, and the College Secretary, George Chance, who lived in London and looked after the College's finances, domestic arrangements, and the supervision of the College steward, a most difficult man named William Lyne. Benson had frequent cause for complaint about Lyne's incompetence; but the Honorary Secretary to the Governors, Lieutenant-Colonel the Hon. Sir Wellington Patrick Talbot, son-in-law of the 14th Earl of Derby, who was one of the most influential of the school's Governors, supported Chance and Lyne and protested that Benson's complaints and his attempts to abolish the unsatisfactory dual system by which Wellington was governed, were an attack on his own position. Benson proposed that the administration of the College should be conducted under a single authority, that of the Headmaster assisted by a Bursar who lived not in London but on the premises. After much acrimonious discussion, Benson eventually had his way.

William Wood himself was offered by Wilberforce's successor as Bishop of Oxford the living of Cropredy near Banbury where he remained for nearly thirty years. He was afterwards Rector of Monks Risborough, then of Rotherfield Greys where he died at the age of ninety in 1919. His widow survived him until shortly before her ninety-second birthday, still thinking fondly of Radley despite all that she had 'suffered in connection with it'.

14

A Rudderless Ship
1871–1879

'For there's not a prank of any degree
But possesses the greatest of charms for me.'

THE MAN CHOSEN in preference to six other candidates to be
Warden of Radley in November 1870, the Revd Charles Martin,
appeared to be ideally suited to his task. Like Sewell, he had
been head of school at Winchester and from there had won a scholarship to New College where he had been awarded a First in Greats.
After a period as a Senior Student and Tutor at Christ Church, he had
left Oxford to teach at Harrow, being, therefore, the first of Radley's
Wardens to have had the experience of being a master at another school
and, indeed, the only one apart from the Wykehamists, Sewell and
Heathcote, to have attended a public school at all. He was married to
a pleasant wife whose domestic interests were such as to make it
unlikely that she would be accused of interference in the manner of the
loquacious Mrs Wood.*

A scholar, a lover of music and an enthusiastic cricketer, Martin was
a considerate man and a thoughtful one. Anxious to increase the

---

*Mrs Martin was the younger daughter of George Moberly, Bishop of Salisbury and
intimate friend of John Keble. She had five sons and four daughters. The sixth child,
who was educated at Marlborough, was William Keble Martin, the distinguished
botanist. His celebrated *Concise British Flora in Colour* was published when he was
eighty-five in 1965, the year in which he married for the second time.

numbers in the school and to enhance its reputation, he did not have to deal with the challenge faced by so many headmasters – opposition from a group of Common Room veterans, settled and conservative: only one of the masters had been on the staff in Sewell's day. This was W.H. Florio Hutchisson, the drawing master, described as 'an old man supposed by his pupils to have been once fabulously rich, formerly an indigo planter, not a great teacher, nor a great artist, but always endeared to his pupils by his kindly ways, and strict abstention from all disciplinary matters outside his own department'. He was, in short, not a man from whom opposition was to be expected; and, in any case, he left within a few months of Martin's arrival.

Such reforms as Martin initiated were not likely to cause revolt. There were alterations in the times of meals, at which the food seems to have remained indifferent. More studies were created; a peculiarly unattractive Infirmary was built; the water supply and drainage were improved; gas was installed in 1871; and Sewell's idea of giving a master responsibility for the social welfare of a number of boys or 'socials' was gradually developed into a system whereby Social Tutors were entrusted with the care of a group of boys who – while not as yet segregated into different houses and still having meals as a school in a common hall – began to consider themselves as an entity more cohesive and mutually dependent than a form.

Yet Martin's reforms did not progress much further than this. Chapel services remained long and frequent; the curriculum, in the past more varied than that of many other public schools, became as narrow as it was elsewhere. Modern languages were taught perfunctorily by a succession of more or less incompetent masters, and there were now no science masters at all. The so-called Laboratory was used for storing hampers, while the Library, to which junior boys were admitted only once a week, was ill-stocked with books and heated by a stove which not only smoked but was even more smelly than the gas burners which cast an uncertain light over the desks in School and the pews in Chapel. Although eleven university scholarships and exhibitions, all at Oxford, were won in the nearly nine years of Martin's Wardenship, the school's reputation for scholarship was still not high, and parents chose to send their brighter sons elsewhere. 'It is quite true,' Warden Norman had observed, 'that many parents have sent their stupid sons to us, and their more intelligent to Harrow or Rugby.' This was still the case.

Not enough parents even of stupid boys chose Radley, though.

Numbers, which stood at seventy-nine when Martin became Warden, fell to seventy-four by the end of his first year;* and this worried him not only for professional but also for personal reasons: Hubbard and the Trustees had reduced the Warden's salary from £600 a year to £500 with a capitation fee of £2 10s. per boy. This compared very unfavourably with the incomes of headmasters at some other schools. At Wellington, Benson had successfully appealed to the Governors to have his salary increased from £800 to about £1,500 a year; at Rugby in 1862 the headmaster's income from various sources was estimated as being £2,967; and at Uppingham by 1908 the Revd H.W. McKenzie was in receipt of £3,150 a year.

Although his income would grow the more boys there were in the school, Martin was reluctant to admit into it what Wood had called 'diseased specimens', boys of decidedly limited intellect or flawed character. Yet the demands of a growing family, his concern to keep Radley alive, and Hubbard's insistence that numbers must be kept up, combined to persuade him to accept pupils whom it would have been more prudent to exclude, including boys expelled from other schools.

The problem would have been less serious had the masters been more dedicated. It was agreed that they were a likeable set of men, far more pleasant and agreeable than the cantankerous denizens of Common Room who had driven Warden Norman to the verge of nervous collapse. For the first time in the school's history a majority of them were not in Holy Orders. Indeed, several of them had the appearance and manner of country gentlemen rather than schoolmasters.

One of these, a former Senior Prefect, H.M. ('Buffy') Evans, a Welshman of private means and landed property, was renowned for his jocularity, his boisterous singing of the songs of the land of his forebears, his manner of strutting about the school with stiff back, chest pushed out and arms straight at his side. He was also renowned for his

---

*Numbers at Wellington, which had opened twelve years after Radley, had already risen from 76 in January 1859 to 110 by October of that year. In 1865 sanction was given for the number of boys to be raised from 250 to 290; and when he relinquished his appointment as headmaster to the Revd E.C. Wickham in 1873, Dr Benson was able to report that Wellington was full. In the year of Benson's resignation, when there were still less than eighty boys at Radley, numbers at Charterhouse in its new buildings at Godalming had risen to 268. There were almost 425 boys at Rugby in the 1870s, 363 at Uppingham in 1873, and 239 at Tonbridge in 1876. Marlborough's numbers rose to 600 in 1880, and numbers at Cheltenham, the largest public school in England after Eton, to 722 in 1868.

love of rowing, shooting and champagne. 'He had an invincible belief in champagne as a cure for all ills,' wrote a member of the First Eight. 'His critics said that he trained the crew on it. He certainly gave us a good deal of it to drink in training.' Another Radley don, an Old Etonian, C.E. Moore, a keen cricketer, kept a hunter and left Radley to become a land agent. Two other masters, F.B. Harvey and C.F. Vincent, were also keen if unorthodox cricketers, Vincent being a dedicated golfer besides and a familiar figure on Radley's first golf-course, laid out in 1871. Yet another master, C.H. Hodges, a huge presence, was a noted athlete and had come near to breaking the University record for putting the shot at Oxford. Indeed, all these men appeared to be more at home on the playing fields than in the classroom, happier when drinking punch between innings in Common Room cricket matches than in attending evensong in Chapel.

Not all the boys shared their enthusiasm for games. Although cricket was compulsory by now, many of them found excuses not to play; and over a third of the boys in the school in the mid-1870s contrived to get leave off football. Tennis was popular enough; but on the river there was more languid rowing and punting or boisterous splashing about than serious training in eights and fours and competitive oarsmanship. Most of the school went to Henley for the first day of the Regatta; but no one expected the Eight to do well.

A member of the 1873 Eight, A.E. Wigan, who was later to qualify as a barrister and to go out to Jamaica where he became a member of the Governor's Privy Council, described a jaunt that year.* After Radley's customary defeat, he and his companions drove back from Henley in a four-in-hand, stopping at Nettlebed to visit the village fair. Here they had an argument with the gypsy in charge of the coconut stall who was knocked out 'amid much bloodshed' by the Captain of Boats, Thomas Hockin, a clergyman's son, soon to achieve fame as a hero of Oxford oarsmen. The next night the driver of the four-in-hand was too drunk to be trusted on the road; he was dragged from the box and held

---

*It was in this year that boys went to the Regatta for the first time in straw hats with the school ribbon instead of the top hats hitherto *de rigueur*. A writer in *The Radleian* expressed his disapproval of the change, the straw hat and its ribbon being so much like those worn by 'low-minded people who go to Henley to watch the Punch and Judy show or listen to barrel organs'. 'The beaver is the hat which the Prince of Wales thinks fit to wear, then let us vie with him in the shine of our nap and go to Henley in that attire.'

down until he passed out, while the stroke of the Eight, a younger son of Sir Thomas Tancred, 7th baronet, drove the coach back to Radley.

With strong personalities like Wigan, Tancred and Hockin to maintain discipline in the school as Prefects, it might have been supposed that Radley was as orderly as the better regulated public schools of the 1870s. But this was scarcely the case. The Prefects were as indulged an élite as they had been in Sewell's time. They had their special dinners and their special privileges; they and they alone were permitted to read newspapers in school hours; they were not expected to work too hard unless they were going in for some university or army examination. They did not find it difficult to obtain permission to go to London by train after 1873 when the railway station was opened at Radley.* The Senior Prefect at Radley was not required to attend early morning or afternoon school unless inclined to do so. He and the other Prefects and the Captains of Games exercised a control over the organization and finances of the school's sporting activities and all its societies which would strike a Prefect of today as quite astonishing.

The Prefects' study – where there was always beer on tap – was a sanctum into which outsiders rarely penetrated except to be beaten with canes or fives bats. From it the Prefect of the Week would emerge to march into School as the bell known as 'Peter' began to toll. At his command of 'Caps, please' the boys – lined up on either side of the long panelled room beneath the honours boards on one side and the high windows on the other – would take off their mortar boards. They would then proceed into Covered Passage, replacing their mortar boards which would be removed again when they passed the Warden standing to receive their salute in Cloister. The Prefects, some of them perhaps in evening dress, the white tassels of their mortar boards distinguishing them from the common run of boys, took pride of place in the procession into Chapel. They marched forward, as one of them recorded, 'like Roman generals in a triumph'.†

This, at least, was the ideal; but in the late 1870s a spirit of rebellion had entered the school. It was not unknown during the procession into

---

*Radley's railway station was at that time the only one built largely for the benefit of a school, apart from that at Wellington which was constructed by the SE Railway at the behest of Wellington's Governors. Christ's Hospital station was built later.
†The forming up of the Chapel procession in School continued until shortly before the First World War when the boys lined up in Covered Passage. Except for what was known as 'Surplice Chapels', the procession was abolished altogether in 1947.

Chapel – the oldest and most revered of Radley customs – for disliked Prefects to be jostled or hissed on their way down Covered Passage, and for their passage to be blocked by boys surging forward to impede their progress. Unpopular boys of lesser degree were liable to be 'lobbed' down the Passage with kicks and buffets; while, after a victory in a school match – not a common event – each member of the winning team was borne aloft on the backs of eight boys to the cheers and roars of the rest.

After Chapel at this time it was common practice for Prefects to retreat to their study for a smoke and a drink, while their juniors were left free to break as many school rules as they liked and to indulge in the most remarkable escapades. Not infrequently they clambered out of their dormitory windows and went off to swim in the river at Sandford; and one night, clothed in makeshift smocks and equipped with a variety of real or pretended farm implements, they marched through the school grounds and out of bounds to roister as yokels in the surrounding countryside. Drinking and smoking were widespread; so was gambling; and a boy who made a book on the Derby was criticized in *The Radleian* not for having set himself up as a bookmaker but for being such a rowdy and incompetent one.

The Radleian, run by the boys without interference from the masters and now far less censorious of 'do-nothings' than it had been in Sewell's time, makes light of practices and misdemeanours which in earlier times would have been severely frowned upon. It was, for instance, understood that boys on the Shop Committee, who took it in turn to stand behind the counter, should be allowed to help themselves to such foodstuffs offered for sale as caught their fancy; and it came as no surprise when the boy charged with the duties of Secretary of Shop, faced with some inexplicable figures in the accounts, excused himself on the grounds that he was not much of a head at mathematics and could not be expected to clear the matter up. It was not until 1879 when George Wharton became Treasurer of Shop that the books were kept with some degree of accuracy.

Several boys preferred to patronize the shop in Radley village, although this was, of course, out of bounds; and *The Radleian* had something to say about this, too:

> 'Tis merry to drink at the baker's shop,
>   Or to buy your pipe at this depot,
> And the woman to tempt you must needs draw 'pop',

Her best lemonade, and you can't say 'no' . . .
But let the dons (heaven bless them) come down with the cane,
For we will continue and do it again:
For there's not a prank of any degree,
But possesses the greatest of charms for me.

With Prefects enjoying their privileges but more or less abandoning their responsibilities, with masters who were either tolerant or ignorant of misbehaviour, and with a number of disruptive boys in the school who should never have been admitted to it, the Warden felt his grip on Radley weakening month by month. He expelled the worst offenders, amongst whom were some members of the Eight which consequently was unable to row at Henley that year. One of the boys expelled, who had already been expelled from another school, returned for the Old Radleian cricket match and, when reprimanded by the Warden, replied insultingly before numerous spectators. The Warden, by now known to the boys as 'the Butcher', and to some of the masters, including 'Buffy' Evans, as 'Flabby Arse', had to endure even more humiliation when, at a prize-giving ceremony, all the boys began to shout and bang the lids of their desks. The Revd T.D. Raikes, who had left the school in 1868 to take up a scholarship at Oriel College and now returned to join the staff, confessed that he could not see how the school, let alone the Warden, could survive.* 'Buffy' Evans, who coached the Eight and had quarrelled with Martin over the management of rowing in the school, was of the same opinion.

It is evident from George Wharton's diary that all was not well between the Warden and Common Room almost from the start. There were 'most disagreeable' and 'stormy' College Meetings; there was a 'row about Athletics'; the Warden behaved 'foolishly'; he was 'in the wrong again'. With F.B. Harvey, a clever, difficult man of stern, heavily bearded visage, Martin's relations were particularly strained. He had never got on well with him; and when Harvey was appointed Bursar in 1873 he took the appointment as an excuse to regard himself as answerable to the Trustees and not to the Warden. When asked by the

---

*T.D. Raikes, in the opinion of a colleague 'a futile little man', was Radley's first married assistant master and the first historian of the school. It was said that his wife ran his Social. He was teased remorselessly in class. One of his pupils later said of him, 'Tommy Raikes I teased unmercifully, for which I often suffer remorse even now. But, really, Raikes was no more fit to be a don than any old woman.'

Warden in Hall one day when he was going to remove a tree which had been blown down and was blocking the drive, Harvey curtly replied, 'When I please.'

The situation could clearly not continue. Nor did it. Following a meeting at the Bank of England – attended by Hubbard, Wharton, by now the longest-serving member of the staff, and by one of the Trustees, Henry Barnett – notice of dismissal was served upon the Bursar. Soon afterwards the Warden announced that he had accepted a living in Norfolk and would leave at the end of the year. He died as rector of another parish in 1910, leaving behind him no record of either complaint about his treatment at Radley or justification of his conduct there.

*

The Trustees of Radley, having regard to the comparative success of similar schools, were anxious to find for their own a headmaster capable of rescuing it from the sad state into which it had fallen. A number of highly successful headmasters had been improving beyond measure the standards of Radley's rivals, and helping to bring into existence schools which, within a few years of their foundation, had far more pupils than Radley had so far been able to attract. Among these men were the vigorous and dynamic E.W. Benson of Wellington, one day to be Archbishop of Canterbury; Frederick Temple of Rugby, another future Archbishop of Canterbury; Henry Whitehead Moss, Kennedy's successor at Shrewsbury where he was to be Headmaster for forty-two years; R.E. Sanderson, for twenty-seven years Head Master of Lancing; J.I. Welldon of Tonbridge; G.G. Bradley of Marlborough; S.A. Pears of Repton; and, above all, Edward Thring, Headmaster of Uppingham from 1853 to 1887.

The son of a wealthy hunting parson from Somerset, Thring had been at Eton in the last two years of the reign of Dr Keate. From Eton, where he had been head of the Collegers, he went as a Scholar to King's College, Cambridge. Elected a Fellow of King's, he left Cambridge for an ill-paid curacy in a working-class parish in Gloucester where he also taught in the National School in the suburbs of the city until he was obliged to go home to Somerset in a state of physical and mental collapse.

Having recouped his health on a tour of the Continent, where he met his German wife, he was appointed to the headmastership of the school at Uppingham whose numbers had dwindled to scarcely more than forty. After his first visit to the school he told a friend, 'I think I have found my life's work today'; and so it proved to be. Helped by the growing demands for secondary education and by the existence of two nearby railway stations, he soon restored the school's flagging discipline and increased its numbers until they reached a predetermined figure of 330, beyond which he firmly refused to increase them, maintaining that a headmaster could not know personally more than this number of pupils at any one time. By the time this figure was reached, by insisting that every boy must receive equal and full attention, that those not academically gifted must have opportunities to succeed in other ways, that they must live in well-designed and attractive buildings, and that education must concern itself with the whole spiritual and moral being of a boy, Thring had created at Uppingham one of the most admired public schools in England, one worthy of serving as a model for the Governors of Clifton College, founded in 1862.

Thring himself had by then become one of the most celebrated headmasters of his time. He was listened to attentively by the Taunton Commission, established in 1864 to investigate those endowed schools with which the Clarendon Commission of 1861 had not been concerned; and, when the Revd John Mitchinson, Headmaster of the King's School, Canterbury, suggested a meeting of headmasters in London, it was Thring's attendance that Mitchinson and his friend, Harper of Sherborne, were most anxious to secure. Thring did attend, was impressed by the other headmasters present, and proposed a regular conference of headmasters, the first of which was held at Uppingham in 1869.

Only fourteen of the thirty-seven headmasters invited on that occasion agreed to attend. But year by year, more and more headmasters realized that it was in their school's interest to go to the conference. Forty-three went to the conference held the next year at Sherborne, fifty to Highgate in 1871. Soon the well-known schools which had been examined by the Clarendon Commission of 1861 decided that it was in their interest to be part of an organization which had originally been founded to oppose the Government's intention to mould all secondary schools of higher academic standard into the pattern of those ancient schools. In 1873 the Revd Charles Martin had become the first Warden of Radley to attend the conference when it was held that year at Winchester.

15

Firm Hands
1880–1896

'There was a good spirit in the school.'

'CERTAINLY VOTE IF you like – but it won't affect my decision.' These abrupt words, addressed to George Wharton at a Common Room Meeting by the recently appointed Warden of Radley, well conveyed the nature of the relationship between himself and his staff. Robert James Wilson had taught at Radley for three years in the 1860s, and his Warden then, William Wood, had had to endure his 'insolence' and the grim humour of his sarcastic tongue. Educated at Bradfield and later at Cheltenham, he had gone to Merton College where he obtained a Second in Greats. After leaving Radley he had taught for a time at Marlborough before returning to Oxford as a Fellow of Merton.

Wilson was now, in 1880, forty years old. Remote, in manner forbidding, in appearance so darkly handsome that he became known as 'Zulu', a teetotaller who rebuffed overtures of friendship, he was a man with whom it would clearly not be wise to trifle. Boys found him alarming and were all the more surprised when, feeling unwell or unhappy on a winter's day, they were invited to tea in the 'Zulu's' drawing-room, offered a hot bath and a warm bed for the night, brought a cup of tea in the morning by his butler and given a glimpse of tenderness they had never expected. The masters, to whom he was 'the Sphinx' rather than 'the Zulu', were not shown such indulgence. The Warden made it plain to them that the easy-going days were over, that they would have to work much harder than they had done in the past, be prepared for change which they might not like but must accept; and they, respecting the man if not much liking him, and recognizing that the survival of the school might well depend on their obedience, submitted to his will.

They agreed to more and longer teaching periods, to an extension of the curriculum to include the reading of English classical literature, and the complete reorganization of the teaching of science, as well as to a wholesale revision of the school's time-table. They submitted to the Warden's monthly examinations, his personal 'Reviews' of all the forms in the school. They accepted the shortening of the weekday Chapel service, only the Precentor registering a mild protest. They welcomed the introduction of a Common Room dinner instead of tea in Hall and the subsequent innovation of Common Room luncheon, George Wharton once again showing a preference for traditional ways by continuing to have his meals in Hall. Yet even Wharton, who could never bring himself to like the Warden, conceded that he had brought a new, invigorating atmosphere into the life of the school which was commented upon by several of the many visitors to Radley whom Wilson, following a Sewellian tradition, invited to it.

New buildings seemed to spring up everywhere. A new Music School appeared, a new Drawing School, a new structure for the Army Class, new classrooms. With the help of almost £1,000 raised by 'Buffy' Evans, mostly from Old Radleians – formed into the Radleian Society at this time – a rackets court was built near Clock Tower; and, with just over £5,000 lent by T.D. Raikes, a new house, designed to accommodate thirty boys, was constructed north-east of Chapel and, much altered and extended over the years, came to be known – as houses did in the development of the system of Socials – by the names of successive Social Tutors.

While new structures were being built, existing ones were being altered and redecorated: Chapel was repainted and its unsightly gas burners replaced by chandeliers; the walls of Hall, formerly decorated with Prefects' banners, were ornamented with shields bearing their families' coats of arms. In the dormitories, the curtains of the cubicles were replaced with sliding doors which were opened each morning after a perfunctory knock by a servitor bearing the traditional can of what was – or was at least supposed to be – a modicum of hot water.

Although pets were banished from school grounds where, occupying an evil-smelling shanty town of cages, kennels and hutches, they had been permitted under previous regimes,* there were numerous activities to occupy the boys' time out of the classroom. Old school societies were rejuvenated and new ones founded, from a Junior Debating Society and a Natural History Society, to a Chess Club and an Ambulance Class. A Radley Mission was founded at St Peter's, London Docks. Choirs sang, school orchestras played; there were sing-songs and 'penny readings' and performances by 'Nigger Minstrels' with banjos and blackened faces. There were plays in Latin, followed by plays in Greek, as well as in French and English, staged in the Gymnasium with the help backstage of professional carpenters and scene shifters, the performances being marred and occasionally rendered almost incomprehensible by the wholesale excision of the female parts.

Games were now compulsory, though watching school games as yet was not; and boys who found excuses for not playing football were liable to be ushered off to the Gymnasium where Mr MacLaren's days were coming to an end but where his exercises were still practised under the eyes of his assistants and lessons were given by a pugilist in the 'noble art of self-defence'.

The Cricket XI began to win more than the occasional match; the Eight won their first heat at Henley in the Ladies' Plate; athletes looked forward to the annual Sports Day; hockey was introduced; squash was played; a new tennis court was laid out near Chapel; the Radley rules of football were abandoned and the rules of Association Football adopted. Prefects played bowls; masters played golf with the help of young boys who bravely preceded them round the course watching for the landing balls.

The new spirit abroad at Radley found expression in the pages of *The Radleian*. No longer was there need for complaints about idlers and loungers, no longer did the magazine's editors write so sardonically of escapades and misdemeanours. The earnestness of the 1880s'

---

*'An edict was issued against the keeping of pet animals, a practice which had grown into the dimensions of a public nuisance,' wrote T.D. Raikes. 'Tame rabbits were discovered busy in the flower-beds, snakes had been surreptitiously introduced (in the owner's pocket) into Chapel, "because they were fond of music", and little companies were seen going down to the river apparently for the sole purpose of giving a pet monkey a gentle airing.'

editors found characteristic expression in the magazine's pages in a pious suggestion that the holidays be shortened so that the Jubilee of 1887 could be suitably celebrated by making Radleians 'better educated citizens'.

That they were better educated than they had been in the recent past was beyond doubt. There was no longer any good reason for the Trustees to complain, as they had complained in Martin's time, of grave defects in the boys' learning, of 'a lack of spirit', of 'a tendency to inaccuracy', of 'failures from carelessness' and 'bad handwriting'. Now such Trustees as attended the irregularly held meetings listened to the Warden's reports with satisfaction, hearing of awards with complacency – sixteen scholarships and exhibitions were won under Wilson, five for science. Turning their attention to financial rather than scholastic matters, the Trustees were gratified to learn in 1887 that the debt to Hubbard had been paid off, that in the following year the numbers in the school had risen to 156, that there was a healthy surplus in the College accounts and that the death of Sir George Bowyer made it possible for the freehold of Radley to be purchased and the temporary buildings of tin and corrugated iron to be replaced with more permanent structures.

Radley had good cause to be grateful to Warden Wilson, yet, when he accepted the wardenship of Keble College in 1888, it could not be said that Radley was sorry to see him go. Not long after his arrival he had been hissed in School for having had bars placed across the windows to enforce the lock-up after nightfall which had been flouted so often in his predecessor's time; and when the possibility of his departure was given out, 'long and loud', so *The Radleian* reported, 'were the cheers that greeted' the announcement. The editor of *The Radleian* made amends for his fellow pupils' rudeness by printing a glowing tribute to Wilson's achievements. The Precentor, who had never overcome his distaste for the man, described the tribute in his journal as 'fulsome flattery', a verdict which other members of Common Room would no doubt have endorsed. It could not be doubted, though, that, uncomfortable as they had felt in his presence, the years that Wilson had been Warden had been of inestimable benefit to the College which they all served.

*

The Radley Common Room now enjoyed a stability it had never known before. Two masters left in 1889, one J.H. Hichens, to teach at

Cheltenham and then to become Headmaster of Wolverhampton Grammar School, the other, T.F. Hobson, to go to Wellington before being appointed Warden of St Edward's, Oxford. One of their replacements, the Revd Arthur Titherington, late Scholar of The Queen's College, left after six years to become Headmaster of Brighton College which had been founded in 1845. But the six other men appointed between 1889 and 1892 remained at Radley for a total of 149 years, two of them staying for over thirty and three for more than twenty.

Most were exceptional men. Five came from Oxford, where a majority had been scholars or exhibitioners; the sixth, F.J. Stone, who was to take over Titherington's Social in 1895, was from King's College, Cambridge. Three of the others were also to take over Socials. E.F. Simpkinson took over T.D. Raikes's in 1895, and F.J. Barmby succeeded H.M. Evans in 1909. A.C.M. Croome, the most distinguished of them all, who took over Orlebar's in 1891, had won a demyship at Magdalen from Wellington. An outstanding athlete and a man of impressive personality and sympathetic understanding, he was, as one of his former pupils said, 'a marvel though a swanker'. Another wrote,

> A.C.M. Croome was an outstanding figure in his day. He had married into the Peerage, and had a very good conceit of himself. A good athlete – it was rumoured that on going to Oxford he had made a bet that he would get five 'blues' before coming down – he succeeded in getting four and a half . . .
>
> He was a good disciplinarian and a good teacher – though no scholar.

The fifth of these long-serving members of Common Room, A.O. Pughe, sometime Scholar of Christ Church, left after twenty-three years' service in 1913, preceded by Lionel James, also a Scholar of Christ Church, who, having joined the staff in 1892, was appointed Headmaster of Monmouth Grammar School and was to publish, after many years' gestation, the biography of his hero, William Sewell, in 1945.

All these men, who helped to guide Radley successfully well into the twentieth century, long outlived the man who had appointed them. This was Henry Lewis Thompson, who was well past middle age at the time of his election and, having failed to obtain the headmasterships for which he had previously applied, at Cheltenham, Marlborough and St Paul's, had seemed unlikely to fulfil the promise of his youth. He had been Captain of the School at Westminster, had taken a First at Christ Church and had become a prominent figure in the Oxford of the 1870s. He had been spoken of with the respect accorded to those two other Oxford notabilities, Henry Liddon, Professor of Exegesis, and Liddon's friend, Charles Dodgson, author of *Formulae of Plane Trigonometry* and, under another name, of a less esoteric work, *Alice in Wonderland*. But, having declined to be considered as a candidate for the bishopric of Cape Town, Thompson had left Oxford for a far from enticing living in Gloucestershire where, instead of the company of the high tables of the University, he was to find himself surrounded by villagers whose days were spent labouring in the fields or with pickaxe in the coal-mines.

With the help of his clever, though unassuming, shy and patient wife – an exceptionally 'plain featured' woman who 'rather resembled a horse', the daughter of Sir James Paget, Sergeant-Surgeon to Queen Victoria, and Vice-Chancellor of London University – Thompson became a great success as a parish priest, to the surprise of some of those who had known him at Oxford. Approachable as well as hard-working, he was capable of delivering sermons very different from those expected from the pulpit of the Oxford University Church of St Mary the Virgin and was much appreciated by the parishioners of Iron Acton whose church he filled to capacity.

His direct and open manner, his politeness and patience, his gifts as an administrator – not Warden Wilson's strongest point – were immediately recognized and appreciated at Radley; and he himself soon felt quite at home. His first term had scarcely begun when he decided that the masters were 'most pleasant and courteous'. 'The place is lovely,' he told a friend, 'even in winter, and the Chapel *very beautiful* . . . The School is full [there were 153 boys at that time] . . . great on the river, and energetic in other respects. The standard of scholarship is not high, but I dare say it may be raised a bit in time.'

Thompson did not say so, but he found the boys less easy to get on with than the masters. Like Sewell, he did not really like boys much, and found their ill behaviour not merely exasperating but on occasions incomprehensible. He was quick to lose his patience with miscreants and tended to mete out severe punishments for quite trivial offences: a boy overheard saying 'damn' and conducted to the Warden for a birching, was told the offence was too serious for corporal punishment and was given a hard and lengthy Greek imposition instead. But the Warden was not disinclined to use the birch when occasion seemed to him to justify it: a boy, the cox of the Eight, was lent a pony to ride back to College from the river by the coach. He was intercepted by the Warden as he rode down Covered Passage. Ordered instantly to dismount, he was ushered away to be severely beaten, then told to 'RIDE that pony back.' Usually, however, the Warden's punishments consisted of writing or translating Greek, a tedious exercise imposed upon two unlucky boys caught talking in the Infirmary where, so the Warden decreed, the rules of dormitory silence should apply.

Part of the trouble was that Thompson had certain highly idiosyncratic mannerisms, a voice that rumbled in his throat and earned him the nickname, 'The Belcher', as well as an uncontrollable habit of sneezing furiously when troubled by hay fever and an easily imitable way of walking, top-hatted and frock-coated, in the Park that made him the butt of boyish jokes of which he was only too painfully aware. As well as 'The Belcher', he was known as 'Puffin' because of the way he expelled his breath when annoyed. His sermons were not appreciated, and his Liberal politics considered highly suspect in a school in which political topics discussed in the Debating Society were never very lively since few boys could ever be found to present other than Conservative views. When a motion such as 'Should the lower classes be educated?' was proposed in the Society it was almost a foregone conclusion that the consensus of opinion would be strongly against it – as, indeed, in this particular case, it was.

Thompson's satisfaction with the College, the naughty boys aside, was much enhanced when the Radley estate was put up for sale by auction and the Trustees were able to buy Radley Hall and 136 acres of surrounding land for £13,000. The Trustees – or Council as they became under a Royal Charter of Incorporation soon after the death of the eighty-five-year-old J.G. Hubbard, by then Lord Addington – could now put their minds to thoughts of new and permanent buildings and to ways of raising money to pay for them. A new Infirmary was opened in 1891; temporary buildings leaning against School were converted into classrooms which more exacting boys of later generations were to know as 'the Slums'. A new house for Evans's, later Barmby's, Social was started in 1896; the building of a new Hall to accommodate 250 boys (there were 186 in 1894) was approved, though this was not completed until 1910; and in November 1893 the foundation stone of a new Chapel was laid by the historian, William Stubbs, formerly Bishop of Chester and, since 1889, Bishop of Oxford.

The architect was Thomas Graham Jackson who had won a scholarship to Wadham from Brighton College and who, fulfilling commission after commission, was to have a hand in the alteration or design of so many buildings in the University that he was to be known as 'Oxford' Jackson. He had also undertaken, and was yet to undertake, work at numerous public schools, including Giggleswick where the chapel is one of his most masterly achievements.

There were many who regretted the passing of the old Chapel, even though it had not been built to last and was, in fact, slowly disintegrating. There were others who protested against the felling of the lovely chestnut trees to clear the site; there were those who complained of the cost – £12,000, a large proportion of the £30,000 spent in all in Warden Thompson's time; and there were those who objected to the wishy-washy colour of the bricks and the generally rather undistinguished design which was not one of Jackson's better works.

The fittings of the old Chapel, including, of course, the fifteenth-century Flemish altarpiece and George Wharton's 'dear organ', having been installed in the interior, the consecration of the new Chapel was celebrated on Gaudy Day, 29 June 1895.

A line of masters and former masters and two past Wardens, the Revd Charles Martin and Dr William Wood, accompanied by Bishop Stubbs, marched in procession to the Chapel door where they were greeted by the Warden and the Council whose principal members now included the Old Radleian, the Earl of Egmont, and the Hon. Pascoe Glyn of the banking family, a Member of Parliament, whose sons had both been Prefects at the school.

After the service – at which the address, delivered by the Bishop, was the same, apart from a few introductory comments, as the one he had delivered some time before at the opening of John Oldrid Scott's chapel at Bradfield – there followed a lunch in a vast marquee where the 560 guests were entertained by the Blue Hungarian Band and then obliged to listen to no fewer than ten speeches.

Gaudy that year was a lively day: photographs show ladies shading their faces with white parasols and the sun throwing shadows across the well-mown grass. More than one of the guests commented upon the good behaviour and friendliness of the boys, the well-mannered attentions of the masters. Parents could consider that the fees – 90 guineas a year for boys admitted under the age of thirteen, 100 guineas and 110 guineas for those under fourteen and fifteen – were well enough spent, though they might have been surprised to learn that the masters' salaries started at no more than £150 as they had done for several years.*

Radley's guests were justified in concluding that the school, compared with similar places, was a pleasant and tolerant place. The boys were not only polite but had a reputation, unusual in their kind, of being clean. Certainly most of them were neatly dressed; indeed it was suggested that more interest was taken in clothes than was altogether desirable. There was still no official uniform and, although parents were required to provide their sons with three suits, all of them 'quite dark', there were wide varieties of cloth and pattern. Ready-made suits were frowned upon; and boys who came from homes in which the social nuances of clothes were an arcane topic were liable to come to the disciplinary attention of the Radley College Toilet Club.

As for the academic standards of the school, parents were led to suppose, with some justification, that these were improving year by year. Warden Wilson had once sardonically remarked to an assistant master on his way to Chapel, 'To-day I have ploughed a boy for Entrance – the first in the history of Radley.' Since then several boys had been refused places on the grounds that they would not be able to keep up to the standards of their contemporaries. Admittedly these standards were not as yet very high; but the teaching at the hands of such masters as Titherington, James, Barmby and Bryans was of a higher and more stimulating quality than had ever been achieved at Radley before, while the school could point with satisfaction to such products of a Radley education – all of whom obtained firsts at Oxford – as Bishop Stubbs's son, Reginald Stubbs, who was to become a Governor of Hong Kong and then of Ceylon, and to Stubbs's contemporaries, K.D. Mackenzie, Scholar of Hertford College, the future Bishop of Brechin, and David Randall-MacIver, the archaeologist. Altogether sixteen university scholarships and exhibitions were won in Thompson's time, more than had ever been won in such a space of time before. It could not be said, however, that Radley was as yet distinguished among public schools for its academic record: it might

---

*Radley was one of the most expensive schools in England. Fees at Wellington, another expensive school, were slightly less at £110 a year. As for salaries, when the foundation of Wellington was being discussed in the early 1850s, £200 to £300 a year was proposed as a suitable starting salary for assistant masters. Masters at Marlborough in 1865 were getting '£300 and upward'.

indeed have been considered that sixteen awards in eight years in a school of getting on for 200 boys was disappointing.

The fact that so very few books were taken out of the Library is an indication that for many boys their interests lay elsewhere. In one term in 1892 all but fifteen of the 493 books borrowed were novels and of these fifty-eight were taken out by masters.*

There could be no doubt that, as at most other public schools then, boys would far rather have played games than read books; and games were now being played at Radley with far more success. In the mid-1860s, when they could rely on the skills of the two Akroyd brothers who afterwards played for Surrey, the Cricket XI had been far more successful than Radley's XIs had ever been in the past. Clifton, Wellington and Bradfield had all been beaten, and this by a school in which only about thirty boys played the game regularly. But in the 1870s, as numbers in the school fell and rowing became increasingly popular, cricket at Radley had been in a sorry state, the College's only opponent from other schools being Bradfield which won almost every match. In the 1880s and 1890s, however, Radley's cricket improved immeasurably: Bradfield was beaten from time to time, once by an innings. Two of the team's players won Blues at Oxford; one of them, L.C.V. Bathurst, afterwards played for Middlesex and for the Gentlemen against the Players at the Oval, the other, R.H. Moss, who went on to teach at Cheltenham and Malvern, played for Lancashire.

At football, also, Radley played far better in the 1890s than they had done in the past, having outgrown an inability to forget the rules of the old Radley game. In 1894 of eleven matches played only one was lost, Bradfield and Lancing both being beaten that year, although these schools had far more boys playing the game from which to select their teams; and in 1899 Malvern, a much bigger school, was beaten for the second time. Two outstanding players in these years were L.W. North, a future Cambridge Blue, and Leonard Cooper, an 'indefatigable goal-keeper', later an Oxford Blue and Captain of the Oxford team, father, grandfather, and great-grandfather of Old Radleians.

On the river the days of perpetual disappointment at Henley were over. Heats were won regularly in the Ladies' Plate; and by 1885 the school had provided Oxford and Cambridge with sixteen Blues, more

---

*When Singleton was Warden he urged boys 'especially to avoid reading novels, than which few occupations more debilitate the intellect'. Singleton also forbade the reading of newspapers by boys.

than any other school except Eton (with 99) and Rugby (with 21). One of these Blues, R.W. Risley, is believed to have been the first man to have rowed four times for his university, a feat later achieved at Cambridge by two other Old Radleians, T.E. Hockin and C.L. Baillieu. Despite erratic coaching by the enthusiastic 'Buffy' Evans, the crews improved year by year, in 1893 reaching the final of the Ladies' Plate at Henley and, though beaten there by Eton, being described, with their rivals, in a newspaper report as the 'two best crews at the Regatta'.

For those who took no pleasure in games, who could not share the almost universal admiration, verging on reverence, for those indulged figures who excelled in them, Radley could still be rather a bleak place, especially in winter when the House and the schoolrooms were fearfully cold, the ink frozen, chilblains a torment and whole forms caught colds. One year almost eighty boys had influenza and three of them died; in 1890 a boy died of pneumonia and in the following year there was another death in the Infirmary, this time of diphtheria. The food remained indifferent – complaints were nevertheless made by some of the boys that the new spoons and forks provided for them to eat it with were not of silver. Breakfast was particularly nasty, with porridge to be had only as an extra if ordered from Shop. As in the past tea was a meagre meal of bread and butter. 'The food was wretched,' one boy wrote, making a general comment: 'at the end of the table I had badly cooked mutton every day for 12 weeks, and I never saw green food.'*

On half-holidays boys would have their own private tea-parties in their studies, when they had them, and in such places as the recesses in School when they did not, making what use they could of the few gas rings provided. Occasionally parties were held in Socials and these Socializings, as they became known, which all boys were expected to attend, were dreary occasions by all accounts, except when an attractive or entertaining Social Tutor's wife could be relied upon to enliven the proceedings. The fields beyond the Park and the whole of the school grounds between the Gymnasium and the Lodge were out of bounds; so was the drive to any boy without leave. Wandering beyond the prescribed limits was a risky adventure and roll-calls had to be

---

*The poor food at Radley in the 1890s was not in the least exceptional. A.A. Milne, who went to Westminster in 1893, said that in all his years there he 'never ceased to be hungry'. A generation later the food at Marlborough, according to the historian John Bowle, was 'atrocious'.

attended with unfailing regularity. Bicycles were forbidden until 1897, long after several other public schools had permitted them, and then they were allowed only to members of the Eight. A few other senior boys were granted permission to bring back bicycles two years later; but it was not until the next century that they became common.

Chapel was out of bounds except at specified times and so, for less obscure reasons, were the cubicles. But this latter rule was scarcely necessary at this time, according to Lord Latymer, who was at Radley between 1889 and 1895. 'There was a good spirit in the school. Small boys, even the nice-looking ones, were left alone by the bigger boys. I cannot say that a certain ugly vice did not exist. It existed, but it was distinctly frowned upon by public opinion, and no small boy was ever made an unwilling victim.' Studies in the House attics were, however, still in use, as they had been from the earliest years of the school's history, and no master by convention ever penetrated into these dark upper regions.

*

'You know I shall have been at Radley for eight years by next Christmas,' Warden Thompson wrote in 1896, confessing himself 'anxious to get rid of school mastering if an opportunity arose'. Soon afterwards the opportunity came: Bishop Stubbs, whose son had had so successful a career at Radley, asked him to join him in Oxford as Vicar of the University Church of St Mary's. Thompson accepted the offer with pleasure. Common Room regretted his departure more than the boys; and hoped that they would be able to get on as well with his successor, the Revd Thomas Field, Headmaster of the King's School, Canterbury.

16

Thomas Field
1897–1913

'Of course we stood in awe of him.'

THOMAS FIELD'S FATHER had been in a poor way of business as a draper in Folkestone. When the business failed the four-year-old Thomas and his mother went to live with a prosperous uncle, a shopkeeper, at Gravesend. Thomas was devoted to his mother, a devout Particular Baptist. She died when he was sixteen, and thereafter, for the rest of his life, he kept by his bedside a photograph of her and of her grave. The uncle was also a strict Particular Baptist and in later years Field related how he had overheard a solemn discussion as to whether one of the shop assistants should be dismissed because she kept a crucifix in her bedroom.

With the help of another uncle, Thomas was sent to school at Faversham where, so precociously remarkable were his talents and personality, that the story was circulated and believed that he became head boy at the age of nine, though the average age of boys in the upper school was fifteen. He displayed the same precocity at the King's School, Canterbury, to which he was sent in 1867 and of which he became head boy when he was only fourteen. And here, in the King's School, in the words of his biographer, 'he attained a reputation as a disciplinarian preserved throughout his career as a headmaster also'.*

---

*Thomas Field appears as Tom Perkins in *Of Human Bondage* by Somerset Maugham who was at the King's School, Canterbury, in the 1880s. Maugham

From the King's School, Field won a scholarship in mathematics to Corpus Christi College, Oxford, where the last vestiges of his Particular Baptist beliefs were dissipated and he became the devoted adherent of the Anglican Church which he always afterwards remained. This devotion was to be central to his work as a headmaster.

Half the undergraduates at Corpus Christi – then the only Oxford college at which attendance at Chapel was not compulsory – went on to take Holy Orders, and Field himself followed their example. After obtaining a First in Greats, he embarked upon his career as a schoolmaster, first at Repton, then, under Montagu Butler, at Harrow where he caused some surprise among boys 'brought up in very low church surroundings' by being the only master among many in Holy Orders who wore a cassock. 'We thought him,' commented one senior boy, 'a terrible ritualist.'

A man of astonishingly retentive memory and of exceptionally eclectic knowledge, he was a peculiarly eccentric teacher, in many ways resembling Andrew Lang of whom it was said that in a course of lessons on the French Revolution he had reached the early Egyptian civilizations by the end of the first term. A Radley boy was to remark of Field that he was 'very interesting' in the classroom but 'generally teaching about something else'.

His appearance was striking [another of his pupils wrote], especially his swarthy complexion and black beard. He filled boys with a certain awe, and he bore some resemblance in aspect, as well as in directness, zeal and enthusiasm, to an Old Testament prophet. Anyone who heard him declaim passages from Isaiah in a scripture lesson, interlarded with a few words of Hebrew, would have recognized a certain spiritual kinship.

Such was the man, energetic, restless, tall, commanding, erudite, unconventional and abrupt, who was installed as Warden of Radley on

---

describes Perkins, as a boy at the school, as 'the son of Perkins, the linen draper . . . The first thing about him was that he was not a gentleman . . . A small dark boy, he looked like a gypsy. He had come to the school with the best scholarship in the endowment, so that his education had cost him nothing. Of course, he was brilliant.' Maugham was not particularly happy at the school, but his ashes were buried in the grounds there at his request. He was generous in his donations to the school, his generosity being maliciously attributed to his dislike of Hugh Walpole, another former pupil and benefactor, whom he satirized as Alroy Kear in *Cakes and Ale*.

30 January 1897, having appeared on a short list of three for the Mastership of Wellington in 1893 when the Revd Bertram Pollock of Marlborough was preferred to 'a Mr Field of King's School, Canterbury', as Wellington's historian dismissively refers to him.

First impressions were not altogether favourable. Boys at Radley found his brusque manner alarming, and at the warning sounds of a deep bass humming and a brisk but heavy step, it was said that they were 'apt to take cover'. When he caught up with them his shafts of sardonic humour were to them as bewildering as his digressive sermons to which, after a time, they stopped listening. His quirks of behaviour and speech were disconcerting and, when the boys became familiar with them, widely imitated. He had a habit of emphasizing his favourite phrases and epithets with a strange prodding movement of his fingers as though he were about to strike a chord *fortissimo* on the piano; he spoke of himself always as 'one'; he sang in Chapel at the top of his not very melodious voice.

Masters also found him irritating on occasions as when, for instance, he referred, as he so often did, to the near perfection of Harrow or of the King's School, Canterbury, implying criticism of Radley, an unwelcome comparison which irked the boys too and once, at a prize-giving in the Gym, elicited sighs and groans. Masters were often as bewildered by him as the boys were. As one of them, Ernest Bryans, wrote, 'His active brain jumped so quickly from point to point as ideas occurred to him, that it was difficult to know exactly where you were.'

Other masters found him exhausting, his temperament too authoritarian, his schemes – which were, as he admitted, always 'buzzing' in his head – not always either desirable or practicable. Most of these masters had been at the school for many years and were perfectly satisfied with the place as it was. A not altogether uncharacteristic example was the champagne-loving 'Buffy' Evans, who had been a Social Tutor since 1879 and was Sub-Warden from 1890 to 1909. He ran his Social in a cavalier manner, bothering little with the younger or less congenial boys, spending far more of his energies on the river than in the classroom, beating real or imagined miscreants almost at random with a fives bat, affecting not to notice the presence of new masters in the Common Room, offering to shake hands with the Warden's wife, the daughter of a Canon of Wells, every time he encountered her, as though she were as much of an outsider at Radley as the £1 a week customarily paid by the Warden for the keep of his lady would suggest she was supposed to be.

The new masters whom Field appointed were men of a different stamp. They included William Johnston Stone, a scholar of King's College, Cambridge, who left in 1899 for Marlborough where he died two years later; William Hamilton Fyfe, Postmaster of Merton, later Sir William Fyfe, who became Headmaster of Christ's Hospital and Vice-Chancellor of Aberdeen University; H.L. Rogers, scholar of Christ Church, later appointed Headmaster of King's College School, Wimbledon; Harold Sloman, scholar of Balliol, afterwards Headmaster of Tonbridge; George Sainton Kaye Butterworth, the composer, who wrote his *Shropshire Lad* rhapsody in the Lodge; and Thomas Roper Spyers, who had won an exhibition to the school, had played in its cricket and football First Elevens, had also played rackets for Oxford, captained the Radley Rangers, the Old Radleian cricket club founded in 1873, and was successively barrister, actor, parson, headmaster of a preparatory school and manager of a hotel before dying in his ninety-third year.

Although these his own appointments were eventually to out-number the masters he inherited, the influence of the old guard was still pervasive in the school. So, too, was the influence of the Council, which remained a decidedly aristocratic body among whose members were, or were soon to be, Lord Northbourne, the Earls of Egmont and Cranbrook and the 7th Duke of Newcastle, none of whom were pre-disposed to get on too well with a Kentish draper's son who treated them with such brisk lack of ceremony. Dr Field was, therefore, unable to carry through as many changes at Radley as he would have liked to do, a failure compounded by his own tendency to lose interest in one of the many schemes busily buzzing in his head when another came into it buzzing more insistently. Even so, the changes wrought in his time were considerable.

Although the Warden considered most modern subjects an 'excrescence', the curriculum was widened to include German as an alternative to Greek. Instead of sitting where they liked for meals in Hall, boys were now required to sit by form and then by Socials, a strong request from masters for meals to be served in the Socials' own houses – on the grounds that Social Tutors were otherwise deprived of the profits from catering earned at other schools – being rejected as 'undesirable and impracticable'. Junior boys were, however, still required to sit towards the middle of the table and, whenever called upon to do so, had to look for and pass up the pots of jam and other privately owned comestibles to their seniors at the heads of the table, a tiresome system, much resented by those called upon to operate it, that remained in operation for well over half a century to come. After the meal, these juniors were also expected to pile up the empty plates which were passed down to them for the purpose; but at least they were now assured of a reasonable helping of meat since the joints were no longer carved by Prefects, notoriously partial in their offerings, but by College servants, the plates being handed round by servitors. Jugs of beer, known as 'swipes', were still placed on the tables – much to the satisfaction of the Hon. D.B.O. Freeman-Mitford, afterwards Lord Redesdale (Nancy Mitford's Uncle Matt in *The Pursuit of Love*) who had an 'insatiable thirst' for it.

> It was supplied to all and sundry [a man who had been at Radley with Lord Redesdale recalled]. But few of us acquired the taste. Mitford sat next to the Prefect at the end of my table in Upper Hall. The servitor who waited on the table was called Bob, and Mitford was for ever calling for 'MORE BEER BOB'. He became known as 'More beer Bob'.

By the end of Field's Wardenship beer had disappeared from tables in Hall after a Senior Prefect, in what was supposed to be a drunken aberration, had hurled a ham at the portrait of the Founder whose features bore the marks of the insult for a long time thereafter.*

*

Although denied the extra money to be gained at other public schools by catering, Social Tutors were now slightly better paid than they had been in the past. Newly appointed masters received £160 a year, rising to £250 a year after ten years; Social Tutors earned about twice as much.

There was more uniformity in the boys' clothes, except in relation to collars, the Prefects being allowed to wear the turn-down collars then in fashion, the less privileged being required to retain their single stick-up collars. The small boys, and all those of whatever age unable to pass into the Upper School, had to wear Eton collars. It was already

---

*This portrait, which still hangs in Hall, is by Julian Drummond who was paid £52 10s. for it. This sum was subscribed by the Fellows and one or two friends; but when William Wood attempted to extract the money due, he was unable to collect all that had been promised. Sewell took the portrait with him when he left Radley and bequeathed it to his brother, the Warden of New College, in his will. James Sewell gave it back to Radley.

customary for gowns to be shabby and torn and for the brims of straw hats to be frayed to suggest long residence at the school. Bowler hats were worn on Sundays, dark blue blazers for going out to play games.

Oxford and Abingdon and all houses beyond the school gates were still out of bounds but otherwise the boys were encouraged to walk in the surrounding countryside, taking with them the Warden's booklet *The Radley District*, or to join an archaeological or historical expedition organized by one of the masters.

'Keepers of School' marched about between the desks as the Lower School did their prep to maintain order and silence, if necessary with canes. As for formal beatings, whereas it had been customary in the past for a Prefect to shout 'All Out' to give warning that a beating was to be administered, such punishment could now officially be given only when sanctioned by the Senior Prefect who was to require another Prefect to be present and have the punishment recorded in a book. Less generally popular innovations were the institution of a compulsory Officers' Training Corps and the requirement that the boys themselves rather than the school servants should clean their studies on Sunday mornings.

Believing that they were still too long for the patience of the ordinary boy, the Warden shortened the already curtailed Chapel services. His attitude towards Radley's Chapel had been made clear in the first sermon he preached in it:

> The life of the school must not be in three separate departments with some boys known as the athletic boys, some as the intellectual boys and some as the religious boys. It is certain that the whole character of games degenerates when they are in any way dissociated from the intellectual life, but there is a worse thing when the services of the Chapel are felt to be foreign and separate from the great flood of earnest activity that goes on outside its walls.

*

The completion of the Chapel in Warden Thompson's time was now followed by a spate of other building. There was a new Laboratory designed by A.R. Tenison, who also drew up plans for a Pavilion and a house for Croome's Social, the centre of which, the arch and tower, still bear Croome's name. There were new studies known as the Market Place, the Market Place originally being a brick arcade, traditionally so called because some long-forgotten master had once asked a group of boys lounging there, 'Why stand ye here all the day idle?'

There was a new boathouse, Evans Memorial Boathouse, designed by C.T. Steward, who had been a Prefect in Warden Thompson's time; there were two new fives courts; and, most impressive of all, there was a fine Hall, T.G. Jackson's best building at Radley, which cost £8,732, and was opened by the Bishop of Oxford in October 1910.

While new buildings appeared, old ones were reconstructed or refurbished. School was extended; a museum which had been shunted about from building to building was found a more permanent home; an aviary was constructed; a comfortable and well-stocked library dedicated to the memory of Dr Wilson was established in the House;* a carved oak case, designed by Jackson, was provided for the organ at a cost of £800; Covered Passage was wainscotted; a memorial window to Warden Sewell was installed in Chapel; an avenue of chestnuts was planted along the front drive;† and nearly 400 other trees were planted in the College grounds.

This programme of building and improvement was made possible by a steady rise in the number of boys at the school, as well as by the generosity of its benefactors. Numbers rose from 159 in 1897 to 200 in 1903 and 258 in 1908.‡

---

*'It may be mentioned here,' wrote A.K. Boyd in his *History of Radley*, 'that no sanction will be given in this book to a deplorable neologism . . . The House throughout these pages will be known as the House, and not by that pretentious, unhistoric and generally unpleasing title "The Mansion".' It is to be regretted that this name, described in Boyd's glossary as 'vulg.', is now universally used and has been given quasi-official sanction in the booklet issued for the guidance of new boys.

†This avenue of chestnuts was known as Addington Avenue, a name described in A.K. Boyd's history as already obsolete in 1947. Since it is the only memorial at Radley to the College's saviour, the name deserves to be revived.

‡Yet Radley was still a comparatively small school, as was Bradfield where there were 288 boys in the Senior School in 1910. There were 493 boys at Wellington in 1898 and 547 by 1910; in 1898 there were 444 at Tonbridge and 586 at Rugby; in 1910 there were 440 at Uppingham; and by 1918 numbers at Cheltenham, after a fall during the war, had risen to 631 and at Marlborough to 700. At that time Radley's numbers had dropped to 230, though they were to rise to 293 in 1924.

17

Novelists and Misfits
1897–1913

'Its High Church character was inimical to the Puritan repression that sometimes
flourishes in schools of the more Protestant type.'

AMONG THE BOYS at Radley in Thomas Field's day, as in earlier
times, there were many whose parents or guardians chose
Radley because of its reputation as a kindly place rather than,
as they might have chosen Winchester, for example, because of its name
for scholarship. One of these boys was Cyril Holland, son of Oscar
Wilde, who came to Radley in 1899. Warden Field had been at Oxford
with Wilde and had, predictably, not much approved of him there; but
he agreed to take the son at Radley on the understanding that none of
the other boys should know who his father was. They never did know;
nor were they enlightened after they left the school: before the edition
published in 1947 the name of Cyril's father was omitted from *The
Radley Register*. The boy himself, who was commanded never to speak
of his father, had been led to believe that he had died, a pretence that
proved difficult to maintain. At the height of the scandal surrounding
his father's name only three or four years before, the boys in the school
had discussed the case endlessly and had emphatically stressed the
word 'wild' as they sang it in Chapel when it came in the hymn:

'Forty days and forty nights,
Thou went fasting in the WI-ELD',

the *i* being sharpened to the acutest point.

In order that Cyril and his brother Vyvyan should not reveal anything by talking together about their family, they were sent to different schools. So Vyvyan, who was, so he said, 'quite determined to
become a Jesuit', was sent to Stonyhurst, while Radley was chosen for
Cyril, who was destined for the Army, since Radley was, in his
brother's words, 'a school well known for athletics'.

Determined, as he put it, to 'be a man', that there should be no cry
of decadent artist, of effeminate aesthete, 'of weak-kneed degenerate'
about him, Cyril set himself the task at Radley of proving his manliness.

> He stroked the Radley Eight in the Ladies' Plate at Henley at the age of
> seventeen [Vyvyan Holland wrote in his memoirs] . . . That year, too, Cyril
> won the mile, the half-mile and the steeplechase in the annual sports and
> received a medal as *victor ludorum*. He was the best swimmer in the school
> [which he also represented in boxing]. He was also a prefect and the head
> of his house.

He went on to Woolwich and then into the Royal Artillery where he
was lonely and unpopular with his brother officers who considered
him pompous and intolerant. 'He would not join in the small-talk of
the mess . . . and they could not understand anyone who spent his leave
in travelling about Europe, studying architecture and visiting art
galleries instead of hunting, shooting, yachting or fishing.' He was
killed in action in 1915.

Many of his contemporaries at Radley were also to be killed in the
First World War. Of those who survived, several gained distinction in
a variety of ways. Orme Sargent became the highly influential
Permanent Under-Secretary at the Foreign Office; Edgar Ludlow-
Hewitt, an air chief marshal and Inspector-General of the Royal Air
Force; R.H.T. Raikes an admiral, and his brother G.T. Raikes a general.
Frederick Witts also became a general; Norman Whatley, Headmaster
of Clifton; Eric Whitworth, Headmaster of Bradfield, then of
Tonbridge; F.J. Nugee, Headmaster of Eastbourne; Arthur Knapp-
Fisher, Professor of Architecture at the Royal College of Art and
Chairman of the Royal Institute of British Architects; Noel St John
Buxton, Hunterian Professor at the Royal College of Surgery;
Douglas Granville Chandor, portrait painter; Eric Gillett, man of
letters; L.H.D. Buxton, scholar; H.J.F. Badeley, 1st Baron Badeley,
Clerk of the Parliaments; V.H. Sutton-Vane, playwright; Harold
Monro, poet; D.C. Dunlop, Bishop of Jarrow; and F.H. (Freddie)

Grisewood, a brilliant broadcaster. Nicholas Hannen, having been apprenticed to Sir Edwin Lutyens, went on the stage where, in his *Who's Who* entry, he described himself as having 'played many parts from Greek Tragedy to Modern Comedy', and gave as his recreation, 'trying to play games'. He had played none with notable success at Radley, though he had been in the Eight in 1900.

Also at Radley with Cyril Holland were Louis Wilkinson, the author known as Louis Marlow, whose novel of Radley, *The Puppets Dallying*, had been preceded by another story about Radley, *Jaspar Tristram* by A.W. Clarke, later Consul-General at Zanzibar, a sad evocation of the torments of adolescent homosexual love.* These two novels were followed by *Young England* by D.B. Cancellor, who wrote it under the name Douglas Strong and who – after a successful and happy career at Radley, where he was Senior Prefect, in the cricket and football first teams and won an exhibition to New College, Oxford – was to be twice wounded before being killed in action within a few months of the end of the war and awarded a posthumous Military Cross.

All these novels, and Marlow's later book, *Swan's Milk* (published in 1924), contain reliable details of the Radley of the time which, according to Marlow – a parson's son, who was there in Evans's Social from 1895 to 1899 – was exceptionally snobbish. Marlow confirmed other reports that there was very little bullying and that quite mild. It was, in fact, 'an unusual public school, with an unusually tolerant majority opinion. The prevailing tone there was aristocratic, although the actual aristocrats were in a minority . . . The tone was different from that at Eton and Harrow, because Radley was a small school, because it was demonstratively High Church, and because it had a sprinkling of delicate and eccentric boys.'

In this atmosphere, 'patrician, tolerant, casual' as it was, 'homosexual attraction' of the kind so painfully experienced by the hero of A.W. Clarke's novel 'was taken for granted, as at other public schools' such as Uppingham where it was fashionable for the bloods to have 'favourites' and where in these years several boys were expelled for homosexual activities. Good looks were 'extremely important' at Radley, 'quite as important as they could be in any girls' school. They

---

*A later and better novel on this theme, Michael Campbell's *Lord Dismiss Us* (1967), is set in St Columba's.

were almost as important as prowess at games or on the river, or as good birth.' There were

> no moral inhibitions at Radley [Marlow averred]. There were continual affairs between the older and younger boys, and they were sometimes highly romantic. They were always of great and universal interest, the favourite theme, indeed, of conversation . . . Occasionally a boy was expelled, but very rarely . . . It was the custom that only the elder boy should be expelled: the 'lady' was severely birched by the Warden . . . The boys' natural susceptibilities were not atrophied nor even blunted by this so prevailing preoccupation of theirs. Most of them would certainly have preferred girls if they could have got them.

As for the snobbery, 'Radley was then an even more intensely snobbish school than England was a country':

> In snobbery the aristocrats among the boys set the tone. No one could have been at Radley at that time without shedding many bourgeois illusions about the ruling caste. The boys who came from the commercial class were made to feel it. 'Macey's father is an *underwriter*' said with ruthless contempt, or 'Hutton's father sells *boots*, the little beast' ejaculated with horror, were observations likely to be imprinted upon young Macey and young Hutton for the rest of their lives. If such boys were good at games or had the kind of character that helps at school they could get on all right in spite of their stigma. But they were always a little despised.
> There was a booklet printed at Radley containing the boys' names and addresses which were always closely inspected for indication of social status. 'Three, Myra Road, Surbiton, good God' . . .
> 'How many servants have you got?' 'Have you a butler?' . . . 'Do you hunt?' . . .
> Of course, under such pressure as Radley brought upon us, we were turned into snobs even if we weren't snobs to start with. The then Warden of Radley was unpopular chiefly because he was a self-made man.

In *Young England*, D.B. Cancellor (Douglas Strong), who was said by one of his fellow officers to have had 'an obsession' about Radley, describes in autobiographical style his hero, Dick Garland, arriving at the school for his first term. He records his fears of being bullied, since he had been told 'such gruesome yarns about bullying' in public schools; but he is much relieved to discover that there is no dreadful bullying to be experienced at Radley.

Garland's social tutor (Cancellor's was F.J. Barmby, 'a master of brilliant and varied gifts', who, at Radley, had lost all the ambition he had had at Oxford) hands him over to the matron, a 'motherly old lady'. She shows him his cubicle in the dormitory, a little room containing 'a bed, chest of drawers and wash-stand complete'. As a scholar he is given a study straight away and buys a second-hand armchair from another boy for half a crown, and also a broken folding one for a penny. He is asked to be one of the Senior Prefect's four fags, an office he willingly accepts because its duties 'were certainly lighter than those of the ordinary fag. Besides, the position held a certain dignity in the eyes of its possessors.'

He soon becomes aware how grand are the 'Caps' who parade arm-in-arm in fours and fives about the school in their fancy waistcoats and bow-ties like gods and are reverenced as such, enjoying 'a licence far beyond their deserts'. 'And, gazing at them' with boundless admiration, as others did too, he makes up his mind to play his footer and fives for all he is worth, and to become an exalted 'Cap' himself. Garland also soon becomes aware that 'there are many friendships formed between big and small boys at Public Schools. Some are mere passing fancies which fade almost before they begin, others are little better than amours, prompted solely by immoral motives and carrying nothing but evil in their train: a few bring great inspiration, and very happy memories.'

Caught smoking a pipe, Garland goes through the usual procedure of being beaten and says to a friend afterwards on their way to Chapel, commenting on the bravado of some of those whom the Prefects had punished with him, 'I can't see the point of saying a beating doesn't hurt when it does.'

'Nor can I. It's mere swank: all beatings hurt.' 'They caught each other's eye as they sat down very gingerly after the Psalm, and got "fifty lines" for laughing in Chapel.'

*

While Field's Radley produced a satisfactory number of boys who went on to achieve distinction in later life, it cannot be said that the school's academic reputation was all that much higher than it had ever been, even though fifty university scholarships and exhibitions were won in the sixteen years of Field's Wardenship and numerous boys passed into Woolwich and Sandhurst. The teaching of mathematics and science, particularly in the lower forms, left much to be desired, while some of the less gifted boys could scarcely be said to be taught at all. A.K. Boyd, who entered the school in 1905, was to become Senior Prefect, win several prizes and scholarships and play in both cricket and football First XIs, began his first term most inauspiciously:

> [He] spent his first period of school at Radley – Divinity on Sunday afternoon – with the Lower Fourth at the top of Croome's Tower (not knowing where else to go); there was a new master present, but the person in charge was a boy of defective intelligence who had been in the form seven terms already; he told the master that they always made tea in Sunday afternoon periods, and proceeded to do so; between the comings and goings the master tried to switch the conversation to Divinity, but everything was against him. Meanwhile almost within earshot Field was doubtless flitting from major project to minor, with a nod to Origen in passing, dipping into the Jewish Calendar, glancing at the early Papacy, and illustrating incidental points with fragments of Hebrew and extracts from *In Memoriam*.

Another Radleian of Boyd's time, Colonel H.B. Morkill, who was to live to be ninety-four years old, described the Spartan conditions of public school life in these years. He recalled the cold of the cubicles in winter, the shallow metal bath (the 'tumby') with its few inches of often icy water, the severe, 'extremely painful' beatings.

Gerald Brenan, author of *The Spanish Labyrinth* and *South from Granada*, was also at Radley at this time; and, so he complained, 'was liable at any moment to be kicked, hit, mobbed, thrown in the bushes, as well as called by every sort of abusive name'. His ill-tempered, sarcastic and unimaginative father, an army officer who had himself been at Haileybury, had wanted Gerald to go to Harrow, but the lists of that school were full and, having gained an exhibition to Radley, he was sent there instead. He had also been offered an exhibition at Winchester, but Radley's reply came first, much to his later regret, though it is doubtful that he would have been happy at any public school.

This could also have been said of C.R.W. Nevinson, the war artist, who was sent in 1903 to Uppingham, a school described by his father, the journalist, H.W. Nevinson, who had himself been at Shrewsbury, as 'very likely not in itself much worse than the average Public School for a boy whose main interest lay in art'. Here the son, so he himself afterwards wrote, was 'kicked, hounded, caned, flogged' and, at the age of fifteen, possessed 'an extensive knowledge of "sexual manifestations"'.

Nevinson's contemporary, the poet, Robert Graves, was equally unhappy at Charterhouse – so unhappy, indeed, that he had recurring dreams of being back there in misery and sent his own son to Oundle as a school he considered, of all others, the most unlike it. When it became known that his name, as it appeared on the school register, was Robert von Ranke Graves, he was accused of being a German Jew; his locker was rifled, his study wrecked and his clothes stolen. The bullying increased when he joined the seven-member Poetry Society, a society disapproved of by many masters since it encouraged friendships between boys of different ages in different houses. But as he was quite good at games and became a skilful boxer, the bullying eventually ceased. Yet his dislike of Charterhouse remained with him for ever; and he never forgot the farewell remark of its Headmaster, 'Well, goodbye Graves, and remember that your best friend is the waste-paper basket.'

Gerald Brenan also took up boxing at Radley but 'without success', he said, blaming the weakness of his shoulder muscles. 'Radley did me immense and permanent harm,' he wrote in his memoirs.

> Even in the worst moments of the war [in which he was awarded both the Military Cross and the Croix de Guerre] I comforted myself with the thought that anyhow I was not at Radley. For those shells and bullets whose noises filled the air were inanimate objects discharged by an impartial hand: they did not come at me dressed in the malignity of the human face . . . I have never once, I believe, dreamed of the war . . . but I have dreamed continually, sometimes for years on end, of this school . . . this detested place.

He took refuge in the Wilson Library, a blessed haven where he delighted in the well-stocked shelves and pored over maps, planning journeys to exotic places, far from Radley; he sought consolation, too, in masturbation until one day, when he was in the Infirmary suffering from influenza, his urine turned red – doubtless a symptom of glomerulonephritis – convincing him that the pamphlet, which was circulated throughout the school warning boys of the likely results of self-abuse, was an authoritative document after all.

Despite his expressed hatred of Radley – which he declined to mention in his *Who's Who* entry, claiming that he had been 'self-educated' – his life was not, in fact, nearly as miserable as he afterwards maintained. He and another boy were taken on bicycle rides by a good-natured and sympathetic master, A.M. Wilson-Green, who introduced them to the pleasures of the Berkshire Downs. He made friends with a clever and extraordinarily ugly boy, H.G. Thornton, who was studying biology and was excused games so that he could go into Oxford for special tuition. 'His private tastes lay in the direction of snails and fossils,' Brenan wrote of Thornton who became a distinguished bacteriologist and a Fellow of the Royal Society. 'For snails we visited Cothill Marsh, where there were some rare ones, and for fossils we ransacked all the quarries and clay-pits within cycling range.'

Nor could Brenan justifiably claim that he had been badly taught at Radley: 'By the end of his first year – summer 1909,' his biographer recorded, 'he had won the form prize, the Divinity Prize, came second in science and maths, first in English and French. He was at once moved into the top form on the Army side. There were several boys of eighteen; the average age was 17.2; Gerald was about to be sixteen. By Easter 1911 he was second in English and fourth in French. He won the Scott Essay Prize every single year, the Divinity Prize again in 1912, and also shared the Old Radleian French Prize.'

*

As a golfer, a keen swimmer and oarsman, a painter in water colours, a cellist, a man interested in natural history and photography, as well as in classics, biblical studies and English literature, the Warden warmly encouraged the pursuit of such extra-curricular activities as those taken up by Thornton and Brenan. The Debating Society was well attended; so was the Natural History Society; *The Radleian* flourished as never before; plays and books were read at meetings of the Senior Intellectual Society; Greek plays were performed; a Rifle Club was founded; a range was created, and rifle-shooting became compulsory. Lecturers from outside the school were welcomed; so, on half-holidays, were entertainers, including a renowned conjuror who astonished the boys by plucking eggs from the Warden's beard, a feat which led an assistant master to ask sardonically if the magician had also contrived to extract a coherent sentence from the same place.

Despite the adulation accorded to the 'Caps' during these years, Radley crews and teams did very poorly. 'Buffy' Evans, who had been coach for thirty-three years when he died in 1909, saw his Eights beaten regularly at Henley. 'It must be admitted,' wrote a later and far more effective coach, the Revd Vyvyan Hope, 'that in his later years his crews were noted more for a pretty style than for hard work.'

The cricket and football teams were no more successful. From time to time there was a victory to celebrate: Bradfield were beaten in excit-

26. The First Eight at Henley in 1863 with the Angel Inn and Henley Rectory on the far bank. Two of this crew took Holy Orders, one became a surgeon, one a Queen's Messenger, one emigrated to New Zealand, three inherited family properties, the ninth, C.G. Perceval, was elected Member of Parliament for Midhurst before succeeding his uncle as 7th Earl of Egmont

25. The Revd R.W. Norman, Fellow 1853–61 and Warden 1861–6

27. Warden Wood with the Sixth Form and Upper Fifth in 1867. Sitting on the steps in the front row are (*from the left*) J.E. Melluish, who won a scholarship to Wadham College, Oxford, and became a master at St Paul's School, A.G. Duncombe who went to Christ Church, T.D. Raikes, scholar of Oriel, assistant master and Social Tutor at Radley and author of *Fifty Years of St Peter's College, Radley*, and the Hon. Harold Gathorne-Hardy, who took a first-class degree at University College and was elected a Fellow of All Souls

28. The Revd George ('Kitty') Wharton, Precentor 1862–1914; a cartoon by F.T. Dalton, Social Tutor (F Social) 1879–86, who later joined the staff of *The Times*

29. The Revd Charles Martin, Warden 1871–9

30. The Warden's sitting-room, a photograph taken on All Saints' Day, 1870

31. Radley Football XII, 1869. The Radley rules gave way to Association in 1881, then to Rugby Union in 1913.
Back row from the left: H.F. Elkington (subsequently a manufacturer), J.C.R. Milns, C.W. Browne-Lecky (Cambridge University VIII, 1873–4; High Sheriff of Londonderry), P.W. Brancker (Cambridge University VIII, 1867; Holy Orders), A.R. Harding (Oxford University VIII, 1867; barrister), Francis Spurling (stockbroker).
Front row from the left: J.A. Randall, H.W.K. Roscoe (barrister), H.M. Evans (Social Tutor at Radley, 1879–1909, Sub-Warden, 1890–1909; succeeded to the Llwynbarried property, 1899), G.H. Gray (Canon and Sacrist, Canterbury Cathedral), E.C.M. Evans.
On the ground: R.C. Parsons (Holy Orders)

32. The Clock Tower, Fives Courts and School, a watercolour by F.T. Dalton, Social Tutor (F Social) 1879–86

33. Social Fours Bumping Races at Sandford, 1888

34. The Revd T.D. Raikes and his Social, *c.* 1887. In 1886 his Social was the first to be built to house all the boys under one roof

35. The Revd R.J. Wilson, Warden 1880–8

36. Middle Hall in the House with High Table on the left. A photograph taken between 1888 and 1893 when wrought-iron chandeliers replaced the inelegant lighting

37. School and lean-to classrooms, 1890; watercolour by an unknown Old Radleian

38. Covered Passage, built in the 1850s, photographed in 1891

39. The Revd H.L. Thompson,
Warden 1889–96

40. Gaudy 1894, a photograph taken from Gallery Dormitory, looking towards Archery
Ground and the Pond

41. A Chapel procession in June 1895 when the Gymnasium was being used for services before the new Chapel was completed

42. The Revd Thomas Field, Warden 1897–1913

43. Boys waiting for the train to Henley at Radley station (built 1873). When this photograph was taken in the 1890s the whole school went to the Regatta

44. The old organ case in Chapel designed by Sir Thomas Graham Jackson, 1897

45. School in 1903. The Fifth and Sixth Form Recesses on the right were joined together in 1904 when the central bay was added to the building. The near recess for the Fifth Form was the scene of fights during 'Bells'. The desks were removed in the 1920s

ing matches in 1908 and 1910 and Westminster in another thrilling match in 1913, the last year in which Association Football was played; but these were isolated victories. Radley could not hope to achieve the successes of Oundle and Uppingham, Eton and Harrow until it became a larger school and until its general tone became less leisurely and easy-going.

*

To the dismay of the Council, however, Radley was shrinking rather than growing. As in Thompson's last years, numbers were falling off at a most disappointing rate, as stories spread of the 'low moral tone' of the school and of a large number of insolent bloods who sat through lessons with no intention of profiting from them. There was also a belief that Radley's earlier reputation as a school where bullying was exceptional rather than habitual had not been justified for some time. The reminiscences of Radleians who were at the school at this time tend to confirm this:

> It was customary for the senior boys to play Bat Fives on the Clock Tower court between 12 and 1 p.m. and, after their game, they would foregather at the foot of the stairs ... and practise forehand and backhand strokes with the bat on the juniors' backsides as they sprinted past.

> I was much bullied [wrote another man, by then Professor of Anatomy at Bristol University] ... Fear became almost fright until I formed a belligerent pact with a co-sufferer, Whitworth-Jones [later to distinguish himself in the Indian Medical Service] by which we kept together and bit like savage little dogs any aggressor – the danger was in being caught singly ...

A third Old Radleian, the son of a clergyman and a clergyman himself, recalled:

> There was a great deal of bullying when I was at Radley. We new boys had to run the gauntlet of the big men's boots down Covered Passage. They stood at the sides and took kicks at you as you ran down ... No, Radley was not a good school in my time.

Bullying at Radley was, however, no worse than it was at most other public schools in the years leading up to, during and immediately after the First World War. There was scarcely a public school in the country where new boys were not required to learn a lexicon of unfamiliar terms and a series of archaic privileges within a certain period and were punished with more or less severity for not having mastered them in time. Nor were there many schools which did not perpetuate such practices as Marlborough's 'basketing' in which the chosen victim – 'perhaps he sported coloured socks too soon, perhaps he smarmed his hair with scented oil' – was 'stripped of most of his clothing, smeared with ink, treacle or paint, then hoisted in one of the two big waste-paper baskets' and pelted with 'darts of sharp pen-nibs'. According to Louis MacNeice, who went to Marlborough soon after his fellow poet, John Betjeman, 'the masters considered this a fine tradition.'

Although he liked it to be supposed that he had been 'basketed' himself – an experience he described with ever-increasing extravagance and hilarity – Betjeman, as another of his contemporaries at Marlborough, the art historian and spy Anthony Blunt, recalled, escaped bullying by his 'marvellous sense of humour and very, very infectious laugh'. 'When the toughs tried to be bloody he simply laughed in their face . . . and they were absolutely routed.'

The capacity to be funny was always a good defence against bullying, as Angus Wilson discovered at Westminster and Cyril Connolly at Eton, where, aged fifteen, he was, according to his own account, 'dirty, inky, miserable, untidy, a bad fag, a coward at games, lazy at work, unpopular with my masters and superiors, anxious to curry favour yet to bully whom I dared'. At the beginning of his career in the school, Godfrey Meynell had been singled out to look after him; and, so Connolly wrote, 'nobody would have believed Meynell could make me stand on a mantelpiece while he brandished a red-hot poker between my feet and said, "What is your name?" "Connolly." "No – what is your real name? Go on, say it." "Ugly." "All right, Ugly, you can come down."'

Having learned to make use of his comic gifts, however, Connolly became popular. He was elected to Pop, formally known as the Eton Society, that self-electing association of twenty or thirty boys who elsewhere would have been school prefects.

Lord Clark, the patron and interpreter of arts, had no such gifts as Connolly's to call upon at Winchester. Travelling there for his first term, he spoke to a boy on the train who did not reply. On arrival at the school he was told to report to the head of his house, who turned out to be the handsome youth he had so thoughtlessly addressed on the train. '"Sport an arse," he said (which in Wykehamist language means "bend over"); and he gave me three or four very painful strokes with a stick. "That will teach you to speak to your seniors," he said. It did.'

'In the twinkling of an eye,' wrote Lord Clark in his autobiography, 'the jolly boy from Wixenford [his preparatory school] became a silent, solitary, inward-turning but still imperfect Wykehamist.'

> On the whole I cannot say that life was agreeable . . . Hunger, chilblains and a perpetually sore bottom. I remember one mid-day meal that consisted solely of the *skins* of boiled potatoes, and on such sordid nourishment we were expected not only to work and play games, but go for two long runs each week . . . Our performances were timed by the prefects, and we were beaten if we took too long. The Athenian cunning, traditional at Eton, would have found some way round these hardships; but Wykehamists are as virtuous as Tamino.
>
> My own personal misfortune was an exceptionally stupid house-master [who] took a great dislike to me because I was not a gentleman, and encouraged his prefects to beat me more, even, than they felt inclined to do.*

At Malvern fags were traditionally denied the use of toasting forks, as Lord Holland had been in the eighteenth century – a tradition that survived well into the 1920s.

> There were generally about eight boys struggling for position at the guttering gas toasters, in a space barely adequate for three. As a result one generally got pushed on to the machines, and burned both the toast and one's hands. In winter chilblains always resulted from this activity, and as soon as one got a chilblain one inevitably acquired a burn on top of it. It was a perilous occupation, in which failure was rewarded with a beating.

Bullied though a number of them undoubtedly were, most boys at Radley, from the turn of the century till the First World War, seem to have been quite happy there, for all the school's discomforts. They remembered getting up at half-past six and at seven o'clock drinking cups of cocoa in Covered Passage; skating on the frozen Pond; taking part in long cross-country runs followed by cold baths in tin tubs; rushing to Shop to buy buns and hoping to avoid Prefects who would

---

*In justice to the Winchester of Lord Clark's day, it should be added that, while there, he won a good scholarship to Trinity College, Oxford.

order them to prepare tea for them in their studies; filling in the date-card – 'a quaint document listing the chief events from 54 BC to the Crimean War' – if they were late for Hall; drinking synthetic lemonade and eating biscuits in Hall between Prep and Evening Chapel; enjoying Social Teas on Saturdays huddled round a classroom fire, and on Sundays apple pie.

What a terribly cold winter my first term was [recalled a man who had been at Radley in these years and later enjoyed a successful career]. Yet we new boys were not allowed to wear overcoats, woollen scarves or gloves – 'the bloods' saw to that. And summer had its disadvantages: no cool flannels or soft collars. We had to wear the same clothes as we wore in winter . . . The evening meal was a dreary affair of bread and butter and tea or coffee, supplemented by such grub as we had in our tuck boxes or ordered from Shop . . . We lived Spartan lives . . . But they were happy days – the happiest in my life. My fondest memories are of 'socialising' on summer evenings – the rooks cawing sleepily – deep shadows on the lawns – and the scent of sweet briar and roses. The end came too soon, far too soon.

By 1913, however, there were only 196 boys at Radley compared with the 258 of 1908. It was the general feeling of the Council that Field was largely responsible for this failure, just as there was a growing feeling in Common Room that after sixteen years as Warden it was time for him to go.

It cannot be said that the Council, having appointed him, had ever given him much support. For many years its members had been dominated by a narrow-minded and outdated oligarchy determined to preserve the least important – or, as some might put it, the most harmful – parts of the Sewell tradition. Nor were the Social Tutors of much help to Field in his work at Radley. As one of his assistant masters said many years later in a paper read to Forum, an informal club of Radley dons:

Social Tutors were at that time appointed strictly on seniority, regardless of qualifications, and only one notorious gentleman was ever passed over. Of Field's seven Social Tutors only two would have had any chance of being appointed in recent times; and the average length of a tenure of all the Social Tutors was 29 years.

If I had to make a report on the school at this time, it might be something like this:

Religion   Negative.
Moral Tone   Pretty low, though word was much worse than deed.

Work	Minimum standards. VI Form lively but frivolous.
Intellectual and Artistic Interests	Nil, except in VI Form and among future VI formers. Public opinion was frankly Philistine.
Games	Undistinguished, especially rowing, which had been ruined by 'Buffy' Evans. The whole school was dominated by the 'blood' system.
Manners	Visiting speakers and others assured us they were excellent.
General	Upper-middle-class social consciousness was pervasive. The boys had a complacent belief in themselves as a social community, but no belief at all in Radley as a school. There were terrific standards of personal cleanliness.

Only too well aware of these defects and conscious, too, of the Council's attitude towards him, Field became even more brusque than was his usual manner with the members of the Council and increasingly autocratic and offhand with a discontented and discordant staff to whom he had rarely troubled to explain his plans and policies.

When he was offered the living of St Mary's, Nottingham, he thought it as well to accept it. There had been a time – had he felt able to bring himself earlier to leave the Radley he loved – when he could have expected an appointment far more impressive than this, the headmastership of a larger school, the Deanery at Canterbury, even a bishopric, perhaps. That time had passed. His astonishing vitality was waning. He was getting on for sixty. After thirteen years in Nottingham he moved to Southwell where he was appointed a Canon of the Minster and where, after a long illness, he died.

18

Warden Selwyn

1913–1917

'He was accused of replacing Radley customs and traditions with foreign ones, probably from Eton.'

THE NEW WARDEN of Radley was twenty-seven years old, the youngest Warden the school had ever had. The son of Dr E.C. Selwyn, who at the age of thirty-four had succeeded Thring as Headmaster of Uppingham, and a great-grandson of Arnold of Rugby, Edward Gordon Selwyn had been Captain of the School at Eton. An extremely intelligent, small and pale young man whose somewhat fleshy features were to earn him the nickname of 'Piggy', he had won all manner of awards: Newcastle Scholar, Ball Scholar, Porson Scholar and Prizeman, Waddington Scholar, Browne's Medallist. A Scholar of King's College, Cambridge, he had taken a First and become President of the Union. He had been appointed a Fellow and Lecturer of Corpus Christi College, Cambridge, in 1909 and a year later had married the daughter of Sir Edwyn Hoskyns, a distinguished divine, Fellow of his College and Bishop of Southwell.

The Council hoped that he would bring a new sense of urgency and vigour to a school which had of late shown symptoms of complacency and ill-discipline as well as what was rather evasively referred to as 'moral decline'. They knew him to be a convinced Liberal with progressive views on education but hoped at the same time to be able to rely on him not to be too revolutionary: they were to be reassured by a speech he was to make at his first Gaudy in which he said that he would take as his motto a notice which he had seen on his way to Radley – '*School – Drive Slowly*'.

At Uppingham his father, also an Old Etonian, had been found a difficult and rather impatient man with what one of his staff called 'a combative personality'. 'He did not suffer fools gladly and it seems that he included a number of the Uppingham Trustees in that category ... His relationships with others for whom he had no great respect or affection were often strained by his biting tongue.' There was something of the same character in his elder son who, undeniably arrogant on occasions, was to be described by the father of a Radley boy as 'the rudest man in Europe'.

Selwyn set to his task with a will, not to say an impatience quite at odds with the policy he had announced at his first Gaudy.

> Armed with the information which he had been given [his first Senior Prefect, A.C. Nugee, recalled], he decided that he must act swiftly ... I think we all knew that all was not well with the moral standards in the school ... So within a few weeks of my appointment I found myself with the unpleasant task of fetching out from their classrooms certain of the most senior and popular boys in the school and taking them to the Warden's study. Some of them we never saw again ... Several of them were either in the 1st football XI or certain to be included ... This drastic action shook the school to its foundations and it was a hard job for those who were loyal to [the Warden] and understood the need for such action, to maintain our position in the face of a growing spirit of revolt.

Having followed the precept of his great-grandfather, Thomas Arnold, who held that 'the first, second and third duty of a headmaster is to get rid of unpromising material', Selwyn then gave careful consideration to ways of improving the standard of work in the middle and lower forms of the school. If a boy did badly over a prolonged period, his form master was required, as at Eton, to hand him a ticket which he was to take to the Warden who, in the words of one culprit, 'acknowledged receipt of it by way of a caning'. This was, however, not a very severe punishment, as the culprit had to acknowledge: 'My beating was really a bit of a farce. Indeed when the Warden had finished he had to inform me of the fact, for I was so unhurt I thought he must have been merely taking aim.'

In the Upper School, the Warden stimulated the teaching of modern languages and science so that boys could specialize more successfully in these subjects. On learning that scarcely more than a quarter of the boys had passed the swimming test, he also introduced compulsory bathing once a week. He allowed the Prefects to wear grey flannel trousers instead of the striped trousers with black coats or blue suits required of lesser boys, but annoyed them by allowing the wearing of 'up-and-down' collars throughout the school – except by the youngest boys who were still required to wear Eton collars – thus abolishing one of the Prefects' most treasured privileges. He also removed the Prefects' right to administer what had been known as 'Octagon beatings', and outlawed the traditional line-up and parade into Chapel, though this was a custom so revered in the school that he felt obliged to restore it.

The Warden's principal problem in gaining acceptance for his reforms was the opposition of Common Room, occupied as it was by a number of masters set in their ways, some of whom had been at the school long before he had been sent as a boy to Eton and three of whom had been Social Tutors before he was born. They resented what they took to be his high-handed manner, his pretence at consulting them over matters upon which he had already come to a decision, often, it was thought, with the help of his wife, a proud woman, condemned as patronizing.

Masters complained to each other of the way in which his published works were put on prominent display in his lodgings to impress visitors; of his habit of wearing his mortar board throughout such hurriedly conducted Common Room meetings as he chose to attend; his printed invitations to Gaudies which came from 'The Warden and Mrs Selwyn', rather than from 'The Warden and Masters'. On one occasion when he complained of there being no one to consult over a particular problem, even his wife being away, Ernest Bryans – a caustic, strict and rigid man, the handsome, heavily moustached driver of a celebrated dog-cart, who had been on the staff since 1882, a Social Tutor since 1884 and Sub-Warden from 1914 – rose in what another master described as 'a cold fury'. 'Trembling with anger', Bryans suggested that in such circumstances it *might* have been supposed that the Warden *might* have considered that the Sub-Warden *might* have been of some help.

The masters, Selwyn decided, had not been supporting Field as they should have been in his later years at the school; and it was not long before he made up his mind that they must support him or leave.

The Revd John Kirkby, a shy and kindly man, who taught mathematics and had been the first Tutor of what was thereafter to be known as E Social,* was asked to give up the Social which had been his since 1879. He resigned soon afterwards and retired to a living in Berkshire. Also required to leave was the tiresomely dogmatic Arthur Pughe, also a mathematician, who had been at Radley since 1890 and had long irritated his colleagues by his bossy parade of knowledge about his own and all other subjects. Then it was time to face the unpleasant task of dislodging the small and wizened seventy-six-year-old 'Kitty' Wharton, now more commonly known as 'The Cat' since his whiskers had turned white and wispy. Wharton had been Tutor of A Social since 1879 and for years an increasingly eccentric Radley institution, celebrated for his theatrical sermons, his uncertain seat on an old mare which he rode into Oxford and his even more uncertain seat on the bicycle which had replaced his creaking tricycle of the 1890s. His rooms in the House were 'a treasure-trove of intimate and small-scale delights', as described by one of those invited to enter them: 'I remember a spinet on which he would play a few bars, some antique gold or silver repeating watches, and when one had tea it was out of beautiful dark blue and gold Royal Worcester cups, a fearsome ordeal for the gangling.'

It was felt impossible to ask Wharton to leave his quarters altogether but it was tentatively suggested that he might see his way to vacating a room he had taken over as a bedroom when his other rooms had become too cluttered for normal occupation. This room, however, he declined to give up. He continued to occupy it and to receive a pension of £100 a year from the Council, as well as free board and lodging, until his death at Radley in 1925.

Modest as it was, Wharton's pension was a sum which the Council could ill afford. The low numbers in the school – soon to drop to 160 – were resulting in a financial crisis so worrying that even the lead was stripped from the roof of the House, sold and replaced by asphalt. Fees were increased to £110 a year for boys entering the school under the age of fourteen, to £120 for others; in addition there were compulsory extras of 12 guineas a year.

Despite these financial troubles, the Warden carried on with his reforms as though money were not a problem, drawing up a plan for wholesale improvements in the buildings which he considered essen-

---

*As well as by the name of the Social Tutor for the time being, Socials were and still are also known by the permanent initials A to H.

tial if parents were to be persuaded to send their sons to Radley rather than to one of those other foundations of the 1840s, Marlborough or Lancing, Cheltenham or Rossall, or to Bradfield (founded in 1850) or to one of the newer schools which had come into existence since the 1850s and which, since the extension of the railway network, were more easily accessible than they would have been in the past: Wellington, Clifton and Haileybury, St Edward's (Oxford), Cranleigh, Malvern, Eastbourne and Denstone. To compete on equal terms with such schools, Selwyn outlined an ambitious scheme of building and improvement which was estimated to cost £30,000. The Council appealed to the Radleian Society to help in raising the money. This was in May 1914. In August war was declared.

The effect on Radley was immediate. Lancelot Vidal, who had been appointed to take over Wharton's Social, left to join the Oxfordshire and Buckinghamshire Light Infantry and was killed in action a few months later. Other masters also left and three of them were killed. Two young men who came to fill the vacancies, A.T. Hedgecock, a Scholar of St John's College, Oxford, and Walter Smale, an Exhibitioner of New College, Oxford, were both in the Army within a few terms, Hedgecock an officer in the Irish guards, Smale in the ranks of the Royal Garrison Artillery, 'without doubt the most improbable soldier of all time'. Several other young masters drilled with Radley's Officers' Training Corps as a preparation for their own war service.

The war soon affected the school in other ways. Trenches were dug in the grounds; lawns gave way to potato patches; boys worked as farm labourers, their extremely modest remuneration being given to charity without passing through their hands. School meals became even less appetizing and nourishing than they had been in the past, although it was some compensation that they were served by maids rather than servitors, most of whom had joined the Army. 'Life tended to be spartan,' recalled a Radleian of those days. 'At night, in the cold weather we went up to bed, and would start by thawing out our face flannels, which were frozen stiff, and thawing the ice in our water-bottles. All the lavatories . . . were frozen for weeks at a time. We all had chilblains.'

This Radleian also recalled the unpalatable wartime breakfasts of the inevitable, unchanging pork pie; the groups of hungry boys loitering around the kitchen or stillroom door, hoping to be given half a loaf by a sympathetic maid; the plopping noise the gas jets made in Chapel as clouds of asbestos fragments fell on the heads of the congregation; musical evenings in the Old Gym, known as 'the tin tabernacle'; the performances there of Gilbert and Sullivan in which a Social Tutor, the Revd F.J. Stone, revealed an unexpected gift for comedy.*

In the course of the war unusual visitors would arrive at Radley for days or weeks on end: soldiers, foreign refugees, members of the Inns of Court Reserve Corps who took over various school buildings and marched amateurishly across the park. *The Radleian* – which was handed out to eager readers from the windows of Pups' Study – brought news of deaths at Ypres and on the Somme, of decorations awarded and exploits achieved: R.L.G. Marix, a Flight Lieutenant in the Royal Naval Air Service, later an Air Vice-Marshal, was awarded the Distinguished Service Order for destroying a Zeppelin by bombing its shed at Düsseldorf from a very low altitude; and O.A. Reid, captain of the 1913 Cricket XI, having been three times wounded, twice mentioned in despatches and awarded Italy's Silver Medal for Valour, eventually won the Victoria Cross as a Major in Mesopotamia.

The boys still at the school anxiously awaited their turn to go to the front, perhaps to win glory, perhaps to die, and in that mood of restless expectancy a spirit of revolt was born.

The masters were not equipped to deal with it. Most of the older ones amongst them got on with the Warden no better now than they had done in the beginning, disagreeing with many of his reforms, and still resenting his failure to discuss them fully with staff. They resented, too, his imposing upon them various unwelcome duties such as that laid upon Tutors of sitting with the boys of their Socials at luncheon in Hall. The younger masters, some of them little older than their

---

*The difficulties of arriving at a fair estimate of the characters of masters long since dead are highlighted by the reminiscences of three men who were in the Revd F.J. Stone's Social during the First World War. To one Mr Stone was 'a cold looking and almost inarticulate bachelor but inwardly a kindly and humane creature . . . He was really beloved by everyone in his Social and kept excellent discipline . . . Because he was such a decent chap, boys felt it would be unsporting to behave badly.' To another Old Radleian who had been a boy in his Social, Mr Stone was a man 'who gave himself completely to the boys, watching over [them] with gentleness and real affection. I do not think I ever saw him angry, and if anything went wrong it was hurt and disappointment he showed not anger . . . He played the 'cello beautifully.' When these passages were read to the ninety-four-year-old Leonard Cooper who had been one of Stone's Prefects, there was a long pause before he replied succinctly, 'Mr Stone was a slimy toad.' As for the cello playing, this witness was once so distressed by the discordant sounds which reached his ears from the room in which Stone practised that he hurled a jar of potted meat at his window.

pupils, came and went with such frequency that the boys had scarcely time to get to know them before they left. Several were quite incapable of keeping order, as, indeed, were some of the older temporary masters: one of these, a clergyman of less than sound mind, lasted for only a week before he was taken away to a mental hospital after preaching a fiery sermon against the Warden in Chapel. A young master, an undergraduate who came over from Oxford every day on a motorcycle to teach mathematics, was peremptorily told by one of his pupils not to demonstrate his sums on the blackboard. When he ignored this unseemly request, the boy produced a revolver from his desk and shot a hole in the chalk marks.

There seem to have been numerous revolvers at Radley at this time: the respectable inhabitants of Sandford were liable to have holes blasted in their bowler hats of a Sunday, and bargees by the Mill became accustomed to having their craft peppered by small arms fire. In the College there were constant eruptions, rowdy altercations and elaborate practical jokes of unprecedented impertinence. One master had to grow accustomed to teaching, or attempting to teach, a classroom full of boys smoking pipes, one entire row of desks occupied by boys all puffing on churchwardens. Another master was interrupted in a class by the entry of a boy smoking a pipe, and wearing a big false red beard. 'Carry on,' the boy – one day to be headmaster of another school – said with breezy condescension, 'I'm the new Warden.'

The real Warden's new broom had provoked the less governable boys in a number of ways. He was 'not popular', wrote one of them in later years. 'He was accused of replacing Radley customs and traditions with foreign ones, probably from Eton.' The manner in which he decreed that rugger should replace soccer as the school's winter game was considered by masters and boys alike as typical of his arrogance. This episode was recounted by the Senior Prefect, A.C. Nugee.

> He consulted the Prefects and asked their opinion. Our unanimous opinion was that the game should be altered, but not just yet to give the school time to get used to the new code. He then consulted the Common Room and received, so we understand, much the same advice. Then he called a meeting of all first Caps who were not Prefects, and the majority at that meeting was against the change ... Nothing more was heard of the proposal for some weeks. But one day at lunch at High Table in Hall – for the Warden had instituted the custom of having some of the senior boys at High Table – I was sitting next to Mrs Selwyn. She asked me if I had seen the notice on the Warden's board. I said that I had not , and asked what it was. She told me

that it said that, beginning at next winter term, the school game would be Rugby. I am afraid that my immediate reply was 'How stupid!' I knew there would be trouble, and trouble there was that evening during bells before Chapel. Certain first Caps dressed up a dummy in football shorts and striped rugger vest and carried it at the double down the length of Covered Passage between the lines of booing and hissing boys. Then they stripped off the rugger vest and disclosed the shirt of the 1st XI and carried it back in triumph to the cheers and applause of the rest of the school . . . Immediately after the service I went to the Warden's study to report to him, and as I was doing so the two prefect ringleaders came in to resign and return their caps of office. It was a miserable affair and left a nasty taste behind it.

The boys had been equally annoyed when, in his only too well justified attack on 'bloodism' in the school, he much reduced the privileges enjoyed by 'Caps' and outlawed the practice of 'ramps', the chairing by running, shouting bearers of a victorious team up and down Covered Passage before Chapel. On one occasion the Warden had himself been jostled by the cheering mob until the Senior Prefect was able to bring the rowdy proceedings to an end. In the autumn of 1915 the Prefects declared their solidarity with the 'Caps' and resigned *en masse*.

By then the Warden had made himself particularly unpopular by his mishandling of what became known as the 'Nunn affair' in which his determination to establish the right of a headmaster to assert his authority over that of a parent in matters relating to school rules led him to act in a way which a more experienced headmaster would have avoided.

The fifteen-year-old boy at the centre of the case, Vivian Nunn, asked for, and was granted, a day's leave to go home to see his brother who was about to sail for India, having just been commissioned in the Royal Field Artillery. When he reached home his brother had not yet arrived, so a telegram was sent by the boy's father to the Warden requesting permission for the boy to stay the night so that Vivian would not miss seeing him. Permission was refused. The boy nevertheless stayed the night, assured by his father that, while he had broken his undertaking to the Warden, he had obeyed his parents and could rely on them for 'seeing him through'. The next morning he returned to the school where he was beaten by the Warden. His father demanded an apology; the Warden declined to give one, whereupon Mr Nunn brought an action for assault against him.

Ellis Hume-Williams, KC, Member of Parliament for the Bassetlaw Division of Nottinghamshire, was briefed to represent Mr Nunn; E.M. Pollock, KC, also a Member of Parliament and later appointed Attorney-General, was briefed on behalf of the defendant. The case, which was heard before Mr Justice Ridley on 20 and 21 October 1915, aroused widespread interest in the popular press. After the jury decided in favour of the plaintiff, but with only ten guineas damages, the Council considered making an appeal but eventually decided against it.

So many letters, most of them abusive, were written to the Warden during and after the Nunn case that he asked the Bursar to open and deal with most of them. One particularly insulting one was written by a peer. To this the Bursar replied that his Lordship might like to know that some unscrupulous person had evidently stolen a quantity of his private writing paper and had used some sheets to write a peculiarly intemperate letter to the Warden. His Lordship, however, would be relieved to learn that the letter had not reached the Warden's eyes.

*

The months immediately before and after the Nunn case were marked at Radley by the worst behaviour that the school had suffered since the 1870s. The Warden thought of resigning and would, perhaps, have gone had not the Council, and in particular the Chairman, the Ven. T.H. Archer Houblon, Archdeacon of Oxford, expressed their confidence in him.

Their support was justified. By the beginning of 1917 there could be no doubt that discipline had been restored; and while the Warden's continuing reforms – such as the institution of fifteen minutes' compulsory Swedish Drill before early school and the replacement of the *Radley Psalter*, to which the boys had grown accustomed in Chapel, by the unfamiliar *Cathedral Psalter** – were widely criticized, there

---

*It was not only because of their habitual conservatism that the boys opposed this change. As A.C. Nugee explained: 'We used a special *Radley Psalter*, the compilation of Dr Field, which was interleaved with pages of his notes. There were many blank spaces in these pages, and they were very handy for recording the really important events of school life – who won the Social competitions, who was Victor Ludorum, and the results of the Bradfield match. Not all the entries were in that harmless vein, and when Gordon Selwyn became Warden, after a cursory glance at some of the psalters, they were all removed and the school went over to the *Cathedral Psalter*.'

was no such opposition to his will as had earlier been displayed. It was not just that the older boys were worried they might not obtain a commission without the Warden's recommendation, it was generally if belatedly recognized that he did have the good of the school at heart, that his reforms were for the most part salutary and overdue, and that, for those who cared to learn, he was an inspiring if demanding teacher. In his short time as Warden, seventeen boys at the school won university scholarships or exhibitions. Also he took an obvious and active interest in many of the school's activities. He spoke in meetings of the Debating Society; he regularly attended the English Essay Society which he had founded; he encouraged the activities of the Musical and Choral Societies; he contributed a poem to *The Radleian*, something which no Warden had done before and only one Warden has done since.

One of his Prefects recalled with shame how, as a younger boy in the school, he had joined in the cheering when the result of the Nunn case was announced; how, following the lead of other boys and some of the masters, he had ostentatiously withdrawn his attention when the Warden, gathering his long, black silk gown around him, mounted the pulpit to preach a sermon in Chapel. He was all the more ashamed of this behaviour because he remembered also how as a nervous new boy, he had been put at his ease when called to the Warden's study. 'He spoke to us in the gentlest and most encouraging terms . . . His voice was soft and not unmelodious, though he had perhaps the faintest suspicion of a hot potato in his mouth . . . He seemed a man of contained and equable temperament, dignified, reserved and powerful, with gentleness and humour never far below the surface.'

Before he left the school this Prefect came to realize the difficulties which the Warden had to face in governing a school in wartime, with a dissident Common Room composed largely of masters either openly hostile or inexperienced, and senior boys anxiously awaiting their time to join the Army: there were no fewer than seven Senior Prefects in just over three years. It was not surprising the Warden was abrupt at times, that often, after leading the stately procession into Hall with some distinguished lady visitor on his arm and uttering in his eloquent way the long, elaborate Latin grace, he would 'sit abstracted and withdrawn throughout the meal'.

For all his good intentions, however, and the good results of many of his policies, Selwyn could not win the regard of the 'Caps'; nor could he compose all his differences with Common Room, differences which were assiduously spread about the school by George Wharton. His final break with Common Room came in December 1917. As with Warden Martin, it came over trouble with the Bursar. The first full-time Bursar, the Revd A.W. Davies, left Radley within a year of his appointment. He was succeeded by H.L. Mullins, the son of an Uppingham master, who had previously been Bursar at Giggleswick. Mullins and the Warden did not get on; and, after less than two years in his new post, having previously been told that he could not be released for military service, Mullins was informed that his resignation was required. A majority of Common Room sided with the Bursar against the Warden, and a letter was addressed to the Council asking that Mullins's services should be retained. The Warden felt that he himself should not remain at Radley in these circumstances and handed in his resignation, giving some authority to a belief, widely held in Oxford, that 'Radley's Common Room always breaks its Wardens.'

The Council accepted the Warden's resignation, but asked him to remain until the summer. He agreed not to leave until Easter; and so was still at Radley when there was further trouble with the 'Caps'.

19

'The Feud'

1917–1918

'A sort of monastery with no fun left.'

THE STORY OF this trouble, 'the Feud' as it came to be called, throws a revealing light on the mores of senior boys at Radley, and at public schools generally at the time.

The end of the Michaelmas term 1917 had seen the departure of the Captain of Boats and both the Senior and Second Prefects. The Prefects were succeeded by H.S. Selous, who was to leave at the end of term to serve in France as an officer in the Queen's Regiment, and J.M. Hawker, who was to take Holy Orders. Both these boys were in the First XV. The Captain of Boats was succeeded by D.E.B. Manning, a strong and forceful character, who was also Captain of Rugger.

Among their fellow senior athletes were several whose interests were almost entirely confined to sporting activities, and to such pleasures as they could enjoy at school before joining the Army. They did as little work as they could for the senior masters and virtually none at all for the younger temporary ones. As soon as they saw that Selous was not exercising his authority as Senior Prefect, they assumed a growing independence. The Second Prefect and three other Prefects, deciding that the authority of their office must be upheld against the 'Bloods', went to Selous to give him their views. But Selous did not want to become involved. His father had been killed in action; his brother had been killed on the anniversary of his father's death, and he had become convinced that he himself would be killed on the second anniversary.

While Selous was virtually *hors de combat*, the senior boys began to divide into two factions, on one side the supporters of the four Prefects who had gone to Selous to protest against the arrogant behaviour of 'the Bloods', and on the other the 'Bloods' themselves who complained that, if their priggish, industrious rivals were allowed to rule the roost, Radley would become 'a sort of monastery with no fun left'.

On the last night of term, between 'bells' for evening Chapel, the school lined up as usual on either side of Covered Passage while the Prefects and 'Caps' paraded up and down the centre arm-in-arm. At the second bell the 'Caps' took their places in the lines while the Prefects returned to the Prefects' Study from which they emerged, in seniority, to walk down between the lines and into Chapel.

On this occasion, one of 'the Bloods' was late, and as he came edging surreptitiously down the line to take up his position, the Second Prefect, who thoroughly disliked him, gave him a kick, as Prefects and 'Caps' often did to scurrying late arrivals. He then punched him in the back hard enough for him to lose his balance and fall to the ground.

Having heard of this insult to one of his henchmen, Manning, the Captain of Boats and of Rugger, called a meeting of his supporters after Chapel and marched them off to Upper Dormitory to avenge the assault by ducking the Second Prefect in a cold bath.

Learning what had happened but evidently unaware of the Second Prefect's provocative kick and punch in Covered Passage, Selwyn had Manning and his friends brought from their beds. Told to remove their dressing gowns and pyjama trousers they were all birched. They were then expelled on the spot.

Soon afterwards the Warden left Radley for the last time, having performed a final service to the school by this summary punishment of 'the Philistines'. 'He went with the admiration and affection of most of us,' wrote a senior scholar. 'We made him a presentation in School on his last day. We were moved and he was moved, restrained and dignified and eloquent as always, but inwardly moved . . . It was clear to me that he was contrasting our friendliness with the mistrust and rancour of his staff.'

The 'Bloods' had been wounded, not killed, however; and the problem they presented, at Radley as in other schools, was to plague a future generation.

Selwyn joined the Army as a chaplain and served on the Italian front where he was mentioned in despatches. From 1921 to 1931 he was Proctor in Convocation and, from 1924 to 1926, Select Preacher at Oxford. He became Dean of Winchester in 1931. In his retirement he came across one of his former Prefects, Leonard Cooper, in a London picture gallery, where he pronounced this not unjustified verdict upon his career at Radley: 'I did all the right things in the wrong way.'

20

Calmer Seas

1918–1924

'Well, are you proud of your old school?'

PRESS REPORTS OF 'the Feud', and stories, much exaggerated in the telling, of Radley's indiscipline, evidently deterred suitable candidates for the Wardenship from coming forward after Selwyn's departure. Before 'the Feud' had reached its rowdy climax, the Council's Selection Committee had offered the appointment to C.H. Blakiston, a strongly recommended Eton master who accepted the offer but then withdrew, ostensibly on grounds of ill health but in reality for reasons less excusable. Regarding the Warden's rooms in the House as unsuitable for a headmaster, he had hoped a separate house would be built for him. When told that this would not be possible he had written to say that Ernest Bryans would have to move out of his house which would be required for the Warden's occupation. Needless to say, this was not acceptable. So Blakiston resigned without ever having taken up his appointment. In 1925 he became Head Master of Lancing where his career must have made the Radley Council thankful that they had been spared his attentions.

In the days of Blakiston's predecessor, the Revd H.T. Bowlby, Lancing had greatly increased its numbers and, thanks at least partly to Bowlby and to some excellent young masters, including J.F. Roxburgh, the future first Headmaster of Stowe, the school had produced some remarkable young men, among them Evelyn Waugh, Tom

Driberg (Lord Bradwell), Lords Trevelyan and Molson, the historian Sir Roger Fulford, the archaeologist Sir Max Mallowan, and the Arctic explorer Gino Watkins. Under the eccentric direction of Cuthbert Blakiston, however, Lancing's reputation and financial position sharply, if temporarily, declined.

Following the withdrawal of his application for the Wardenship at Radley the Council looked urgently about for another candidate, while Bryans, the Sub-Warden, acted as caretaker. Several men of varying attainments were approached, including a distinguished master from Eton who, having been interviewed by the outspoken and intimidating Bryans, took the train back to Eton and promptly withdrew his application. Also considered was William Hamilton Fyfe, who had taught at Radley for a short time in Field's day. Fyfe, however, preferred to remain at Merton College, where he was a Fellow, until, in 1919, he accepted the headmastership of Christ's Hospital.

The Radley Council then provisionally decided to offer the Wardenship to the Headmaster of one of the smaller public schools. But when the Warden of St Edward's, Oxford, the Revd W.H. Ferguson, heard about this proposal he 'knew enough about the man to be quite sure that his appointment would be disastrous for Radley; indeed at that juncture it might have been fatal'. Ferguson expressed these views to the Ven. T.H. Archer Houblon, who was on both the Radley and St Edward's Councils, and suggested that Houblon should consult a master on the staff of St Edward's, a 'very sane and trust-worthy man', who had served under the new candidate. As a result of that interview the offer was withdrawn by the Council, and the appointment was given instead to the Revd Adam Fox, an assistant master at Lancing, where Ferguson had also taught before moving on to St Edward's. The Council hoped that they had found a man who would restore a sense of harmony, even of serenity, to the Radley scene.

*

Other schools were beginning to settle down after the difficulties and unrest of the years of the First World War. Their relative contentment is reflected in a collection of reminiscences of fellow writers edited by the novelist, Graham Greene, who had been at Berkhamsted where his father was Headmaster. Greene himself had not been happy at Berkhamsted and had since come to the conclusion that the public school system was doomed. Evidently he had hoped that the contributors to his symposium would recount impressions of their school lives similar to his own and would come to the same conclusion as to the future of the system. To ask writers was, at least, more likely to elicit such responses than to ask, say, generals. Field Marshal Montgomery was 'very happy' at St Paul's; General Horrocks 'enjoyed his time [at Uppingham] enormously'; Lord Wavell, who chose Winchester as the second of his viscountcy titles, 'could not have found a happier *milieu*'. For Lord Alexander, Harrow became 'a fond memory'.

While not so unreservedly contented at their schools, Greene's writers were far from being as condemnatory as he had no doubt hoped they would be. To be sure, Derek Verschoyle was not complimentary about Malvern, though he had to admit that he knew 'very few boys who left Malvern unconvinced of its virtues'; William Plomer did not greatly care for Dr David's Rugby; and Harold Nicolson had no affection for Wellington, while admitting that it was, by the time he wrote his article, a very different place from the school it had been in his day and confessing, also, that he was 'conscious of a marked distaste for those who had not benefited by a public school education'.

Yet L.P. Hartley had good words to say of Harrow where 'we had a great deal of freedom and a great deal of leisure' and where he was 'never up to a master who did not in a greater or lesser degree attempt to understand as well as to teach one'. Anthony Powell enjoyed his days at Eton where – despite its reputation in those days for fierce corporal punishment – he himself was never beaten, and where, though 'quite ludicrously bad at games and none too high up in the school', he was elected a member of his House Library through the intercession of friends. And W.H. Auden was quite content at Gresham's School, Holt, though he strongly disapproved of its system of maintaining discipline by obliging boys to promise not to swear, to smoke or to say or do 'anything indecent', and to report those who did not confess to these sins themselves. The buildings were comfortable, fagging extremely light, the food adequate, and 'all the staff were conscientious'. Much the same could be said of Radley in the days of Adam Fox.

Fox was a Wykehamist like Sewell but, unlike Sewell, a man known to be an experienced and effective teacher. He had taken his degree at University College, Oxford, in 1906 and had then spent twelve years at Lancing, during the last five of which he had been a housemaster.

'The Adam', as he was known there, was well liked at Lancing where he had commanded the Officers' Training Corps in the war, and came to Radley with a reputation for friendliness, approachability, originality of mind and eccentric unpredictability. Three anecdotes about him, related by one of his successors as Warden, give an indication of his character:

> He came to stay a night at Radley – and to preach next morning. Before dinner I offered him a glass of sherry: 'Thanks, no,' he said: 'I seldom drink, and then only to excess.' The second is this – he was persuaded once to go to address a Youth Rally (not at all his 'cup of tea'); as he boarded the taxi to take him there, he said despairingly, 'Well, I don't know what I have to say to them except that I hope they'll soon grow up.' And here's the third – he is recorded to have begun a sermon thus – 'Now all of you know ...' pause: 'Well, most of you know ...' pause; '*Some* of you know ...' long pause: 'Perhaps *none* of you know ...'

Another characteristic anecdote was related by D.C. Somervell who had him to stay at Tonbridge. When Somervell said he really ought to go out to watch his House play cricket, which he found rather a bore, 'Oh, no,' Fox responded. 'I always think watching cricket is one of the more agreeable ways of wasting time, like going to church.'

'Fox was one of those who loved to make other people happy,' wrote A.K. Boyd who, after service in the Machine Gun Corps, came to Radley as a master at this time, 'and those who had requests to make found in him a charming habit of giving more than was asked. Yet there was a disciplinarian underneath who could be stern and even angry when the need arose ... Transparent sincerity, a complete absence of *amour-propre*, and a notable goodness were other qualities which went to make up the personality of Radley's new Warden.'

A sound scholar and accomplished poet – he later became Professor of Poetry at Oxford – he was not so rigorous and painstaking a teacher as Selwyn but his lessons were always interesting and stimulating, and he succeeded in attracting to the school a new generation of masters who were to help him build up its reputation and restore the good behaviour which Radley, like all other schools more or less, had lost during the war. In a way, Fox was too successful in attracting good men to Radley, since a number of the best went on to become headmasters or second masters of other schools, F.C. Doherty to Oakham, then to Lancing, E.K. Stephenson to Farnborough School, H.W.F. Franklin to Epsom College, Basil Handford to Lancing, F.J. Nugee to Eastbourne.

However, Nugee, who had been one of Field's most effective Senior Prefects – the only boy to have held that office for two years – remained at Radley for almost twenty years before taking up his appointment at Eastbourne, and for fourteen of those years was a notably efficient Sub-Warden.* Another Old Radleian, G.T. Hellard, who had taught at Winchester before coming to Radley, also stayed for almost twenty years. A.K. Boyd stayed for thirty-three years and was Social Tutor for six of them. Four other Social Tutors, the Revd Vyvyan Hope, Theodore Cocks, Stephen Paton and R.E. Eason, all remained until the 1950s or 1960s, Eason, a former Bible Clerk of All Souls, Oxford, remaining until 1962, having been Sub-Warden for the previous ten years. The former Gunner Smale and Lieutenant Hedgecock, Selwyn's appointments, who both returned to be given Socials, stayed for twenty-two and twenty-four years respectively.

Walter Smale was to become a Radley institution like 'Kitty' Wharton and an eccentric character such as most, if not all, public schools take pride in possessing.†

He was a huge and ugly bachelor who was very much one of the few remaining real pre-First World War editions of a schoolmaster [wrote Peggy Gardiner, the wife of one of his colleagues, recalling Smale's character and idiosyncrasies without undue exaggeration]. He bellowed like a bull at everyone, never spoke to a new master for at least two years, and never

---

*Although F.J. Nugee, whose father had been at Eton, was the first of the Nugees to come to Radley, he was continuing a tradition to rival that of the Raikes family. The five sons of his forebear, the Revd E.T. Richards, an Old Etonian High Church friend of Keble and Pusey, were among the school's earliest pupils. Nugee's two brothers were also at Radley, the younger of these being A.C. Nugee, Senior Prefect in Warden Selwyn's troubled early terms; the elder, G.T. Nugee, also a Senior Prefect, was the father of E.G. Nugee whose four sons were all at Radley in their turn.

†As is often the case, these two eccentrics did not get on well together. 'One day when I was riding my bicycle into Abingdon I had a very bad fall,' Wharton once told Smale; 'and do you know, Mr Smale, that when the doctor saw the cut, he said he could see right through to the brain.'

Smale paused for a moment, eyeing Wharton closely before replying, 'Very reassuring, Mr Wharton.'

at all if he had the misfortune to have been at Cambridge* [Smale himself, a Salopian, had been an Exhibitioner of New College, Oxford]. He bullied in a kindly way the boys in his house and took delight in saying he could not remember anybody's name . . . It was obviously a great favour to be asked to dinner and [when we were asked, my husband] impressed on me the importance of the occasion and that on no account must I mention certain touchy things such as going abroad or any other school . . . Naturally I was in a dither of nerves when I arrived . . . and was ushered into the drawing-room, a vast, bleak room with a fireplace with a gloomy fire of about two pieces of coal smoking away without enthusiasm. I was trying to warm my feet which were already frozen when there was suddenly a noise as of thunder in heaven and a voice of stentorian tones shouted, 'Mind my mother, dear girl.' My host stood in the doorway pointing with a shaking figure at the mantelpiece to a small silver casket . . . 'That is my mother, she died six months ago and I had her cremated and I cannot make up my mind whether to bury her or keep her here – Have a drink, dear girl' . . . Gradually I got to know him much better and came to love him as a very lonely man.

Despite the meagre fire in his drawing-room, Smale lived in some comfort at Radley, with a good cellar and two attentive servants. But the food served at his table was unremarkable when it was not actually unpalatable. He insisted on buying the ingredients for his dinner parties in Oxford personally, looking for bargains, often settling for pigeons, and always telling his guests exactly how much he had paid for them.

In his earlier years at Radley, Smale was less of a law unto himself

---

*Peggy Gardiner's husband, a graduate of Christ's College, Cambridge, came in for this treatment when he first arrived at Radley in 1930. On first entering Common Room, he found Smale at one end of the table, the Revd Vyvyan Hope at the other. 'I hear they've appointed a Cambridge man to the staff,' observed Smale. 'Ruddy scientist, too,' responded Hope. They both then slowly turned round to look at him before continuing with their meal.

Mrs Gardiner herself suffered similar embarrassment: 'As the most junior wife, I had no allocated seat in Chapel and used to sit up in the organ gallery. One of the housemaster's wives had a seat downstairs and very kindly told me that I could always use it when she was unable to go to Chapel, so for several Sundays I was delighted to sit somewhere where I could hear and see the beautiful service much better than upstairs. Then the blow fell; [my husband] came home to lunch one day looking furious and worried. He had been approached by [a senior master] who told him that it was a most peculiar and unwarranted piece of impertinence for me to sit in that seat when *his* wife had never been offered it.'

and willingly co-operated with his fellow members of Common Room. With the support of these members, Fox faced the problems encountered by so many schools of the time – inadequate buildings for rising numbers, inadequate sums to pay for them, and married masters needing houses for their families and more generous salaries to support them. At Radley, in Fox's first years, masters' starting salaries were increased to £200 a year with free board and lodging, then to £220 in 1922. At the same time fees were also increased: to £165 in 1919 and to £180 in 1921. These increases had no adverse effects on steadily growing numbers which reached 293 in 1924.

Increasing though they were, Radley's numbers were still well below those of most of the school's rivals. In representative years in the 1920s there were 381 boys at Bradfield, 383 at Lancing (though numbers here were to fall to 265 by 1935), 513 at Uppingham, 589 at Rugby, 722 at Cheltenham and 750 at Marlborough. Fees at Radley, on the other hand, were appreciably more than those charged at most other public schools of comparable standing. In the early 1920s parents were paying 105 guineas a year at Bradfield, £142 a year at Stonyhurst and £162 at Cheltenham, although Uppingham's fees at £186 a year were slightly more than Radley's. At Lancing, in deference to Woodard's aims, fees were still no more than £186 a year in 1946, with places offered to the sons of clergy at £120.

Encouraged by the growth of the school and by hopes – soon realized – that public schools would gain exemption from tax as charitable institutions, the Council undertook much building and rebuilding at Radley. Houses and bungalows were constructed for masters and other members of staff; a new boathouse was erected, largely through the efforts of the brusque, dynamic and persistent Vyvyan Hope who was to do so much for the school in other ways.

South of Chapel a house was built for F.J. Nugee's Social (B), later to be occupied by Morgan's (G); and the Wilson Library, moved to new quarters on the ground floor of the House, was opened by the Prince of Wales who had lunch with the Warden, played squash with the Senior Prefect and recalled a previous visit to Radley when, as an Oxford undergraduate, he had come over with Magdalen College Second XI to play football. He had not played very well according to A.C. Nugee, 'but he had tremendous courage. There had been a shot at our goal which failed to score. He charged down straight at the goalkeeper as he cleared, and the ball came at the Prince's face. Instinctively he put his hands up to protect himself and so committed a technical foul. I saw the master acting as referee put the whistle to his mouth to blow for a free kick, but when he realized who the player was he didn't blow.'*

On the Prince's second visit to Radley, he once again met the courtly Mr Wharton who had entertained him to coffee on his previous visit and, in response to some remark about the old man's precious chairs, which, the Prince noticed, were covered in a material similar to that used for upholstering at the Petit Trianon, Wharton had responded with practised deference, 'That, if I may say so, is remarkably observant of your Royal Highness.'

*

When the new Wilson Library was officially opened by the Prince of Wales in 1924, thought had already been given to the building of a war memorial with a large part of a War Memorial Fund of some £17,000, a proportion of which was to be devoted to scholarships for boys whose fathers had been killed or disabled in the war. On the inside walls of the memorial were to be inscribed the names of those 219 Old Radleians who had given their lives, a large number of whom had been decorated. In all, Old Radleians won 117 Military Crosses, 57 Distinguished Service Orders, four Air Force Crosses, two Distinguished Service Crosses, one Distinguished Flying Cross and one Victoria Cross. For a school of 213 boys in 1913 this was a remarkable achievement. The King's School, Canterbury, prided itself on slightly fewer decorations than Radley's number, and this was a school of some 250 boys. Tonbridge, a school of over 400, won rather more DSOs but only about a third as many MCs.

The design of Radley's War Memorial, which took the form of an Archway at the top of the drive, was entrusted to the architect of the school's Chapel and Hall, T.G. Jackson,† by now Sir Thomas and

---

*The Prince had shown himself to be no better at cricket than he was at football when he had come over to play for the Magdalen Second XI in the summer: 'He made some golf shots at a few balls, one of which he hit and so broke his duck. Then he received a straight one and so got out.'
†T.G. Jackson also designed the South African War Memorial in Chapel. The figure of St George is by Sir George Frampton. This and the window above it are memorials to Major-General Sir E.R.P. Woodgate, who died of wounds received at Spion Kop. He was one of nine Old Radleians killed out of 160 who had served in the Boer War, a higher number it was believed than any other school in proportion to its size.

a venerable member of his profession, well into his eighties. Its foundation stone was laid in 1921 by Sir Theodore Cook, a former Senior Prefect, man of letters, sportsman, Oxford rowing blue and captain of the English fencing team.

Ten months later the building was opened by Field Marshal Sir William Robertson, who had risen from the ranks to his present eminent position. The Field Marshal was accompanied by Major-General Sir Philip Nash, an Old Radleian who had been Inspector-General of Transportation on the Western Front. After the ceremony they returned to London together and on the way Robertson, who according to Nash had 'an uncanny power of judging men', suddenly asked, 'Well, Nash, are you proud of your old school?' 'Of course I am,' Nash replied. 'Well,' said Robertson with a bluntness characteristic of the troop-sergeant he had once been, 'you have no reason to be. It's all wrong.'

Whether or not the comment was at that time justified, either because the school was socially divisive or incompetently run, there could be no doubt that Fox and his Common Room were working hard to make it a better place, to improve scholarship, and to restore the pleasant, friendly atmosphere it had enjoyed before the war. The duration of lessons was reduced from one hour to three quarters; but in these shortened periods boys were kept diligently to their tasks to obtain the new School and Higher School Certificates. It cannot be said, however, that Radley won a high reputation for scholarship in Fox's six years of office. It seemed to many, indeed, that out-of-form activities were pursued with much more enthusiasm than lessons. Meetings of the Debating Society were regularly held; and the high standard of public speaking, demonstrated by the contestants for the prize presented by the Revd R.H.C. Birt, a Social Tutor during the war years, delighted parents at successive Gaudies. There was a well-attended poetry reading by the Old Radleian, H.E. Monro, founder and editor of the *Poetry Review*, whose *Collected Poems* were edited by T.S. Eliot. And on Saturday evenings throughout the school from study after study there emanated the strains of music on gramophone records, while the Gymnasium was packed for cinema shows, performances by the school's jazz bands, brass bands and dance bands, and for occasional dances.

At the boys' dances there were naturally no female partners, though the Warden, following Sewell's example, did give a proper dance at the end of the Christmas term in 1921. This was held in Hall and many of the older boys were invited. The Warden also asked ladies to Sunday luncheon with a frequency unmatched by any of his predecessors other than his fellow bachelor, William Sewell; and to make the long procession, arm in arm with a master from the House to Hall, less of an ordeal for ladies in their hobble skirts, he shortened the customary route. He thought it as well, however, not to shorten the traditional tedious Latin grace, though he did reduce the time the boys spent in Chapel on weekdays to twenty minutes.

With enthusiastic encouragement from the new Precentor, Leslie Huggins – an organ scholar of Balliol – and the Succentor, W.N. McKie – later organist at Westminster Abbey – music at Radley flourished, having been rather neglected since the resignation of George Wharton who was once seen fleeing from Chapel with his fingers in his ears after a particularly discordant performance on the organ. The school orchestra was revived, as well as a military band, and most Socials had their own orchestras. Huggins awarded a cup for the winner of a Unison Singing Competition, known thereafter as 'the Social Shout'.

Games were played with energy but no striking success. Defeats of Radley's First XV were more common than victories. So were defeats on the cricket field, even though there were some excellent players in the First XI, including R.E. Yates, E.T.B. Meyrick-Jones, C.E.A. Worsley, who was to play for Northamptonshire, A.E. Blair, whose average was over 50 in his three years in the XI, and F.C. Dawnay, twice Blair's partner in the finals of the Public Schools Rackets at Queen's.

By the beginning of 1924 it was clear that the Warden's health was failing. He had persistent and acutely painful headaches, suffered intermittently from neuralgia and, after a short convalescence away from the school, returned to it only to fall ill again with pleurisy. His resignation that year caused widespread regret. He left Radley to recoup his health in South Africa, returning in 1929 to become in time Archdeacon of Westminster.

He had been an extremely well-liked headmaster as well as an effective one. The school had not yet achieved as high a reputation in the educational field as the Council had hoped; but its numbers were steadily rising and the troubles of the past seemed over for good. There were grounds for hope that a new Warden, helped by a Common Room united at last in the interests of Radley, would be able to build successfully on secure foundations and demonstrate to the outside world that Field Marshal Robertson's condemnatory verdict could no longer be upheld.

Part II

21

The Advent of Canon Ferguson

1925–1933

'We are all impressed by the good tone and manners of the boys.'

THE PROBLEMS OF making progress within the traditions of
Radley were now in the hands of Fox's successor, the Revd
William Harold Ferguson, who, like Fox, had been a master at
Lancing before being appointed Warden of St Edward's, Oxford, when
that school had entered a critical period in its history.

Years later Ferguson related the story of how he came to Radley
from St Edward's where he had been Warden for twelve years. He was,
he said, a friend of the Ven. T.H. Archer Houblon who had gone to
seek his advice about some of the hundred-odd applicants who had
answered the advertisement for Adam Fox's successor. Houblon said
that the Council were not satisfied with any of the six candidates who
had been interviewed and that they were thinking of placing another
advertisement. Soon afterwards Ferguson met Ernest Bryans, the
former Sub-Warden of Radley, now also on the Radley Council.
Bryans said to him, 'Why don't *you* go to Radley?'

I replied, 'Because I haven't been asked' [Ferguson recalled]. I suppose that
Bryans must have talked to Archer Houblon, for very soon the latter
appeared in my study and asked whether I would go to Radley if the
Council invited me. I agreed provided that the Council clearly understood

that I was not applying for the post & that I was not in competition with anyone else.

When he heard that Ferguson was being considered for the appointment, the Provost of Worcester College resigned from the Council on the grounds that, as Warden of the very High Church St Edward's, Ferguson might well lead Radley in the same extreme direction and that his academic qualifications were, in any case, not of a sufficiently high standard. At least one other member of the Council also objected to Ferguson on grounds of his dubious scholarship; but at the special meeting of the Council called to interview him, the members were sufficiently impressed by his manner and his answers to their questions to approve his appointment by twelve votes to nine.

Ferguson was then fifty-one years old, a dignified, impressive, handsome man with a wide, firm mouth and penetrating eyes beneath thick black eyebrows. He had been educated at Magdalen College School and Keble College; and in the brief, reserved entry he submitted for inclusion in *Who's Who* he gave his father's name and provenance as William Ferguson, Leeds, and his recreations as music and golf. He was unmarried and brought to Radley as hostesses two cousins of kindly temperament.

At St Edward's, Ferguson had shown himself to be a model of industry who nevertheless could bring himself to delegate tasks and authority to other men and give them confidence to carry them through without interference. He displayed these qualities at Radley from the beginning. He was a most indifferent teacher; but he concerned himself with all matters of the school's administration, making a point of receiving a report from the Senior Prefect before he went to bed every night, and working closely with the man appointed as school Comptroller.

This man, C.D. Crozier, was recommended to Ferguson by the Hon. Sir Stafford Cripps, a Wykehamist member of the Council from 1923 to 1929. A barrister who had been a lieutenant-colonel in the Royal Artillery, Crozier used to maintain that one of his principal reasons for coming to Radley was to fulfil his ambition of playing the violin in an orchestra. He seemed, however – and was, indeed, to prove – eminently suited to the post, though it was to be hoped that, as an extremely trenchant as well as endearing man, he would not have occasion to make use of a subject of which he had specialized knowledge, the properties and uses of high explosives. He was, however, to give Common Room 'an occasional whiff of grapeshot' and to be none too tactful in his dealings with Council.* The boys, however, appreciated his custom of marching about Hall to ask if they had any complaints in the manner of a duty officer in an army barracks.

In a school still increasing in numbers, which were to rise from 304 to 389 by the end of Ferguson's Wardenship, there was much work for the Bursar and the Finance Committee of the Council to do in the adaptation of existing accommodation and the provision of new buildings to meet the needs of this large increase. The urgent need for such improvements had been emphasized by Inspectors of the Oxford and Cambridge Examination Board who reported on Radley soon after Warden Ferguson's appointment.

*

The Inspectors were 'all impressed by the good tone and manners of the boys, and the evidence that the discipline of the school was of the best kind'. The boys were 'open and friendly', neat in appearance and punctual in their attendance in class. It had to be admitted, however, that they were often inattentive during lessons which they evidently regarded 'without great enthusiasm'. Their work was often 'badly prepared'; and there was 'an attitude of polite but obvious indifference'.

Various reasons were offered for the boys' 'polite boredom and refusal to think': 'It may be that a higher standard should be required for entrance to the school, or that bad work is not sufficiently penalized, or that many boys came from rich or unintellectual homes, or that preparation is interrupted by music and various distractions, and the time for work is generally diminished by excess of holidays.'

---

*It had originally been intended that Crozier as Comptroller should co-operate with the Bursar, Mullins; but as Crozier inevitably encroached upon the Bursar's sphere, Mullins found his position intolerable, particularly so as Crozier made no attempt to disguise his low opinion of 'the silly old fool'. Mullins appealed to the Council without success, then consulted his father-in-law who was a solicitor, and eventually decided that he would have to go. He believed that the Warden instructed the editor of *The Radleian* not to mention his departure. Certainly the 1928 *Radleian* carries no reference to Mullins's thirteen years at the school. He was afterwards Bursar at St Bees but had to leave that school four years later when it was so badly affected by the slump that it was in danger of closing down. He remained thereafter out of work, apart from temporary wartime employment, until his death in 1949. Ernest Bryans used to say that in all the many years he had been on the Radley Council since 1920, the only suggestion of his that had ever been adopted was the change of Colonel Crozier's official title from Comptroller to Bursar after Mullins's departure.

Whatever the reasons, the Inspectors concluded that 'a boy who will work will get excellent teaching at Radley, but there is evidently something which tends to make the boy's own part much less satisfactory than it should be.'

The masters were found to be, almost without exception, more than adequate. There were 22 of them for the 304 boys, 'not an unsatisfactory' proportion; and, while not allowing 'much margin either for the purchase of books or for travel', their salaries were 'not low in comparison with those paid at all but a few schools . . . The salaries range from £220 to £500 per annum (with residence or an allowance of £100); four House Masters receive £800; the Sub-Warden and Masters who are "Social Tutors" receive £100 per annum extra.'

Few of these masters came in for serious criticism. Mr Boyd's manner was 'rather monotonous' and his lessons were 'too much like cramming, while the boys showed little interest' in them; some 'became sleepy and others restive'. Mr Hellard 'seemed not to pursue one train of thought long enough and to jump violently from one subject to another of quite a different character'; the Inspector fancied that he made him nervous. Mr Rawlinson also seemed 'very nervous' and did not yet know how to 'deal with difficulties of teaching and discipline'; he appeared 'to lack the buoyancy and sense of humour required for school work'. Mr Paton was 'equally inexperienced' but was 'lively to the point of impatience', 'vigorous and interesting'. The other masters mentioned by name came in for almost universal commendation: Mr Nugee was a 'very good teacher'; Mr Eason, 'a very promising young teacher' who had 'all the natural gifts of a form-master'; Mr Watkins gave 'the best lesson in literature' that the Inspector had heard. Mr Wilson-Green was 'a seasoned teacher and a conscientious worker'. Mr Smale was 'a pleasure to hear'; he 'kept the class interested from beginning to end'.

The school's curriculum, however, was far from satisfactory; and a 'thorough reconstruction of the time-table [was] very necessary': the complete omission of science from some forms was 'most unfortunate'; the arrangement by which a boy who took German or Spanish dropped all history was 'a very extraordinary one'. In English lessons it was 'obvious that there was little or no organization of the course'; while 'a little boldness in aiming at the cultivation of mathematics for its own sake would improve the general mathematical tone of the school'.

As for the school's buildings and equipment, these came in for much harsh criticism. Many of the classrooms were badly ventilated, the atmosphere in them becoming 'very close and even unpleasant' and the unpleasantness being 'aggravated by an escape of gas in many of the rooms'. There were a great many interesting pictures, busts and engravings but these were scattered about the school in no kind of order, and were badly placed and hung. There was no swimming bath and the chemistry and physics laboratories were both 'quite inadequate'. Arrangements for the practising of music were unsatisfactory; and most studies were very small: 'in some of these two boys have to work, though there is not too much room for one. It would be impossible for both to write at the same time.'

In finding the money to carry out the Inspectors' recommendations for raising the standard of Radley's facilities – a problem faced by all schools with small or no endowments – much ingenuity would be required. Fees were raised in 1928 to £185 plus an entrance fee of five guineas, these entrance fees being placed, together with registration fees and various other sums, into an Endowment Fund. It was to be years, however, before this Fund was sufficient to pay for a building programme on the scale envisaged; and, in the meantime, there were rival claims on the generosity of Old Radleians and other possible supporters of the school when in 1930 a Land Fund Appeal was launched, largely at the instigation of Vyvyan Hope who pursued its aims and potential contributors with his customary energy.

The purchase of the open land around the College was considered of even more pressing urgency than the building of new premises within its bounds; for, if this land were to fall into the hands of speculators and building developers, Sewell's vision of a school in lovely countryside awakening a boy's awareness to beauty in general would come to nothing.

A boy walking to Abingdon one day was offered a lift by Mr Hope in his car:

> He kept stopping and getting out and taking photographs of various houses along the route – He would ask me, 'Which is the uglier of those two houses?' 'That one, Sir. Why?' 'Don't ask any questions. Get back in.' It turned out that he was doing this in order to persuade the Council to buy up much of the land that was being developed to the detriment of the Radley scene.

The Council were well aware of the danger. Parcel after parcel of land around the school was bought as soon as it came onto the market, until, by the end of 1937, the College's estate had been increased from 140 to 740 acres.* The surroundings of the school were thus protected from mutilation while, with the enormous increase in the value of building land, the Council had secured an investment which, in future years, would be put to excellent use.

Limited as their resources were, the Council approved the new buildings which the growing school demanded. In later years the Warden paid tribute to the Council's 'courage and foresight': 'At my first meeting I ventured to warn them that unless they were prepared to plunge heavily they would have on their hands a second-class school, unable through lack of equipment and modern improvements, to satisfy the educational demands of the day. They nobly responded.'

The General Strike of 1926 followed by the financial crisis of the early 1930s halted this development for a time; but by the end of Ferguson's Wardenship four new houses had been built for masters and one for the Bursar; a Music School and Armoury had been constructed. Shop, its finances now supervised by the industrious Hope, was enlarged and a range of buildings was constructed between Shop and Memorial Arch, including guest rooms for Old Radleians with whom Hope – as the highly efficient and conscientious Honorary Secretary of the Radleian Society – kept closely in touch, constantly adding details to the index cards he kept for all of them, and later, during the Second World War, arranging for parcels to be sent to those who had been taken prisoner.

A large new block, providing classrooms and accommodation for a Social, completed at a cost of £32,700, was opened by M.R. James, the Provost of Eton, better known to posterity as a writer of ghost stories; and this new house made it possible to reorganize the four Socials still housed in the old College buildings into three, each one more comfortably accommodated than in the past. Other houses were enlarged and improved; the creeper was pulled off walls to prevent rats clambering up behind the leaves; paths were asphalted, grass cut, hedges trimmed. Trees were planted, including the Edward VIII Clump behind the First XI Pavilion, a rare memorial of that King's brief reign; while the much-loved Dormitory Clump, severely lopped, was saved from total extinction by a protest from the Radley Rangers who learned of its impending demise during their annual match against the school.

---

*The school today owns about 875 acres.

Nearly all the new buildings were designed by two Old Radleians, H.I. Merriman and A.B. Knapp-Fisher, both of them boys in Stone's Social in Warden Field's time. These two architects also collaborated on plans for a house for the Warden into which Ferguson moved in 1935. Designed in what Sir Osbert Lancaster might have described as Wentworth Golf-Course Georgian, it cost £9,000: today a similar house would cost about £450,000. Two years after its completion a further £17,000 was spent on laboratories designed in a Modernist style by W.G. Newton, architect of a similar structure at Marlborough, a former editor of the *Architectural Review* and, according to *The Times*, 'one of the most scholarly architects of his time'. Such laboratories, if built today, would cost about £700,000. Altogether, it has been estimated that the cost of the building and improvements undertaken at Radley between 1925 and 1937 represents an outlay in present-day terms of close to £8 million, an astonishing sum for an unendowed school.*

*

While all this building was in mind or in progress, determined attempts were being made to create what was to be referred to as a 'New Radley', a concept much discussed by various younger members of Common Room and some of their senior colleagues who were dissatisfied with the school as it then was. The masters whom Ferguson inherited in 1925 included some who had been there for many years; but these had gradually disappeared. 'Kitty' Wharton, still occupying his cluttered rooms in the House, had died at the age of eighty-seven; and his strange collection of assorted treasures – together with the celebrated watch which he had delighted in showing to those who had never before seen its operations, as well as to many who had seen them countless times – had been sold at auction. Guy Newman had retired to a parish in Devon; Wilson-Green, who had been appointed to the staff in 1905, had gone to live in Abingdon where he became Mayor in 1937.

A new generation of masters had taken their place; and among them were some remarkable men. J.C. Nowell Smith, the son of a head-

---

*Although there is no corroboration in the Radley Archives, it is believed that the Vestey family made contributions to these building costs. The Hon. William Vestey, son of the 2nd Lord Vestey, a splendid athlete who was killed in action in Italy in 1944, was at Radley from 1925 to 1930.

master of Sherborne, led an extremely active life at Radley until he was killed in a car crash in France in 1937; T.L.B. Huskinson was an eccentric and entertaining art master who, in the words of the Warden's successor, 'blew into Radley like a breath of fresh air, looking as if he'd come straight from the race-course'; Robert Heuzé Hogg, formerly a practising barrister, taught modern languages. Although some of his colleagues considered Hogg a most unsuitable schoolmaster, one describing him as 'straw-stuffed' and another as 'an amazingly successful impostor', Hogg was much liked by the boys whom he taught with politeness and courtesy. Clement Morgan, scholar of Hertford College, the son of a Welsh clergyman, became a dedicated Social Tutor of forceful personality and Sub-Warden for fourteen years. A.A.M. Gardiner, W.G. Morgan, a former rugger international, R.L.C. Southam and Ranulph Waye were four other highly capable and understanding masters, all of whom became Social Tutors.

Ivor Gilliat, whom Ferguson, at Nugee's prompting, trusted not to repeat the offence which had led to his leaving his previous appointment at Bradfield – and to his never being given a Social at Radley – was an inspired teacher of history to less clever boys, a passionate cricketer and, in a later Wardenship, a dedicated Honorary Secretary of the Radleian Society. The Revd Hugh Brodie was a most unparsonical chaplain from 1930 until he joined the Royal Naval Volunteer Reserve in 1940. Above all there was Charles Wrinch, an exciting and inspiring teacher of English whose name is more often mentioned with affection and admiration than that of any other master by Old Radleians who were at the school in his time. As with Timothy Tosswill at Rugby (Treadmill in A.N. Wilson's *Incline our Hearts*), H.F.W. Holmes at Sherborne, D.C. Somervell at Tonbridge, Arthur Marshall at Oundle, Stacy Colman and Frank McEachran at Shrewsbury, J.B. Poynton at Winchester, Roxburgh at Lancing and Stowe, Charles Wrinch's influence was a lasting one on all those whom he taught.

It was such new masters as Wrinch and Brodie – who had discussed Radley's problems and their possible cures while walking on the Sussex Downs together in 1931 – and certain of Warden Fox's appointees, including Kenneth Boyd and Stephen Paton – who decided that Radley must be given a fresh impetus, transformed from what Charles Wrinch described as a 'glorious country club for both young and older men' into a more serious, purposeful school. They instituted a discussion group, whose members were to read papers to each other, and, encouraged by Clement Morgan, they created what became known as a 'Steering Committee', to co-ordinate their ideas and put them into practice.*

'In spite of notable advances since the First Great War,' Boyd wrote, 'it was felt that some flaw resided in the Radley way of life which was keeping the School from reaching the heights.'

---

*Clem Morgan and Wrinch had attended a schoolmasters' conference at Harrow in 1931 and it was then that they had been inspired by the spirit of reform. These conferences had been initiated by T.F. Coade, a master at Harrow when the great educationist, Cyril Norwood, was Headmaster. In 1932 Coade left Harrow to become Headmaster of Bryanston, which had been founded four years before. When he left Bryanston in 1959 the school had been recognized as a remarkable institution, where the relationship between masters and boys was more relaxed than in most other more conventional schools and where there were more opportunities for the creative uses of free time. When charged with allowing the boys 'to do what they like', Coade responded that 'they like what they do'.

22

'The New Radley'

1933

'The scholarships and the Ladies' Plate will come hand in hand.'

O N 13 JULY 1933, in John Nugee's drawing-room, A.K. Boyd
read an important paper to a number of like-minded
members of Common Room, setting out what he took to be
the problems the school faced and proposing certain remedies.

By then various reforms had been initiated at Radley; but most
of these were modest, even superficial. On the grounds that the
College could no longer afford such extravagances as the Victory
Gaudy of 1919 which had cost over £400, it was decided that future
Gaudies should be more informal occasions: the Gaudy lunch was
abolished; instead guests could either bring a picnic or buy a buffet
meal in a marquee; Cake Sunday, a College festival invented by
Sewell, on which simnel cakes were distributed, was also done away
with.

Cold baths were made compulsory all the year round; it was forbidden to take books into Hall; grey flannel trousers became regula-
tion wear; trilby hats replaced bowlers on Sundays and in Oxford.
'Checks' were introduced instead of 'lines' as a punishment, one
'check' involving 'labour detention', several 'checks' a beating. Of
more consequence, and largely at the instigation of S.H. Paton and
John Nugee, assistant tutors – known as Sub-Tutors – were initiated at
this time so that promising young masters should be given opportunities for closer involvement with boys outside the classroom. Most of

the Sub-Tutors first appointed became Social Tutors in due course and three became headmasters.

Boyd and Wrinch, Brodie and Morgan, Nugee and Paton and those masters who shared their views were convinced that these reforms did not go nearly far enough. Boyd prefaced his dissertation that evening in Nugee's drawing-room by declaring that he would speak with a frankness and directness about his own school which he would not use 'in any other gathering of this size in the world'.

> I believe [he continued] that, for better or worse, masters play a much more important part in the formation and handing on of school tradition than is commonly supposed, and that if there is anything in Radley which we would have otherwise, we must all bear a considerable portion of the blame for its origin and perpetuation . . . Much that I say will be highly controversial, and some of it will be deliberately provocative.

Boyd reminded his audience of William Sewell's purpose in founding Radley and painted a perhaps over-rosy picture of the boys the school then produced, quoting among other encomia the Earl of Kellie's letter to the founder praising the education provided by Sewell's Radley: 'You treated the boys as Christians and as gentlemen, and trusted to their honour; and the result was that nothing false or dishonourable would for a moment have been tolerated by the boys themselves . . . The system of education at Radley was perfect . . . '

As Boyd admitted, it is tempting to extract cynical amusement from Lord Kellie's description of the moral and social paragons produced by Sewell's Radley; and he had to confess that Kellie himself, having claimed a second title in the defunct Earldom of Mar, achieved no distinction in later life which he 'presumably passed in contemplating the perfection of his education, only breaking the reverie to make arrangements for sending his son and heir to Eton'.* Yet 'the fact remains that a remarkable headmaster' did achieve 'remarkable results in his pursuit of a remarkable, if rather limited, ideal'.

Boyd then went on to compare the more or less legendary output of the Sewell era with the Radleians of more recent years; and in doing so

---

*Lord Kellie's choice of school for his son is reminiscent of Stanley Baldwin's. It is well known that when Baldwin, an Old Harrovian, became Prime Minister in 1923 he is said to have wanted to appoint a Cabinet of which 'Harrow could be proud'. He did so to the extent of appointing no fewer than six Old Harrovians to it. What is perhaps not so well known is that he sent both of his sons to Eton.

he felt obliged to conclude that all pretensions to moral uplift had disappeared. The middle-aged product of the school was 'agreeable, tolerant, kindly, pleasant to have about the house, and doing a quiet job of work'. He did not aspire to charm, content with being nice. He was a slave to good form and 'like most public school boys' a Philistine and frequently a snob. Lacking aggressive ambition, he was 'permeated by the country-house spirit which was breathed over Radleians in their impressive youth'.

Since the 1914–18 war, Radleians had been quite content to grow up much like their fathers, but since they were born into a world very different from the world of their fathers this must give cause for alarm. Remaining 'friendly, polite and easy to deal with', they were 'strangely class-conscious', referred to the 'lower classes' in a manner which 'in modern times has become the prerogative of great ladies in farcical comedy'. 'Their worst fault is an unhealthy complacency. They have been told so often that a public school education provides a good manner and the power of leadership that . . . they have become convinced that four years spent passively at a public school will give them all they need for life.'

Boyd then drew his audience's attention to the unpalatable fact that extremely few Old Radleians had achieved a distinction in life which had made their name familiar to the man in the street. It was frequently stated, he said, that the three senior admirals on the active list were all Old Radleians, but it was surely 'almost a confession' of weakness that this fact should have been so widely advertised: one of the admirals had been at Radley for two years, the others for two terms each.

Boyd gave a list of fourteen names of men whom he considered to be the most distinguished deceased Radleians. Not one of them could be said to have achieved national fame and, apart from the South African statesman, J.X. Merriman, only three of them (Boyd Alexander, the African traveller and ornithologist, S.H. Reynolds, Warden Singleton's critic, and E.R.P. Woodgate, the General killed at Spion Kop) had found their way into the *Dictionary of National Biography*.

Of the twelve men whom Boyd listed as the most distinguished Radleians living in 1933, only three (Sir Robert Hodgson, Air Chief Marshal Sir Edgar Ludlow-Hewitt and Sir Reginald Stubbs, colonial governor) are in the *Dictionary of National Biography*. Boyd did not include in his list Gerald Brenan who had not at that time published his best-known works; but having regard to what Brenan thought and wrote about Radley, he was probably not tempted to do so anyway.

'There are very few schools,' Boyd was compelled to conclude, 'whose clientele has such advantages as Radley, in the way of wealth and opportunity, which, in proportion to its numbers, cannot produce a far more distinguished list.' In pursuance of his argument he took the trouble to examine 3,000 entries in *Who's Who*, taking three continuous batches of 1,000 each from three different parts of the 1926 volume. His table is given in Appendix 1.

> There is no reason to dwell on the school's academic record [Boyd's paper continues]. We are only too well aware of the facts in recent years. The school started with an academic bang... Since then, on the average, Oxford and Cambridge combined have received from Radley one man capable of taking a first every other year ... In the field of sport (with the exception of rowing) Radleians have been even more undistinguished than in learning. It is not that the record of Radley is the record of a bad school. But it is not the record of a first grade school, which is what Radley ought to be. It is equalled or surpassed by many schools which the Radleian would hold in complacent contempt.

Boyd believed that the principal reason why Radley was not a first-class school was its ingrained tradition not of idleness, though that used to exist, but of denigration of intellectual development 'as a thing not worth striving for'. There was 'a complete absence of intellectual pride, intellectual ambition, and any scheme of intellectual values whatever'.

For this sad state of affairs he blamed, first of all, the Council, most of whose members were not only ill qualified to serve on any educational authority but were also far too ready to perpetuate all that was 'worst in the "Christian and gentleman" tradition of static Sewellism'. Their self-satisfaction was strongly reinforced by many of the Old Radleian parents who helped 'to perpetuate the same, complacent, hopelessly unintellectual tradition'.

Then there were the Radley masters. Assuring those in his audience that these strictures did not apply to them, Boyd castigated others, 'undistinguished nonentities', who had no faith in Radley and were only too ready to voice discontent, who had absorbed the lotus which 'grows so beautifully on Radley soil'.

Boyd also found fault with the religious teaching at Radley which he believed to have been demoralizing in its message that faith was more important than works. He could 'say with certainty that whatever religion might have done to the Radley boy in the past, it had not made him religious'.

Boyd wondered whether there was not yet another cause of Radley's malaise, a 'purely physical cause'. How was it possible to account for the 'disparity with Sherborne and Downside at football, with Shrewsbury at rowing, the rarity of outstanding athletes, the repeated failure of young star athletes to fulfil their promise'? It was sometimes suggested that the air of the Thames Valley was not conducive to athletic prowess; but the success of Eton at rowing and St Edward's at rugger soon disposed of that theory. Boyd instead advanced the views that constipation, perhaps induced by the hard water, might be held responsible, or insufficient sleep, or – a common belief among schoolmasters of his generation – 'self-abuse on a large scale'. He believed that this widespread masturbation was 'induced by the cubicle system'.

Sewell had instituted the cubicle system in the belief that it would encourage the boys to say their prayers; but, since there was 'no evidence that it encouraged any such practice', and 'not even the best informed housemaster can be sure that he knows the truth about self-abuse', Boyd proposed that, as the system served no useful purpose and was responsible for harmful practices, it would be worth scrapping it 'on the off chance that it might affect the situation'.*

In proposing cures for Radley's troubles, Boyd emphasized that 'sporadic offensives in the classroom' were useless. First, the low standard of entry to Radley, rendered necessary by the official policy of securing material prosperity without regard to educational responsibilities, should be reconsidered. Then, the system of grading a boy's work by marks should be abolished throughout the school since 'the competitive spirit in work had hardly anything to be said for it. A boy's true rival is not the rest of his form, but his second-best self.'

As an alternative, Boyd proposed a system already applied at Marlborough, the marking of written work by Greek alphabetical symbols, α, β, γ with appropriate pluses and minuses. At the same time the weekly order should be replaced by a report on the boy's industry and willingness to learn.

---

*It seemed to the wife of one long-serving member of Common Room that in the 1940s and 1950s 'all of the masters still seemed obsessed by the threat of "self-abuse"'.

Boyd concluded his discourse by turning to the 'overwhelming prestige attached by authority to games'. An athlete himself as well as a scholar, he condemned unreservedly the rewards of 'prestige, authority, privileges, sartorial distinctions and remission of work' conferred upon boys with little other than athletic prowess to recommend them. To maintain that boys would not do their best for the school without material rewards was to 'give away the whole case for the educational value of games'.

'The cry of myopic Old Radleians (which finds its echo in the Radleians of 1933) "We can do without the scholarships, if we can win the Ladies' Plate" is the baying of dogs at the moon,' Boyd concluded. 'When Radleians fulfil themselves intellectually, the scholarships and the Ladies' Plate will come hand in hand.'

Boyd's audience, who had been expecting a paper on a quite different subject, perhaps on the production of plays, on which he was one day to write an excellent book, were profoundly impressed by his words and sat up until after midnight discussing them. As one of them put it, they 'planned immediate action'; and each of them was delegated to approach a colleague, Brodie to tackle Hope, and Nugee to approach the Warden whom he found sympathetic and co-operative. Soon afterwards the Warden proclaimed the aims of the Steering Committee and the concept of the 'New Radley' to the boys with notable success. 'Yer fellers,' he told them, addressing them in his usual way. 'No more bloods.'

After further discussions, certain reforms were eventually taken in hand. In future no boy who was not in the Sixth or Remove (the former Lower Sixth) could be made a Prefect; the Sixth were to have their own permanent classroom; many of the privileges hitherto accorded to 'Caps' were withdrawn; marks, except for examinations, were to be replaced by Greek symbols. Masters were to complete weekly reports on their pupils' progress and general attitudes towards work. Extra half-holidays for Saints' Days were to be no more, though there were to be three half-holidays during the summer term instead; gramophones and wirelesses were banned. Boys were to rest on their beds every day for half an hour after lunch; they were to be weighed and measured twice a term.

Some of these reforms aroused the scorn of certain masters who considered the zeal displayed by the 'Steering Committee' to be pretentious if not absurd and who derided the efforts of its members to give birth to the 'New Radley'. When one day Vyvyan

Hope noticed that the masters involved in the movement for reform were not following the queue into Chapel, he had been heard to remark to another don, T.E.E. Cocks, 'I suppose they are all at a meeting of that damned snobbery club.' Thereafter its members always referred to their association as the Damned Snobbery Club, the D.S.C., and such minutes as they kept were headed with these initials.

23

'The Finest Headmaster'

1933–1937

'He retained to the last the open mind of youth.'

WHEN BOYD'S IMPORTANT and influential paper was read, Ferguson had been Warden for some eight years and was to be in office for four more years to come. He was well aware of most of the faults to which Boyd had drawn attention, in particular to what he called 'the Radley disease known as "Bloodism"'.

Ferguson never succeeded in eradicating the disease entirely; its symptoms were to linger on for year after year, as, indeed, they did in most other schools. The disease was not nearly as virulent, of course, as it had been at the beginning of the century when, at Charterhouse, for example, 'the bloods of the Eleven ruled the school and dictated the school customs', despising the weeds of the Sixth Form:

> Oh, we are the bloods of the place.
>   We shine with superior grace
> At the goal or the wicket, at footer or cricket,
>   And nothing our pride can efface.
> The worms of the Sixth we despise . . .
>   We count them as dirt in our eyes.

Yet in the 1920s and 1930s, as the historian of Bradfield observed, games at that school, 'as at most public schools, were still a sacred cow and to "skunk them" as it was called, was an offence of such seriousness that it was punished by Librarying', that is to say by a beating in the library by the Senior Prefect in the presence of all the other Prefects. One boy 'skunked' games as a deliberate protest against their being compulsory. When summoned to the Library, he appeared carrying in each hand a large, antiquated and loaded pistol. He then ran away, to be discovered later in Slough, and did not return again to Bradfield. He was killed in action in 1942. No attempt was made to follow up his protest.

At Uppingham, too, 'philoathleticism' had been 'rampant' when the Revd E.G. Selwyn's father, Dr E.C. Selwyn, Edward Thring's successor, was Headmaster there, 'more so,' Uppingham's historian has observed, 'than at any other time in its history, though the 1920s and 1930s must run it close'. This was true also of Rugby where the morally earnest and narrowly puritanical John Percival, Headmaster from 1887 to 1895, had attempted to extend the iron discipline of his rule to the suppression of 'bloodism', by abolishing undesirable privileges and certain sartorial distinctions enjoyed by boys who excelled at games but at little else. By the 1930s, however, 'bloodism' at Rugby was still rife. When the sixth-form council known as the Levee pressed repeatedly for the abolition of house caps, although supported by Hugh Lyon, Headmaster from 1931 to 1948, it was repeatedly vetoed by the housemasters. It has been suggested that Shrewsbury was almost unique in being immune from the disease of 'bloodism'. In other schools, Shrewsbury's historian, Basil Oldham, has remarked, 'athletic distinction has often tended to develop idolization. This does not seem ever to have been a characteristic of Shrewsbury . . . The School's traditional dislike of what Shrewsbury calls "lift" – that is the assumption of airs and self-importance – does seem to have preserved it from excessive worship of athletic success.'

Charles Wrinch, however, who was a boy at Shrewsbury soon after the First World War, does not believe that Shrewsbury was as free from bloodism as Oldham suggests. Certainly in Wrinch's house the official head prefect had to give place to a leading games player 'not known for his intelligence'. Simon Langdale, a former Headmaster of Shrewsbury, comments, 'Charles Wrinch is right . . . It's different now in all schools, principally, I think, because boarding school is so much less a "closed world" than it was. Being good at games is still prestigious but it's not the be-all and end-all of life.'

In Warden Ferguson's time at Radley the worship of athletic success was certainly diminished. By the 1930s 'the Bloods' no longer left classrooms after the Prefects and before anyone else as they had done in the 1920s. But the Warden had to acknowledge his failure in stamping out the excessive distinctions accorded them in many other respects.

Ferguson was, however, triumphantly successful in carrying out another reform close to his heart, in vastly improving the Chapel services. In discussions about these services with the Council before he arrived at Radley he was warned that 'he would only break [his] head and heart in attempting to raise the standard of congregational singing.'

> It says much for the willing co-operation of the school, even in my earliest days before I knew the boys [he wrote], that at my first congregational practice I had them all going full blast in five minutes. It is amusing to look back on that occasion . . . A member of the Council came to Sunday evensong very early in the term. As we sat down for the first lesson he whispered to me, 'It's a miracle.' But, of course, it wasn't really . . . I found the Radley boys wonderfully responsive to any suggestions so long as they understood the reasons for them.

An Old Radleian who was at the school in Ferguson's time well remembers the talks of the Warden in Hall: 'He would address us as "yer fellers" and either congratulate us on recent achievements or berate us. "I was thrilled with your singing last Sunday, yer fellers," he would say, and we glowed for we knew that this was a thing near his heart. On other occasions we felt sometimes that we had let him down, and we went away inspired to do better . . . He was a great personality.' 'He was certainly a pioneer in getting public schools really to sing in chapel,' according to Robin Miller, later Director of Music at other schools. 'I myself later found myself striding up and down the aisle, both at Ardingly and later at Oundle, and much of my technique and routines was derived from his splendid example.'

His decision to conduct congregational practice personally and to undertake other duties which had previously been the preserve of the Precentor had an unfortunate consequence, however: it was generally supposed to be one of the principal reasons why Leslie Huggins decided to leave Radley in 1928 and move, as Director of Music, to Stowe where he was to be seen on occasions playing the organ in his hunting-pink and where he deeply gratified John

Roxburgh by leaving a large sum of money for the building of a music school.*

Having lost Huggins, however, Ferguson chose well in appointing his successor, Sydney Watson, an organ scholar of Keble College, who joined the staff as Precentor in 1929 and was immediately recognized by his pupils as 'a great and patient teacher, particularly of those not so brilliant as himself'. 'I think my allocation to him for piano lessons was a turning point in my life,' wrote one of those pupils who became a musician himself. 'I instantly responded to him and his values became mine.' In the words of an obituary sent from Radley to *The Times*, there was in Ferguson's time a 'real resurgence of the school's musical tradition'. 'Not only does Radley owe much to the calm and purposeful administration which gave the school a period of prosperity hitherto unequalled,' this obituary continued, 'but colleagues and pupils alike value highly the memory of that dignified figure and kindly presence which lives for them under the affectionate name of Fergie.'

The obituarist did not strain the truth when he declared that Ferguson's

> talent for headmastership was as remarkable as it was unobtrusive. The simple formula for appointments to his staff: 'I must have men that will fit in', was applied with a deep personal insight; and he was never afraid to delegate responsibility. In his twelve years at Radley he was the sponsor of a vast programme of building and development. But he was no mere devotee of bricks and mortar: his period as Warden was marked by a real educational renaissance. Though he was himself neither a great scholar nor an educational pioneer, and became Warden at the age of 52, he retained to the last the open mind of youth, and could be easily won over for experiment.†

---

*Leslie Huggins, described as 'the great reformer of Radley music', was awarded the Military Cross in the Second World War and is believed to have been the only Doctor of Music to have also been a Master of Fox Hounds. His nephew Jeremy Huggins, the actor Jeremy Brett (who was himself at Eton), sent his son David, son of Anna Massey, to Radley.

†An example of Ferguson's openness of mind is provided by G.B. Stanger in his account of the formation of the Radley College Dance Band in the mid-1930s. 'Before getting his approval,' wrote Stanger, at that time Senior Prefect, 'we had to give the Warden a sample of our wares. This we did in the Music School; we gave him a rendering of Duke Ellington's "Mood Indigo". I am quite sure he did not like it; but he was very polite and told us to carry on with his blessing.' A photograph of this band taken in 1934 shows, amongst others, the future Professor of Russian at Oxford (John Fennell) next to a future member of the London Philharmonic Orchestra (Edward Harley), both on trumpet (see Plate 59).

Another tribute to Ferguson, all the more convincing since it was offered in private by a member of the Radley Council who had voted against his appointment, was that of Norman Whatley, the Old Radleian Headmaster of Clifton:

> I still don't see how, when I voted against Ferguson, I could have done otherwise. He had personality and manner; he was very lucky in his staff and handled it excellently (much better than he had done at St Edward's where most of the staff were not enthusiastic about him); and he was almost scandalously successful with preparatory school headmasters (he never attended the H[ead] M[asters'] C[onference] if it clashed, as it nearly always did, with the I.A.P.S. Conference). He had 'immorality' on the brain at St Edward's, and, to judge from a talk with us, in his early years at Radley.
>
> His qualifications seemed all right for running successfully an intellectually alive school which needed some good moral and personal influence. But he did not seem to have the qualities required for giving Radley what Radley needed. And yet he did it.

John Nugee's verdict, overheard at a meeting of the Headmasters' Conference, was shorter and characteristically forthright: 'He couldn't teach and he couldn't preach but he was the finest headmaster I've known.'

*

In 1937 Ferguson left Radley – where, like Thomas Field before him, he had loved both the work and the place – to become Canon and Precentor of Salisbury Cathedral, conscious that he had reached an age when he had lost the drive of his earlier years at Radley and that the Steering Committee were, in truth, now directing the affairs of the school rather than himself. He had been married in Chapel four years before, at the age of fifty-nine, to a bride far younger than himself, the only reigning Warden to have been married since Heathcote who had also left Radley for Salisbury. He died at Littlehampton on 18 October 1950 when his successor at Radley, J.C.V. Wilkes, was nearing the end of his own career there.

24

J.C.V. Wilkes

1937–1939

'Not at all like a normal headmaster.'

JOHN COMYN VAUGHAN Wilkes was the son of the headmaster of St Cyprian's preparatory school at Eastbourne of which establishment George Orwell and Cyril Connolly gave such gruesome accounts. Like Orwell and Connolly, Wilkes was sent to Eton where he won a classical scholarship to Trinity College, Oxford. Here he took first-class honours in both Classical Moderations and Literae Humaniores and won a half-Blue for Golf. In 1925 he was appointed a master at Eton and five years later became Master in College. His wife, whom he married soon after coming to Radley, was Joan, youngest daughter of Dr Cyril Alington, Dean of Durham, a former Headmaster of Eton, whose second daughter was married to Alec Douglas-Home, later Prime Minister, a contemporary of Wilkes at Eton. John Wilkes's career as Master in College was briefly summarized in a recent essay on Wilkes's successor at Eton, Walter Hamilton, later Headmaster of Rugby:

> John Wilkes had been considered by the 'aesthetes' as an improvement, if a limited one, on H.K. [Hugh Marsden], by the intellectuals duller but less narrow-minded, and by the athletes a poor bargain. No one disliked him, for he was a most kindly man; but perhaps because he was shy he kept himself at a distance from his scholars, and he was thought nothing like so approachable as he later came to be at Radley.

After an informal lunch with two senior members of the Radley Council, the Very Revd E.L. Henderson, Dean of Salisbury, the Council's chairman, and P.K. Hodgson, a former Private Secretary to the Duke of York, both Old Radleians, Wilkes was interviewed by other members of the Council. One of these was Sir Stephen Gaselee, an ardent High Churchman, classical scholar and librarian at the Foreign Office who was celebrated for his archaic tailcoat, spats, red socks and Old Etonian bow-tie. He submitted the nervous candidate to what Wilkes called 'some pretty stiff questions on my churchmanship'.

Wilkes paid his first visit to Radley in the middle of a December fog. He was conducted round the buildings by two masters who, he admitted, both frightened him even more than Sir Stephen Gaselee had done. These were A.T. Hedgecock, Warden Selwyn's first appointment, a Social Tutor since 1919, head of the science department, a kindly man at heart but one with the manner of the Irish Guards lieutenant he had been in the First World War, and the Revd Vyvyan Hope, the forthright, sardonic and energetic bachelor whose numerous, dedicated services to Radley ranged far beyond his duties as Social Tutor and the teaching of mathematics.

On his next visit Wilkes met Clement Morgan, recently appointed a Social Tutor, with whom he had a pleasant lunch and less unsettling conversation than he had had with Hedgecock and Hope on his previous visit. He also met the forty-six-year-old Radleian, John Nugee, Sub-Warden since 1924, to whom he felt drawn at once, though he was rather startled by the candid comments which Nugee made in his bluff and artless way on some of his colleagues who seemed to be well within earshot. Wilkes was introduced also to Nugee's wife, Lucy, 'a wonderful person', who had been struck down with polio shortly before they were married and had spent the rest of her life in a wheelchair. Nugee never went anywhere without her if he could help it, pushing her briskly along, paying scant attention either to the traffic in the roads they crossed or to dawdling pedestrians on the pavement.

Conversations with these men, and a subsequent visit to Radley during which he saw Charles Wrinch's production of *King Lear*, persuaded Wilkes that Radley was not at all the school he had expected it to be. Coming from Eton, where he had been as a boy and master for seventeen years, he had supposed that all other schools, necessarily inferior, were very much like one another. 'I vaguely thought of their inmates as rather hearty, rather callow and immature, narrow and provincial in outlook,' he wrote later; 'hidebound in tradition – and rather barbarous tradition at that – suspicious of change; living under a sort of iron discipline of law and custom which stifled initiative, left little freedom of thought and action.' Yet, even before his arrival as Warden, he had come to realize that he 'would have to revise all [his] preconceived ideas of Radley'.

When he did arrive his first impression was 'the amazing courtesy of the boys and the ease with which they moved in adult company'; he was also impressed by the friendliness of most of the masters. He began to understand what his predecessor had meant when referring to 'the lovely lotus land of Radley'. Indeed, he was to come to believe, 'after cautious comparing of notes with other Head Masters who had been plagued with difficult colleagues, or jealous housemasters; or tiresome wives, or Old Boys who have never grown up (and they are generally the ones who haunt a school and try to control its policy) . . . that being Warden of Radley is the easiest and the pleasantest assignment of its kind in England. Almost *too* easy, perhaps.' He felt as Warden Field had felt a generation before when, throwing up his arms as though in triumph, he had declared, 'No one could fail to be happy here.'

Although Wilkes brought to Radley an Etonian cast of mind, as Selwyn had done before him, unlike Selwyn he immediately showed himself anxious to obtain the co-operation and understanding of Common Room in what he perceived to be Radley's needs for the future.*

The Warden's relations with Common Room were not at first as harmonious as he had hoped they would be after his early meetings with its members. In his predecessor's last months the Steering Committee's ideas had become increasingly influential in the school's affairs; but their emphasis on the directing and monitoring of the boys in the manner of John Percival at Clifton and Rugby ran counter to

---

*Among Wilkes's Etonian importations was 'Chambers', a daily mid-morning gathering of masters. 'Such a gathering was badly needed,' Charles Wrinch comments. 'The Common Room was almost solely a place in which to eat and read occasional notices before he came. "Chambers" was admirably centripetal.' Wilkes would also have liked to import from Eton a scholars' Social like Eton's College; but this was strongly opposed by his brother-in-law, Alec Douglas-Home, a member of the Radley Council from 1943 to 1949. Wilkes did, however, after discussion with Common Room, adopt the silk cassock and gown worn by lay Provosts of Eton. William Sewell's aim had been to create 'a Christian Eton': John Wilkes was in some ways a Sewell *redivivus*.

Wilkes's own Etonian belief in the need for allowing them more freedom to use their own time in their own way. It was supposed that a member of the Council, distrustful of the influence of the 'Damned Snobbery Club', had told him, 'You must break the Soviet'; and certainly he would not allow the 'Club's' beliefs to disturb his own. He instituted a Board of Studies under his own chairmanship, which held meetings in his own house; and he made it clear that the Warden was, indeed, to be head master.

Boyd, Wrinch and Morgan and most of the other assistant masters got on with him perfectly well, though with some of them relations with the new Warden became increasingly uneasy. He was 'never an easy man to talk to', one of them said. 'One seldom felt that the topic one was talking about was really engaging his full attention.' His relationship was particularly difficult with Stephen Paton, the first member of Common Room to have a modern language degree, who was deeply unhappy about the Warden's attitude towards the teaching of German and Spanish which, so Paton thought, he saw as inimical to the proper study of Greek.

For some years Wilkes and Paton remained at odds with each other; but when the question of modern languages was resolved in Paton's favour, and Wilkes agreed to the inclusion of Russian and Italian in the curriculum, suspicion and hostility were eventually transformed into trust and friendship.

Wilkes's own ideas for Radley's future were described by one of his own senior masters:

> In brief terms, this is what the Warden set out to do for the Radley boy: to free him from unnecessary restrictions, and give him self-reliance and initiative; to make him willing and able to teach himself, and to work without supervision; to submit him constantly to the influence of the first rate in literature, art, and music; to encourage him to mix easily in all grades of society; to inspire him with a desire to serve those who needed service; to release him from the last inhibitions of monastic life; to make him eager to express what is best in himself in the medium which offered him most scope . . . It was no revolutionary policy; previous Wardens would have endorsed much of it, though only Sewell would have accepted it all. What was novel was the intense and practical manner in which it was applied – universally, immediately and without regard to obstacles.

Wilkes himself said that he wanted to 'raise the school's academic standards (what headmaster doesn't?), to make [his] colleagues and their charges more dissatisfied with themselves and with things as they were'. He was well aware how much his predecessor had done for the school: 'he had been a great builder, a great reformer, a man of vision and energy'; the school's debt to him was 'enormous'. Yet 'no headmaster sets a pattern for his successor to follow, or leaves behind a "finished product" (heaven forbid)'.

> Ferguson had done much [Wilkes continued] and was the first to admit that there was much more to be done ... I wanted to see more freedom for both masters and boys to initiate, to experiment, to take more risks, to take more responsibility – to be, shall I say, a little more unconventional.

In attempting to fulfil his aims, there were many obstacles to overcome and one of these in the early part of Wilkes's career at Radley was the instability of Common Room. The industrious Nowell Smith had recently been killed in a car crash in France; the most experienced of the Social Tutors, F.P. Stevenson, had a nervous breakdown in the Warden's first term and was subsequently also killed in a car crash; next year, the Sub-Warden was appointed Headmaster of Eastbourne College. That year also Colonel Crozier, who, like Nugee, had done so much for the school, retired as Bursar to be replaced by Charles Jenner who, on commenting to the bursar of an Oxford college, 'I suppose all one needs for this job is common sense and tact?' received the reply, 'Yes, but not too much tact.'* A.G. Macpherson, who had been a Social Tutor for over twenty years, died unexpectedly in 1938; and G.T. Hellard, who had been one of Adam Fox's first appointments and was now over sixty and deafer than ever, had to leave the staff.

The new Warden accepted most of these losses with apparent equanimity. There were those, indeed, who found in his manner a certain complacency underlying his bustling liveliness. He was undeniably and unthinkingly self-centred. Years later the charming and much loved mother of his children recalled a train journey from Leeds: on his retirement from Radley, by then ordained, he had been offered

---

*Charles Jenner, who, incidentally, had been one of Wilkes's father's pupils at St Cyprian's and was an intimate friend of John Wilkes himself, was certainly not noted for his tact at Radley. During the fuel crisis of 1947 when, in that bitterly cold winter, masters taught in overcoats in classrooms which were kept, in the national interest, only a little above freezing, Boyd was appalled to discover the Bursar's office so overheated by a blazing gas fire that the Bursar himself was working in shirt-sleeves.

the living of Hunslet. They had been to look at the parish and its vicar-age. Distressed by the insalubrity of this depressing suburb of the industrial city, Joan Wilkes had been appalled to hear her husband say, without a word of consultation, that he supposed they could be in by Easter. Later he declined two suffragan bishoprics without informing her that he had been offered either of them.

Yet he was a thoughtless rather than an inconsiderate and selfish man, often appearing unaware of the impression he was creating upon others, as is frequently the case with those who have had a limited experience of life and people outside a cloistered world. He was uneasy with the more reserved as well as with the most ebullient members of Common Room and with some of the dons' wives, one of whom described him as 'arrogant' and regretted that he never looked her in the eye but always over her shoulder. He was also awkward and even shy with the younger boys in the school. One of these, now in his seventies, remembers, more clearly than any other encounter with him, a talk he gave to a gathering of new boys. The Warden, as embar-rassed as the boys in front of him, persistently twisted a handkerchief between his fingers as he touched hesitatingly on the subject of masturbation, a supposedly widespread practice that seemed to disturb him unduly: his last Senior Prefect recalls walking with him one day in the rose garden of the Warden's House when he was sud-denly asked, 'Ahh . . . John . . . Do you masturbate?'

Frequently Wilkes aroused pity and compassion as well as affection in the boys: 'There was a talk by [the Warden] today on Standards and Values, very good stuff, but badly delivered. We all, I think, go hot and cold whenever he begins groping unsuccessfully for his words . . . I feel sorry for him sometimes.'

On surer ground, however, the Warden was confident and capable of exercising a pleasant charm, warmed by a ready laugh – described by one don's wife as a 'nervous giggle' – and heightened by an excep-tionally retentive memory which enabled him to comment on the interests or achievements of boys who were as surprised as they were pleased to learn that the Warden even knew their names. One of his Prefects, John Livingstone, who later became his curate at Hunslet, said that he was 'not at all like a normal headmaster'.

I remember a fast moving figure with darting eyes and what seemed to be a very young face, popping oddly up like a doll out of a vast silk cassock and gown; a curious uniform for a layman, as Warden Wilkes then was.

Unlike so many of the dons who had a nickname indicative of something funny in their character or surname, all that the Warden acquired was a contraction of his title ['the Dun']: he seemed, like the Royal Family at that time, to be beyond nicknames; and also like the Royal Family to have only a title, no surname of his own.* While in cassock he undoubtedly impressed a small boy as a religious figure – there seemed nothing odd in his preaching sermons – he did not for all that seem to have the priestly (or more correctly, apostolic) authority which the Oxford Movement idealized.

As for his teaching, he was enthusiastic, but it was 'not a perfectly communicated enthusiasm, largely because he never got to the end of any sentence; a fresh and even more exciting idea having come to him before his vocal machinery could process the preceding messages'. In an effort to achieve an easier relationship with the younger boys he tried teaching a junior form; but he soon abandoned this practice, explaining that he 'couldn't stop them talking'.

Nor could he stop them teasing him, though he was often unaware that they were doing so. Knowing only too well his nervous habit of twisting his handkerchief around in his fingers as though it were a piece of string, they would place a length of string on his desk in class and wait eagerly for him to pick it up and start twisting it about, as sooner or later he was sure to do. And once, when delivering a serious admonition after lunch in Hall, he actually tore his handkerchief. A boy who was there remembers 'the loud ripple of applause at this event'.

Stories of the Warden's absent-mindedness were numerous. Frequently he forgot to take any money with him when going to a Council meeting in London, had to borrow some and usually forgot to pay it back. When the Sub-Warden, Nugee's successor Clem Morgan, had a sabbatical leave and Wilkes took over his Social, vacating the Warden's house for three young bachelor masters, he returned one day to the house to fetch some things he needed. A few days later one of these bachelors was surprised to see his best suit appear in Common Room. 'Oh, really, Scottie, I am sorry,' the Warden said when challenged about the appropriation. 'I saw it in my wardrobe and thought, "what a very nice suit. It's funny I don't remember buying

---

*Most members of Common Room referred to him in private as 'W.W.' for Warden Wilkes. In Morgan's Social some boys called him 'Bacon' – at Eton, like Warden Selwyn, he had been known as 'Piggy' – but this was an epithet that never caught on generally.

it."' Then there was the celebrated occasion when, during one of the services held in Chapel for Radley children, he 'sang forth with familiar vigour' the hymn 'All things bright and beautiful', oblivious of the fact that the organ was playing 'Onward Christian Soldiers'.

One of his Senior Prefects, and later England cricket captain, E.R. Dexter, was once overheard remarking to some visitors he was showing round the Wilson Library, that the Warden was 'a comic figure'.

*

To his work at Radley Wilkes brought a seemingly inexhaustible energy as well as a real talent for methodical organization. Problems were brushed aside with a visionary-like impatience, which some of the more conservative and practical members of Common Room found exasperating.

Within a few weeks of his arrival he had made it known that while he considered that the classics, particularly Greek, were not being as well taught as they should be, certain modern subjects should be given a more honoured place in the curriculum which should at the same time be widened to include new studies such as agriculture and carpentry. 'I will not have it said,' he was once heard to remark provocatively, 'that classics is more important than woodwork.' Boys should be encouraged to work on their own, in the manner of undergraduates rather than pupils at a preparatory school, and to carry out 'projects' as a means to this end.

In this matter his views resembled those of his contemporary, J.F. Wolfenden, Headmaster of Uppingham, who had told his house masters in 1935 that boys must be given enough time to develop their own individual interests and had asked them, 'Do we encourage boys to think too highly of athletic success to the exclusion of some other things?' Such demands for personal freedom echoed those of William Temple, Headmaster of Repton between 1910 and 1914, who had declared, 'There is no way of teaching boys to work for themselves except by giving them the chance to be idle; there is no way of teaching boys to use time except by giving them the chance to waste it.' But such convictions ran counter to the earlier belief, so firmly held by John Percival at Rugby who had insisted that boys were to be watched every minute of the day and who had ensured that at his school there was 'no place for the boy of unusual tastes'.

While insisting that boys should be encouraged to work on their own, the Warden also proposed that the standard of Common Entrance, already rather higher than it had been in the recent past, should be raised still further. Free places were to be offered to boys from other schools in the county, in the manner of Sewell's 'decimal' system, after consultation with the County Education Committee. Eventually thirteen boys were accepted at Radley but, although the school was able to report the experiment as wholly satisfactory, the county was not one of those that was to choose to spend money on sending boys to independent boarding schools.

The Radley Common Room had scarcely had time to accustom itself to the ideas of the new Warden when, in his second term, government inspectors were invited to the school to assess its performance. Three of the masters were so appalled by this intrusion that they took to their beds at the Inspectors' approach and did not return to duty until they had left. The imminent arrival of the Inspectors made 'the great Smale' in particular, in the Warden's words, 'flutter and gibber with alarm'. But at least, when they did arrive, they were not accorded the treatment which colleagues of theirs met at Eton where they found that every single history class was lugubriously studying the Black Death and where the Inspector of the school's classical teaching – espied at the back of his form by the burly master, C.M. Wells, for six years in the England Rugby Football XV – was greeted with the furious words, 'Who the deuce are you? *Get out!*' An Inspector at Radley, however, on complaining that some of the boys in an art class were so badly placed that they had to crane their necks like giraffes to see the blackboard, was surprised to receive the reply, 'Well, *giraffes-manship* is what I am trying to teach them.'

The Inspectors were generally polite in their assessment, if not enthusiastic:

> The general standard of work in the Main School seems reasonably satis-factory without being in any way distinguished. In the Sixth Form also the same assessment holds good; there are capable boys but the general level of work does not seem to rise above that indicated by the University record of the last three years, in which six Classical scholarships and one History Demyship have been gained. It would be a healthy sign if other subjects began to be represented in the scholarship lists.

While this Inspectors' report would not have persuaded many pre-paratory school headmasters – had they learned of its contents – to urge parents to send their clever sons to Radley, they were no doubt impressed to learn that the leader of the inspection, R.H. Barrow, decided that he could not do better than send his own son there. As the Warden observed, 'one cannot think of a higher compliment to a school than that.'*

As the Inspectors had noticed, exceptional encouragement was given at Radley to extra-curricular activities. There were, or were soon to be, flourishing societies for those interested in, for instance, painting, poetry, antiquities, films, campanology, philately, chess, model railways and model aeroplanes. The Warden himself revived Sewell's Shakespeare Society and attended its weekly meetings; his wife presided over meetings of a Pantechnicon Society. The Warden also attended meetings of the Literary Society and read a paper in his first term.†

To address Radley's societies in Warden Wilkes's time, a wide variety of speakers came to the school, C.S. Lewis and Anna Freud in one week, followed by the Regius Professor of Divinity at Oxford, the Master of Balliol and Dorothy L. Sayers.

The Dramatic Society staged some highly professional performances, memorably *Pride and Prejudice* in which the Senior Prefect, Peter Way, took the part of Mr Collins so well that a younger member of his Social recalled the performance half a century later as one of the most vivid memories of his schooldays. Every year there was a Drama Festival; and every year also a Junior Dramatic Society staged productions of a quality to rival those of their seniors. Sophocles was performed in Greek and Molière in French. On All Saints' Days the masters put on a variety show known as the Dons' Plays, sketches of often hilarious incompetence in which generations of Radleians have delighted and which the Radleians of Wilkes's day chiefly remember for the songs traditionally called for and sung with

---

*Barrow also agreed to serve on the Radley Council, as, indeed, did two other men who took part in a later government inspection in 1955, D.B. Briggs and M.W. Pritchard.

†This Society, which celebrated its centenary in 1988, has been one of Radley's liveliest since the presidency was assumed by Charles Wrinch in 1933. Under the succeeding presidencies of other Radley masters, among them Kenneth Boyd, Peter Way and Barry Webb (biographer of Edmund Blunden), the reading of plays has been superseded by the reading of members' papers, by original contributions from such promising young Radley poets and critics as Andrew Motion and Stephen Romer, and by talks by visiting speakers.

a combination of mock reluctance and surprised delight by that most popular and revered of Radley masters, Charles Wrinch.

The school's musical traditions, so warmly supported by Warden Ferguson, were well maintained under the direction of Ronald Dussek, the Precentor, and D.C. Hammond-Chambers-Borgnis, Succentor, who succeeded in eliciting a moving performance of Handel's *Messiah* by the whole school in Chapel. Two musicians more dissimilar than Borgnis and Dussek it would have been scarcely possible to find. Borgnis was an Old Radleian, a fine and sensitive pianist, a keen cricketer, and an organ scholar of Corpus Christi College, Cambridge, who would have been quite at home accompanying Vivaldi in the *salone* of a Venetian palazzo, and was, indeed, perfectly at ease playing to the Queen Mother in her wartime house at Badminton. The other was 'a more eccentric character, a great-grandson, it was said, of "the great Dussek"* ... He and his wife were faithful adherents of what might almost be called a sect which advocated a school of singing called "Sinus Tone Production."' 'He would chatter on maddeningly in rehearsals while we rattled our keys,' recalls one of his pupils, 'but the music he gave us was both technically and often intellectually stretching. Sinus Tone Production seems to be a bit of a mystery, but there was something at that time about the quality of some of the trebles ... Interestingly it was "done" to be in the choir ... even the "lads" would stay in it when their voices broke.'

For all his endearing foibles, Dussek, assisted by the urbane Hammond-Chambers-Borgnis, ensured that music at Radley did not suffer under his direction, as so many feared it would after Sydney Watson departed in 1933 to become organist at New College, then Master of Music at Winchester and afterwards Precentor of Eton and Professor at the Royal College of Music. Indeed, music flourished at Radley and those with musical tastes found Dussek – as Maurits Sillem, the future conductor did – a masterly and inspiring teacher, 'a wise man with a profound instinct for the psychology of musicians'.

---

*'The great Dussek', Jan Ladislaw Dussek, the Bohemian pianist and composer (1760–1812), was a member of a distinguished family of musicians. Ronald Dussek's son, John, an Old Radleian, became Director of Music at Oakham School. Ronald Dussek's wife, Winifred Machin, a sister of the Headmaster of Bilton Grange, was a relative of Warden Ferguson. John Dussek's son, Michael, who came to Radley in 1971, is a pianist of distinction.

46. A Greek play, *The Frogs* by Aristophanes, being performed at the Clock Tower Fives Courts in 1900. The scene is the Palace of Pluto; the contest between the dramatists Euripides and Aeschylus. Nicholas Hannen played the part of Dionysus

47. A Latin play, *Rudens* by Plautus

48. The Revd E.G. Selwyn, Warden 1913–18

49. Warden Selwyn and his Prefects, 1913. Nine of the twelve Prefects in this photograph were either killed or wounded in the First World War. *Back row from t[he] left*: A.C. Nugee (Lieutenant, Rif[le] Brigade, wounded); M.S. Richardson (Captain, Royal Welch Fusiliers, died of wounds); T.P. Gibbons (MC, Captain, Hertfordshire Regiment, killed in action); G.H.C. Adams (Second Lieutenant, Suffolk Regiment, killed in action); H.W.S. Cotton (Captain, Cheshire Regiment, wounded); A.H. Bennett (Capta[in] Devon Regiment). *Middle row fr[om] the left*: R.C. Keller (Captain, Hampshire Regiment); O.A. Rei[d] (VC, Major, The King's Regimen[t,] wounded three times); E.H. Whitfield, (MC, Captain, Oxfordshire and Buckinghamshi[re] Light Infantry, wounded); L.A. Westmore (Second Lieutenant, Hampshire Regiment, killed in action). *Seated*: S.J.S. Groves (Captain, York and Lancaster Regiment, wounded); E.V.K. Bryant

50. A shooting range was started south-west of the Pond in 1906 when compulsory rifle-shooting began under the guidance of a don, the Revd A.W. Davies, Commanding Officer OTC 1909–15

51. The presentation ceremony of the Radley College Motor Ambulances, 1915.
The boys, Old Radleians and others subscribed to the cost

52. Bryans's Social Platoon, OTC, 1919

53. Glass panel engraved by Laurence Whistler and installed in the Music School in 1986 in memory of George Butterworth, a music master at Radley 1909–10, who was killed in the First World War. He wrote his *Shropshire Lad* rhapsody while living at the Lodge

54. The Revd Canon Adam Fox, Warden 1918–24

55. The Cloister looking towards the House, c. 1920. The Museum of animal, vegetable and mineral specimens, which was then displayed here, had had several previous homes in different parts of the school. Having been moved ten times its exhibits were eventually dispersed

56. A parade of 'bloods' outside Memorial Arch, 1925. They were members of the Swallows, an unofficial club which became the Radley Swallows Rugby Football Club the next year

57. The Prince of Wales – who played squash with the Senior Prefect, G.C.A. Adams (who later played cricket for Hampshire) – opened the Wilson Library in 1924. The Warden, Canon Adam Fox, is on the Prince's right; F.J. Nugee, Commanding Officer OTC, on his left. Walter Smale (Tutor of H Social), the Librarian, is on the far left behind the Warden. Sitting next to Nugee is P.K. Hodgson (Radley, 1898–1902), later Private Secretary to the Duke of York. The man behind Hodgson is A.B. Knapp-Fisher (Radley, 1902–5), the architect, who designed the Wilson Library equipment. He later became Professor of Architecture at the Royal College of Art

58. Canon W.H. Ferguson,
Warden of Radley 1925–37;
a portrait by James Gunn

59. The Radley College Dance Band in 1934. *From the left*: saxophone, Peter Windle
(later an architect); piano, T.C. Harvey (Private Secretary to the Queen 1946–51); clarinet,
G.B. Stanger (managing director, Burmah Shell Refineries, Bombay); drums, Derrick
Howell (aeroplane pilot, killed in an accident 1937); bassoon, Peter Cooke (major, Royal
Engineers); trombone, John Thomas (South African police); trumpet, John Fennell
(Professor of Russian, Oxford University); saxophone, Charles Coles (director, game
conservancy); trumpet, Daker Harley (London Philharmonic Orchestra)

Vyvyan Hope would not have a word said against him; though that was supposed to be largely because he attributed the cure of his migraines to Dussek's 'Sinus Tone Production'.*

*

In his earnest and untiring endeavours to provide Radleians with a more liberal education than they had hitherto enjoyed, the Warden was helped by what had become a strong if occasionally exasperated staff. The men appointed by Fox were now old hands; those who had come in the early years of Ferguson's time were scarcely less so; but the masters appointed by Wilkes were soon assimilated into a Common Room as united as a Radley Common Room had ever been. Among these new arrivals were E.J. Scott-Snell, an eccentric art master, generally clothed in tight purple corduroy trousers and a green corduroy jacket, to whom numerous men are now grateful for helping them to appreciate and understand works of art; W.J. Llewellyn Jones, an energetic rowing coach from Monkton Combe, who aroused an interest in science in boys to whom the subject had previously seemed tedious; H.J.R. Barker, a geographer from Christ Church and a physical training enthusiast whom everyone liked; and the Revd Ronald Lunt.

Lunt, the son of the Bishop of Ripon, later Bishop of Salisbury, had been a King's Scholar at Eton and had gained a First in Greats at Oxford. A tall and handsome young man of impressive presence, he had not considered becoming a schoolmaster until one Sunday in October 1931 a don at his Oxford college invited him to lunch to meet Charles Wrinch and the Radley chaplain, Hugh Brodie. 'I have always looked on that day,' Lunt wrote much later, 'as deciding my whole career.' He warmed to Wrinch at once, saw him subsequently quite often in Oxford, visited Radley on several occasions, learned what the Steering Committee were trying to do, heard about its moving spirits,

---

*Borgnis had hoped to succeed Dussek as Precentor and was bitterly disappointed when A.D. Caesar was chosen instead, unfairly blaming Dussek for his rejection. He was, however, subsequently to be very happy at Eton. Caesar proved to be an excellent choice for Radley where he 'imparted a new impetus and a new sensitivity to the whole range of Radley music', until his departure in 1959 to become, eventually, the Sub-Dean of Her Majesty's Chapels Royal. His assistant, as Succentor, was Standish Lester who also commanded the Combined Cadet Force and became an outstanding Director of Music at Shrewsbury.

in particular Clement Morgan; and one day he was presented to Warden Ferguson, 'a delightful, fatherly, vague, warm figure'.

Lunt was not to stay at Radley long, but was thereafter remembered with gratitude by the boys he taught; and to the success of his subsequent career as the dedicated if autocratic, abrasive and on occasions extremely difficult Chief Master of King Edward's School, Birmingham, his early experiences at Radley contributed much.

The new spirit and direction which such masters as Llewellyn Jones and Ronald Lunt helped to infuse into teaching at Radley was to be reflected in the number of university scholarships and exhibitions – over forty of them – which the school won in the Warden's first decade. Sporting achievements were less creditable. The Cricket XI had done well in the late 1920s and early 1930s with the help of such good cricketers as P.I. Van der Gucht, who afterwards played for Gloucestershire, W.H. Vestey, and H.P. Dinwiddy who led his team to victory in nine out of their ten school matches in 1931 and 1932. But, apart from the XI of 1937 which defeated all those of other schools apart from Sherborne's which was held to a draw, the cricket teams had since been disappointing. So, excepting that of 1936, which lost only to Stowe, were the Rugger XVs that had seemed to promise so well in Warden Ferguson's time when Stowe and Downside were both beaten for the first time.

On 2 July 1938, however, all the defeats in other sports seemed unimportant when, having last reached the final in 1925, the Eight, coached by R.E. Eason, won the Ladies' Plate at Henley, a victory which excited the school immeasurably and so thrilled the umpire, himself an Old Radleian, that he threw his cap into the river. The brilliant stroke of this crew, Peter Fanning, was soon afterwards killed in action, serving with the Coldstream Guards. Three other members of the victorious crew – J.W. Arkell, Major, Indian Army, C.D.F. Kaye and G.E. Chandler, both pilot officers – were also killed.

25

Schools in Wartime

1939–1945

'It was not all so harmonious as the correspondence in The Radleian would suggest.'

THE EXPECTATION OF war in 1938 had led to the construction for each Social of a concrete shelter – in which there was to be much illicit smoking in the coming years – but the outbreak of hostilities in September the next year provoked such a sudden flurry of activity it was as though there had been no warning of war's approach. Trenches were dug; sandbags filled; work began on a machine-gun emplacement at the main gate. Windows were painted over or blacked out by curtains; lights were dimmed; and the College bells were silenced. A hundred boys arrived from Colet Court, St Paul's Preparatory School in London; thirty more came from a crammer's establishment, in the wake of a coachload of expectant mothers who fortunately stayed only one night, but were soon followed by a party of mothers and their children, one of the mothers having fifteen noisy offspring whom she bossily insisted must be housed together. These were soon all removed elsewhere.

Already the school had been hard put to it to find accommodation for the more than four hundred boys it by now contained; and, until the old, decrepit organ had been dismantled and new seats provided in the vacated organ loft, there had had to be separate services in Chapel for Seniors and Juniors.

Now Radley was more congested than ever. The Warden had temporarily to give up his house to the crammers and take up quarters in the old Warden's Lodgings; the preparatory school boys were dispersed all over the place from Shop to the Pavilion and the Music School. There had to be different sittings for meals in Hall and boys were called upon to perform all kinds of menial duties which would have appalled the boys of Sewell's Radley.

There were further problems to come.

*

At the beginning of May 1940, the Warden, who had just returned from honeymoon in Ireland, received a telegram from John Nugee, Headmaster of Eastbourne College, asking if he could bring his school to Radley. For some time the Warden had been fearing that Radley itself might have to move should the Government require the premises for other purposes. Indeed, later on that year he received a telegram reading: 'Cancel instructions to move school to Pitlochry', a retraction of orders which had never been received.

Many other schools were not so fortunate as Radley. Cheltenham was obliged for a long time to leave Gloucestershire for Shropshire where its former Headmaster, H.H. Hardy, was now Headmaster of Shrewsbury. Uppingham was obliged for over six years to act as host to Kingswood School, Bath, and while the union was described as one of the entirely 'successful marriages', there were occasional displays of antagonism between the black-coated Uppingham boys and their less regimented sports-jacketed guests, as when, for instance, a group of Kingswood boys cheered for Rugby School at a football match against their hosts.

Tonbridge School had to share its premises briefly with Dulwich and when the time for parting came, it was 'to the relief of both schools'. The King's School, Canterbury, had to go to two hotels and several houses in Cornwall where 'there were no classrooms, no laboratories, no playing fields and for the first term all teaching had to be done out of doors'. Malvern's buildings were requisitioned twice and it was feared that the school would have to close down until it was offered hospitality first by the Duke of Marlborough at Blenheim Palace, then by Harrow.

For a year Repton had to find room for King Edward's School, Birmingham, which returned home thankfully after what the *O.E. Gazette* called its 'Reptonian captivity'. Westminster School moved to

Lancing and Hurstpierpoint, then to Exeter, then to various houses in Herefordshire, while parts of the school's buildings in London were destroyed by bombs and its financial losses mounted until they reached £400,000. Meanwhile Gresham's School went to Newquay, Clifton to Cornwall, and the City of London School to Marlborough where the two schools took scarcely any notice of each other. One Marlburian recalled, 'We entirely ignored the London boys; to this day I am ashamed we were not more hospitable'; and an old City of London boy, Sir Kingsley Amis, wrote in his memoirs: '[We] received little comfort or friendliness from the Marlborough College boys who remained entirely aloof.'

A happier relationship was enjoyed when the Quaker school, Bootham, was evacuated to another school in Yorkshire, the Roman Catholic Ampleforth. At a farewell dinner the well-received opening speech delivered on behalf of the Quakers began, 'Friends, Romans, Countrymen.'

The Warden of Radley – who had received a visit from some rather uncommunicative officials from the Ministry of Health on the look-out for suitable buildings to requisition as a hospital – did not hesitate when the request from Eastbourne was received. He wired back immediately, 'Come as soon as you like'; and, with the help of the Bursar, he set about making arrangements to accommodate the evacuees, many of whom were to sleep in the new Gymnasium which had fortunately just been completed. Others were to be found room in Radley Vicarage, at Wick Hall, the nearby house of an Old Radleian, William Dockar-Drysdale, at Nuneham Park – from which the boys were ferried every day across the river – in the accommodation vacated by Smale's Social, in the House's drawing-room which was converted into a dormitory, in a disused laboratory and even in a Scout hut. School was to become Eastbourne's dining-hall.

The first draft of boys, for whom Eastbourne was to pay a fee of £20 a term each, arrived at Radley railway station a few days later, having spent most of the previous night in air-raid shelters.

While they were taking their turns firewatching on the roof of the House, the Warden and the Headmaster discussed the problem of sharing the limited facilities which Radley had to offer.

The plan that emerged was to pool our teaching resources, and make the two schools one unit for teaching [the Warden recalled], to combine their orchestras and various societies etc, but to remain separate in Chapel and on the playing fields.*

The system worked quite well; and, as numbers in both schools fell, with boys leaving a term or two earlier than usual to join the armed forces, the difficulties of accommodation became less acute. By the summer of 1942, when Radley's numbers had fallen to 338, and Eastbourne's to 174, it was possible to arrange a single time-table.

Several Radley masters had left to join the forces, three of them never to return: Pilot Officer Barker was killed in action in 1940; Squadron-Leader E.H. Moss, DFC, who had come to Radley from Trinity College, Oxford, never returned from a raid on Nuremberg; Lieutenant C.B. Colvile was killed while serving with the Royal Welch Fusiliers. Other masters returned from the war but not to Radley. Among these were the Revd Hugh Brodie who, after service as a chaplain in the Royal Naval Volunteer Reserve, became headmaster of a preparatory school in Dublin, and the Revd Ronald Lunt who had won a Military Cross while serving as a chaplain with the 201 Guards Brigade. Two of those who did return to Radley were Ivor Gilliat, a former Major in the Royal Berkshire Regiment, and W.J. Llewellyn Jones, a Major in the Royal Fusiliers.

During their absence, various vacancies on the staff were filled by a succession of temporary teachers young and old, by the Warden's wife, and by Sheila, Clem Morgan's wife, who was asked to take over a French class. When she approached the head of the modern languages department for some guidance as to what to teach them, she received the impatient, curt directive, 'Oh, I should teach them

---

*At first the two schools had shared services in Chapel and this had not worked well, as Eastbourne's historian explained: 'Sharing Chapels did not on the whole prove satisfactory and soon came to an end, and this was especially the case when it came to Holy Communion on a Sunday, a service which Eastbourne had always treated with a pleasing informality, but which in the case of Radley involved the wearing of full academic dress by the staff and an advance to the altar rails in order of seniority.' The Warden treasured 'the memory of an occasion during the brief time when Radley and Eastbourne came to Chapel together, Radley on the Warden's side, Eastbourne on the other. It was the custom of Eastbourne to remain seated on the entrance of the masters, while it is Radley's to rise. Each school sturdily stuck to its custom at the first service of this kind, but the Prefects of each school, anxious to be courteous to their rivals, adopted their ways, so that Radley Prefects sat down again and the Eastbourne Prefects rose as the dons proceeded to their seats.'

French.' She and Mrs Wilkes were both treated by the boys, if not by all the masters, with 'great consideration and also with considerable chivalry'.

There were, however, some temporary teachers – 'weird birds of passage', as the Warden referred to them – who found the maintenance of order in the classroom quite beyond them. One of these was a distinguished history don from Exeter College, C.T. Atkinson, who bicycled over from Oxford, a basket on his handlebars piled high with books. One day he confided to the Warden in a bemused kind of way that his medieval group, which had started with fourteen boys, had mysteriously dwindled to four. Another temporary master was a small Irishman, R.B. McDowell, an authority on Irish history, an inspired teacher of those who wished to be taught, and a future Professor of Oratory.

Who could ever forget that excitable little Irishman called McDowell [wrote one of his pupils]. He was very short, both in stature and sight, and spoke in a strong accent in a squeaky voice. Although a distinguished historian he had no idea whatsoever what to do with a room full of lively schoolboys most of whom singularly failed to share his undoubted enthusiasm for his subject. He was lucky if he got 50 per cent attendance at his early morning pre-breakfast periods, and the number of replies when he called the roll bore no resemblance whatsoever to the number of pupils before him.

An ill-disposed view of the attitude which some Radley boys adopted towards their work during the war was presented by S.P.B. Mais, the novelist, critic and broadcaster, who taught at Radley from 1941 to 1945, and was, like McDowell, distressed by the offhand manner in which he was dismissed after the war was over. Before devoting himself to writing he had been a master at Rossall, Tonbridge and Sherborne (where he taught Alec Waugh, author of the once notorious novel of public school life, *Loom of Youth*). He was a gifted teacher, though most reluctant to teach the set books. One of his Radley pupils considered him 'one of the best teachers [he] had ever sat under'. Yet in his autobiographical novel, *Caper Sauce*, which is based on his experiences at Radley, Mais's fictional self does not find most boys as stimulating as they found him. In this novel he presents Peregrine Mallory, a broadcaster who has taught at Wellington, being greeted by the Headmaster of Lunbury (Radley), 'one of the younger and most efficient headmasters' who is thought to be 'using Lunbury as a stepping stone to Eton'. The Headmaster explains to Mallory that these are tiresome times for Lunbury: the school is sharing its premises with Shersby (Eastbourne) and it is

> a difficult business entertaining another school . . . the two schools working at different times. We are, as you know, a high Anglican foundation. Shersby, alas, is Evangelical, very low indeed. That causes a complication. The two schools naturally play their games apart, the two staffs combine for teaching purposes, and the classes are mixed. It will be interesting to see if you as an outsider can always tell the difference.

Mallory finds the young Lunbury boys impertinent and facetious, as difficult to control as he finds the Prefects rude and disdainful. 'The great Public School tradition that had made it a sin to work except under compulsion, that made it a virtue always to get away with a minimum, was as strong as ever.' Mallory is eventually driven to cow his form into submission by force.

The indifferent attitude towards learning and the keen interest shown in games at Lunbury may well have reflected some attitudes of mind at Radley, though they are also based upon Mais's experiences of another public school at which he taught for two months in 1940 and in which, so he was led to complain in an article in the *New Statesman and Nation*, 'everything was the same as it had been in 1920 and everything was wrong'.

A less jaundiced and, so far as Radley is concerned, a more realistic view of 'a public school in wartime' is given in the unpublished recollections of Robert Cyril Storrs, an Eastbourne master who taught at Radley throughout the period of his school's stay there.

He arrived at Radley thankful to find one of the senior masters was T.E.E. Cocks, a 'great friend' of his at Westminster, and pleased, too, to find that the Eastbourne masters, their pay drastically reduced in order to keep their school alive, were all to be 'honorary members of the Radley high table and well looked after'. He was grateful also that the Radley cellars, 'so well stocked and enlarged by John Nugee when Sub-Warden', were open to them. This, unfortunately, did not last long. 'When things became difficult, this privilege was confined to Radley masters and the tuckshop also only served their limited supplies to them.'

> We worked together, each class a mixture of the two schools [Storrs recalled]. The front desks would be occupied by the Radley boys in grey,

the back desks by the Eastbourne boys in blue.* They never quarrelled, but seldom mixed. When lessons were over, we were quite separate schools . . .

To start with we had our own tables in the Radley dining-hall, but their eating habits were so different from ours that this did not last long. The Radley dons, as they called themselves . . . behaved very like Oxford dons . . . They had their High Table, and their boys' behaviour below did not seem to concern them.† Our housemasters begged leave to eat with their houses, but this worried the Radley dons and indeed the kitchen staff, because we found their method of serving food rather disorganized. So we persuaded the Bursar to provide food for us in a separate hall, the old school Hall at the opposite end of the cloisters . . .

Storrs did not find 'a great deal of difference between the boys' of the two schools, though the Radley boys were more polite, 'almost excessively' so. 'If a Radley boy arrived late for a lesson, he would stand at the door, bow to the master, and try to give a lengthy description of how sorry he was for being late. An Eastbourne boy would tend to slip in and hope to take his place without being noticed or causing a disturbance.'

In the village Radley boys would remove their caps well in advance of an encounter and 'hold them out in front of them as they bowed their way past', whereas Eastbourne boys would 'not exactly slink past, but would go by with a touch of the cap'.

Deferential and polite as they were to their own and Eastbourne masters, Radley boys, so Storrs thought, held themselves aloof from the domestic staff. The wife of one man told Mrs Storrs that in all the thirty years her husband had worked at Radley 'hardly any boy or master had taken any notice of him', whereas he had 'got to know all the Eastbourne staff and the boys had made great friends with him'.

---

*Generally speaking the Radley boys sat in front when a Radley master was teaching, and at the back when being taught by an Eastbourne master.
†It had, however, concerned a pre-war Senior Prefect, Athol Campbell, who was so disgusted by the sight of the behaviour in Hall of the members of his own Social that he made them wear bibs until their table manners improved. It was not only the table manners of Radley boys in Hall which were to be lamented. When the eyes of authority were averted in Hall, a favourite pursuit was trying to flick pats of margarine onto the ceiling or over the beams. Also, boys would drop as many cherry stones as possible onto the centre aisle before the Warden led guests from Hall after lunch.

As for the Radley dons, who met daily in the Senior Common Room and held a monthly meeting in the Warden's lodgings to hear talks by distinguished educationists and to discuss education in general, Storrs and several of his colleagues 'got the impression that they were more fond of talking about education than carrying the theories discussed into practice'.

> We were also shocked [Storrs wrote] at what seemed disloyalty to the Warden, their saying 'yes' to his face and then running him down behind his back.
>
> One particular episode struck me forcibly. A senior Radley boy, a scientist, told his father, an influential member of the Radley Council, that the Eastbourne masters taught him well, and that the Radley masters were useless. I reckon it was because of this that the Warden sacked the senior science master and appointed another – a rather unsuitable one – from another school.* At our daily common-room meeting, he explained his action by saying that the master he had sacked had not co-operated in ARP and other war work. Actually he was within a year or two of retiring and not very fit. At the meeting we were all embarrassed by the behaviour of a number of Radley dons who just turned their backs on the Warden while he was talking and muttered their displeasure.

'It would be mean to complain about Wilkes,' Storrs added, 'but it would be fair to say that it was not all that easy to work under someone with such a volatile brain. He seemed to love changing things about and . . . changes were made by little notices pinned to the Warden's board in Covered Passage. Such a notice might read: "In future Friday's timetable will be exchanged with Tuesday's . . . " The Warden reckoned this kept people on their toes; actually it just irritated them.' It irritated Radley masters as well as those from Eastbourne. 'At the time of the greatest overcrowding,' wrote the widow of one of them, 'when classes were having to play Cox and Box to get into the classrooms, and Radley had to play games while Eastbourne was taught, the Warden arranged for periods to begin and end at times which no one could remember – 9.35 or 11.55 and so on.'

---

*The sacked master was A.T. Hedgecock, a Social Tutor from 1919 to 1938, who left Radley in 1943. Notoriously eccentric, he was suffering from diabetes, though he managed to keep it well in hand. It should be said in his defence that one of his pupils, David Jamison, who became a distinguished physiologist, considered him a 'very good physics teacher'.

Nugee would never interfere [Storrs continued]. He had been Sub-Warden at Radley for many years when Wilkes was appointed Warden . . . Often at Radley, Nugee's staff were a little impatient with his tact, but looking back on it all, it is also clear that Nugee's quiet diplomacy was one of the main reasons for Eastbourne's five years of peace in war.

Wilkes paid similar tributes to Nugee, as Nugee himself did to Wilkes. There can be no doubt that the friendly manner of the one and the tact of the other were to an extent responsible for the generally happy atmosphere that existed between the two schools for these five years. To deal with any difficulties that might arise between them a committee of two Radley and two Eastbourne masters was appointed. They met regularly but found no work to do.

*

That the Eastbourne boys were contented enough during the war years at Radley, despite the unpleasant and unwelcome duties that the times demanded, the anxiety and unhappiness caused by concern for friends and families whose lives were in danger – as well as devastating reports of sudden death – is confirmed by their reminiscences. Extracts taken at random from a number of these provide an authentic if some-times contradictory picture of wartime Radley as seen through Eastbourne eyes.

I remember the great welcome from Radleians; some lent us bikes to see the junior boys [at Nuneham Park] . . . Several of the senior Radley boys invited Eastbourne boys to share their studies . . . The immediate feeling after the move was of a loss of independence, and of being cut off from the outside world. At Eastbourne part of the town and shops had always been in bounds to the boys, at Radley the shops were miles away . . . The biggest single difference we found from Eastbourne was the food. We did not like either the food . . . mainly bread, potatoes and fried eggs . . . or communal feeding . . . Cold winters were the norm . . . Most of us suffered from chilblains . . .

All I remember of my first year or two was endless hours spent by the gas range making toast and preparing tea for prefects and cleaning their rugger boots and corps boots . . .

The wretched fags spent their lives hanging round the door of the Prep Room [Social Hall] waiting for the next summons to avoid being last in the rush, so it was quite impossible to settle down to any other activity . . .

I used to escape with my fishing rod either to the banks of the Thames to fish for roach, dace and chub, or to the Radley College Pond which in those days was full of pike and perch . . . We also spent a lot of time trapping moles . . . I remember the marvellous playing fields stretching endlessly away towards the wood in the far distance . . . Compared with Eastbourne, Radley's sports facilities seemed quite amazing. A 9-hole golf-course, squash courts and a rackets court whereas we had only Rugby fives . . . Rowing on the Thames was a delight after the narrow confines of the Cuckmere . . . I was mad about shooting in those days and we had to find a member of staff to supervise us. I remember making our Chaplain, Charles Neate's life an absolute misery by pestering him to come and supervise us. Although he had no interest whatsoever in shooting, he cheerfully spent hours watching us. What a delightful man he was. After the war he became [Chaplain and later] Sub-Warden of Radley for many years.

Liberty in one's spare time was a contrast from Eastbourne. Here at Radley we could cycle to Oxford or where we wished. Curiously, Radley were not allowed personal radios, so we had to hand ours in . . .

We shared classes with Radleians who seemed to consider themselves rather superior to us Eastbourne intruders . . . It was not all so harmonious as the correspondence in *The Radleian* would suggest.

It was certainly the case that in the lower forms Radley and Eastbourne boys did not get on as well as some accounts indicate. A man who was a Radley Prefect at this time recalls:

As one became older friendships between the two schools did form. But there was considerable enmity in the lower schools. It would be put about on the grape-vine that there would be a confrontation, say in Radley Wood on Sunday afternoon. The favourite weapons used to be catapults . . . and it was fortunate more injuries were not sustained. Also, on one occasion, a Radley boy wearing a scarf covering a bandage over a boil was ambushed by 'the bogos' (I do not know how this name for the Eastbournians originated) and he was suspended by the scarf over a tree branch. Luckily he was rescued in time as he had become unconscious.

On the whole Eastbourne College was tolerated, but I think rather looked down on in a snobbish manner by Radleians as intermingling did not really take place.* In classes I can clearly remember 'bogos' being ridiculed quite openly.

*

---

*But then intermingling was still uncommon between Radleians themselves in different Socials. It is still fairly uncommon, though no longer discouraged.

The reminiscences and letters of Radleians provide a picture similar to that given by Eastbourne boys of a school quite content, despite the rivalries, occasional confrontations, difficulties and hardships of the time. There are, of course, complaints about the need to carry out domestic duties, to work on the land and dig on the ploughed up golf-course, to turn out on cold nights for black-out patrols, to practise fire drill, to hurry down to the shelters when the air-raid warning sounded, to parade with the short-lived Local Defence Volunteers, later to be known as the Home Guard, or with the Air Cadet Corps, the Sea Training Corps or the Junior Training Corps. This last, an increasingly efficient force under the command of a master, Major Ranulph Waye, elicited from Lieutenant-General Sir Bernard Paget, Commander-in-Chief, Home Forces – whose two sons were at Radley, one of whom, while still only a lieutenant, was to be awarded the DSO after winning the Croix de Guerre – the verdict that it was the best contingent he had ever seen.

Boys were sometimes hungry, and, as in earlier times, would appear from the surrounding countryside with carcasses of strange animals in their hands. They were often also cold, wearing scarves in Hall where the heating system had irreparably broken down; and, no longer required to wear stiff collars or gowns or, indeed, any uniform at all, they dressed themselves more or less as they chose. Yet cheerfulness kept breaking through.

There were fairly frequent holidays when boys cycled to Oxford, Wallingford or Abingdon, took picnics into the woods and enjoyed boating parties on the river. Several boys kept ferrets and went rabbiting; others went beagling with a pack started in 1940. Working on nearby farms occupied many afternoon hours; so did 'manual digging' on 'Social plots'; so, too, did the acquisition of 'standards', every boy being required to obtain at least five in some athletic track or field event.

There were ping-pong tournaments and contests between Socials, singing contests still known as 'Social Shouts' and rowing races known as 'Social Fours'; there were film shows and concerts and regular school and Social plays. There were occasional tea-parties given by the Warden at which a great attraction was Mrs Wilkes, 'very untidy and wears frightful clothes and an awful girl's hat but has a kind face and is really very nice'. There were still numerous societies: one boy belonged not only to the Aeronautical Society, the Stamp Club, the Junior Scientific Society and the Political Society, but also to the

Poetry Society whose members vied with each other to get their verse printed in *The Emergency Ration* or *The College Block*, two publications which had sprung up now that a greatly reduced *Radleian* appeared only once a term. This boy also belonged to the Junior Literary Society and to the Canterbury Club, a society which was devoted to the reading and discussing of plays and poems but which seems to have spent much time also in debating the future of public schools, the consensus after one meeting being that 'even if we won the war the public schools could not survive without government help'.

Many boys appear to have found their wartime duties more agreeable than irksome, and their training with the Corps a necessary duty in order to pass Certificate A, a useful step towards the commission in the Army to which so many of them aspired. The days of Corps parades and drill were also not so much dreaded now that battledress was beginning to be worn and there was no more struggling with the buttons and puttees of the OTC uniform. Field-days with the Corps were generally enjoyed; so were 'lighting patrols' which took boys out at night looking for chinks in black-out curtains. Boys also enjoyed their nights on duty with the Upper Thames Patrol whose members patrolled the Park with rifles from the Corps armoury and ten rounds of ammunition each and helped in the river patrol in the motor launch, *Lusimus*, used for coaching.

For those brave enough to take advantage of it, a patrol towards Sandford Lock afforded the opportunity of a pint of beer in the public house there. One boy who had 'no experience of alcohol', was taken there by his companion and was 'completely smashed for the rest of the watch'. An apprehensive boy, he afterwards dreaded being discovered and therefore beaten, just as he feared that his brother – with whom he shared a cubicle as brothers did – would be discovered taking swigs of gin from a bottle he kept concealed under his bed.

He never was beaten. In fact, beatings were not common then, though five 'checks' or 'faults' still rendered the culprit liable to one. One day in 1943, Martin Blake, having already been given three checks for various offences including 'leaving lights on', received two more 'for not getting the Ovaltine bread'. He felt 'quite calm' as he awaited his punishment and was 'unafraid when entering Social Hall'. 'It hardly hurt at all a few minutes after the event,' he wrote in his diary after the beating. 'I got six strokes. I feel one up on all the other chaps with four checks or over, as I have got it all over and can look forward to the end of term in peace.' 'My backside,' he added the next day, 'is rather more uncomfortable now than it was yesterday.'

Other old customs lingered on: one boy tells his parents of his pleasure at being allowed to wear brown shoes on entering the Sixth Form; another recounts his bravado on walking across the area known as Pups' Court sacred to the feet of Prefects; many complain about the lavatories and coldness of 'those awful latrines without doors near the Clock Tower' – one of those who did so afterwards said that they had haunted him all his later life, though he was spared the indignity of sitting on a lavatory to make it warm enough for a Prefect, as he might well have been called upon to do as a fag in the 1920s.

The disappearance of the College servitors and the advent of women servants in Hall is a subject of frequent comment in the letters and memoirs of the period. One famously voluptuous woman servant was known as 'the Resister', though why she had earned the sobriquet and what or whom she was supposed to have resisted never became clear. The number of women servants employed was not large, and boys themselves were called upon to act as waiters in Hall as well as to clean their cubicles and make their own beds.

Preoccupied as they generally are with the experiences of school life, these letters from Radleians from time to time reveal their awareness of a world outside in the throes of a devastating war: 'An O.R. called Chandler [G.E. Chandler] was brought down in flames in Belgium a few days ago. That sort of thing brings the war very close. I knew him quite well . . . He was very nice. His brother is here now, and looks very forlorn, poor chap.'

26

Centenary
1945–1950

'With a little extra joviality.'

ON 8 MAY 1945 Radley celebrated the German surrender at
Lüneburg Heath four days before. In the morning there was
a voluntary thanksgiving service in Chapel and – as it had
been for a previous voluntary service on the day of the Normandy
landings, when 'practically the whole College was there' – the 'place
was packed'. As darkness fell a huge bonfire was lit: and, as the flames
reached the stuffed figure of Hitler on the top of it, rounds of blank
ammunition and detonators, stolen from an American store, exploded
spectacularly and dangerously in the Führer's straw entrails. 'The
assembled crowd sang timidly for a few minutes,' wrote one of the
spectators, 'then grew a bit more cheerful, joined together arm-in-arm
and rushed frenziedly round the fire, and finally went quite mad,
people joining into serried bands and charging helter-skelter round the
place, sweeping all and everyone before them, people rushing about
brandishing carbide torches, people mobbing girls – of which there
was quite a profusion – and everyone yelling songs for all they were
worth. The Dun, Clem, all the Dons and wives were in the midst of all
this and got hustled more than once.'

In the following months life gradually returned to normal and
numbers in the school, which had stood at 341 in 1944, rose to 407 in
the summer of 1946. Masters who had completed their military service
returned to Radley; so did Charles Wrinch, who had left four years

before to become Headmaster of Raynes Park County School and who, as on previous occasions, found it impossible to resist the lure of Radley, making a habit of returning, as Clem Morgan used to say, soon after having accepted a leaving present. W.R. Smale, a gunner in the First World War, did not survive the Second: overwhelmed with grief at the disbandment of his Social, which had meant so much to him – and perhaps aware that his history teaching had become, in the words of one of his colleagues, 'sadly digressive' – he had, 'with great care and preparation' and having previously been to Chapel, gassed himself in 1941 in the Cottage to which he had regretfully to withdraw, leaving a pathetic suicide note which read, 'I am so lonely . . . '*

Two hundred and twenty Radleians did not come home, a loss higher by one than the school had suffered in the First World War. One George Cross and 28 DSOs had been won, 13 DSCs, 78 MCs and six DFCs, one of these being awarded to Squadron-Leader O.L.S. Philpot, a Prefect and member of the 1931 Eight, the author of *Stolen Journey*, who escaped from a German prisoner of war camp by means of a tunnel dug under cover of a movable vaulting horse. The George Cross had been awarded to the Earl of Suffolk and Berkshire, who had been killed in London in 1941 with his woman secretary and driver while trying to defuse a bomb.†

Over £30,000 was subscribed to a War Memorial fund, most of which was to be spent on scholarships, a relatively small amount being devoted to a stone tablet, inscribed with the names of those who had been killed, which was placed inside the War Memorial Arch opposite the tablet with the names of those who had fallen in the earlier war.

As the end of the war had come into sight, there had been more

---

*His suicide had long been expected, since he himself had often hinted at it. When an Old Radleian, Peter Stuart, who had returned to the school to visit him while on leave from the Merchant Navy, admired a print of Christ Church on the wall of his drawing-room, Smale immediately took it down and gave it to him as though it was a parting gift. On hearing of Smale's death, Clem Morgan's immediate response was, 'Oh, so he's done it at last.'

†The number of decorations awarded to Old Radleians compares very favourably with that of other schools. The record could not bear comparison with that of Cheltenham which has thirteen Victoria Crosses on its roll of honour. Nor could it bear comparison with the record of Wellingtonians who, between 1859 and 1948, won 15 VCs, 638 DSOs, 34 DSCs, 678 MCs, 46 DFCs and two DFMs. But to take a school of Radley's size, the record of Bradfield – whose numbers were 381 in 1929 – shows 19 DSOs, 38 MCs, 25 DFCs, two AFCs, 9 DSCs and two GMs.

encouraging results on the playing fields and the river. In November 1943 Martin Blake had written in his diary of the sad state of Radley rugger and of the efforts made to improve it. By next season, however, the tide had turned. The First XV beat Wellington and Cheltenham for the first time and seemed certain to beat Eastbourne when, in a thrilling match, an Eastbourne boy, who had failed Common Entrance to Radley, took his side to victory with a startling drop goal. In 1945 the Eight beat Eton and won the Hedsor Cup at Henley; the Cricket XI in 1947 was the best for several years, compensating for that humiliating day towards the beginning of the war when, in a match against a Royal Air Force team from Abingdon, the First XI scored 14 against a total of 250 for three declared. In 1948 E.R. Dexter, later to captain Sussex and England, came to Radley to join another fine cricketer, A.C. Walton, who went on to captain the Oxford XI and play for Middlesex.

Dexter was 'the most magnificent boy athlete' the Warden had ever known. Not only a splendid cricketer, he was also a fine golfer, a first-class rackets player, a brilliant fly-half on the rugger field; and, without any particular training, he won the hundred yards and quarter mile at Radley, breaking the school records for both events. He was also a more than competent pianist; and, had he not left young, would certainly have won a scholarship to Cambridge. John Scott, who succeeded him as Senior Prefect, was an even better rugby player, eventually finding a place in the England team.

*

In 1947, the year before Dexter arrived at Radley, the school celebrated its centenary. On St Columba's Day, 9 June – a fine summer afternoon after an alarmingly cold and overcast morning – a large gathering of notabilities converged on Radley, among them – in a display of episcopacy which would have delighted Sewell – the Archbishop of Canterbury, the Rt. Hon. and Most Revd G.F. Fisher, the former Headmaster of Repton, and nine bishops, including K.E. Kirk, the Bishop of Oxford, as well as assorted deans and generals and the Princess Elizabeth, then twenty-one years old and shortly to be married.

There were processions and fanfares of trumpets, speeches and receptions. There was a service of commemoration in Chapel, an inspection of a guard of honour; the Senior Prefect, F.G. Wells, who had just won a scholarship to King's College, Cambridge, gave an address in Latin; the Princess responded, in English. She was entertained to tea in the Prefects' Study where, accompanied by two members of the Royal Household, Lady Katherine Seymour and the Old Radleian, Major Thomas Harvey, she seemed quite at ease, taking part in a not too strained conversation and eating strawberries and cream with a spoon which was later shown to visitors together with a plate on which she had 'politely left the remains of a strawberry'. After her departure from Radley – sent on her way with loud cheers which more than made up for the scattered clapping and 'dignified, rather half-hearted cheer' with which she had been greeted – the Council gave a dinner to the masters in School. In the evening the school's history was recalled in a performance of *Radley Retrospect*, devised and directed by A.K. Boyd, Charles Wrinch and R.T. King, and partially narrated by Freddie Grisewood and John Livingstone, a Prefect who not only 'had a beautiful voice', in the Warden's words, 'but the most aristocratic presence'. The orchestra, consisting mainly of Old Radleians, was enthusiastically conducted by Ronald Dussek 'quite coherently, if with a little extra joviality' attributed to the sherry and champagne consumed at the dons' dinner in School. Fireworks flashed and exploded above the floodlit House; and the whole school sang the Radley song, *Lusimus*, the music of which had been written years before by Dr Monk, the Latin words by William Sewell incongruously emphasizing the happy prospect of leaving school at the end of term rather than the pride in belonging to it.

There were hitches, as was to be expected: the Princess was twenty minutes late, a delay that 'harrowed' the Warden, so an onlooker thought as he watched him 'waiting nervously' with Dean Henderson on the steps of the House, the Dean himself, the proudest of Old Radleians, 'nearly dying with joy', as Charles Wrinch described him, 'in short advance of his actual death, appropriately on a visit to Radley a few months later'. The guard of honour was lost for a time when it was most needed; the Warden's son, instructed to present a large bouquet of flowers to the Princess, delivered them solemnly into the hands of his mother; the oldest living Radleian, the founder's nephew, the ninety-seven-year-old Revd Arthur Sewell, was unable to attend as he had hoped to do;* and Nicholas Hannen, the Old Radleian actor,

---

*The Revd Arthur Sewell took the opportunity of his own centenary, six years before his death, of asking that his grandson should be educated at Radley free, a request that the Warden felt unable to refuse.

had great difficulty in remembering J.H. Fawcett's admirable lines in *Radley Retrospect*.

This was a problem not experienced by John Livingstone in reciting a prologue of verses in heroic couplets which Boyd had vainly attempted to extract from various Old Radleian poets who all declined the task. They had eventually been supplied by Dr Alington who, approached by his son-in-law, the Warden, indignantly replied that the request was absurd as he had no first-hand knowledge of the school – which could surely find its own poet for the purpose – but who, nevertheless, despatched a more than adequate prologue by return of post.

Despite minor misfortunes, the St Columba's Day celebrations were an undoubted success. So was the subsequent inspection of the Junior Training Corps by Field Marshal Montgomery, even though he lost his temper with some Swedish visitors who followed him about clicking at him with their cameras and were upbraided furiously for their impertinence. Afterwards, in calmer mood, he gave the boys a half-hour's talk, making plain how he had achieved his brilliant victory at El Alamein with the help of a map drawn on a blackboard which is now preserved in the Imperial War Museum.*

The French General, Jean de Lattre de Tassigny, was a more difficult guest. He arrived with two aides-de-camp, one a cheerful Frenchman, the other a 'gaunt and haggard' English officer who seemed worn out by the responsibilities of serving so demanding a master. Although the General spoke in perfect English to the boys he met, he insisted that the masters and their wives speak French to him at the Warden's dinner party, an obligation which only Clem Morgan's wife, Sheila, could adequately fulfil.

Among the other guests at the Warden's dinner party was George

---

*During the war Montgomery had met Llewellyn Jones who for a time had commanded a battalion of the Royal Fusiliers. They met again at Henley Regatta in the early 1950s. Montgomery (who was himself at St Paul's and sent his only son to Winchester) took great interest in the Radley crew, especially in a Norwegian boy, Ole Fegth, who was to row for Norway and become Norwegian Sculling Champion. Montgomery sent presents of Turkish delight and chocolates to Llewellyn Jones for the Radley Eight. On sending the Turkish delight he said the cox was not to have any until he had his hair cut; and on sending 'a large box of Swiss Chocolate' after the crew's victory in the Princess Elizabeth Cup at Henley in 1952 he added, 'It is more than a box; it is a sort of minor crate and contains enough chocolate to last the entire crew for several months! I suggest you might see it is wisely consumed.'

Mallaby who had recently been appointed Chairman of the Council in succession to Wilfrid Raikes, Dean Henderson's successor. Raikes, a member of a Radley dynasty which has supplied no fewer than twenty-five names to the latest edition of *The Radley Register*, was a man of unfailing not to say exhausting energy, quite capable of making telephone calls at two o'clock in the morning before he went to bed, or at seven on rising. Mallaby, also an Old Radleian, a former Senior Prefect, a master at Clifton and St Edward's and Headmaster at St Bees before eventually in 1957 becoming High Commissioner in New Zealand and First Civil Service Commissioner, did not choose to go to bed so late as Wilfrid Raikes. He left the Warden's dinner party at the same time as the other guests for a bedroom at the house of W.G. Morgan (later Stewart-Morgan), whose cheerful and amusing Welsh company Mallaby no doubt preferred to that of the awkward, hawk-faced French General. Mallaby was in bed when the General, Raikes-like, decided he wanted to talk to him. A call was made to Morgan's house: Sir George was in bed and would not stir. The General, so the Warden recalled, 'of course took it out on the poor English aide-de-camp . . . He was not an easy guest.'

*

There were other days and nights of the post-war years of his Wardenship to which Wilkes looked back unwillingly, not all of them mentioned in his 'Confessions of a Lotus-Eater' or the 'Rambling Reminiscences' which he wrote when his work at Radley was done.

There were the days when he had to consider reports of the disorderly behaviour of Radley boys at Henley Regatta which the whole school was then allowed to attend until the Eight were defeated. On occasions, according to a man who was at Radley from 1947 to 1952, this disorderliness was 'extraordinary – many Radley boys were to be seen reeling drunkenly in the streets, and the vandalism on the special train was worthy of the worst soccer hooligans'.

Being on sabbatical leave the Warden was not at Radley in November 1950 when a series of mysterious fires broke out at different places in the school, when the wail of the siren sent boys running to their Socials for roll-call, and fire-engines from Abingdon and Oxford came roaring up the drive. The police had to be called in and boys had to write down where they were at the time of the outbreaks and produce two witnesses to corroborate their alibis. Eventually the arsonist was found, and expelled. He was a boy who had been seen on the fire-engine, directing the driver to the fire, and had allegedly given as his alibi, 'on holiday in Barbados'.*

The Warden did, however, have to deal with the distressing case of Hildred Carlisle, the fourteen-year-old son and nephew of former Prefects, who ran away in his pyjamas and dressing gown and was found hiding in a barn in the College grounds by a Prefect from whom he managed to escape, losing his slippers in the struggle. He was later seen eight miles from Radley at South Moreton where a man chased him; but again he escaped, leaping across a barbed wire fence and turning to wave to his pursuers. At 11.15 that night he was found asleep in a hayrick on a farm at Didcot with straw stuffed inside his pyjama jacket to keep him warm. He was driven back to the school by the Warden whose car was pursued by a reporter from the *Daily Express*. 'He would not say why he ran away,' the *Daily Telegraph* reported on 24 February 1949, 'but stated that he intended making his way to London.' It was said that he was about to be beaten, or that he had been bullied, or both.

As there was not so much beating, so there was not so much bullying at Radley at this time compared with the punishments and humiliation inflicted at several other public schools. Yet, while many boys who were at Radley in the 1930s can recall not a single instance of physical bullying of any kind, it is idle to suppose that there was none in the 1940s and 1950s. Indeed, the photographer Dmitri Kasterine, who was at Radley from 1945 to 1950, described that period in the school's history as one of 'bad food, no heat, intense heartiness and much bullying'.

Unpleasant initiation ceremonies were still conducted in certain

---

*The fire-raiser's name was, ironically, the same as that of the celebrated Superintendent of the Metropolitan Fire Brigade who was immortalized in Gilbert and Sullivan's *Iolanthe*. The boy had been known as an arsonist at his preparatory school, a fact which had not been divulged to the authorities at Radley.

There had been similar outbreaks of arson in 1903 at Eton when two boys had been killed in the flames. The culprit, who had been heard to declare, 'Isn't it a jolly blaze?' was caught lighting another fire a few nights later. Expelled from Eton, he went on, according to Tim Card, to a reasonably successful career as a journalist. The Radley arsonist died in 1988, having gone to work as an agricultural officer in Kenya. With apparently unconscious irony his obituarist wrote of him, 'He was best known in Kenya for his work in the police force where his bravery in dealing with dangerous criminals was unmatched. Wherever there was a robbery, or fire, [he] was there, always armed, and always ready.'

Socials, mainly in those where the Tutors were bachelors. New boys, after about three weeks of peace, would be chased around the tops of the partitions which divided the desks and cupboards in the social halls and pelted with books in their unsteady progress. Boys who fell off were pushed beneath a barrier of waste-paper baskets and chairs with legs interlocked so that it was impossible to escape until released. The unfortunate prisoner would then have missed Chapel or supper and might well be officially punished for his absence.

'There was also a chimney in these social halls,' a man who was a Prefect in the 1940s remembers, 'and another test was to "clean the chimney". The boy would be required to force himself up as far as possible, about two or three feet off the ground and rattle a broomhead in the chimney, thus bringing down a load of soot on his head. At the same time he would be assaulted from below by all sorts of broom handles ... According to how these tests went it was decided how wet the boy was considered to be and whether or not he would be marked out for future ragging.' The compilers of a survey of Old Radleians living in Australia in 1955 – which reported that 70 per cent of those questioned had come across instances of physical bullying during their school careers – revealed that similar unpleasant ceremonies were still practised a decade after those described by this former prefect. 'The most extreme bullying we heard about,' the compilers of this survey wrote, 'was in the 1950s when boys were crucified, forced to lift iron grates above their heads and were made to run through tables whilst being kicked.'

*

When the time for his leaving Radley approached, the Warden was thankful that he would never again have to deal with such examples of bullying as came to his notice; and thankful, too, that never again would he have to dismiss such a master as the one who had answered a summons to his house in expectation of being asked to take over the next Social that fell vacant and who 'screamed' at him when he discovered why the Warden had really sent for him. Nor would he have to compose such rows as had erupted when one Social (Hedgecock's) objected to moving into College and another (Morgan's) objected to moving out, and when certain elderly Old Radleians vented their fury with the Warden for having invited that 'inveterate socialist and class-traitor', the Hon. Sir Stafford Cripps, Chancellor of the Exchequer in Clement Attlee's Labour Government – and for six years an active and effective member of the Radley Council – to speak to the school's Political Society.

Nor would he ever again have to deliver such a rebuke as he had to inflict upon the choir after a sermon by the Bishop of Salisbury which, having lasted twenty-five minutes, had sent several of their members to sleep and driven others to read books or drop pennies on the floor. Nor yet would he have to administer such a beating as he had to do on the occasion of the 'Great Gym Beating' as described in a letter from Alexander Bowlby, Old Radleian artist and author of *The Recollections of Rifleman Bowlby*: 'There was a new gym master who was unaware that it was a tradition to cut gym on the day before the term ended, so he reported all 150+ boys who cut it to the Warden. Who duly beat us all! I didn't appreciate the waiting. But Vaughan Wilkes was his delightful self when I finally got in there. We had a pleasant little chat, he then beat me, and wished me a very happy holiday!'

The Warden was also much relieved that he would never again feel obliged to call the whole school together and threaten dire reprisals if a confession was not forthcoming, as he had done after a marquee, erected for Gaudy Day, had been slashed all the way round with a very sharp knife – a knife which, he subsequently discovered, had been wielded by his seven-year-old son.

Wilkes's pleasant memories of his Wardenship, however, far outweighed the sad. He recalled with deep affection his Senior Prefects, and mourned the loss of those killed in the war, in particular Robin Whitehead, 'so forceful, so humorous, bursting with zest for life', and John Hamilton, 'so incredibly handsome and with the same golden voice as his father' (the Dean of Windsor), and Athol Campbell – 'Why can't all boys,' he once said to his wife, 'be like Athol Campbell?' Wilkes recalled, too, the masters of whom he had grown particularly fond, among them Clem Morgan with his 'wonderful sense of the ridiculous', the tears coursing freely down his cheeks when amused or moved; and he told the story of Morgan and another Social Tutor, R.L.C. Southam, an extremely large and exuberant man, going to the cinema in Paris after an excellent lunch to see, of all films and for the second time, *Little Lord Fauntleroy*. 'After a time Clem felt a queer stoppage in the throat and was conscious of those tell-tale tears gathering in his eyes: he looked at Robin beside him – and saw enormous tears sliding down those enormous cheeks.'

Wilkes took a great pride in the younger men he had appointed to the staff, especially those who had been Prefects at Radley before or during the early part of the war, Peter Way, Peter Stuart and D.T.M. Birks; and in Neill Fisher, a former pupil of his at Eton, and Christopher Ellis, also an Etonian pupil, who had appeared at Radley one day in the shabbiest garments asking to borrow some trousers and a coat so that he could have lunch in Hall, explaining that he was a naval commando on an endurance course.

> I asked him what he hoped to do when the war ended [Wilkes wrote]. He said he didn't know: and I said, 'Why not come here to teach Arts and Crafts and a little Mathematics?' He seemed at the time to regard this as an absurd idea – but twelve months or so later he asked me, 'Had I been serious in the suggestion?' . . . He joined us when demobilized [having won the George Medal for bomb disposal on Malta]. In some ways he proved the most remarkable schoolmaster I have ever known . . . One of Britain's leading yachtsmen, he started our sailing club – and we had home made craft to sail in; he started the Marionette Theatre; he introduced us to pottery . . . He was an enormous influence for good at Radley.

Throughout his time as Warden, Wilkes laid great emphasis on the kind of activities which came under Ellis's enthusiastic direction: in the school's prospectus issued in those years there are more words under the heading, 'Societies, etc.' than under any other, including 'Curriculum'. Some of these societies were listed alphabetically: 'Angling, Antiquarian, Archery, Campanological, Debating, Dramatic, Farming, Literary, Madrigal, Mountaineering, Musical, Natural History, Photographic, Political, Sailing, Scientific, Shakespeare'. As for 'Drawing, Painting, Printing and Pottery', prospective parents were assured that any boys who wished could learn these skills in their spare time.

All of the school's societies and clubs were actively encouraged by the Warden who attended the meetings of some of them, and who wrote warm letters of congratulations to the producers of the school plays, taking particular pleasure and pride in Charles Wrinch's production of *Comus* and Sophocles's *Philoctetes* (a 'marked success', in the opinion of *The Times*), A.K. Boyd's *The Critic*, and in his own presentation of the *Bacchae* of Euripides at which an appreciative Gilbert Murray, most revered of Greek scholars, was in the audience.

27

A Widening Gulf

1950–1954

'A priest first and a schoolmaster second.'

THERE WERE TIMES when Wilkes thought that, despite all their advantages, the activities which the boys were encouraged to undertake might interfere with their success in the examinations whose demands he so much resented. He sometimes feared that these activities might, indeed, account for what he felt was an increasingly unsatisfactory attitude among the boys, particularly in the lower forms, towards their work in class. He had felt obliged to ask a meeting of Common Room to consider the causes of this.

> There are no doubt many causes [he thought], some beyond our control (e.g. the War, and in particular the early leaving age which removes boys before their minds are mature, so that there is no longer the influence of senior boys who have outgrown a childish attitude, seeping down into the school). Connected with it there is further, I believe, a less satisfactory relationship between boys and Common Room – it seems that there is a feeling in the school that they are in opposite camps. Moreover there is a tendency in the school to magnify the importance of the athlete and to depreciate that of the scholar and of the boy with scholarly or cultural interests.

By the end of his Wardenship, Wilkes could comfort himself with the reflection that most of these strictures were no longer valid. At games the school was much more successful: in 1952 and 1953 the cricket team won match after match under the inspiring direction of Ivor Gilliat, centuries being scored against Bradfield and Westminster by Dexter, and against Eastbourne by C.E.B.L. Carr and Leo Cooper. The First XV, coached by Guy Stewart-Morgan, scored a total of 95 points in three consecutive matches. Between 1951 and 1953 they won all school matches save one in each year. At Henley the Eight, coached by Llewellyn Jones, assisted briefly by Joe Bailey, won the Princess Elizabeth Cup in 1952 and reached the final of the Ladies' Plate the next year. The relationship between masters and boys had improved immeasurably; and the boys had a much more positive attitude towards their work: ten scholarships and exhibitions at Oxford and Cambridge were won in a single post-war year, one of them by J.C. Wolton, a boy with 'the most charm of all those charmers' who occupied the office of Senior Prefect in Wilkes's time.

Services in Chapel, and the religious life of the school generally, had much altered for the better, so Wilkes thought, in the last years of his Wardenship. He had been patient with the Chaplain he had inherited, Hugh Brodie – a gifted but lazy man not much liked in the school or by the Common Room wives – a High Churchman who would have liked to introduce into Chapel services a ritual that could well have offended many parents. Wilkes had subsequently shown great acumen in appointing the Revd R.C. Howard, later Headmaster of Hurstpierpoint, as Chaplain in 1943, and the Revd Charles Neate, 'Chrome Dome', a much admired, not to say beloved figure, as Chaplain in 1949.

Furthermore, Radley was now, the Warden felt sure, a happy school;*

---

*In a poll carried out by *The Petreian* in 1947, almost 90 per cent of the boys questioned said that they were happy. In that same poll, incidentally, 80 per cent of boys said that they would vote Conservative. True to this tradition, Radley boys generally had not objected to the reintroduction of gowns in July 1947, nor to the restoration of the Prefects' banners in Hall; and in the *Petreian* poll only a very small majority objected to the reintroduction of surplices. A later poll, conducted by *The Radleian* in 1957, confirmed the continuing conservatism of Radley boys: 82 per cent approved of fagging and 77 per cent of compulsory games; 67 per cent approved of compulsory weekday Chapel and 70 per cent of surplices. Only 27 per cent of boys would have preferred co-education. 80 per cent considered that the Conservative Government was 'morally justified in staying in office despite the change in public opinion', and 55 per cent would have suppressed the *Daily Worker*. In a similar poll conducted in 1993 there was less support for the Conservatives and considerably more for the Liberals. 41 per cent of those who answered the questionnaire supported the reintroduction of corporal punishment and 46 per cent of capital punishment. 90 per cent approved of sex before marriage.

it was also beginning to turn out young men who were to play a far more positive role in their country's life than those of impeccable manners and irreproachable unpretentiousness for which the school had been renowned in the early 1930s when Dennis Price, the actor, Lord Shackleton, the explorer and Labour minister, and Leslie Scarman, the Lord of Appeal in Ordinary, were rare exceptions to a general rule.

From Wilkes's Radley came – to name a few from widely different spheres of activity – Sir Philip Shelbourne, Chairman of Samuel Montagu and Company and later of Britoil; Sir Patrick Nairne, Permanent Secretary of the Department of Health and Social Security, and, later, Master of St Catherine's College, Oxford, and Chancellor of the University of Essex; General Sir Richard Worsley; Peter Cook, writer and entertainer; Michael Elliott, a brilliant theatrical producer who died young before the great fame predicted for him; Sir Donald Hawley, High Commissioner in Malaysia; Sir Peter Laurence, HM Ambassador in Ankara; Sir Derek Thomas, HM Ambassador in Rome; Lord Justice Stuart-Smith; Michael Westmacott, a member of the Mount Everest Expedition of 1953; Lord Carlisle of Bucklow, Secretary of State for Education and Science, 1979–81, and Sir David Craig, Marshal of the Royal Air Force, whose affection for his old school was reflected in the title he chose when created a peer, Lord Craig of Radley.

*

After the Warden's ordination on 4 May 1946, he felt increasingly drawn to pastoral work, though doubting that he was really qualified to undertake it. As he put it in a confidential letter to A.K. Boyd, he wanted to be 'a priest first and a schoolmaster second', and at the beginning of March 1948 he broached the proposition that he might hand over to the Sub-Warden some of his administrative work 'in favour of purely pastoral work'. This was not a solution that recommended itself to Boyd who could not believe that it would be possible for Morgan to take over much of the administrative burden while the Warden remained 'the source of policy'. 'The other danger,' Boyd continued in his response to Wilkes's letter, 'is, I think, even more serious.' This was the question of religious teaching and religious practice in the school.

By then various members of Common Room had for some time had misgivings about the High Church tradition which Hugh Brodie had favoured and wished to secure, even to elaborate, and which was close to the Warden's own heart. There was talk of a growing 'Protestant underworld' in Common Room.

'I don't know whether you know,' Boyd's letter went on, 'but it is undoubtedly true – that a gulf is forming between religious practice in the school and the feelings of those who are expected to co-operate in the religious teaching. The gulf is pretty wide already, and I have a fear that if you devoted yourself mainly to the chaplaincy and pastoral work this gulf would widen and widen.'

'I am disturbed by what you say,' Wilkes wrote in reply. 'Of course I have been conscious in a dim sort of way of the sort of "gulf" of which you speak: but have been, and still am, at a loss to understand its cause and nature . . . I am sadly aware that – no doubt largely through my fault – there is little support in Common Room for what we are trying to do, or at any rate for the way we are trying to do it.' There was certainly little support for what was described by one of his masters as the 'oddest enactment of his last years', the requirement of a passage of scripture being read and discussed at the beginning of the first period '*every day*, whoever was teaching and whatever the subject'.

There was another problem for the Warden also: 'I confess, too, to feeling stale – to finding it more and more irksome to do many of the ordinary tasks that fall to my lot, and to a longing for a new field, where perhaps drooping energies may revive.' He yearned for his new life as a priest; and, as he had been influenced in the past by Bishop Carey, Eastbourne's wartime Chaplain, who had lived in his lodgings for a year or so, so now and later he was persuaded to share the beliefs of Dr Kenneth Kirk, the High Church Bishop of Oxford, as well as those of Father Graham of the Mirfield Community, the Community of the Resurrection, which had been founded in the 1890s by the then Vicar of Radley, the Anglo-Catholic Charles Gore, first Principal of Pusey House, Oxford.

As time went by the Warden became sadly and increasingly conscious that his relationship with Common Room was far from as close as it had been in the earlier, happier days of Morgan's sub-wardenship. Morgan, whom he regarded with the most affectionate friendship – and who had often acted as mediator between the Warden and his Common Room critics – left in 1952 to become Headmaster of Michaelhouse, Natal, South Africa, having decided that he had been at Radley too long and was now too old to become Warden himself as he would have dearly liked to do, believing he could settle the differences which had lately arisen.

In the year of Morgan's departure, A.K. Boyd retired. R.L.C. Southam had died suddenly two years before; Hope and Rawlinson had both retired earlier; Wrinch was on the verge of leaving again. The Bursar, Charles Jenner, had left in 1949, much to the relief of several members of Common Room and, in particular, Vyvyan Hope who had declared in exasperation, 'This school is run by a fool and a knave; I leave you to decide which is which.'* Neither of Jenner's immediate successors stayed long. The new masters appointed had not yet found that confidence and spirit they were later to display, though this did not apply either to David Goldsmith, who joined the staff in 1950, or to Patrick Taylor, a scholar of Brasenose College and brilliant teacher of mathematics, who became Headmaster of Salisbury Cathedral Choir School.

The Warden left Radley for the parish of Hunslet in 1954, having courageously declined a middle-class parish in Finchley and having some years before failed to obtain the Headmastership of Shrewsbury for which he had been short-listed and to which he had been assured by one of the school governors he would almost certainly be appointed.

Before leaving for Hunslet he reiterated his belief that he had grown stale of late, 'stale and tired and rather slothful', and that a 'change of occupation [would] make it possible to recover some of the zest of the past'. He confessed that another factor influencing him to leave – apart from the feeling that it was 'better to get out before you're thrown out' – was 'the feeling of frustration induced by the present examination system and the demands of the Universities'.

Voicing a complaint shared by many headmasters both then and now, Wilkes wrote:

> Schools are to-day, it seems to me, in chains . . . I don't want boys of 16½ to 18½ to work desperately hard; I think those who do too often become the squeezed orange that is the despair of so many University dons. He should I believe work in a *leisurely* way – instead of being in a constant rush all the time: 'scholar' by derivation implies leisure. But what he *must* do is to be fastidious in what he undertakes . . . I've felt that the sort of training that counts and is being given in the workshops at Radley is potentially and often actually perhaps a better training than they are getting in the class-

---

*Hope's low opinion of the Warden was by then well known. A man who was in his Social in the 1940s wrote, 'I despised Wilkes only because my Social Tutor (Hope) despised him so blatantly, and we thought we must be loyal to the Social. Wilkes was always most kind and generous to me personally, and I now know better.'

room, not because the teachers in the classroom are less conscious of the desirability of accuracy, fastidiousness and thoroughness, but because all the time they have this examination incubus to compete with. 'A' level is the enemy of scholarship . . .

The Master of Marlborough, in a paper read to the Chaplains' Conference last September, gave a memorable description of the true ends of education at a public school. He spoke of three stages: – in the first we try to equip the boy with *knowledge*: in the second with *understanding*: and in the third to encourage him to learn *wisdom*: we give him the tools: then teach him to use them: then give him the opportunity of creating something with them. To learn, to criticize what he learns – and finally to relate what he has learnt and criticized to the whole of the environment. There is no time now for the last stage in our school life – and little for the second.

Years later, his duties as a parish priest over, and having retired to Herefordshire, Wilkes returned to the same theme: 'What then do I think is the true end, goal, purpose of education? . . . I believe that the right answer to this has been given by a Belgian Jewess, Simone Weil, in a remarkable essay. She says that the true end is to develop the capacity to *attend* . . . [By this] she meant to train us to give our *whole* attention to something (or somebody) other than ourselves . . . She went on to say that what we study, attend to, is relatively unimportant, so long as the subject (or rather this object of our attention) makes the maximum demands on us.' Wilkes felt that modern education, geared as it was to the demands of the examination system, made the realization of this ideal impossible; and he had, he confessed, with these demands imposed upon him, given up hope of making Radley the school he would have liked to see it become.

The school which he had helped to make was, however, a far more successful and well-regarded place than his apparent disappointment led him to suppose. Radley's historian, A.K. Boyd, in his reflective retirement expressed the opinion that John Wilkes was the best Warden that Radley had had to that date. 'In spite of the wear and tear and stress imposed on subordinates by service under an experimental-ist of inexhaustible energy,' Boyd wrote eight years after Wilkes's departure,

I believe that the period will finally be accounted the second great age of Radley . . . It had extraordinary affinities with the days of Sewell (with the important difference that Wilkes had no streak of the charlatan in him) . . . The Philistinism of the Radley boy, which had dwindled and died in the Ferguson era, was nailed in its coffin . . . But the tendency to treat the school as a university had one serious adverse effect; while the advance in scholarship in the more intellectual spheres was indeed remarkable, Wilkes had little understanding of the mind of the common boy and indeed little interest in it; most of the advance in the standards of work among the normal and sub-normal gained under Ferguson was allowed to fall away.

One of his former House Prefects, Jeremy Ward, added his tribute to the 'civilizing influence' which Wilkes had had upon the school in the late 1940s and early 1950s when the masters in charge of all eight Socials came to the end of their time as Social Tutors and were replaced by younger men better able to deal with such bullying as had infected certain Socials since the war. By the time Wilkes left the school bullying was not, of course, extinct – his own son was badly bullied and tied to a table in his social hall – but it was as uncommon as it had been in the late 1930s.

The Radley handed over to his successor was well described in a Ministry of Education report which, based upon an inspection of the school carried out a few months after his departure, was much more complimentary about Radley than the report which had been made after his arrival. The report of February and March 1955 paid tribute to John Wilkes's 'devotion and leadership' in guiding Radley in a period 'largely taken up with difficulties, common to all schools, caused by the war and its aftermath'.

He had inherited a school of 400 boys and, after a fall in numbers to 338 during the war, had bequeathed one of 429 to his successor. The academic standards of the school had risen markedly during the seventeen years of his Wardenship. 'Radley's record in winning open awards at the universities in the last ten years is very satisfactory,' the Inspectors reported, 'and reflects both on the ability of the boys and the skill of their teachers. In this period 53 awards have been gained, 22 at Oxford and 31 at Cambridge. The distribution is as follows: classics 19, history 12, mathematics 8, science 4, music 4, modern languages 2, English 1. In addition two boys gained a Dreyer Exhibition at Lincoln College, Oxford, and one a Rustat Exhibition at Jesus College, Cambridge.'

The Inspectors had some mild criticism to make of the standard of work and 'a certain absence of stimulating and incisive teaching' in the lower forms; but in general the masters – whom the Inspectors did not name – were commended as being thorough and stimulating, special praise being accorded to the senior English master (P.D.L. Way) who

60. Drawings by Anthony Hill of Radley in the 1930s

a. School

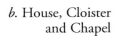

b. House, Cloister and Chapel

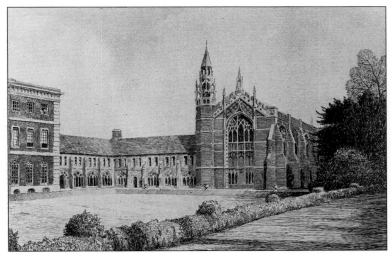

c. Dormitory Clump with Memorial Arch on the left and Croome's Arch and Tower on the right

61. School in 1926, by then no longer used for classes but for assemblies and roll-calls at
start of term. The antlers and animal skulls on the wall were presented to the school by
Major Chauncy Stigand, an Old Radleian, colonial administrator and big-game hunter,
who was Governor of the Upper Nile Province in 1916 and was killed in action in the
Sudan against the Ahiab tribe, 1919

62. The Revd J.C. Vaughan Wilkes, Warden 1937–54

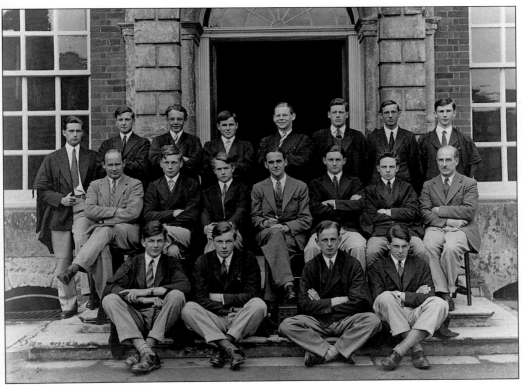

63. The Radley College Amateur Dramatic Society, 1937. Charles Wrinch is in the centre of the middle row. On his far left is A.C. Rawlinson, assistant master 1921–47; and on his far right A.A.M. Gardiner, assistant master from 1930 and Social Tutor 1945–60

64. The Radley Eight winning the Ladies' Plate in 1938, beating Pembroke College, Cambridge, in the Final by 1¼ lengths. The time of 6 mins. 56 secs. was two seconds faster than that of the winning London crew in the Grand. Four members of the Radley crew were killed in the War: J.W. Arkell (MC, Major, Indian Army), C.D.F. Kaye (Pilot Officer, RAF), G.E. Chandler (Pilot Officer, RAF) and P.L. Fanning (Captain, Coldstream Guards). The other members of the crew were C.H. Gray, D.H. Richards, E.M. Sturges, J.D. Eveleigh and D.E.G. Beazley

Training for All at Radley

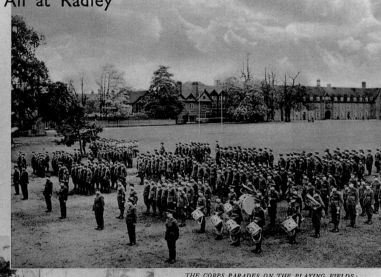

EVERY boy at Radley receives some form of military training from his first term, though he does not come on to the establishment of the Corps till he is fifteen. Most boys get their Certificate " A " before they are seventeen and thus qualify to act as instructors for their last year at school. In addition to this important work, the senior boys may specialise in either the Air or Signalling Sections. The Corps is fortunate in having well-equipped premises and 600 acres of ground around the College suitable for all kinds of training. About fifty of the senior boys are members of the Home Guard and provide a patrol for duty every night.

THE CORPS PARADES ON THE PLAYING FIELDS:
At the back on the left can be seen the small contingent of boys under fifteen who are not quite old enough to be in the Corps.

SIGNALLERS AT WORK: Cadets interested in this branch of the Corps training have ample opportunity and equipment to become efficient. In these pictures cadets are using short-wave radio and a Morse daylight lamp.

COATS OFF : Field work includes digging trenches for use as a section post. The lance-corporal stands guard and the sergeant makes notes.

65. 'Training for All at Radley', a page from the *Illustrated London News*,
8 November 1940, showing the Corps on parade,
signallers at work and boys digging trenches

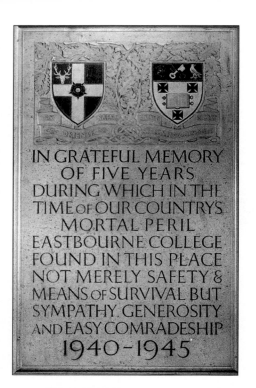

IN GRATEFUL MEMORY
OF FIVE YEARS
DURING WHICH IN THE
TIME of OUR COUNTRYS
MORTAL PERIL
EASTBOURNE COLLEGE
FOUND IN THIS PLACE
NOT MERELY SAFETY &
MEANS of SURVIVAL BUT
SYMPATHY. GENEROSITY
AND EASY COMRADESHIP
1940-1945

66. A plaque in the Cloisters
commemorating Eastbourne College's
exile at Radley, 1940–5

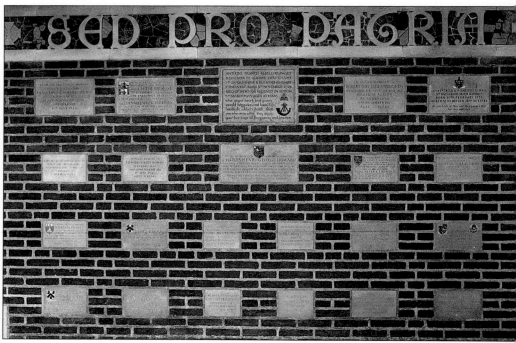

67. Tablets in the Cloisters commemorating some of the Old Radleians who lost their
lives in the Second World War, including the Earl of Suffolk and Berkshire, GC, and
A.F.M. Paget, son of General Sir Bernard Paget, who was awarded the Croix de Guerre
and the DSO at the age of twenty-one

68. Princess Elizabeth visits Radley for the school's centenary, 9 June 1947.
She is accompanied by Warden Wilkes. Behind them is the Very Revd E.L. Henderson,
Dean of Salisbury and Chairman of the Radley Council, with the Warden's wife,
Joan, daughter of the Very Revd C.A. Alington, Headmaster of Eton 1916–33

69. Field Marshal Viscount Montgomery inspecting the Corps on 17 June 1947 with the
Commanding Officer Major, later Lieutenant-Colonel Ranulph Waye, an assistant master
at Radley from 1933 and Social Tutor 1948–62. Behind Waye is Captain R.L.C. Southam,
assistant master from 1931 and Social Tutor 1938–50. Behind Southam are
Dean Henderson and Warden Wilkes. The four cadets nearest to the camera are
C.H. Rogers-Coltman (a farmer and High Sheriff of Shropshire), F.M. Godfrey
(chemical engineer), M.E. Found (member of Lloyds) and C.E.W. Saunders
(farmer and Deputy-Lieutenant of Cambridgeshire). The Sergeant standing to
attention in front of them is G.F.B. Birdwood (surgeon)

70. Drawing of Shop by Bryan de Grineau in the *Illustrated London News*, 1947

71. Radley College Beagles, 1949

had returned to the school in 1952, to the three history masters (R.T. King, J.V.P. Thompson and Paul Crowson, all of them Social Tutors), to the veteran classics master (T.E.E. Cocks), and to N.R. Eyres and L.P.E. Taylor of the mathematics department, in which 'great progress had been made since 1937'. These and other Radley masters 'handled their classes with good humour and seemed to be on excellent terms with them'.

Their basic salaries were not high at £340 a year (compared with £220 a year in 1936), rising by annual increments of £15 for five years and thereafter £25 to £620 after fifteen years' service; but allowances were 'numerous', a married Social Tutor, for example, having an additional salary of £240, a messing allowance of £100, servants' allowance of £160 and entertainment allowance of £50, as well as free lodging, fuel, light and laundry.

As for their pupils: the present Radleian 'appeared to be a boy with a natural friendliness and courtesy, capable of expressing his opinions with point and vivacity and in no way limited in his interests to his own community'. His relations with his school's 'devoted staff' were marked by friendliness and mutual respect 'in a community that sets value on these things'. There were numerous opportunities to pursue intellectual and artistic interests outside the classroom; while the school's reputation for music teaching and musical and choral performances remained deservedly high.*

'School and Social life seems to be nicely balanced,' the Inspectors' report concluded. 'Within the Social the boy can claim a due measure of privacy and live on close terms with his fellows in a small community: the Sunday evening custom of "socializing" in the Tutors' rooms epitomizes this close relationship.† The vitality of the boys and the

---

*In a report written in 1944, Wilkes had suggested, 'The three things Radley does best at present are rowing, the drama and music. It would be foolish not to continue to aim at high standards in these . . . I believe myself that Music and Drama are of more value "educationally" than most, if not all, subjects – especially for boys who are not scholars by nature.'

†'Socializing' took various forms. Sometimes it was a kind of *conversazione*; at others, plays or books were read or games were played: 'We had socializing with Borgnis [the Succentor] this evening,' wrote Martin Blake in his diary, 'and acted the best sharards [charades] I have ever participated in.' Prized invitations were those to 'socialize' with Ivor Gilliat, the cricket coach and history master, who provided not only excellent food but also entertained his young guests to songs and loud, inexpert piano playing.

environment in which they live here suggest that there need be no incompatibility between a rich and interesting school life and exacting standards in the classroom. In striving towards a more complete fusion of the two, Radley will continue to add to its considerable reputation.'

28

Another Etonian
1954

'The school was a bit below par.'

THE 1950S WERE said to be a bad time for recruiting good men for responsible posts, the war having taken its toll of some of the best and kept others from obtaining the experience they might otherwise have enjoyed. If this were indeed so, it seems not to have applied to the search for headmasters, as several public schools discovered. In 1952 Thomas Garnett left Charterhouse for Marlborough where he put into practice his belief that 'the most important of a headmaster's tasks' is choosing good assistant masters and where no fewer than ten of his 1957 Common Room were to become headmasters themselves. These included Donald Wright at Shrewsbury, John Sharp at Rossall, Ian Beer at Ellesmere, Lancing and Harrow, and Dennis Silk at Radley.

The year after Garnett went to Marlborough a man who was also to have a profound influence on that school, John Dancy, left Winchester to become Head Master of Lancing. Instructed to improve Lancing's academic standards, he soon showed himself determined to do far more than that. An ambitious, occasionally acerbic and often impatient man in his early thirties, whose impatience may well have been exacerbated by the polio which left him with a limp and intermittent pain, Dancy was a Wykehamist and graduate of New College. Before returning to teach at Winchester, he had been a lecturer in classics at Wadham. He was not a comfortable man to work under. Certainly one of Lancing's older assistant masters, Basil Handford, the school's historian, did not find him so:

> Doubtless Lancing seemed too easy-going and informal after Winchester . . . Consequently he reintroduced a formality and authoritarianism which was on its way out. Thus masters were required to wear gowns at High Table in Hall; the informal open day was replaced by a formal speech day and prize-giving, at which the masters were required to sit behind the Head Master . . . academically robed . . . At the first, during his speech, he remarked with a smile that he hoped to teach the old dogs some new tricks; the audience laughed and the masters muttered about arrogance.

Nine of these masters were dismissed or resigned in the first year. The rest were subsequently told that sixty was the retirement age. There was talk of 'Dancy's Inferno'. Extensive changes were made in the curriculum; numerical marks and form orders – those bugbears condemned by A.K. Boyd at Radley in the early 1930s – were reintroduced; fees were increased while automatic subsidies for the sons of clergy were abolished; and the standard of Common Entrance was raised.

In 1961 John Dancy left to become Master of Marlborough; but there could be no doubt that, in the years he had been at Lancing, he had succeeded in making it both a more rigorous and more successful school, and with that success he had himself become a less rigorous and more companionable man. His staff's initial repugnance had been transformed into a wary respect.

At Bradfield also, a classical scholar in his thirties had helped to raise intellectual standards while at the same time increasing both numbers and fees – in Bradfield's case from 377 to 444 and from £284 to £711. This was Anthony Chenevix-Trench, formerly a housemaster at Shrewsbury where he himself had been at school, and a prisoner of war of the Japanese from 1942 to 1945. Small in stature, Chenevix-Trench could be as formidable as Dancy, but in general had a more relaxed and easy-going manner. The staff, according to an appreciation of him in the *Bradfield School Chronicle* on his departure to be Headmaster of Eton in 1963, found him 'wonderfully approachable'.

At Oundle, where Dick Knight became Headmaster in 1956, the problem was not so much to make an easy-going school more disciplined – as Dancy had seen his duty to be at Lancing – but to make a stiffly regimented school less tightly structured. Knight had been on the staff at Marlborough since 1945, and, apart from Garnett, who was a few months his senior, he was the oldest of the headmasters appointed in the 1950s so far mentioned in this chapter. There were those, indeed, who considered forty-two to be rather too old to tackle so demanding a new career – John Ounsted had become Headmaster of Leighton Park School in 1948 before he was thirty. But, once installed at Oundle, Knight dispelled all doubts as to his capabilities. He set to work with a will, reforming the curriculum and widening the scope of sixth-form work, modifying rules about dress and compulsory chapel, allowing senior boys to choose whether or not to join the Combined Cadet Force, abolishing fagging and much reducing the number of prefects' beatings.

He would have liked to do more; but there was a limit to how much could be done in a school so bound to the traditions and ethos which that great and zealous Headmaster from 1892 to 1922, F.W. Sanderson, had imposed upon it. Knight was 'delightful to work with', commented one of his staff after he had left Oundle to become Headmaster of Monkton Combe in 1968. 'He raised academic standards and abolished a lot of pettifogging rules. But the school was difficult to handle and he lacked that streak of ruthlessness that every headmaster should have.'

Ruthlessness he may have lacked; but it could not be denied that Knight guided Oundle's fortunes through difficult times with remarkable success. So, too, did John Carleton guide those of Westminster where he became Head Master the year after Knight went to Oundle. An astute and kindly man, Carleton was, as Westminster's historian suggested, ideally suited to meet the challenges of the times. His 'benign and avuncular presence soothed passions that a more overtly managing Head Master might well have inflamed . . . His own sense of the place had been fashioned before the war, and radical policies were neither needed nor expected.'

Carleton's predecessor at Westminster was Walter Hamilton who, when he left to succeed Sir Arthur fforde at Rugby in 1957, was the first Head Master of Westminster ever to have left the hallowed precincts of Dean's Yard to become headmaster of another school. He was also the first man for a quarter of a century to be appointed Headmaster of Rugby who was not himself an Old Rugbeian. In fact, as one Old Rugbeian put it, 'it must be the first time they have appointed the right man since Arnold.' Hamilton had doubts about going to Rugby, but these had been dispelled by Sir Robert Birley, the

Old Rugbeian Headmaster of Eton, whom Hamilton had known well when serving as Wilkes's successor as Master-in-College.

Hamilton proved to be all that Birley had hoped for Rugby, a lucid and inspiring teacher, a remarkably effective preacher, humorous, humane and, when occasion demanded, unnervingly formidable. He was not made welcome on arrival: greeted with slogans such as 'go back to Westminster, Wally', and with the chapel lectern being removed to the middle of the School Close draped in lavatory paper, he had also been outraged at the weekly chapel practice – 'at which behaviour had been notoriously bad' – to hear all the hymn books 'banged shut in concerted unison'. Walter Hamilton's 'roar of disapproval shocked seven hundred boys into stunned silence'. By the time he left Rugby to become Master of Magdalene College, Cambridge, such behaviour had become almost unthinkable.

*

These six men, Garnett, Dancy, Chenevix-Trench, Knight, Carleton and Hamilton, were just a few of those, all distinguished in their different ways, who were appointed to headmasterships of public schools in the 1950s. A seventh was the highly respected Frank Fisher, son of the Archbishop of Canterbury and Headmaster of Repton, who was appointed Warden of St Edward's in 1954 and became Master of Wellington in 1966.* An eighth was appointed Warden of Radley in 1954. At forty-six he was older than all of them and doubts were expressed both at the time and subsequently that his appointment came too late in a career which had involved six years of arduous war service.

This man was Wyndham Macbeth Moir Milligan. The son of a London doctor of Scottish Presbyterian descent, he had been to

---

*Frank Fisher was largely instrumental in forming the 'Rugby Group', an association of broadly similar public schools founded to exchange ideas, pool knowledge and discuss common problems. There were originally fourteen schools but the numbers expanded as a headmaster of one of these schools moved to one which was not in the group and brought his new school into it. Headmasters and bursars meet three times a year; but other members of their respective staffs, such as departmental heads and senior housemasters, also have meetings. The schools which are now members of the Rugby Group are Bradfield, Charterhouse, Cheltenham, Clifton, Haileybury, Harrow, Malvern, Monkton Combe, Oundle, Radley, Repton, Rugby, St Edward's, Shrewsbury, Stowe, Uppingham, Wellington and Winchester.

Sherborne and Caius College, Cambridge, where he had read medicine before changing to classics and gaining a double first. Appointed an assistant master at Eton in 1932, he had become a highly successful housemaster there. During the Second World War he served with distinction as a major in the Scots Guards. The award of the MBE in 1945 was followed by that of the Territorial Decoration in 1947. He was married to an accomplished musician, Helen Cassavetti. They had two sons and two daughters and were to have another son at Radley. He gave his recreations in *Who's Who* as shooting, tennis and rackets, his clubs as the Guards and the Bath, both of them establishments of pronounced Conservative leanings.

A good-looking, well-dressed man of great charm, it was considered that he would exercise that charm to good effect upon parents as well as preparatory school headmasters and that his easy manner and social assurance would heal the rifts between Warden and Common Room which had opened up during his predecessor's last months in office when it had become increasingly obvious that John Wilkes was anxious to start another life. It was also hoped that Milligan was the man to carry out that reformation, rationalization and consolidation which the Radley Council felt the school now needed.

The suggestion that he should stand for the Wardenship of Radley had come to Milligan 'out of the blue', to use his own words, from Sir George Mallaby. His candidature had been warmly supported by another member of the Council, an Old Radleian, John Harvey, a former fellow officer in the Scots Guards, who had argued strongly against the proposition that the last thing Radley needed was yet another Eton master who might turn Radley into a second-rate version of that school. When, after being interviewed, Milligan was offered the post, he accepted it without much hesitation. He had been very happy at Eton, where he had got to know well the parents of all the boys in his house, several of them former Guards officers like himself, and had gone to stay with some of them in the holidays from time to time. But he is, so he says himself, the sort of person who, once he has chosen a career, wants to get to the top of it. To become Warden of Radley, therefore, was an opportunity of advancement he did not want to turn down. Yet, having accepted the appointment, he admitted to feeling rather nervous and apprehensive.

When he took his wife to see the house in which they were to live at Radley, his first reaction was of profound disappointment. It was not at all an attractive house, he thought; besides, it was in 'a terrible state' inside. 'As we came out,' he said, 'we almost sat down and cried on the doorstep.' There were other misgivings to come.

The boys could not have been more friendly and helpful. They were 'very well-mannered', much like the 'better sort of Etonians in that kind of way'. But not all the masters were as welcoming. There had been a short interregnum between Wilkes's departure and Milligan's arrival and, during this interregnum, Eason as Sub-Warden had been in charge. There was a feeling that 'the school was a bit below par'. It might have been taken as a reflection on these faltering standards that, whereas in the list of schools obtaining scholarships and exhibitions at Oxford and Cambridge in 1953–4 published in the *Oxford Magazine* Radley comes quite high on the list, on a par with Rugby, Shrewsbury and Ampleforth, and above Sherborne, Stowe, Repton and Wellington; in the list published the next year Radley does not appear at all.

Among the members of Common Room who thought Milligan was not the right man to restore the school's vitality and academic standing, was the formidable figure of Ivor Gilliat, still an inveterate party-giver, a man with much influence among other members of Common Room and one who – Milligan felt with some justification – strongly inculcated his own views, enthusiasms and prejudices in the boys he taught and entertained.

Charles Wrinch retired early upon Milligan's arrival, telling him 'in his most delightful way' that he 'couldn't face another Warden'; and Milligan could not but regret that Gilliat had decided not to go too. As it was, Gilliat remained at Radley until 1963, 'a real problem', as the Warden described him, 'a great thorn' in his side, a 'difficulty' he had been warned about before coming to Radley. To an observation made to him in later years that Ivor Gilliat had a very strong and persuasive personality and that he must have been a burdensome character to contend with Milligan replied with deep feeling, 'Oh, my goodness, yes!' Much trouble would have been avoided, so several members of Common Room thought at the time, if Milligan had directly confronted Gilliat 'with the Warden's full authority'.

The Warden was thankful at least that the Bursar, K.W. Ross-Hurst, a former lieutenant-colonel in the Gurkha Rifles, was a person after his own heart, a small, tough man, rather like a Gurkha himself, with whom he could escape from the cares of his office on shooting expeditions in the Park. When Ross-Hurst died, Milligan paid him tribute in *The Radleian* in a moving poem, the first verse to be contributed to the magazine by a Warden since Selwyn's time. It was a tribute to a friend not to a bursar, and rightly so, since, as a member of the Radley Council was later to observe, 'Ross-Hurst was a thoroughly nice man, [but] it has to be said he was not a good bursar. His grasp of financial matters was distinctly limited . . . This weakness unfortunately served to compound the fact that, for all his other merits – and I liked him and think on the whole he was a good Warden – financial judgement was not one of Milligan's strong points either.'

Indeed, it was not too much to say that Milligan had 'no financial sense at all. If the bank was prepared to lend money, that was good enough for him: he wasn't too concerned about how to repay it.' Building was begun before money was available to pay for it; fees paid in advance were being appropriated and spent before the boys arrived at the school; Radley was sliding ever deeper into debt. The Chairman of the Council, Admiral Sir Guy Russell, asked a younger colleague more expert in financial matters than himself what he thought of the school's accounts. 'As far as I am concerned, Mr Chairman, the accounts are as clear as mud.' According to another member of Council, the 'combination of Milligan and Ross-Hurst was nearly disastrous for Radley'.

Warden Milligan's relations with the Council were predictably never satisfactory. He had got on well with the Chairman, Mallaby, and even better with Lord Hodson, the Old Cheltonian Lord Justice of Appeal who succeeded Mallaby in 1957. Hodson was, indeed, a 'wonderful man', 'a terribly nice chap'. But there were certain other members of the Council whom Milligan thought should not have been appointed to it. 'They weren't very helpful,' he considered, 'and weren't really interested' in the school. They 'never worried' him, but he always felt that he did not have their full support. He readily conceded that this was his fault quite as much as, if not more than, theirs, since, having been appointed to run the school, he 'intended to run it without reference to them'. 'I don't suppose I was ever very popular with the Council,' he admitted, 'because I really didn't consult them . . . and they didn't know what I was doing.' A member of Council confirmed that this was certainly so. The relationship between Warden and Council was friendly enough but the Council's opinion was not sought 'on anything the Warden had decided to do. He didn't believe they had anything to offer anyway.'

To help him decide what needed to be done at Radley, the Warden turned instead to a team of Ministry of Education Inspectors soon after his installation as Warden. These Inspectors made one suggestion which he immediately seized upon as an opportunity both to exercise his undoubted organizational talents and to make life more rewarding for the younger boys in the school.

29

A Change of Direction
1954–1968

'Their time was increasingly regimented.'

THE INSPECTORS' GENERALLY favourable comments on the school were offset by criticism of the teaching of the lower forms. Milligan immediately set about the task of answering the Inspectors' complaints: the teaching of these lower forms was in future to be more closely subjected to syllabuses; there were to be five morning lessons instead of four, while time spent on out-of-form activities was to be curtailed; the workshops were to be used for specific purposes by specific boys and not – as appeared to the new Warden to have been the case during Wilkes's regime – as a means of indulging a hobby or seeking some kind of unspecified fulfilment. Junior College Plays were not encouraged and after 1961 they lapsed altogether; the early afternoon break from half-past twelve to half-past one was abolished; the boys' industry and progress were to be recorded by masters on report cards which were to be submitted every fortnight to the Warden who was to set a monthly Latin Grammar paper for all boys in forms working for their O levels. Masters were encouraged to bring to the Warden's direct notice any case of idleness or indiscipline, much to the annoyance of Social Tutors who felt bypassed.

While all boys were thus required to work harder, the junior boys were allowed more time to do so by a simultaneous reduction in their age-old duties as fags. They were also spared much of the bullying at

the hands of their immediate seniors who, more actively and purpose-
fully occupied than in the past, had little leisure to indulge in practices
which had been all too common in recent years. In short Milligan was
bent upon providing a programme of professionally efficient teaching
within a 'framework of efficient order'.

The Warden's immediate reforms and methods were not, of course,
universally welcomed in Common Room. Social Tutors resented his
encouraging assistant masters to come to him rather than to them with
complaints about boys in their Socials. They objected to what they saw
as his gathering of power into his own hands; his treatment of Radley
almost as though it were a preparatory school which he had bought, or
his house at Eton or even a company of the Scots Guards; his reluctance to allow the senior boys the freedoms and responsibilities they
had enjoyed under his predecessor. 'Senior boys, as well as the juniors,
found that their industry was liable to detailed scrutiny from the
Warden,' wrote one of his more experienced Social Tutors, Paul
Crowson, who had come to Radley in 1945 and was to be described by
Milligan's successor as the 'greatest schoolmaster' he had ever known.

> Their time was increasingly regimented, their creative activities, though
> never forbidden, ran counter to a current of official displeasure ... The pre-
> dominant trend of policy showed itself among School Prefects and House
> Prefects. Of them it had once been said: 'A housemaster who thinks that he
> runs his House is wrong; either it is run by his prefects or it is not run at
> all.' This responsible order of near adults felt increasingly that their duties
> were reduced to nursemaiding and to the keeping of lists. Warden Milligan
> was trading an amelioration of the junior lot for an impoverishment of the
> senior; his achievement meant that the juniors had, on the whole, a better
> deal and an easier time and that the post-O-level seniors were increasingly
> restless, anxious to leave and loath to undertake responsibility for their
> community.

Paul Crowson disagreed with the then educational orthodoxy
which held that life must be made as pleasant as reasonably possible
for the younger child in the tenderest of his formative years. He
himself argued that schoolboys, and, indeed, people in general, are
most happy when experience indicates that the present is better than
the past and that the future will be better still. He suggested that whatever may have been the limitations of Radley when he joined the staff
– and however unpleasant life may have been for the newcomer – with
every term, 'and notwithstanding puberty, there came amelioration,

until for the senior boy the combination of intellectual stimulus, athletic excitement and very wide responsibility made up so interesting a life that boys were in no hurry to leave but stayed on well beyond academic necessity until they were 18½ or 19'.

Unfortunately the attitudes of mind prevalent amongst the older boys at public schools in the mid-1950s and 1960s – not to mention the increasing pressure of public examination results and their importance in university entrance – combined to dissuade them from seeking positions of authority at school. Warden Milligan was well aware of these pressures and attitudes. So were the young masters who were appointed to the staff in the fourteen years he spent at Radley. Among these were Hamish Aird and David Hardy, both of whom had a high regard for him. 'I remember those times as being very good fun,' Hamish Aird recalled in 1996: 'lots of young, lively colleagues; and the older members of Common Room seemed remarkably friendly and welcoming. To the young dons Wyndham [Milligan] was a warm father-figure whom we were fond of. Not at all distant. He came into Common Room every evening for a gin and mixed and informal conversation . . . The boys were affable and ready to work; but exams weren't regarded as being as important as now.'

'As a new don at Radley,' David Hardy added, 'I found Milligan most supportive and friendly . . . It was one of his principles never to praise anyone verbally in public but it was astonishing how much he knew and noticed of what one did, and a really thoughtful and appreciative letter would always appear in one's pigeon-hole.'

In an interview he gave after his retirement, Milligan identified as his principal benefaction to the school during these years the high quality of the men he brought to teach there. Michael Meredith, an inspiring English teacher who became housemaster at Eton, and Jeremy Tatum, the polymath head of physics, who left for the University of British Columbia, both came to Radley in his time. In 1960 came R.L. Howard, a fine oarsman who was to do so much for Radley rowing; while the next year Christopher Turner, who had been appointed by Wilkes and bequeathed a strong boat club to Howard, left Radley to become Senior Classics Master at Charterhouse, then Headmaster of Dean Close School, Cheltenham, and, after that, Headmaster of Stowe.

Several other masters, appointed by Milligan, also went on eventually to become headmasters. Among these were David Skipper (Ellesmere, later Merchant Taylors'), Peter Thomson (Emanuel),

Simon Langdale (Eastbourne, later Shrewsbury), John Moore (King's, Worcester), Anthony Hudson (Pangbourne), Malcolm Robinson (Queen's, Taunton, and Abbotsholme), Graham Garrett (Wellingborough), J.H.F. Doulton (Elizabeth College, Guernsey), Brian Wilson (Campbell College, Belfast), John Evans (Strode's School, Egham) and Richard Morgan (Cheltenham). James Batten, the barrister and Rugby coach, so many of whose pupils became judges and QCs, left after fifteen years at Radley to be Headmaster of King's, Taunton.

When masters departed, the Warden, while sorry to lose them, readily accepted that it was in their interests to seek advancement elsewhere. They were more than adequately replaced, Milligan justifiably priding himself on having an exceptional ability to 'spot winners', an ability he attributed, as much else in his career, to his army experiences.

The salaries offered to these men, increased somewhat of late, still compared unfavourably, however, with those to be earned at many of the schools from which they came or to which they went. Moreover, while Radley had an enviable stock of housing, remuneration in kind, which had formerly constituted so large a part of assistant masters' salaries, was much reduced; so were allowances paid for specialized work such as that undertaken by Social Tutors, while pensions were totally inadequate. The increases in the salary scales were, therefore, illusory rather than real, particularly so because of the income tax which had to be paid on the cash salaries and which remuneration in kind escaped. Furthermore, salaries were paid two months in arrears. A master who came to Radley in 1959 at the age of twenty-two received his first pay cheque for the first two months of the academic year on 1 November. It was for £64 (£94 less £30 for accommodation and food). Even when he became a Social Tutor in 1968 his basic salary had only just reached £1,000 a year. Salaries and allowances, rarely a bone of contention in the past, thus became one now.

So also did the Warden's attitude towards certain extra-curricular activities. This did not apply to music in which he, like his wife, was deeply interested. In 1959 Donald Paine was appointed Precentor and W.H.C. Langrish Succentor in succession to Standish Lester. Soon afterwards, the Revd Charles Neate, who had resigned as Chaplain in 1958 to become vicar of a parish in Bournemouth, returned to Radley as Sub-Warden, while a young man with strong liturgical tastes, Michael Jenkins, later became Chaplain. These four men, with the Warden's encouragement, brought congregational singing in Chapel to a pitch of excellence it had not reached since the heydays of Warden

Ferguson, while many of those who studied and practised music under Donald Paine found the first stirrings of a lifelong enthusiasm. Some became professional musicians of exceptional gifts, among them Michael Dussek, Richard Deakin, the violinist, David Pountney, Director of Productions at the English National Opera and Robert King, conductor and harpsichordist, founder of The King's Consort and biographer of Henry Purcell.

While Warden Milligan looked with a constantly benevolent eye upon music at Radley, and upon the concerts given by the College Music Society in association with St Helen's School, Abingdon, he did not do so upon that other activity, less orderly and more experimental, which Warden Wilkes had believed to be, with music, an art in which Radley could take pride in excelling. John Wilkes had gone out of his way to encourage the production of plays, making time to attend their performances, regularly writing to Kenneth Boyd and Charles Wrinch to congratulate them on their productions and going to the dress rehearsal of Peter Way's production of *The Alchemist* only hours before leaving Radley for the last time. Warden Milligan by contrast seemed to regard schoolboy interest in the theatre with a kind of horror and, when he could, found excuses for not attending schoolboy productions, although he did sanction the formation, under the supervision of a master, Kenneth Brookman, of a film society which not only held showings of films but also had some success in making them: one of these, a film about the First Eight, being shown on Independent Television, another, *Reflections on the 139th Psalm*, winning a special prize from the British Film Institute. A leading member of the Film Society was Michael Reeves who became a highly original film maker and would, no doubt, have become one of the industry's most successful directors had he not died at the age of twenty-six soon after completing his last film, *Witchfinder General*.

Tolerant though he was of the activities of the Film Society, the Warden could never extend similar understanding to drama, despite the fine performances given in these years under the direction of Peter Way and James Batten, notably of *Edward II*, *Our Town* and *Hamlet*, and such productions of Greek plays as Brian Wilson's of the *Bacchae* of Euripides. A question addressed to the Warden as to whether or not he thought acting and the productions of plays had a useful place in an adolescent's education was met with an emphatic '*No!*'

*

Much as he was liked by the younger dons, Milligan did not enjoy an untroubled relationship with some senior members of Common Room. His attitude of mind did not appeal, for example, to Llewellyn Jones who used to quarrel with him 'right, left and centre'; while A.A.M. Gardiner, a shy, abrupt, though highly regarded Social Tutor, thought that he would not have been given a Social had he not already had one when Milligan arrived. James Batten, though always grateful to the Warden for making him his first appointment and for listening so patiently to his ideas, often, so he says, 'disagreed with his style of leadership and his decisions'.

As with the Council, so with a large proportion of Old Radleians – many of them Gilliat's friends or supporters – his relations were not of the best. Unlike his successor, who took great care to win their approval, he regarded them without enthusiasm and in their company he was ill at ease, even gauche, a figure far removed in its false *bonhomie* from the maestro of the cocktail party, moving with practised grace from group to group with just the right words and manners for each.

Even his sternest critics who complained of his urbane, almost effusive manner – which others thought was part of his charm and which gave rise to the epithet by which the boys knew him amongst themselves – could not deny that Milligan was extremely hard-working, conscientious, kind and good-natured, taking the trouble to know the Christian names not only of the boys but also – in marked contrast to John Wilkes – of the domestic staff and the gardeners, and going out of his way to be friendly to the people of Radley village. He was generous with his time and understanding with boys in distress; and over these and, indeed, over boys in general he exercised a strong personal influence.

He was never afraid of taking unpopular decisions, some of which greatly eased the path for his successor. For example, he closed down the Radley Club in Wapping which had been founded in 1910 as part of the Radley Mission – a necessary move, he considered, in view of the current decline in public order – and channelled the social work formerly done there into similar work in the Radley area. For the same reason he stopped the traditional outing of the whole school to Henley Regatta where the misbehaviour of some boys, while not so disgraceful as it had been on occasions in the late 1940s, remained inexcusable and, when reported in the press, did much damage to the school's reputation.

At the beginning of his term of office he had received complaints about the behaviour of rival groups of high-spirited Radleians and Etonians in what was described in the *Daily Express* as 'a fairground brawl'. According to the gossip columnist, 'William Hickey', the brawl was provoked by Eton: 'Trouble between the two schools started on opening day when Eton boys (who were not required to wear their school colours) started knocking off the jazzy cerise-and-white boaters worn by their rivals.'

'Eton made an umbrella charge at the Radley boaters, in revenge for an attack upon them last time they played cricket at Radley,' 'Tanfield's Diary' reported in the *Daily Mail* the next day. '"It was a right do," said one of the attendants at the fairground where battle was joined. "Everyone forgot the dodgems. They preferred watching the young gentlemen."'

Milligan also ended the All Saints' Day gathering which, in the words of one of his staff, 'had been an Old Radleian occasion for as long as anyone could remember, but it had become a stag party with more "sluicing" *chez* Ivor Gilliat than was proper in a school.' Milligan carried the unpopularity of ending it, in order that, as Paul Crowson says, 'his successor could develop an alternative'.

Towards the end of his time at Radley Milligan's grip on the school began to falter as his mind became occupied with other matters and his hip, shortly to be replaced, gave him increasing pain, suffered characteristically without complaint.

After his retirement various criticisms of his regime were privately expressed, as indeed they had been of John Wilkes's. Yet such criticisms ignore the benefits which Milligan bestowed upon Radley in the fourteen years of his Wardenship. In this time the boys – for whose welfare and interests he had always been principally concerned – had reason to be grateful for the cautious liberalization of the school's regime at a time of disturbing social unrest which at some other schools led to widespread expulsions. Private fagging came to an end; the kind of bullying which some boys had had to endure in the mid-1950s was no longer tolerated in most Socials when Prefects or Tutors became aware of it. 'Bloodism' which, in Milligan's words, had been dying down when he became Warden was, he believed, dead by the time he left, and had certainly had no encouragement from him, since his own interest in athletic triumphs was limited: he rarely accompanied the school's teams when they left to play against other schools: and he admitted to being deeply thankful that the school both rowed and played cricket as this meant that if he was not present at a cricket match it could be supposed that he was by the river and if he was not watching the Eight it might be thought he was on the Pitch.

If not as actively encouraged as they had been by past Wardens, the school's teams and eights performed with credit in his time. At Henley the First Eight reached the semi-final of the Princess Elizabeth Cup in 1956 and 1966; in 1961 they were beaten in the quarter final by King's School, Canterbury, and in 1965 by Emanuel by half a length in the then record time of 6 minutes 44 seconds. In 1962 they successively beat Shrewsbury, St Edward's, St Paul's, Hampton Grammar School and Pangbourne to win the event for the second time.

In the fourteen years of Milligan's Wardenship, the First Cricket XI won over twice as many school matches as they lost; and from 1957 to 1960 and in 1963 the First XI were unbeaten in all their school matches, much credit for this being due to Ivor Gilliat: in the words of Simon Langdale, who succeeded him as master in charge of cricket, 'one of the outstanding schoolboy coaches of all time'.

The First Rugby Football XV were not quite so successful. They beat Eastbourne, however, in nine of their annual matches, Cheltenham in seven, Wellington in six, St Edward's and Stowe in five, Pangbourne and Uppingham in four and Sherborne in three. In 1963 all these schools, apart from Eastbourne, were defeated in their matches with Radley.

The Hockey First XIs did almost as well as the Cricket XIs. They won over half as many school matches as they lost. In 1960 they were undefeated. In 1965 they did not lose a school match.

'In the 1950s,' wrote Kenneth Brookman, the physics master who had been a candidate for the British Olympic athletics team,

> sport was pursued with greater energy and more passion than any other activity, including lessons, not only at Radley but many other great public schools. Neither Warden Wilkes nor Warden Milligan wished this to be so, but the intensity of interest in sport was greater than at many corresponding schools. Rowing, Rugby and Cricket were the major trinity, with honourable apostolic places for Rackets, Hockey and Fives. There was, however, sufficient tolerance for outstanding individuals, like R.W. Stoughton-Harris [a master since 1955] with gymnastics, to add to the list, provided they did not try to usurp the places already reserved for other activities.

At athletics, Radley was particularly distinguished in these years. D.T.M. Birks, who had won the discus at the Public Schools Athletic

Meeting in 1938, was a highly effective coach. So too was Kenneth Brookman, and it was at Radley in these years that C.E.B.L. Carr and R.A. Lane – the son of a Radley master, subsequently himself a master at Millfield and afterwards at Epsom – acquired the skills that were to make them national schools champions at the shot-put and the javelin respectively.

*

In his retirement, Milligan confessed to being thankful that he left Radley when he did. His relations with certain senior members of Common Room had deteriorated to such an extent that, when David Hardy went to say goodbye to him, he found him in a 'sad and embittered mood'. One phrase he used, Hardy has never forgotten: 'Those bloody, bloody men!' In his own words he 'got out just in time', for 1968 was '*the* bad year'. 'Things came to a head; and behaviour which you never saw in the school before' was almost commonplace. He himself had to talk to boys whose 'hair was all over the place', since Social Tutors were 'not terribly helpful in that sort of way'. He was well aware that some of the comments expressed in recent years by successive editors of *The Radleian* and *The Petreian* were not altogether unjustified:

> There is a certain ineffectiveness about the Radleian; he drifts along in a cloud of pleasant egoism and refuses to face the duty he owes to himself as much as to the community . . . People should never be at a loss for something to do, especially when surrounded by such a diversity of opportunities as there are at Radley. But the fact to be faced is that many are, and the place where it is most noticeable is [among the junior boys in] Social Hall . . . This unwillingness to work really hard and to partake enthusiastically in every aspect of College life is preventing our academic achievement from fulfilling its potential . . . It is becoming increasingly difficult to get anyone to show more than a casual interest in anything . . . Those in the upper part of College are beginning to lose all interest in Radley . . . There no longer exists at Radley the inbred courtesy for which the school had a justifiably good reputation a short time ago.

While accepting that these self-analytical strictures had an element of truth, the Warden was not prepared to agree that the Radleians of the 1960s were any more prone to indifference than boys at other public schools. He remained convinced that public schools in general had a vital part to play in giving boys the opportunity of learning to live in a community and having 'to give and take as they will in later life'. 'The second thing,' he maintained in an interview given towards the end of his time at Radley, 'is that in a public school a boy gets a much fuller education in the sense that his potentialities can be drawn out of him . . . The third benefit – a by-product of boarding – is that he is permanently in contact with older people whom he can look to for help at any time . . . The master–boy relationship is vitally important.'

To a question as to how valid was the criticism that Radleians were 'nice but ineffective', the Warden answered emphatically: 'It is absolute nonsense – certainly in the modern Radleian. I think the reason for attributing to Radleians this mythical attitude could be that they have often been credited with charm and good manners, and there are people who are suspicious of a charming manner.'

In his last term the Warden was distressed to receive a number of letters complaining about the rude and inconsiderate behaviour of some fifth-form boys who had been taken to the Royal Shakespeare Theatre at Stratford. One of these letters ended, 'I am surprised that a letter of this nature should be necessary with regard to pupils from a school of such standing.' If such rowdyism were to erupt again in the coming decade, as seemed not improbable at Radley as at other public schools, the Warden could be thankful that it was his 'successor who would have to deal with it'.

At least Milligan could feel satisfied that he would hand over to his successor a school of manageable size in which it was 'possible to know everybody', a school which he was proud to say was 'beautifully kept' like the private country estate of Sewell's ideal, with 'lawns rather than concrete and without a proliferation of signposts everywhere', an academically respectable school which sent a satisfactorily high proportion of its leavers to university at a time when places were increasingly difficult to win. In the Michaelmas term following his departure the school was offered more places at universities than ever before. Milligan could, above all, be satisfied that he left the boys' future in the hands of what he could honestly describe, despite his occasional and sometimes painful disagreements with them, as a 'first-class staff', a Common Room which his successor was to describe as 'marvellous'. He himself could take credit for having steered Radley successfully through an exceptionally difficult period in public school history: his achievements were to be seen as far more commendable than he was given credit for at the time.

It was later held not to be an extravagant claim when a newcomer to Common Room said, a few months before the Warden left to become Principal of Wolsey Hall, Oxford, 'I feel this school to be so organized and poised that a very little change of direction will bring it to greatness.'

Yet there was little doubt that a change *was* needed. In 1967 Council discussed the possibility of the Warden remaining in office for a further period, it being then understood that he wished to do so. But, concerned as they were about the financial state of the school and other matters, it was agreed that the Chairman was right in suggesting that Milligan had had 'his full stint'. Milligan was then over sixty years old, tired and not in good health. There was a feeling that he would have done well to have retired earlier, as he no doubt would have done had he not had a young family to consider. As it was, Radley was standing still. The school's stock was falling with preparatory schools and its numbers were soon to be reduced to 443. It was agreed that a new dynamic helmsman was required.

30

A Master from Marlborough
1968–1972

'You're not going to find this school very easy, Sir.'

DOUBLE BLUE IS Radley Head.' Under this headline on 25 September 1967 the *Daily Telegraph* informed its readers that Mr Dennis Silk, the Cricket and Rugby Blue, a thirty-five-year-old housemaster at Marlborough College, had been appointed to succeed Mr W.M.M. Milligan as Warden of Radley College. 'Mr Silk was educated at Christ's Hospital, and Sidney Sussex College, Cambridge,' the newspaper's Education Correspondent continued. 'He captained Cambridge at cricket in 1955 and played rugby for the University in 1953 and 1954.'

This brief announcement did scant justice to what had already been a remarkable career. Dennis Raoul Whitehall Silk was born on 8 October 1931 in the town of Eureka on the coast of northern California. His mother was Spanish, his father, the Revd Dr Claude Whitehall Silk, a medical missionary working amongst the Stoney Indians of the mountainous hinterland. When he was four years old his mother died and his father sailed home to England with his four children to share a home with his mother and two of his sisters in Primrose Hill. Dennis, the youngest of the children, was sent at the age of ten to Christ's Hospital where in due course he became head boy. One of his friends at this school recalls an occasion that demonstrated the young Silk's quick wit. With several other boys without tickets they were on a train journey from Worthing back to Horsham when the ticket inspector was seen approaching their compartment. 'Let us pray,' whispered Silk, falling to his knees, his head bent to the carriage floor. The others followed suit, so that when the inspector appeared and saw the kneeling figures in their blue cassocks, instead of calling out 'Tickets please,' he uttered an apology for disturbing their devotions.

At Cambridge Silk won a half-Blue for Rugby fives as well as Blues for cricket and rugger; but he did not neglect his studies, taking an upper Second in History. At the same time he made several good friends, including another Old Blue, Edmund Blunden, whom he had first met when Blunden came to Christ's Hospital to play for the old boys against the school. Blunden introduced him to his fellow poet and cricket enthusiast, the naturally reclusive Old Marlburian, Siegfried Sassoon; and, 'from that moment', so Silk says, he enjoyed an 'absolutely perfect friendship' with Sassoon for the last thirteen years of the poet's life. He became something of an authority on his works and formed a friendship with the editor of Sassoon's diaries, the publisher Sir Rupert Hart-Davis.

A more intimate friend of his own age was Ian Beer, captain of the Cambridge XV, who had been at Whitgift and who, like Silk, was approached by T.R. Garnett, the recently appointed Master of Marlborough, with an offer to join his staff there. Garnett had gone to Cambridge to look for possible Marlborough masters and had knocked on Silk's door. Silk, who had been playing squash, was drying himself on the hearthrug before a gas fire. Thinking it was a friend he called out, 'Come in'; and Garnett, 'totally unabashed', conducted the interview with a naked candidate.

Before accepting Garnett's offer of an appointment at Marlborough, Silk approached two other schools, Cheltenham and Radley. To keep the appointment at Cheltenham on the only day that the Headmaster, the Revd A.G.G.C. Pentreath, could see him, he had to miss playing for Cambridge at Cardiff Arms Park, something he 'had longed to do'. So he was naturally much disappointed to discover on his arrival at Cheltenham that the Headmaster had forgotten he was coming, and he was consequently not at his best during his interview with the Assistant Chaplain.

At Radley his interview with Warden Milligan was rather more promising. He 'immediately and absolutely fell in love with the place', but 'swallowed hard' when told that the salary at the school (which, he was subsequently led to believe, had in the past 'rather relied on people with private incomes') would be no more than £320 a year. The income of £650 a year offered at Marlborough seemed princely by comparison, particularly so as the perquisites were more generous, too. Besides, Marlborough was, like Radley, an attractive place and at that time, in Silk's words, 'such a good school, a purposeful school, full of distinguished teachers and that marvellous leavening of the sons of clergy, really good boys who were not too rich . . . all mixed up with some quite rich boys who were also very nice'. It did not take long for him to make up his mind to go to Marlborough with his friend, Ian Beer.

> There was so much they had in common [Garnett wrote years later]. I was fond of quoting the remark of an Old Marlburian, at that time the only Protestant judge on the High Court of Eire [who] told me, 'When I was at Marlborough there were many very sane, very sound, and very dull masters and the only one who ever taught me anything was mad.' (This was another Irishman, who taught History backwards, starting from the present.) Both Dennis and Ian would have been on the side of madness: they were never dull.

Garnett was not to be disappointed in either of his choices. Ian Beer was to go on to be Headmaster of Ellesmere College, then of Lancing, then of Harrow. Silk, appointed a junior housemaster with what was described as 'almost indecent haste', was an immediate success at Marlborough. Renowned as he was as an athlete – he played cricket as an opening bat for Somerset in the holidays, went on three tours with the MCC and was also, with J.F. Pretlove, Amateur Rugby Fives Doubles Champion several times – there was, as Garnett said, nothing narrow about his interests. He 'subscribed to the dictum that, to someone actually playing a game, it should matter more than anything else in the world, but that when it is over it should come low down on the scale of importance'. He brought as much enthusiasm to the printing by the Marlborough College Press of an edition of Siegfried Sassoon's poems as he did to the coaching of the Colts' cricket eleven.

While still at Marlborough he married Diana Milton, modest, friendly and appealing, yet as eager for her husband to succeed in his career as he was himself, and, as she was to show at Radley, untiring in her efforts to help him, regularly attending plays, concerts, chapel services and acting as a hostess at once attentive and relaxed. By the time the chance of being appointed Warden of Radley came, the Silks had had three children, two daughters and a son: another son was to be born at Radley. His two rivals on the short list were his friend, Ian

Beer, and John Kendall-Carpenter, Headmaster of Cranbrook, who had played rugger for England and who was to become Headmaster of Eastbourne, then of Wellington School, Somerset. Silk felt his chances were slim with two such rivals on the short list, both of them 'excellent practising headmasters'.

Yet, 'maybe,' as he said years later, 'going in for the interview without any hope at all relaxed me a bit.' In any event, he was as surprised as he was pleased when he was selected and had some cause to be surprised since it had been proposed in the initial brief given to the Selection Committee that the candidate to be sought should already be a headmaster, should have obtained a first-class honours degree, and, other things being equal, should be in Holy Orders. These qualifications Dennis Silk failed to offer in every particular. But the Chairman of the Council, Admiral the Hon. Sir Guy Russell, and his colleagues were fully confident they had found the right man, the one doubtful member of the Council being Lord Shackleton who had gone on from Radley to Magdalen College, Oxford, and who argued that an Oxford man should be chosen.

As soon as he learned of his appointment the new Warden went out of his way to talk to anyone who he thought might be able to give him useful advice about Radley, its past and probable future, the problems he was likely to have to face, the improvements which were needed, the innovations which were required or were to be avoided, and the men with whom he would have to work.

The prognostications were not encouraging. Milligan himself had warned him that there were going to be difficult times ahead, scarcely to be avoided in a period of general student revolt; and the Senior Prefect, whom he and his wife took out to dinner before his first term began, obviously wanted to say something and then suddenly blurted out, 'You're not going to find this school very easy, Sir.'

With these warnings in mind, he set out from the beginning to impress upon the members of Common Room that he saw himself as *primus inter pares*. 'This,' he told them more than once, 'is not my school, it is *our* school.' He emphasized this at both his first Common Room meeting and his first Tutors' meeting by drawing masters into the discussion, asking them to explain certain proposals, while keeping firm control of the proceedings in a manner that showed how well he had briefed himself before appearing before them in a body.

Breaking with tradition, he invited all the assistant masters to be present at his first address to the whole school; and this address, so one of them said, demonstrated a capacity to communicate with 'every one of his listeners. He made contact, not by what he said but by the type of emotion with which he said it.'

Writing a few months after the new Warden's installation, this master reiterated his admiration for Silk's 'concern to reach out to as many individuals and groups as possible: he sees many boys about their work; he is pleased to be form master of a Shell form, he helps with Rugger on Big Side and on less exalted League Games.' On the first Thursday of his first term, 'despite his 36 years', he turned out with Big Side for twenty minutes and 'jinked his way casually through the ranks which had vowed to bring him down'.

On or near their birthdays all boys were invited to the Warden's House for a chat. 'Little boys would have a cup of cocoa or a glass of Coca-Cola,' Silk recalled. 'I think I must have drunk more Coca-Cola than any other grown-up in England. Then, with an older boy, perhaps we'd have a glass of port like two old gentlemen.' When they were ill he visited them in the Infirmary or in hospital in Oxford; and he took the trouble to remember their Christian names. There was a certain guile in this, he admitted: 'Of course, in a small school like Radley you felt you jolly well ought to know their Christian names and one is always glad if someone takes the trouble to mention your name. But my theory was that if you knew a boy's Christian name, he would think, my God! what else does he know about me? It was very good for discipline.'

The discipline of the school was a matter which the Warden had to deal with at the very outset of his career at Radley when cases of merciless bullying came to light.

*

Although bullying was far less prevalent in public schools than it had been in earlier times, it had not yet been eradicated; and many men who were at school in the 1950s and 1960s have recounted painful experiences.

At Eton, Sir Winston Churchill's grandson would be suddenly surrounded by boys who, as he described it, 'would strip one and get a rubber-soled slipper, and say "Take that for being a shit! Take that for being a son of a bitch! Take that for being Winston Bloody Churchill."' The Prince of Wales was similarly bullied at Gordonstoun for being the son of the Queen of England, although, according to Eric Anderson, an assistant master there in the Prince's time, Gordonstoun was 'not nearly as tough a school as it and other people liked to make out'. And it has certainly not been so since Mark Pyper, a Wykehamist and convinced proponent of co-education, was appointed Head-master.

At Bedales, in the late 1960s, according to Polly Mortimer, 'there was a lot of bullying, especially among the boys. They had terrible rituals, used to hang people upside-down out of windows. The girls' bullying was more psychological.'

A report submitted in 1993 by the chief inspector for Oxfordshire's Social Services found that about 5 per cent of the boys at Pangbourne said they were bullied 'often or most of the time'; but the average was over 6 per cent in other schools. At Pangbourne the most prevalent sort of bullying was 'verbal abuse'; there was a certain amount of phys-ical bullying, though initiation ceremonies such as 'bog-washing', in which boys' heads were pushed down lavatory basins, and 'divisional scrubs', in which they were blackened with boot polish, were said to be 'part of the folklore of the past'. Most parents were perfectly satis-fied with the school and some 'were clear that bullying and teasing were a good preparation for later life'.

Reports and experiences such as these could be cited in the histories of most schools for the 1950s and 1960s; but cases of serious bullying were becoming increasingly isolated, and often much exaggerated in the telling as, apparently, were the widely publicized 1995 reports of boys being hung upside-down from windows and being sexually assaulted with broom handles at Fettes. Andrew Marr, political com-mentator for the *Independent*, who lists his recreations as 'whining and dining', wrote light-heartedly in the *Spectator*:

> As a former [1970s] pupil of Loretto, the main rival to Fettes, I am per-plexed at stories of assaults . . . One always assumed things at 'Fetish', as the crenellated madhouse was known, were much, much more barbarous than that. They certainly were with us. Newspapers report in scandalized tones that the Fettes regime 'has left one boy mentally scarred for life'. Only one? And only mentally? Fettes must be losing its touch.

However, Magnus Linklater, former editor of the *Scotsman*, who was himself at Eton, took the trouble to investigate the reports and came to the conclusion that much of the evidence was distorted, 'some charges were ten years old, others untrue.'

The bullying at Radley in 1968 was not to be dismissed, however, and, in view of the growing infrequency of reports of serious and persistent bullying in other English public schools all the more disturbing. When he heard it and learned that in one Social in particular it had become systematic, that boys were actually being given electric shocks, and that, at the same time, there was widespread illicit drinking, the Warden decided he must act firmly and at once.

On a Saturday evening in the second week of his first term he suddenly announced there would be a fire practice at half-past ten. There were muttered complaints that this was too early in the term and too early in the evening to test the boys' night-drill. 'But by 10.45 every Social had had its routine fire roll-call so that before midnight, Social Tutors were interviewing all the pub-crawlers and sky-larkers whose casual indiscipline had taken hold of the school during the previous twelve months.' Three boys were too drunk to get out of bed.

The Warden spoke severely to the Prefects and told the Sub-Warden, 'There's got to be a showdown. It won't be fair to the boys unless they know where they stand on this.' The next morning he had the whole school assembled in Hall. He confessed that his knees felt like jelly and his mouth was 'as dry as sandpaper'. 'I went into Hall,' he said, 'and I called the names of the three boys who had been incapably drunk and who were also known to be bullies in the house of bullies. I dressed them down publicly and then I told them, "Right, you three. Get out of Hall now and go and wait on my doorstep" – this was in the days when boys were still beaten and these boys *were* beaten – I was shaking, I remember. I was shaking like a leaf. But boys who later left and came back said, "You know, we were shaking, too." Which,' the Warden added, laughing, 'retrospectively gratified me . . . Those three boys erred again within a fortnight and were all expelled.' Soon afterwards two other boys were expelled for what a newspaper described as 'a naughty night out' with two girls from a local comprehensive school.

The Warden acted just as firmly and just as swiftly on the last day of his first year when he learned that posters had been put up in Oxford inviting hippies and others so inclined to sabotage the end-of-term Gaudy at Radley by turning it into a pop festival. 'Within one hour the Warden had himself collected all the posters,'* his Sub-Warden

---

*In case any visitors should arrive despite the removal of the posters the Sub-Warden stood at the entrance to College. A few did arrive and were given an extended tour of the buildings and grounds which left them 'in a somewhat bemused state'.

recorded; 'within three hours he had discovered which boys were the saboteurs. How did he manage this? By knowing each separate boy individually and knowing also the patterns of companionship which they all maintained.'

In the same way he discovered who were the culprits when he received a complaint that certain of his boys had behaved badly on a train, smoking and swearing. He immediately drove them all to Maidenhead to apologize in person to their affronted fellow passengers. On another occasion he drove some boys to another school to apologize for damaging a changing room there after an away match: in his hurry to get there he was stopped by the police for speeding.

It was not long before the school came to realize that the Warden meant what he said, that he was not a man to be trifled with, that tolerant, easy-going, even suave as he contrived generally to appear, when his rules were flouted or his strong sense of decorum was outraged, his eyes would grow hard behind the glinting lenses of his spectacles and the mouth set firmly above the heavy lantern jaw.

Much of the trouble in the early months of his Wardenship he attributed to the fact that some Social Tutors had grown too old and weary to run their houses as they should have been run. For example, the Tutor of the Social in which the worst cases of bullying had occurred 'had served Radley marvellously in the past'; but by 1968 he was 'too tired to know about – probably didn't want to know about – the things that were going on in his Social, or to understand the divisions, inspired by electronic music, which were opening up between generations'.

The Warden was only too well aware of the strains and demands of a public school master's life at this time. He himself, though a man of astonishing stamina, was taking sleeping pills within a fortnight of starting work at Radley; and for twenty-three years he was unable to sleep unless he took two Mogadons every night. He has described being Warden as 'like peering over the lip of a volcano'.

*

As with so many headmasters, Dennis Silk's trials in his early years were exacerbated by his having to make himself free to be questioned four times daily by prospective parents, many of whom arrived with written lists of more or less demanding questions – 'and very boring it was, too.' When asked in later life to help choose a headmaster, one of the essential qualities he looked for was a sound physique: 'Is this man going to last physically? I asked myself. I have seen some fine men killed, well not killed literally; but their judgement went because they were so constantly tried and tired.'

From the very first at Radley he 'set out', in his own words,

> to get into the houses young men, with attractive committed wives, who worked for the boys; since what makes a public school attractive to parents is the quality of housemasters and the young married man of talent with the sap rising rather than the older man to whom the appointment was given as a reward for past services. These men are tired and the boys run rings round them . . . And I said to the Council, 'If this school is going to work, we've got to have young men living in nice houses on the campus'; and I said to the young men themselves, 'You live in a lovely house, you've got four months' holiday a year. So, in term-time you will work a seven-day week and you will be available for the boys – in accordance with the old Radley tradition of socializing – at weekends, and you'll make friends with them, and entertain them, to a kitchen supper or something like that.' The essence of Radley is the very good relationship that I believe there nearly always has been between boys and dons.*

The Warden himself took great trouble to show himself as being concerned in the boys' welfare. He did not want to usurp what he took to be the Social Tutors' responsibility, as Wyndham Milligan had been accused of doing. But he displayed an interest, more often real than assumed, in nearly all of the school's multifarious activities from brass rubbing to photography. He was President of the Coarse Fishing Club and of the Experimental Farmers; he attended the Sixth Form dances and undertook to act as censor of the end of term revue; he rarely missed a school or Social play or a musical performance; he never missed that Sewellian revival, Declamations, his favourite competition, nor the Creative Hobbies Competition which he himself instituted for boys with talents lying in that direction rather than in academic studies and which attracted exhibits from over 450 boys.† It was always his

---

*Most public schools take pride in this relationship and some historians of public schools have chosen to suppose it is not shared by others: 'Nothing,' wrote R. St C. Talboys, David Newsome's predecessor as historian of Wellington, 'has ever seemed to impair the easy and delightful relationship between boys and masters which, as I believe, is a trait peculiar to Wellington.'

†The increasing academic demands made upon boys has in recent times led to a certain decline in the amount of time they can spend on their 'creative hobbies', though electronics and video making have developed strongly in the past five years under Max Horsey. At the same time, and largely for the same reason, it has become much harder for dons to teach things not directly related to the syllabus.

contention that every boy had some talent or quality, something individual to him that must be developed. 'A boy who turned bowls in the woodwork department,' so one of his Sub-Wardens contended, 'was just as important as the First XV hooker.'

He encouraged the retention of the school beagles and he took over a new Radley society, Tattersalls, which had been founded by a keen racing man, David Goldsmith, a Social Tutor since 1958, and in which several members were the sons of racehorse trainers, some of them, including Kim Bailey and Oliver Sherwood, becoming successful trainers themselves. The only school activities which the Warden, who had himself been excused National Service on medical grounds, did not support assiduously were those of the Combined Cadet Force which, like all CCFs, had, under the direction of G.L. Treglown and Richard Pollard, changed greatly in recent years, with numbers much reduced and a new emphasis on adventure training.* When Silk visited their camp in 1985 it was the first time he had done so in sixteen years.

That the Warden found time to interest himself in so many of the school's activities seemed astonishing to those who knew how much he undertook to do outside it. Indeed, there were those who saw in his reluctance to refuse an invitation a weakness in his conduct as Warden. Not only was he a Justice of the Peace, a governor of several other schools, active on MCC committees and in public school politics, he was also in constant demand socially. 'The man had the stamina of an ox,' said one of his assistant masters. 'But it became quite difficult for staff to see him because he was so hectic.' However, another of his masters commented, 'He was rarely away for the night; and, when on the campus, he was totally accessible. There was no question of going through a secretary before seeing him. You knocked on the door and went in. The boys had the same access as dons to him. He was formidable but approachable.'

The Warden took care to listen to the boys' opinions about the running of the school, to involve them in the same kind of way in which he involved their parents who were invited to meetings at Radley to discuss their sons' academic courses, their university opportunities and future careers. When in 1981 he instituted a Warden's

---

*The Radley College Combined Cadet Force was judged by a 1996 Inspectors' Report to be one of the best in the country. Richard Pollard holds the rank of Lieutenant-Colonel, the highest obtainable in the CCF.

Advisory Committee, he included amongst its members – as well as the Sub-Warden, the Bursar, Assistant Bursar, Caterer, the Senior Prefect, three masters, the wife of a master, a matron and the Second Master, an office he had initiated for advice on long-term planning for his friend, A.L. Dowding – eight senior boys, one from each Social, elected by the boys from candidates put forward by their Social Tutors.

The matters discussed by this Committee ranged far and wide, from the obviously important to what might have been dismissed as trivial had it not been considered important by the boys themselves. They included the maintenance of buildings and their architecture, changes in the curriculum and in extra-curricular activities, clothes and leisure wear in Oxford, the possibility of relaxing the rules against smoking for boys over sixteen, the use of the Letters Board and of telephones, House Prefects' ties, the failings of the hairdresser, the frequency of Sixth Form dances, pop concerts and amplifiers, the wearing of gowns for exams, the need for Chapel attendance checks, hats ('a needless frivolity', in the Warden's opinion, 'encouraging ostentation'), expulsions and Old Boy status, the Rising Bell ('The only purpose the bell served was to keep traditions going. It was agreed that next term for the first month the bell will not be rung and the situation reviewed in the light of the experiment').

To all matters the Warden gave the patient, full attention of a man who had rapidly established himself as a most effective headmaster, a worthy successor to Canon Ferguson whom he considered the greatest of his predecessors. 'It is marvellous to feel the transformation of the school,' one of his staff remarked in the early years of Dennis Silk's Wardenship, 'the sense of direction, the *continuing* sense of confidence. The Warden arrived with such a reputation and to such a fund of goodwill, that one was driven to fear that something must be wrong somewhere.'

Another observer was also concerned that there might be 'clouds on the horizon'. As a man 'feeling his way into a new position, coming to grips with a new job, the Warden [had so far] not put a foot wrong'. But 'for the long haul, the pace is too hot, the burden which he is taking on is too heavy . . . He must find a good cruising speed – unload jobs onto the rest of us . . . Secondly, for the long haul the Warden has not yet demonstrated that he possesses the necessary vision . . . He cares very much about his job, he cares about the boys individually, he has his own simple faith, but these attributes will, I think, become repetitive and threadbare and unconvincing unless they are rooted in greater

72. Extracts from the Punishment Books, 1868 and 1977

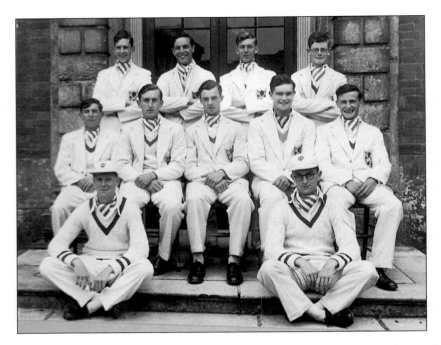

73. The First Cricket XI, 1952. The captain, A.C. Walton, later played for Oxford University and Middlesex. E.R. Dexter, on his right, played for Cambridge, Sussex and England. The other members of the team are, from the left: (*standing*) J.B. Gleave, Leo Cooper, J.S.M. Scott, M.W.G. Duff; (*middle row*) R.R. Davies, C.E.B.L. Carr, J.S. Waddilove; (*sitting on step*) E.C.H. Huddy, T.I. Perkins

74. Boys in Hall, 1956

75. W.M.M. Milligan,
Warden 1954–68

76. First XI fielding practice with Ivor Gilliat, assistant master 1937–63

77. A *Daily Mail* photograph of members of Radley College Boat Club in training

78. The Combined Cadet Force witnessing a fly past by Chipmunks in 1959, the first by any Cadet air section in the country. The pilots are Corporals Richard Bradbury, M.H.B. Snelling and P.M.Cowley

79. A study in F Social in the 1960s. The boys are A.L. Robinson and R.J.S. Bucknall

80. Guests at the Old Radleian dinner, 1971. *From the left*: Warden Milligan, Warden Wilkes, the Revd V. Hope, Warden Fox and Warden Silk

81. Boys on the Radley Oak, *c.* 1971; a tree of extreme though unknown antiquity,
said to have been rejected as timber for naval building in the Napoleonic Wars
being already unsound

82. D.R.W. Silk, Warden 1968–91

83. A shot taken in class of the mathematics teacher and Social Tutor, D.F. Goldsmith, who appeared prominently in the BBC television series *Public School* shown in 1980

84. James Male, world rackets champion, as a boy at the school

85. Peter Cook, entertainer

86. Ted Dexter, cricketer, Captain of Cambridge University, Sussex and England

87. Lord Scarman, Lord of Appeal in Ordinary; Chairman of the Law Commission, 1965–72

depth of philosophical grasp than has yet appeared. The greater depth may well be there. One suspects that it must be . . .' The future would show whether or not these apprehensions were justified.

Some six years after these reservations were expressed, the master who had set them down returned to a consideration of Dennis Silk and, far from being disillusioned, decided that it was clear to all his colleagues '(or nearly all) that [they had] a very remarkable head-master'.

'Dennis Silk arrived at a difficult time,' wrote another of his masters, who went on to become headmaster of a leading public school himself.

> But he came with a clear set of principles and a clear sense of where he was going. He set out his stall with a conviction that was lacking in most heads at that time. He really was a rock against which the storm could beat. Dons and boys could disagree with him but he offered them something positive to disagree with and no one doubted his commitment to Radley or his strength. The result was an enormous upsurge of interest amongst prep schools and parents. Not only did the numbers begin to rise dramatically but the quality of the intake improved markedly. Radley began getting many more talented pupils, not least from amongst those who might previously have gone to Marlborough.

Extravagant as parts of these appreciations might seem, it reflected the opinion which was by then generally held of Dennis Silk in the educational world at large and was still to be held as his work at Radley became more widely appreciated. When he had become well known in that world various other headmasters were asked by the *Observer* to name which of their colleagues they most admired. The Revd Dominic Milroy of Ampleforth mentioned a former Headmaster of that school, Father Paul Nevill, 'a sort of Renaissance Man, a man of unself-conscious learning, immense natural authority and huge humour'. Brian Gaskill of Millfield chose the Old Radleian Douglas Whiting of Cheadle Hulme, 'a Christian man with a good sense of humour, nicely balanced with dignity and bucketloads of charm'. Michael Mavor of Gordonstoun suggested Christopher Everett of Tonbridge, 'an expert in all sorts of fields but very conscious of making others feel their views matter. He has a passion for hard work, and he's one of the few people I know who enjoys reading government bills. I like him because he's an optimist and is always looking for the best in people. He was an out-standing chairman of the Headmasters' Conference. The only possible criticism I, as a Scotsman, could level at him is that he's a dyed-in-the-wool Southerner. When he came up to visit Gordonstoun, he wondered whether he needed a passport.'

Euan MacAlpine of Bedales wrote that 'the problem with heads is that they perform their tasks well away from the public eye – except for a certain ex-head of Westminster . . . I admire John Thorn (ex-Winchester) for his compassion and understanding of staff and pupils on an individual basis. He also managed to convince the heads of Headmasters' Conference schools that the Arts should have a central place in schools.'

It was generally conceded, however, that if one man were to be singled out, the 'headmasters' headmaster' was Dennis Silk. As that 'certain ex-head of Westminster' himself, the brilliant and entertaining publicist, John Rae, observed:

> Dennis Silk, who is the Warden of Radley College, runs a very good school. His pupils are valued individuals; there's purposefulness and good order there . . . He's managed to create in Radley one of the outstanding schools of the mainland. He has brought Radley up to being, after Eton, the most sought-after school in England. He's a more traditional head; the kind who emphasizes hard work, good manners and good appearance.

Gratified as he was to read this verdict, Silk took greater pleasure in the praise bestowed upon his work at Radley by a man who had done so much for it in the past and who had sworn never to return, consistently refusing all invitations to do so. This was Vyvyan Hope who had gone to live in Exeter where his energies were devoted to the maintenance of the cathedral on whose history and architecture he had become an acknowledged expert. Just before his departure from Radley, Peter Stuart had said to Hope that he trusted he would soon return. No, never, Hope had replied in his typically abrupt manner: he supposed the place would get on perfectly well without him and it would hurt his pride to see that that was, indeed, the case. So, since Mahomet would not go to the mountain, the mountain must go to Mahomet. The Warden went to Exeter, asked to be shown round the cathedral and persuaded the eighty-three-year-old Hope to come back to Radley one weekend to stay in the Warden's House. On leaving Radley after his visit, the old man leaned out of the railway carriage window to say goodbye to his host upon whom, most uncharacteristically, he bestowed a heartfelt compliment, 'Warden, I give you alpha.'

31

The Radley Appeal Road Show
1972–1978

'We should look to the wider world horizons.'

FROM THE BEGINNING the Warden had shown himself eager to help provide the school with the buildings and facilities which would allow it to compete successfully with all other public schools in the country. He believed it to be essential to turn what was still in many ways a Victorian school into a school for the 1990s. 'It was a strange thing to me,' he said later, 'that such a fashionable school, so full of the sons of – well, let's face it – rich people, was content to put up with some of the facilities, or lack of facilities, that they had.'

An appeal for funds had already been made in the early 1960s; but this had brought in far less money than had been expected, partly because of Warden Milligan's uneasy relations with Old Radleians, mainly because the professional consultants employed were far from satisfactory. Moreover, the money that was raised was not spent as wisely as it should have been, while expensive projects were put in hand before funds were available to pay for them. By the late 1960s the level of the debts which the school owed to its bankers, and the foreseen difficulty of repaying them, were causing deep concern to many members of the Council.

In Warden Silk's time it was found possible to pay off these debts by the sale of land while property prices were high. These sales initially raised £1.25 million, a figure considerably more than that which would have been realized had they taken place when they were first proposed. There were two reasons for this delay: first there was the intervention of the science master, Hugh Cardwell, an expert on Radley history, who strongly opposed the sales and spoke eloquently against them at the public enquiry held to determine whether or not they might go ahead. Secondly, the school's solicitors, very shortly before the auction, discovered that the land to be sold was subject to restrictive covenants. So the auction had to be cancelled and there was a long delay before the legal difficulties were resolved and the sales could proceed. The delay was of enormous benefit to Radley, for, had the land been sold in 1970 as intended, it would have fetched about £10,000 an acre. By the time it was sold two years later the sudden boom in building land had raised the price to no less than £45,000 an acre.

The acquisition of this large amount of capital was fortunately accompanied by a transformation in the management of Radley's finances, a transformation due not only to two excellent Bursars but also to a Council most of whose members were far more financially competent than any Council had been in the past. Two hard-working members in particular, both Old Radleians, brought an acumen and fiscal ability to the school's affairs which had hitherto been sadly lacking. These were the forceful and astute David Rae Smith, senior partner of Deloitte Haskins and Sells, chartered accountants, who had, in the words of one of his colleagues, 'not only the experience but also the character and determination to change attitudes and bring Radley up to date financially . . . Under his far-sighted and firm guidance revenue surpluses replaced losses, past debts were paid off and the proceeds of land sales divided prudently between development needs and the establishment, for the first time in Radley's history, of a significant Endowment Fund.' His achievements can be compared to those of Lord Addington in the last century. He was well supported by the equally capable John Pattisson, a Director of Hanson Trust Limited, who had, in a significant change in the Council's composition, been nominated to it by the Radleian Society as one of their two representatives at the age of thirty-four and had subsequently been invited to stay on as a full member.

Guided by these men and others the Council initiated an entirely new approach to Radley's finances, managing investments more effectively, building up scholarship funds, and ensuring that the school was run profitably for the benefit of future generations of boys.

The land sales were supervised by the Bursar, Sir Kerr Bovell, a former Inspector-General of Police in Nigeria and prisoner of war in Changi gaol, Singapore, who had come to Radley (from the Bursar's Office at Worksop College) at the same time as the Warden, with whom he was on terms of intimate friendship. It was all the more worrying and distressing for the Warden, therefore, when Bovell developed cancer and died after a ten months' illness, bravely endured, in 1973. Fortunately for Radley the Warden was able to replace Bovell with a chartered surveyor of great energy and varied accomplishments, M.M. Jones, who had been a highly successful Bursar at the Dragon School, Oxford, and at Shrewsbury. A classical scholar of Trinity College, Oxford, where he won a half-Blue for real tennis, Jones was to become Chairman of the Bursars' Association in 1978 and, in the words of his obituary in *The Times*, 'the doyen of public school bursars . . . That Radley is today [September 1995] among the most secure public schools in the land is due in no small measure to Jones's foresight and perspicacity.'

He had met Dennis Silk playing rackets and the two men had immediately warmed to each other.* Silk had explained Radley's financial position which at that time was precarious: the school was, in fact, losing more money than any other public school of its size and reputation. As Bovell had said, Radley was trying to be a Rolls-Royce school on a Mini engine. Steps had been taken to increase the number of boys and to prune the staff, but there was much work yet to be done.

With the help of A.E. Money, the Appeal Secretary who had joined the staff in 1958 and, having been a most efficient Secretary of the Radleian Society, was to become an equally painstaking Archivist and President of the Society, the Warden and his new Bursar set about the time-consuming task of raising the money to secure Radley's position and make it one of the most enviably equipped schools in England. A fresh appeal was launched; numerous meetings and dinners were attended by the Warden and his wife who travelled all over the country and even to New York, spreading the word of Radley's need in what Sir Patrick Nairne, Chairman of the Friends of Radley College Trust, called the 'Silk Radley Appeal Road Show'. Money alone wrote 4,000 letters by hand; Susan Brown, daughter of A.A.M. Gardiner (after

---

*Traditionally since the appointment of Colonel Crozier, the relationship between Warden and Bursar at Radley has been exceptionally close, personally as well as professionally – Jenner and Wilkes; Ross-Hurst and Milligan; Kerr Bovell and Jones and Silk.

Wharton, the longest ever serving Radley don), worked diligently in the Radleian Society office. The boys also helped to raise money by obtaining sponsors for such events as charity walks, a pram run to Paris, which brought in £2,500, and an Appeal Day fête.

Targets set were reached and passed; by October 1978 the Friends of Radley Appeal had already raised well over £500,000; and gradually, under the Bursar's watchful and discerning eye, despite the soaring rate of inflation in the construction industry, old buildings were renovated and extended and new ones constructed. Socials were refurbished, dormitories reconstructed and flats created for masters, the boys often being called in to help, as, for instance, with scraping down the panels in School, the Warden also lending a hand and – taking some ridicule for it – dressed for the part. Eventually sufficient accommodation was provided for each Social to have a living-in Sub-Tutor.

Meanwhile School was renovated for meetings, exhibitions, conferences and concerts, largely by the efforts of boys and dons, and was placed under the administration of an Arts Council supervised by Peter Way who – handing over the English Department to Chris Brown – became Head of Drama. A fine centre for arts and crafts, complete with an engineering workshop and known as the Sewell Centre, was opened on 13 September 1979 by Sir Patrick Nairne who had had much to do with its inception, the spirit of Sewell himself appearing in a clever and delightfully amusing masque, *Lusimasque*, written and directed by Peter Way with music by the Precentor, Donald Paine, which was performed in celebration of the occasion.

Five years later, in October 1984, the Science Building, completely renovated, extended and rendered less stark in appearance, with a new lecture theatre, a library and a refitted computer room, was opened by Mrs Thatcher, a week after she had survived the bomb attack by the IRA on the hotel in Brighton where she and other members of the Conservative Party were staying. She reminded the school that she had been brought to Radley eleven years before when Secretary of State for Education, by her friend, Airey Neave, Member of Parliament for Abingdon and on the Radley Council. On this occasion, as Prime Minister, she wistfully expressed the hope – patently not shared by her husband – that she would return in another eleven years 'in the same position as today'.

The Old Gym and cricket pavilion were both also restored, the swimming pool overhauled, the Chapel roof renewed, scruffy exteriors repainted, Covered Passage redecorated, trees and bushes planted under the direction of the landscape gardener, Penny Slocock. There were new squash courts and classrooms, housing for kitchen staff, a paperback shop, a new professionally designed golf-course, even a ladies' powder room. A new biology department had already been opened in 1975.

Following the announcement of several fresh projects, the Music School, which had been built in 1928 for a school of 334 and now had to cater for 580, was extended. There also appeared a sports centre, complete with a covered swimming pool, finished at a cost of £750,000 in forty-four weeks. In 1984 a new armoury was built; in 1988 a modern language block; and in 1989 an extension to the Sewell Centre. In that year also the Warden opened a new Reprographics Centre, and work began on an all-weather hockey pitch which provided twelve tennis courts for the summer months. In 1991, when over £10 million had been spent on Radley over the past twenty years, a concert hall was named after the Warden who had done so much to help raise the money to bring all these buildings and improvements about.

*

The Warden was anxious that Radley's new concert hall, the sports centre, and others of the College's new amenities should not be seen as being for the use of Radleians only. He had always laid stress upon the need for sharing them with the local community which in the past had tended to regard Radley as an isolated area of selfish privilege looking down upon the surrounding world. 'In my view,' the Warden once wrote to his fellow members of the Appeal Committee, 'one of the real hopes for the future of independent schools is that they should be seen to be integral members of their local communities, sharing with local people and local schools the good things they have.' 'As we seek to open our doors to our neighbours locally in sporting and cultural ways,' he added in one of the annual letters he wrote to Old Radleians, 'it will always be vital that we should look to the wider world horizons and to the needs of others.' He was pleased to be able to say in another of his annual letters that most of the boys themselves agreed with him in these beliefs. They wanted to be part of a wider community and were 'not happy at being a separated privileged élite in their ivory tower'.

Accordingly the Warden – warmly supported by David Rae Smith, as Chairman of the Council, though not at first by all members of Common Room – welcomed suggestions that the school's facilities and grounds should be made available whenever possible to all sorts of outside organizations on a scale undreamt of in the past, not only for idealistic but also for financial reasons to help with the upkeep of the facilities. Eventually some fifty outside clubs were making use of the sports centre; others used tennis and squash courts and the golf-course; the village cricket team played matches on the pitch; the police used the rifle range, children from local schools the gymnasium. When the outdoor swimming pool had been constructed it had deliberately been made a yard longer than the recognized length for competitive swimming, so as to deter outside clubs from asking to use it. When it was refurbished the opportunity was taken to make it of the standard length of 25 metres.

Fêtes were held for local and national charities; and during summer holidays the school was made available to such organizations as the National Youth Orchestra. On other occasions hundreds of children from maintained schools spent a week each at Radley as boarders on football coaching and other courses; and a total of ten thousand people on five consecutive evenings were welcomed to 'Music at Oxford' fireworks concerts on Pups' Field with College Pond in the background. Exchange visits were made with maintained schools in Watford, Walsall and Wantage.

As never before boys gave time and money to charitable enterprises. Fairs were held for St John's Ambulance, Sue Ryder Homes and Great Ormond Street Hospital. An 'Ethiopia Week' raised £3,000. As the Warden said in one of the letters he wrote each term to parents, 'the social services work of the boys remains one of the most well sub-scribed activities in the College.' Several boys gave up their time to visit old people in the village – 'granny bashing' as they called it – an act of kindness as demanding in its way as the cross-Channel rowing under-taken for sufferers from spina bifida. The Warden told parents of the delighted surprise of a man who had come to talk to the boys about various electronic aids which he had invented for the handicapped and who was 'overwhelmed' by the amount of money collected at Radley to help further his work. The Warden – conscious of the fact that most of the money raised for charity by the boys' Charity Committee through sponsored walks and other activities came ultimately from their parents' pockets – proposed that the boys should undertake two days' hard work to earn the money themselves. Over 350 boys responded to this challenge, just as they had responded, if without noticeable enthusiasm, to the Warden's suggestion that they should plant 2½ acres of potatoes to provide the College with the 36 tons of them they consumed each year.

*

Some parents feared that all these charitable enterprises might affect their sons' examination results and disappoint their hopes of gaining acceptance at a university. But the Warden's letters reassured them. Year after year the school's A level and O level results were appreciably better than those of most of the schools which were considered their principal rivals.

In 1969 over three quarters of O level subjects were passed and thereafter the pass rate, with occasional slight lapses, rose steadily, reaching 95 per cent in 1984. In two years in the 1980s the O level results were better than those of any other school in the country. When GCSE replaced O level in 1988 the results were even better: the pass rate was over 95 per cent in 1989, only one boy in 119 failing in French. The next year the results were much the same.

A level results were quite as good as those for O levels partly because boys, realizing their importance, accepted the necessity of doing work in the holidays, even if not the two hours' reading of a morning which the Warden regularly proposed to their parents as a minimum. In 1980 the A level pass rate was 90 per cent, 40 per cent being at grades A and B. By 1983 the hoped-for 50 per cent of A and B grades was achieved with a comfortable margin; by 1988 the pass rate had reached 97 per cent with 53 per cent at A and B.

When A level results were first published in the 1990s it was possible to compare Radley's achievements with those of other schools. In the tables published in *The Times* in 1991 the school's position was listed as eighth in the eighteen schools in the Rugby Group and was to rise regularly thereafter.

These satisfying examination results owed much to an exceptionally capable Common Room, among whose members – in addition to those who became headmasters and are mentioned elsewhere – were Barry Webb, Edmund Blunden's biographer, an inspired teacher of Shakespeare who went on to become a don at St Peter's College, Oxford; Richard Smail, a fine classicist as well as gifted English teacher; Michael Lewis, whose partnership with Guy Waller produced a number of chemistry textbooks; David Hardy and David Fielding, gifted teachers of biology and geology respectively; Charles Hastings and Garry Wiseman, outstanding mathematics masters; and Peter

283

Wilkins who was responsible for the development of the Sewell Centre.

Radley's highly satisfactory A level results in the late 1980s were reflected in the numbers of places obtained, and of scholarships and exhibitions awarded, at Oxford and Cambridge, despite increasing competition now that there were between four and five candidates for each place, many formerly male colleges having become co-educational, and several colleges giving priority to applicants from maintained schools in cases where the qualifications offered were much the same. Even so, about 70 per cent of all Radley College leavers went on to higher education, an increasing number to the newer universities. In 1976 Radleians gained 32 places at such universities compared with 30 at Oxford and Cambridge; in 1980 the ratio was 27 for Oxbridge and 37 for other universities. In addition that year thirteen boys went to polytechnics, art schools or agricultural colleges. In 1974 eight university scholarships and exhibitions were awarded, in 1983 fourteen, a respectable proportion in mathematics and scientific subjects.*

*

Much more thought had been given by then to the teaching of scientific subjects than had been the case in the past. Ever since the publication of Darwin's *Origin of Species* in 1859 there had been pressing demands for the proper teaching of science in public schools. The educational theorist, Herbert Spencer, had strongly advocated it; so too had T.H. Huxley who declared that 'the whole circle of the sciences [was] even more completely ignored in the higher than the lower schools.' So, too, had Dean Farrar, a master at Harrow and author of *Eric, or Little by Little*, whose paper 'On the Teaching of Science in the Public Schools' had led to the formation of a committee to examine the problem. Some progress had thereafter been made: a modern side was started at Harrow in 1869 and a master at Rugby, J.M. Wilson, author of *On Teaching Natural Science in Schools*, succeeded in introducing science into that school's curriculum.

But science long remained a suspect subject, while for reasons which Monckton Milnes condemned as pure snobbery, 'the teaching of the Greeks and Romans remained the basis of education'. Indeed, it was still widely held by the defenders of the classics that they were the only

---

*For places obtained at universities in more recent years see Appendix 2.

'doorway to intellect, taste, manners and beauty, and thus the best anti-dote to commercial ideals'.

It was this kind of attitude which so deeply aroused the scorn and animosity of H.G. Wells, who declared that England's 'imitative imperialism and solemn puerility is to be found, if not precisely upon the playing fields of Eton, in the mental and moral quality of the men who staff the public schools'. G.B. Shaw, in agreement with Wells, pro-posed that 'Eton, Harrow, Winchester . . . and their cheaper and more pernicious imitators should be razed to the ground and their founda-tions sown with salt.' For Shaw and Wells the only public school capable of producing men educated for the future was Oundle under W.H. Sanderson who had been called in by the Grocers' Company to establish the teaching of technical and scientific subjects on a sound basis and to reform a school in which, as he found, 'the majority of the boys learnt little except that vague limited gregariousness known as *esprit de corps*, cricketing sentiment, and a gentlemanly habit of mind'. And since, as Sanderson said, 'boys have only one characteristic in com-mon – their dislike to any change', and since he had not himself been to a public school, spoke with a north country accent and was believed to wear a made-up bow-tie, it was some time before his greatness as a reforming headmaster was generally recognized.

While science and engineering were firmly and respectably estab-lished in the curriculum at Oundle by the time of Sanderson's retire-ment as Headmaster in 1922, it was to be many years before other schools followed Oundle's lead. As late as 1948 a Radley boy had com-plained of the necessity of having to go to lessons in science, 'a subject for pharmacists and such like'. Less than a generation later, however, science was beginning to take its rightful place as a subject quite as important as the Humanities; and there was increasing demand for the teaching of such new disciplines as computer science, engineering science, business studies, design and statistics, as well as economics and politics.

The introduction of some of these subjects into the curriculum was not at first successful at Radley. The teaching of engineering and woodwork, for example, initially produced disappointing results; but after the sudden departure of one master at short notice and the even-tual departure of another who was more of a politician than teacher, these subjects were more rewardingly taught, while chemistry, for long considered a subject to be avoided at all costs as boring, if not, indeed, rather vulgar, became a popular subject under David Skipper and R.C.

Usherwood: every boy in Usherwood's set got an A grade at his first attempt at A level in 1975, a year in which 75 candidates sat for A levels in chemistry, 25 of whom got As. Biology had for many years been taught in the Sixth Form only. With the appointment of David Hardy in 1962 it was soon offered as an optional subject to O level and quickly grew in popularity so that by about 1970 over 60 per cent of boys in the Lower School were taking the subject and new laboratories were opened to accommodate them. By 1974 all boys in the Lower School were taking biology, chemistry and physics to O level and still do so.

*

Much thought was given in these years not only to the teaching of scientific subjects, not only to the increasingly severe demands of university entrance, but also to the careers which boys were likely to pursue on leaving school. The duties of the Director of Sixth Form Studies and of the Careers Master became of greater importance year by year. So did the teams from the Public Schools Appointments Bureau which came to Radley to give the older boys aptitude tests; and so, too, did such events as the Joint Services Day, which allowed boys to consider the advantages of a career in one of the armed forces, and the annual Industry Conference, designed to encourage boys to consider careers in industry.

The number of boys leaving Radley and other public schools to enter upon commercial careers, either directly upon leaving or after university, has been increasing for many years. It has been argued that in the past the sons of businessmen were transformed by their public school education into 'effete and soft-hearted "gentlemen"', and that public schools were thus at least partially responsible for Britain's industrial decline. In his *Collapse of British Power* (1972) Correlli Barnett maintained that the ethos of the public schools, their narrow curricula, their 'moulds of conformity and orthodoxy', their 'neglect of the contemporary world', the 'uncritical patriotism' indoctrinated in some of them, the importance attached to games as a 'powerful instrument for inculcating common responses, common values and outlook', and the tendency in games reports to elevate 'pluck' and 'playing up' above skill, intelligence and initiative were all factors contributing to the national collapse of which he complained.

Making similar points, Professor Martin Weiner, author of *English Culture and the Decline of the Industrial Spirit*, has argued that for all their vaunted independence, the public schools through new institutions like the Headmasters' Conference, converged on a common model. Despite the absence of state intervention, they came to constitute a system, one that separated the next generation of the upper class from the basis of Britain's world position – technology and business ... Public schools gradually relaxed their entrance barriers. Boys from commercial and industrial families, however, were admitted only if they disavowed their background and their class. However many businessmen's sons entered, few future businessmen emerged from these schools, and those who did were 'civilized'; that is detached from the single-minded pursuit of production and profit.

In his more recent *Capitalism, Culture and Decline in Britain*, Professor W.D. Rubinstein has effectively demolished this argument and shown that, far from discouraging their pupils to go into business, public schools actually sent more and more pupils into the most dynamic area of the economy; and that, while many businessmen did not send their sons to public schools, those that did usually found their sons perfectly content to follow them into business life.

Before the First World War prominent businessmen, however rich they or their parents might have been, had rarely been to a public school. A study of the Lord Mayors of six major English cities in the years leading up to 1914 revealed that of 378 men serving in this position

> just 17 (4.5 per cent) attended either a Clarendon School or another leading boarding school (such as Clifton or Radley) and only 26 others (6.9 per cent) attended any public school at all . . . It thus seems extraordinarily unlikely from all of this evidence that the very limited percentage of the northern élite who were educated at a public school down to the First World War could possibly have been responsible for Britain's industrial decline, even if the public schools induced all of the anti-business and anti-industrial qualities often assigned to them.

Moreover, many bankers and those engaged in established financial and commercial activities did go to public schools. Indeed, a recent study has shown that over 80 per cent of the merchant banking and clearing banking chairmen holding office between 1900 and 1972 did so.

Research undertaken by Professor Rubinstein into the fathers of public school boys, and the subsequent careers of their sons at eight leading public schools, from about the time of Radley's foundation until 1900, has shown that the sons of businessmen, in the great majority of cases, themselves became businessmen, just as the sons of professional men usually took up a professional career. 'The intergenerational shift from business to the professions was amazingly small, despite all the anti-business, anti-entrepreneurial influences the public schools are constantly alleged to engender.'

Other academic studies have confirmed the steady rise, since the early nineteenth century, of the numbers of public school boys making careers in business. In 1820–9 the percentage of Wykehamists going into business was only 6.4 per cent; in 1900–9 it had risen to 27.9 per cent. The figures for Clifton and Marlborough since their foundation show a remarkably similar rise. A survey of 2,035 Old Etonians leaving between 1967 and 1977 showed that as many as 450 had gone into accountancy, stockbroking, insurance or some form of banking. A study of 460 company chairmen holding office between 1905 and 1970 revealed that 66 per cent had been to public school; and of the eighteen Directors of the Bank of England in 1983, all but three had been to one. It is not true to say, however, that independent schools consciously educate their pupils for any particular career. A survey conducted at Shrewsbury for the period 1972–82 showed that the most popular subject read at university by Salopians was engineering in its various forms. Yet it appeared that fewer than half those who read this subject became engineers.*

---

*For the occupations of Old Radleians compared with those of Old Etonians and Old Wellingtonians see Appendix 3.

32

The Film and the Dons
1979–1981

'A risky strategy.'

IN 1979 THE Warden of Radley was faced with a difficult choice. Radley and two other schools, Sedbergh and Canford, had been suggested by the Independent Schools Information Service as the setting for a proposed television documentary series to be entitled 'Public School'. Radley would have no right to censor the films when made, nor to veto their showing to an audience which was likely to number over three million. Obviously the director of the film would want to make it lively entertainment as well as informative; and obviously, too, there would be a danger of trivial events being given undue prominence, of weaknesses being exaggerated, of problems inherent in public school life being sensationalized. Also there was the question of how naturally or awkwardly boys and staff would react when under the gaze of cameramen, soundmen, electricians and all the paraphernalia of television.

The producer and his team were anxious that the film should be made at Radley rather than at the other two schools largely because Radley was only an hour or so down the motorway and they would be able to get back to London easily at weekends during the ten months during which shooting was to take place; also Radley was not far from the home of the programme's director, Richard Denton.

But the Warden, intrigued as he was by the opportunity presented, was apprehensive about the effects which the film might have upon the reputation of the school. He did not like the idea of the television team being in the school for so long; and he feared that situations or even disasters might be artificially created for the sake of entertainment. It was not long, however, before the Warden, urged by Tim Devlin, National Director of the Independent Schools Information Service, began to believe that it would do more good than harm for the film to be made at Radley, not only for independent education as a whole but for boarding in particular and for Radley above all. He recalls a conversation in which Devlin pressed him not to turn down the opportunity of receiving ten million pounds' worth of free advertising.

The Warden also spoke to the Chairman of the Council, David Rae Smith, who, after hearing more about the proposal, said, 'Well, we're satisfied that it's not just knocking copy they're trying to make, but a serious attempt. And, as we're proud of Radley and know we've got something pretty good here, we shouldn't be frightened. We should do it. But it's got to go to Council obviously.'

The Council were not unanimous in approving it. Some members were annoyed by the Warden's having gone so far in agreeing to the film being made before consulting them, though no firm commitment had yet been made. Indeed, one of them resigned. Others, however, including John Pattisson, gave the Warden their support; and so, strongly urged on by Rae Smith, a majority gave the project their backing. Common Room also agreed that the film should be made, only two members being against it, the majority believing, as one master put it, that 'if any school was to be televised it might as well be ours' and that, in any case, it 'might be rather amusing'.

When informing the parents of his decision, the Warden added that, although it was all going to be rather unpleasant, he was agreeing to the film being made at Radley 'for the sake of the English public school'.

The result was not as calamitous as might have been feared; but, as the Warden himself observed, it fell short of doing Radley justice. 'Where was the dedicated teaching and the hard academic work?' he felt constrained to ask. 'Where was the pastoral care, only fleetingly glimpsed but so central to the whole being of College? . . . Trivialities were enlarged, mainstream events ignored.'

'It was the untypical that was given prominence,' observed Barry Webb in an article in the *Listener*. 'Nobody would know that we are in fact a community, that we actually teach and boys work; we engage in cultural pursuits; we have some forty families living in the grounds.'*

'But,' the Warden added, 'let us be fair and reflect on [the director's] problems. He had to be his own man, working in a world which has no love for the old establishment and its values ... In the event he had plenty of our opponents baying for his blood from the left, and many "Radley people" baying for his blood from the right ... Full marks to him for enraging both sides ... I only hope it will do more good than harm.'

Most critics were inclined to doubt that this hope would be fulfilled. Joan Bakewell, writing in *The Times*, complained that the series gave 'no serious analysis'. There was no sign of the lonely or unhappy boy, she complained after voicing comments that would no doubt have been modified had she written after the end of the series rather than on the basis of the early programmes. 'What about the uncompetitive, the introspective, the difficult? What happens to a community so introverted? ...'

Were Radley masters never jealous or frustrated, she felt compelled to ask. 'Schoolmastering is just acting,' she quoted David Goldsmith as having said; and she went on to say that his part in the film might well have been played by Robertson Hare. He was 'full of film comedy japes such as doubling prep whenever Ipswich lost at home, and setting maths questions about how many furlongs there were in the July Cup. If he couldn't remember your name, he called you "vile boy". It wouldn't go down well at the local comprehensive, that's for sure.'

'Radley College has other actors on its staff,' she continued: 'The chaplain seemed to be played by Alan Bennett.'

---

*Ever since William Sewell emphasized the importance of introducing ladies into the society of Radley, women have played an essential part in the life of the school, not only as dons' wives but, in more recent years, as such gifted and patient teachers as Miss Rhona Parkinson – who taught the piano for fifty-six years between 1925 and 1981 under six Precentors – and as matrons. Some matrons, indeed, have left more vivid memories in the minds of men they once treated or nursed than the masters who taught them. Three, in particular, were renowned for a decidedly formidable manner combined with remarkable skills as diagnosticians and the kindest of hearts – Miss B.A. Gibson, College Matron for twenty-five years until 1930; her successor, Miss Walpole-Simmons, whose Christian name was never known and whose perceived duties included keeping an eye on the appearance of her charges' tutors and the state of their clothes, and Miss Jean Boddy who ran the Infirmary for thirty-two years until 1974 and rarely missed a rugger match, a regatta or a Common Room drinks party.

It was arguably true that Goldsmith came across as something of a buffoon rather than the gifted and highly successful teacher of mathematics that he was, and that the Chaplain she mentioned, a much respected man, appeared as condescending. It was also claimed that the Warden, uneasy in his part, gave an impression of ingratiating unctuousness instead of sincerity and understanding in dealing with boys. The *Daily Telegraph* wrote of the 'omnipresent Warden with a chin like the Rock of Ages'.

The boys themselves shocked many Old Radleians by their accents. Few spoke, it was observed, 'as well-educated, middle-class boys were expected to speak, and certainly not as most of the masters did'. This, of course, was not peculiar to Radley. As Eric Anderson, Headmaster of Eton, said in an interview in 1993, 'there was a time here when the fashionable thing was to talk as nearly like people from an inner city as you could.' Anderson was talking of the 1960s; but the fashion lingered at Radley as elsewhere.

However, the effects of the Radley film were not as adverse for the school as many Old Radleians had feared. No boy's name was withdrawn as a consequence of it; preparatory school headmasters continued to recommend the school with the same degree of warmth as before the film's showing; it almost became necessary to employ another secretary to deal with the eighty extra letters a week that arrived at the school over the next four months; there were far more applications for places than could possibly be considered. As the Warden observed, the 'overall effect was that Radley, which few of the general public had heard about, became a famous school whether we liked it or not'.*

*

The Warden, who once advanced the opinion that perhaps his 'most important job [was] to find the right people to teach at Radley', was as skilful as his predecessor had been in his choice of assistant masters.

---

*'It's a risky strategy,' commented Stephen Winkley, Headmaster of Uppingham in 1995, 'but Radley College never looked back after featuring in a documentary series, warts and all.' Gordonstoun had by then admitted a television documentary team to make a similar film; and Winkley supported proposals to bring the benefits of boarding schools to wider audiences. The possibility of commissioning a television boarding school soap opera or radio drama series was discussed at the Headmasters' Conference that year.

Several members of his Common Room, appointed by Wyndham Milligan – among them Simon Langdale, Brian Wilson and Richard Morgan, all future headmasters – had come to Radley on the recommendation of a remarkable man, Jock Burnett, a close friend of both Milligan and Silk.

Bursar of Magdalene College, Cambridge, and editor of the *Public Schools Yearbook*, Burnett had a knowledge of public schools which was positively encyclopaedic and his high regard for Radley, of whose Council he was long a member, was responsible for persuading the numerous young men – many of them, like himself, keen fives players – whom he induced to take up schoolmastering to put Radley at the top of their list of schools whose staff they would most like to join. Burnett had, indeed, warmly supported the candidature of Dennis Silk for the Wardenship of Radley, a choice endorsed by an overwhelming majority of the other members of the Council.

A high proportion of assistant masters appointed by Dennis Silk went on to become headmasters themselves. Christopher Hirst (another protégé of Jock Burnett's) went to Kelly College and afterwards Sedbergh, Michael Featherstone to Ryde School, Guy Waller to Lord Wandsworth's College then Cranleigh, Peter Johnson to Wrekin, Michael Cuthbertson to Monkton Combe, Maurice Lynn to the Oratory, Chris Brown to Norwich and Patrick Denham to Solihull.

Silk was also adept in persuading unsuccessful masters to leave. There was one, Hugh Cardwell, who had once been an excellent if idiosyncratic science master, but, as he grew older, seemed to be 'marking time' and teaching mainly those parts of the syllabus that appealed to his own brilliant but erratic mind. Consequently the chemistry department was thought to have fallen into such a low state that it was decided he must be relieved of it for the sake of the boys, despite the good work he had done in the past not only in the class-room but also in his encouragement of the planting and maintenance of Radley's fine trees. When Cardwell – 'a prickly man at the best of times', in the words of one of his colleagues – learned that his name had been omitted from a list of those entitled to a salary increase, he went to remonstrate personally and crossly with Warden Silk who, having, so he once said, received more letters of complaint from worried parents about Cardwell's teaching than upon any other subject, smoothly replied, 'I can't quite make out what you do here.' Cardwell resigned soon afterwards.

Anxious as he was to ensure that Common Room should be staffed by promising young men eager to show their mettle, the Warden also brought to Radley masters of proven ability such as Harry Ferrar, the retired Second Master of King's School, Worcester, who was appointed Head of Modern Languages, as well as men with experience and training from outside the world of education. Among these were Christopher Hirst, who had trained as a banker in Chile, and A.L. Dowding, who had been in the oil industry after taking degrees at both Oxford and Cambridge, and had been captain of the Oxford University Cricket Club two years before Silk captained Cambridge at Lord's. Athletic accomplishments and enthusiasm were also important considerations to the Warden who was concerned that his Common Room should be well stocked with men like Dowding and Hirst who were prepared to encourage and coach boys playing games, it being an axiom of the Warden's that 'boys who are fit and well exercised seem to do better in all spheres of life than boys who are not.'

The principal sports remained rugger, hockey, cricket and rowing but the opportunities for playing other games and taking part in other athletic activities were remarkable. There were excellent facilities for playing court games, rackets as well as squash, fives and tennis. By 1990 there were twenty-three tennis courts and over a hundred boys were playing in various teams for the club. Over these court games Michael Dean, one of the best royal tennis players in England, held a watching brief, and in 1986 the first fives team won all their nine matches and the school's squash team swept aside virtually all opposition.

As well as these court games, boys could play badminton, lacrosse and basketball; they could learn judo and karate, practise archery as well as swim all the year round. They could play golf on a reconstituted course, they could fence and go beagling and sailing, take part in athletics matches and cross-country runs, even, after 1990, in polo matches. And, from 1967, they could join the Radley College Sub-Aqua Club, one of the first school clubs of its kind, from which boy divers helped with the excavation of the Tudor ship, *Mary Rose*, for three successive years and were present at the raising of the vessel in 1982.

As the Warden was proud to relate in his letters to parents and Old Radleians, there were many successes to record: the victories of James Male, the world rackets champion, and of Julian Snow, British real tennis champion; the triumph of the gymnasts in 1976 when they were public school champions for the second year running; the winning of the West of England Public Schools golf trophy in 1987; the undefeated records of the athletics and cross-country teams – as well as the fives, rackets and squash teams – in 1989, the year in which a horse trained by the Old Radleian Kim Bailey won the Grand National.

At hockey, cricket and rugger, Radley consolidated a reputation as one of the major games schools. In March 1980 the Warden could report that Radley's hockey club had three unbeaten teams, and in 1982 that the First Hockey XI, coached by Michael Featherstone and captained by James Male, were unbeaten in their school matches, as were eight other school hockey teams. In 1985 another undefeated season was recorded.

Reports of the rugger season were also favourable: in 1979 the First XV – whose coaching had been taken over by Peter Johnson and Guy Waller from Batten's successor, Anthony Hudson – lost only one match, while the Junior Colts were the Oxfordshire champions. In 1982 the First XV was 'perhaps the best ever', losing only to Sherborne, while the Second XV were unbeaten. The next year also the First XV lost only one match while the Junior Colts were again the Oxfordshire champions. In 1985 – when there were four Old Radleians playing in the Varsity match at Twickenham – the First XV lost only to Wellington and Harrow; in 1989 Rugby were beaten 32–0; and in 1990 they won every match they played for the first time in the school's history, defeating their two greatest rivals, Sherborne and Wellington.

Results at cricket, which was under the guidance of Christopher Hirst, were equally encouraging after 1972, with Michael Glover, captain of the First XI, scoring almost 1,000 runs that year. The 1975 season was the best that the First XI – captained by the all-rounder Nigel Popplewell who went on to play for Cambridge and Somerset – had had since the golden days of Dexter and Carr, Walton and Cooper, losing only to Harrow. The next year the Lord's Taverners' Cup for teams under sixteen years of age – a Cup competed for by 1,300 schools – was won for the third time in four years. In 1977 the First XI were unbeaten. In 1984 the school scored its first ever victory over Harrow; in 1986 the First and Second XIs were both unbeaten and Rory Stormonth-Darling emerged as one of the best medium pace bowlers in Radley's history. In 1987, another unbeaten season, Harrow were again defeated, so were Eton on Agar's Plough. Two years later the First XI enjoyed a season of splendid victories, M.J. Lowrey scoring centuries against Eton and Harrow in the same week. The 1991 Cricket XI was again an outstanding one.

So was the 1969 First Eight which won the National Schools Regatta and the National Youth Championships and represented Great Britain in the World Youth Rowing Championships. Another good year for Radley rowing followed in 1974 when the First Eight won the event for schools at Henley. Two years later a huge crew, six of them over six foot three inches, were beaten by Shrewsbury in the final of that event. The following year also the First Eight were beaten in the final at Henley by St Edward's. Between 1965 and 1975 Radley provided more university oarsmen at Oxford and Cambridge than any other school.

In 1981, a year in which the Boat Club – now expertly coached by Jock Mullard and, from 1987 to 1990, by David Hardy – won more trophies than ever before in its history, the First Eight were victorious in the National Schools Regatta at Nottingham and the next year they reached the final of the special race for schools at Henley. They won this event for the first time in 1974, winning it again in 1987 and for the third time in 1988.

Even more pleasing to the Warden than the matches and races won by the College's teams and crews were the number of boys eager to play games or row every afternoon, as well as the large numbers of teams representing the school at different levels, and of dons – as many as thirty – willing to coach and supervise them: it was not unusual for sixteen rugger XVs, from the First down to the Midgets', to take the field simultaneously. On one characteristic afternoon in March 1982, as well as a squash match against St Edward's, a bridge match against Harrow and a rackets match against Malvern, teams were playing golf against Eton, running cross-country against Winchester and fencing against Wellington. In November 1981 about half the entire school, that was to say twenty-two rugger XVs, took the field against Wellington, in a fairly regular fixture. Wellington usually won; but were defeated for once in 1986 when twenty-one XVs played a match and eleven of them were victorious. After these matches, so the Warden said, in which 'everyone had been exercised', it was a pleasure to walk through College: 'the boys would look at you, smile, tease you, all the things you like boys to do.' Rugger was the only game that all boys were expected to play; but almost half the school chose to play golf, even more played squash, and almost as many tennis.

*

So Radley was clearly a healthy school; but the appearance of the boys was far from being as tidy as the scrupulous Warden would have liked it to be, though it was incomparably tidier than it had been when he first took up his appointment. He repeatedly sought the co-operation of parents in his ceaseless endeavours to improve the look of the boys, whom he described as often to be seen with scruffy, down-at-heel shoes, unkempt hair and shirts with collars too tight to be buttoned at the neck. In letter after letter he urged parents to send their sons back to school with shoe cleaning equipment and shirts that fitted them; and he asked them to be sure to supply them with 'plain dark suits as requested rather than the exact opposite' and with brown shoes that were 'brown not yellow'. On several occasions he was obliged to complain of boys appearing with hair dyed in garish colours and cut into weird shapes 'in the "punk' manner', on which he was 'not very keen to say the least'. Even so, the appearance of Radley boys at this time was, in the words of a Social Tutor who went on to become Headmaster of another leading public school, 'probably tidier than anywhere else . . . The Warden did go on about it all to parents but he was as successful as any headmaster in England on this front.'

The Warden also felt obliged to tell parents how difficult it was to stop boys smoking and drinking in term-time if they smoked and drank freely in the holidays. Excessive drinking he considered to be 'just about the most serious national problem'; and certainly more boys were at that time expelled from public schools for drunkenness than for any other reason. It was with this problem in mind, and hoping to reduce the amount of illicit drinking in studies, that in 1970 he instituted a Junior Common Room in the cellars below the House where boys over seventeen were allowed to have up to one pint of beer each on three days a week. This privilege was not known to have been abused for some twenty years; but when it was, the Junior Common Room was closed and three boys were expelled.

Despite these expulsions, the Warden soon had further occasion to complain not only about boys returning to the school drunk after Leave-Away, but also about dyed hair and 'silly hair cuts' as well as the general sloppiness of dress. There was also, he maintained, far too much swearing in the school; there were cases of boys sniffing vaporizers and thinning fluids; and chewing as well as smoking tobacco. Worse than these offences, so he had to report in the summer of 1980, a number of boys were caught stealing cassette tapes, records and fishing tackle in shops in Oxford and Abingdon and were selling some of them at cut prices in the school. At the same time nearly 250 books were stolen from the school's paperback bookshop.

The responsibility rests squarely on my shoulders as Warden [Silk wrote] and I have learned some bitter lessons, which will, I trust, enable us all to make the school a stronger and better place. We had become too easy-going about leave to visit Abingdon and Oxford and were turning a blind eye to non-regulation clothing outside the College which enabled boys to blend too easily into the background. Above all I feel that the standards of personal integrity, courtesy, language and general self-discipline which we would want to see have been allowed to slide. We all know the difficulties in a society which worships affluence, where many of the young have far too many costly possessions and have experienced too much too early and find all the restrictions of school a great bore.

Yet, despite all his efforts to stop it, the Warden felt compelled two years later to report that there was 'still far too much stealing in the school'.*

*

An Old Radleian of Warden Milligan's time visiting the school in the middle of Warden Silk's term of office would have noticed many changes apart from the proliferation of new buildings. The boys were more competitive both at work and games; they also, to the Warden's demanding taste and constant regret, seemed less well-mannered; they were certainly far better fed.

Early on in his Wardenship Silk had decided to do as St Edward's had done three years before, to introduce self-service catering in Hall. Many members of Common Room were opposed to this change; but the Warden was insistent and persuasive. He pointed out that at Eastbourne waste was six times less than it had been under the old system, mainly because the boys had a choice between three main

---

*In a speech to the Headmasters' Conference, John Rae – already regarded with suspicion by many of his fellow headmasters for what was taken to be an undisguised eagerness to keep himself and his school in the public eye, as well as to make Westminster more successful than its rivals – declared with a characteristic candour that shocked his audience, 'There is not a public school where a pocket calculator can be left for five minutes before it disappears.'

This was not such a wildly exaggerated observation as some of his audience liked to suppose. Warden Silk has spoken of the reassurance to be enjoyed at meetings of the Rugby Group where, on one occasion, a headmaster asked, 'I wonder if we could talk about stealing for a moment?' 'God! You've got it too, have you,' another headmaster said. 'Wonderful!' The other fourteen headmasters present were asked to raise their hands if stealing was a problem in their schools. Fourteen hands went up.

dishes; he also emphasized the advantages of informality with dons sitting amongst the boys, boys from different Socials at the same tables, and wives and children of the staff having their meals with them.

So, in the summer holidays of 1969, work began on the conversion of the kitchen and Hall; and even as the boys were returning to Radley for the start of the next term, the Bursar was driving to Reading to collect the five hundred necessary trays. The new arrangement proved an immediate success, even though there were disadvantages at Radley in the loss of a sense of community, of a place in which to make announcements to the school as a whole, and in the marked deterioration of table manners, never of the politest here or, indeed, at other public schools, few of which now have any other form of catering.

The returning Old Radleian would also have become aware not only of an increasing concern to do well in examinations but of a crowded and more demanding time-table, of new subjects being constantly introduced into the curriculum, and of new methods of teaching them. Computers were becoming more common than blackboards. In the new Modern Language Block, for example, each classroom had instant access through satellite to programmes in French, German, Italian and Spanish.

The Warden was aware that amid all this activity, with the fading importance attached to subjects which had been considered of paramount consequence in the past – Warden Milligan's Latin Grammar paper had been replaced by an English one, for instance, and Latin was no longer a compulsory subject in Common Entrance – there was a loss of 'some invaluable time for contemplation and recreation'. Yet, when it was suggested to him that boys were being put under too much pressure, while insistent that Radley should never become 'an academic hot house' but aim to produce 'the broadly based all-rounder', he remained 'unrepentant about the policy of maximum activity because the world outside is a world of increasing pressure, and developing resistance to pressure is now a very important part of education'. 'Maximum activity' also helped to keep boys out of trouble while still at school.

The Warden never lost sight of the need for Radley to become less secluded from the outside world. He welcomed suggestions that some of the school's musicians and gymnasts should visit Scandinavia and that the College Eight should go to race abroad. He was pleased to have American and Malaysian boys in the Sixth Form and to welcome pupils from maintained schools, though well aware of the problems of boys from poor homes being educated for a time with the sons of parents who were comparatively rich. When the historian, J.V.P. Thompson, formerly a Radley don, a forceful, rich, eccentric bachelor, offered a large sum of money to establish scholarships for boys of good but not brilliant academic standard who might bring other gifts and enthusiasms to enrich the life of the school, Silk replied, 'To take a boy from a completely different background and make him a guinea-pig imposes too big a strain in the holidays in my opinion. In a school like my own, Christ's Hospital, a common denominator of poverty was fine. We were *all* in it together and felt as one. One "poor boy" among several hundred affluent boys can come sadly unstuck, and we ought to remember that it is vital that we take as few risks as possible as we have to live with our "mistakes" for at least four years and a half.'

Yet he was delighted when, in his last year at the school, his leaving present, at his own request, took the form of an award scheme to enable talented but impoverished boys to have the benefit of a Radley education; and he was highly gratified when £430,000 of the £500,000 needed to establish means-tested scholarships for five deserving boys likely to 'enrich the life of the school' was raised within four months.

The Warden was also pleased to welcome to the school a wide variety of people from the outside world to give talks and lectures, to chair discussions and to judge competitions. From all walks of life they came, trade union officials and industrialists, politicians and actors, sportsmen· and novelists, Sir Clement Freud and the Metropolitan Police Commissioner, Sir Robert Mark, Sir Geoffrey Howe and Sir Leon Brittan, Ted Hughes, Vernon Scannell and Piers Paul Read, Jon Stallworthy, Bernard Levin, Jeremy Paxman, David Suchet, Sue Lawley and Sir Robin Day, the last two of whom sent sons to Radley.

The Old Radleians returning to the school after twenty years – indeed one coming back to look at it after a lapse of over fifty – would find as much that was familiar as was new. Societies were still thriving and new ones emerging, including a Philosophical Society and Symposium (a gathering of boys and adults with general cultural interests which, thanks to the endeavours of Chris Brown, the inspiration behind the venture, was addressed by such speakers as Alan Bennett, Tom Stoppard, Christopher Hampton and Humphrey Carpenter), as well as a new debating society which put the Warden on trial for 'running an establishment contrary to the best interests of the nation' and then acquitted him by 291 votes to nine. *The Radleian* remained a useful though rather uninspired publication, now issued once a year instead of every term; new magazines, *Broadsheet, Radley Arts Magazine, Copyright* and *Symposium,* printed original work of varying quality and occasional excellence.

Music under the direction of Paine's successors – particularly the innovative Robert Gower – flourished, if it did not always excel in quality, and was warmly encouraged by the Warden as well as by several members of Common Room. There were more concerts than there had ever been – forty-one musical occasions of some kind in a single term in 1980. The madrigal choir gave performances of exceptional virtuosity. The Chapel choir sang in cathedrals all over the country, while Robert Gower scoured choir schools to bring talented musicians to Radley and also secured the services of highly regarded teachers. The Choral Society gave concerts in Oxford Town Hall and elsewhere with Downe House, St Helen's, Abingdon and other girls' schools. Orchestral concerts were given with St Edward's and with Cheltenham. There was a wind band; there was a brass band; a dance band and a jazz band. Numerous boys played the guitar and can now take an A level in electronic music.

Drama revived with the active encouragement of Peter Way, who proposed drama competitions and additional subject drama classes, and of the Warden who described theatrical performances as 'the best team game we offer; they engage so many people so fully, in so many different ways'. In Peter Way's last year, before he handed over the department to James Hare, who had been a professional actor – and was memorably to produce at Radley his own adaptation of Piers Paul Read's *Alive* – there were no fewer than four school plays as well as the usual Social plays; in one term in 1982 there had been twenty-eight different productions. Boys had given excellent performances in plays as diverse as *Hamlet* and *Oh, What a Lovely War!, Waiting for Godot* and *Conduct Unbecoming, Le Bourgeois Gentilhomme, The Royal Hunt of the Sun* and *Billy Budd.* When James Hare arrived, according to one of his colleagues, drama 'suddenly became popular and exciting . . . He was less cerebral than his predecessor but readier to take risks both in the emotional content and import of his plays and in his stage-craft. He was not, however, a headmaster's man: a bit scruffy and he encouraged the rebels to join his productions. But, oddly enough, in an era of emphasis on games and competitiveness in all areas he was one of the main civilizing influences on Radleians in the 1980s.'

Having reintroduced the Dons' Plays, which had been allowed to lapse in Milligan's day, Peter Way continued to stage, write and produce a succession of highly amusing entertainments until November 1982. With all this theatrical activity engaging so many boys, the Warden's banning of pocket television sets, and of all larger sets except the main set in each Social, were deprivations not too widely resented.

Chapel too remained an important part of school life. Yet, while insisting upon the importance of the school sitting, praying and singing together, the Warden was aware of the danger of making services too long. So, although attendance was compulsory, the evening weekday service lasted no more than ten minutes after supper. On Sundays the boys had to attend either a said Communion at eight o'clock or, at 9.45, a sung Communion which was attended also by various dons and their children of all ages. In the mid-1980s as many as 150 boys were regularly and voluntarily attending Candlelight Communion in Chapel on Friday evenings.

33

Punishments and Misdemeanours

1970–1990

'A growing distaste for beating.'

THE PROBLEM OF misdemeanours was one which all public schools faced. In most of them beating by Prefects had gradually died out, as it had done at Radley in Warden Milligan's time after boys in Peter Stuart's and Peter Way's Socials who had been asked to be Head of Social, had consented to undertake this responsibility only on condition that they would never be required to beat another boy.

With reference to corporal punishment, Warden Silk had this to say in 1982:

> When I started schoolmastering beating was a regular form of punishment and a fairly salutary one. I certainly used it as a housemaster occasionally. I find myself less inclined to use it now as a punishment and in fact have not beaten a boy for about five years. I feel that this is partly due to a growing distaste in me for beating as a form of punishment and also partly from the fear that if it should ever go wrong in any way the 'press hounds' would love a juicy 'beating story'.

This fear was certainly justified. When it was revealed in *The Times* in 1994 that a forthcoming history of Eton would expose what the newspaper's headline referred to as Anthony Chenevix-Trench's 'fondness for drink and the cane', the alleged behaviour of this former headmaster was spread all over the press for several days. A letter in *The Times* on 29 April lamented the fact that over a quarter of all published letters printed the day before had been 'given over to the habits, seamy or otherwise, of a deceased schoolmaster'; while an Old Salopian columnist in the *Observer* wrote a piece under the headline 'Sadism and a Career Move' in which it was suggested that 'when influential parents started asking questions, the Eton authorities panicked and sacked Chenevix-Trench. But the extraordinary thing was that it did not stop him being given yet another headmastership at the Scottish school, Fettes, where he remained until his death ... Whatever else, the sequence of events is scarcely a very good advertisement for the public school system.'

Chenevix-Trench's merits and abilities, his qualities as a teacher, his achievements at Shrewsbury and Bradfield, the reforms he carried out at Eton without undue damage to the school's ancient traditions, were all largely forgotten, except by some of his former pupils at Shrewsbury and Bradfield, as well as at Eton, who rose to his defence.

'The small section [of Tim Card's *Eton Renewed*] that has excited most public interest is where it records that Anthony Chenevix-Trench was too fond of the bottle and the birch,' wrote Philip Howard, *The Times*'s former literary editor, himself an Old Etonian. 'Trench's fondness for the rod was not news at Eton at the time. Trench was a reforming head who improved the academic standards of the school and reduced its social exclusiveness. But ... he himself remarked after one of his beatings, "A good thing the NSPCC does not know anything about it."' Lord Charteris, Provost of Eton from 1978 to 1991, has said that one of the ways in which the school has improved since he was there in the twenties is that 'the boys no longer go in fear of being beaten.' 'Anthony Chenevix-Trench gave the last flourish to the ancient practice,' Howard added. 'Corporal punishment faded away after him because it was seen by the boys to be ridiculous as well as barbaric.'

It was later to be seen as actually criminal, and a master who inflicted it might well find himself accused of assault under the 1989 Children Act. In 1992 a former pupil at Brighton College, who had been beaten by the Headmaster for alleged bullying, sued for damages in a case before the Court of Human Rights, and received an out-of-court settlement of £8,000 from the Government which also had to pay £12,000 in legal costs.

The problem of finding sufficiently severe punishments to replace beating is one which all boys' boarding schools have had to face, particularly since the Children Act of 1989 which has made Social Tutors wary even of sending boys on early morning runs and has led to some boys finding their duties as Prefects very difficult. The ultimate deterrent remains expulsion or the kind of rustication imposed upon the entire fifth form of St Mary's, Wantage, fifty-one girls in all, who were sent home in the summer of 1994 after riotous end-of-exam celebrations got out of hand. That same summer at Cheltenham – whose distinguished alumnus, Lindsay Anderson, the son of a general, celebrated a far more violent riot in his film, *If* – fines, varying from £10 to £30, were imposed on various boys who ruined the traditional school photograph by making horrid faces at the camera, the more wild the expression, as judged by the deputy head, the heavier the fine.

To a doctor who was making a study of the smoking habits of ex-public school boys and who asked in 1982 what kind of punishments would be inflicted on boys caught smoking and thus liable in the past to beating, the Warden of Radley replied:

> So far as punishments for smoking are concerned these vary a great deal from house to house and there is no accepted norm, though they are stepped up for recidivists. One thing we do not do, however, is to fine boys for it because that simply comes out of the parental pocket. We would be more likely to gate a boy (stop him from going into Oxford for a period of time) and set him extra work to do at inconvenient moments like Saturday evening and Sunday. Another punishment might be sending a boy out on a run at an inconvenient moment (7.00 a.m.!).

These were, and have remained, the kind of punishments inflicted for most offences, though for more serious misdemeanours, such as drug abuse, a boy would be expelled.*

---

*

*Such punishments as were inflicted for smoking seem to have had as little effect at Radley as at other schools. Roderick Newall, the Old Radleian former army officer, who was found guilty of having murdered his parents in 1987, was alleged to have been a regular and heavy smoker in his days at Radley. 'He was much fitter than anyone else in the crew [the Second Eight],' a contemporary of his was reported as saying, 'although he smoked non-stop.'

As at other schools, many boys still smoke surreptitiously at Radley. 'We try to discourage it on health grounds,' the present Warden says. 'You've got to keep smoking and alcohol under control . . . but the drugs problem is totally different.'

As with drug taking, it is difficult for school authorities to be certain about the incidence of homosexual practices amongst their charges. From a number of published memoirs it would appear that in the recent past they were rife. At the beginning of the last war, the historian and biographer Alistair Horne was sent to Stowe, where the 'exquisite Palladian buildings were distinctly seedy inside', where the 'dormitories were spartan and freezing, the food terrible' and the school uniform of grey flannel made the 500 boys 'look like a ghost herd of baby elephants'. Here, although he was plagued by 'one notable thug' who 'made up for a low IQ by torturing his wretched mice', what bullying there was, was 'less institutionalized' than it had been at his preparatory school, Ludgrove.

> Instead, it was supplanted by the other 'B' that plagued British public school life – buggery. It came from the top to bottom, in a manner of speaking. The admirable and greatly respected founding headmaster, J.F. Roxburgh, a man with a passion for the classical ethos in all aspects, was probably a sublimated homosexual, (though none of us knew it at the time) ... The numerous classical temples and copses of Stowe fairly vibrated with the love that dares not speak its name.

Horne's near contemporary, the novelist Simon Raven, who was expelled from Charterhouse for what was referred to as 'the usual thing', implies that the 'usual thing' was not at all uncommon at the school in the early 1940s, nor was expulsion for it considered all that disgraceful. 'Never, after my expulsion,' he wrote, 'did anybody so much as raise an eyebrow when the thing was mentioned. Most people merely giggled.' Certainly it did not stand in the way of his taking up a scholarship at King's College, Cambridge.

There are accounts similar to Horne's of widespread homosexuality in various schools in many other autobiographies and in novels based on public school experiences. To take one example at random: in his reminiscences Billy Mitton records, 'It was the custom on Sunday night for one side of the dormitory [at Lancing] to visit each other, the purpose – mutual masturbation. It was considered bad form to express any reticence. I remember very clearly coming back from a cross-country run and saying "I am really too tired" – to be greeted with the most horrendous silence and cold stares.'

Yet for most boys at boarding schools in the 1960s – as earlier and later – such homosexual feelings as were stirred in them were of a romantic rather than a physical nature. Even that most wildly pro-

88. The opening of the Laboratory Extension by the Prime Minister, Margaret Thatcher, in 1984, one week after the Brighton bomb attack by the IRA. The Warden, Dennis Silk, is on the right of the picture, next to Denis Thatcher

89. The First XV in 1990 when, for the first time, all matches were won, Shiplake, Pangbourne, Stowe, Marlborough, Abingdon, St Edward's, Cheltenham, Wellington, Sherborne, Harrow and Rugby all being defeated

90. A boy sketching in Chapel; a photograph by Ian Ellis, Head of Art

91. The West End of Chapel; a photograph by Paul Kilsby, former Head of Art

92. John Nugee, assistant master 1919–38; Social Tutor (B), 1924–38; Headmaster of Eastbourne College, 1938–56

93. Charles Wrinch at a scout camp. Appointed an assistant master in 1928, he left in 1930, returned 1932, left in 1942 to become Headmaster of Raynes Park County School, returned in 1946, retired in 1954

94. Clement Morgan from a drawing by Christopher Ellis. Appointed an assistant master in 1928, Morgan was a Social Tutor from 1936 and Sub-Warden 1938–52, when he left to become headmaster of Michaelhouse, South Africa

95. Peter Way, assistant master from 1952 and Social Tutor 1963–73

96. Richard Morgan, Warden from 1991

97. The 1995 Cricket XI who beat St Edward's, Eton, Abingdon, Marlborough, Bradfield and Winchester, and drew with Wellington, Cheltenham and Harrow

98. Hudson's Social (F), 1985

99. Spens's Social (B) (and cups), 1993

100. Covered Passage, 1996

101. Cloisters, 1996

102. Aerial photograph of Radley College buildings

miscuous of homosexuals, Tom Driberg, although drawn to seeking out working-men in public lavatories in the holidays, seems to have been circumspect in his relationships with other boys at Lancing, his 'sexual restlessness' there, in the words of his biographer, being 'expressed mostly in words rather than deeds'. It was not until his final year, when he was head of his house and deputy head of the school, that he made overtures to a boy in his dormitory who promptly reported him to the housemaster. For the sake of his recently widowed mother, he was not expelled but required by the kindly Headmaster, Henry Bowlby, to work and sleep by himself in a small bed-sitting-room until the end of term. He was then sent to a crammer's which helped him win a scholarship to Christ Church where the apprehensive Dean was assured by Bowlby that there was 'no reasonable probability of a recurrence of this morbid state'.

This was a woeful misjudgement. But most boys who have homosexual relationships at boarding school, either of a passive or active nature, become entirely heterosexual in later life; and, while still at school, resume their friendship with girl-friends quite naturally in the holidays. 'I tend to have sexual feelings towards other boys later in the term,' wrote one seventeen-year-old public schoolboy. 'When we return home this is forgotten. I am not worried.'

A comprehensive survey undertaken by the Wellcome Trust found that 'former boarding-school pupils were only slightly more likely than day-school children to report having had a homosexual partner in the past five years.' 'Boarding school seems to provide greater opportunities for homosexual experience but it seems to have little or no effect on behaviour in later life.'

Over a century before, an Old Etonian had come to this conclusion from his own observation. Provoked by a speech made in 1881 by the Headmaster of Clifton, James Wilson, who argued that homosexual activity in adolescents resulted in moral instability and physical decrepitude, he protested:

I have in my mind's eye a list – a long one I regret to say – of those at my school who were unfortunately conspicuous in this particular manner . . . [But] those very boys have become Cabinet Ministers, Statesmen, Officers, Clergymen, Country Gentlemen etc . . . They are nearly all of them fathers of thriving families, respected and prosperous . . . the moral to be pointed is, that happily an evil so difficult to cure is not so disastrous in its results. How many boys, or rather men, can Mr Wilson point to who owe their ruin to the immorality he talks of?

As Richard Ollard, author of one of the most perceptive of the very many books on Eton, has commented, 'Homosexuality among adolescents is as old as the hills. What changes is fashion and emphasis in morality and discipline.'

In his chapter 'Sex in Single-Sex Schools' in *The Hothouse Society* (1968) Dr Royston Lambert, founder of the Research Unit into Boarding Education, concluded that 'serious sexual activity in the upper reaches [of single-sex schools] is confined to a small minority. There may be more of it than the school authorities know, but much less of it than is commonly supposed.' Some public schools, so Dr Lambert was led to believe, did have a problem. One sixteen-year-old boy told him, 'There is no doubt in the houses a surprisingly large amount of homosexual behaviour. My house certainly seems to have got rather out of hand, anyway. The housemaster was obviously quite out of touch with the situation and a great scandal arose when he walked in on a fairly minor incident.' A rather older boy, a prefect in another school, said, 'With no females around everybody seems to be talking about lush boys, and heterosexuality seems to be frowned on while homosexuality is approved. Pictures of girls are equalled by pictures of boys in the school and photographs of nude boys from the film, *Lord of the Flies*.' 'Some boys at the top of the school congregate in the Hall after supper,' yet another boy averred, 'and stand there talking about "crushes" and "queers" and all the "lushes" and "thrushes" of the school. I think this is shocking.'

Romantic attachments, however, were far more common and generally tolerated: 'The first thing on my mind is when I will see my little friend who I've had a crush on for a year or so. Incidentally that is all it ever has been. By the way our ages are 14½ and 18 nearly.' 'There isn't a lot of homosexuality in the school; of course there is some, but there are some very close friendships . . . Nothing sexual goes on.' 'I have never done anything sexual with Thompson, although I have had my arm round him and he has put his head on my shoulder in an affectionate way, while alone, underneath the trees in the games field.'

A more recent survey than Dr Lambert's, Alisdare Hickson's *The Poisoned Bowl: Sex, Repression and the Public School System* (1995), proposed the thesis that 'every aspect of boarding life from school sports to school architecture' has for the last 150 years been 'decisively influenced by homophobia'. Yet for many if not most of the former public school boys whom the author interviewed, or who replied by letter to his enquiries, homosexuality seems to have been of little consequence in their schooldays. Some characteristic recollections are these: 'I can recall only one case in which any matter of a remotely homosexual character arose' (of Cheltenham in the 1920s). 'I hardly ever recall hearing of, let alone coming across, instances of buggery' (Bryanston in the 1930s). 'We knew very little about sex or sexuality . . . As for homosexual masters I think I can identify three: all remarkably interesting people [who] kept a clear distinction between their interest in boys and anything physical' (Clifton in the 1950s). 'If we had been told that a certain boy was homosexual, the reaction would have been bland indifference' (Gresham's, 1940s). 'Homosexual relationships were, as far as I know, all romantic and non-physical' (Radley, 1940). 'There were lots of romantic friendships . . . pure and unrequited' (Downside, 1950s). 'Most schoolboy crushes were sentimental not physical . . . The vast majority of apparent homosexuals discarded [such inclinations] as soon as they left school or during the holidays' (Eton, 1950s).

The actor Patrick Macnee, who had wanted to go to Radley but was sent instead to Eton in the 1930s, affirmed in an interview with Danny Danziger (*Eton Voices*, 1988) that while 'you had very close relationships with boys' there 'was no buggery at Eton'; and the publisher Anthony Blond was quoted in the same book as saying that at Eton, where his house was 'run on terror . . . fear of failing, fear of being beaten', he had 'crushes on other boys, but he never expressed them in any way . . . The headmaster once remarked, "My boys are often amorous, seldom erotic."'

Men at Radley since the 1930s agree that active homosexuality there was rare, buggery very rare, mutual masturbation rather less so, though as at other schools there was much rumbustious horseplay in studies, and romantic attachments were common enough. The diary of a boy who was at Radley in the mid-1940s gives a delightful and touching account of such a friendship. He and his friend went for long walks together, had tea in each other's studies, accompanied each other to Chapel for Communion. So close was their friendship that the Social Tutor of one of them thought it as well to talk to the boy about it, much to his indignation. They remained close friends after leaving Radley; they both became schoolmasters, married and had children.

Today such attachments are 'certainly not on', an experienced Radley don reports. 'They would be looked on as really absurd ... The whole attitude towards the gay world is more aggressively anti than ever ... A fair number of sixth formers will have regular girl-friends these days, often in the Oxford area, whom they will visit on Saturday evenings.'

34

Co-education

'Is there not, after all, something to be said for teaching teenage boys and girls separately?'

I T WAS SUGGESTED at one time that the problem of homosexuality in public schools, such as it was seen to be, would be largely solved if they became co-educational. Marlborough, one of the first public schools to do so, had taken a few girls into the Sixth Form in 1968. All of them were either sisters of boys already at the school or daughters of masters; but in the years that followed, in pursuit of a scheme that the Master, John Dancy, hoped would 'consolidate the liberal position', girls with no connection with Marlborough were admitted, and by 1977 there were ninety-one girls in the school, all in the Sixth Form, constituting 10 per cent of the total. Not all the masters approved of the innovation. One of them, having asked the class to give their names and receiving the answers, 'Smith, Jones, Brown, Elizabeth Clough', interrupted the roll-call at this point, 'Hyphenated, I presume?'

But the general opinion that the experiment had proved a success was shared by the girls themselves, one of whom carried out a survey which showed that 83 per cent considered that they had gained in confidence and 79 per cent believed that they were better taught at Marlborough than they had been at their previous girls' schools to which only 15 per cent had ever wanted to return. So successful, indeed, had the introduction of girls to Marlborough's Sixth Form proved that, when he became Master, Roger Ellis would have liked to make the school fully co-educational, but Old Marlburians, parents and the boys of the school, as well as a majority of Common Room, were opposed to the idea which was, for the moment, dropped.

However, the advantages of having girls in the Sixth Form had by then been perceived by other schools. Charterhouse, Wellington and St Edward's, Oxford, all followed Marlborough's example. So did Lancing which began to accept girls in 1970 when a local girls' school closed its Sixth Form; but, as at Marlborough, a proposal that the school should become fully co-educational was not accepted, though a house for girl boarders was built at Lancing in 1977 and another soon followed it. At Uppingham the first girl, a daughter of the Second Master, arrived as a day girl in the Sixth Form in 1973; a few other girls followed her; but it was not until the economic crisis led to a dramatic increase in Uppingham school fees that a decision was taken to admit girls as boarders at Sixth Form level and the Sanatorium was converted to accommodate them. By September 1976 fifty girls had been admitted to this boarding house, and the school's historian considered that, all in all, the experiment had proved a success:

> The most immediate results were the improvements in the choir and the theatre . . . A high percentage of girls play musical instruments, and the most able girls intellectually doubled the chances of winning university awards and the best 'A' level grades. There were distinct social advantages too; when in the 1950s it was first thought desirable, or necessary that boys should be given some chance each term of seeing the opposite sex, and dances were arranged with local girls' schools, the boys behaved at times like hungry wolves. Now with girls always around them, they began to behave in a more natural and civilized fashion.

Not all girls who entered the Sixth Form of boys' boarding schools in the 1970s and 1980s would agree that the boys behaved in this way on their arrival. A girl who went to Rugby in 1986 described the majority of the boys there as 'aggressive, bored, under-developed social cripples who couldn't talk to girls and tormented them instead. We were the objects of their conflicting emotions: teenage lust mixed with fear . . . Wary of being ostracized by their peers for abandoning their mates, the boys were too scared to approach us.' A decade later, it is generally agreed, girls at Rugby have become so acceptable as to appear a natural part of the scene, even though the appointment in 1995 of Louise Woolcock as head girl (to reign jointly with a boy) provoked widespread and well-publicized protests from the conservative male community on the ostensible grounds that a girl who had been at the school for only nine months could not possibly understand it well enough to justify her appointment and be the main point of contact between staff and pupils.

By the time of Louise Woolcock's appointment several schools had decided to admit girls at thirteen and thus become fully co-educational, in many cases the decision being taken for financial reasons as much as for any others. For example at Malvern, although numbers were holding up better than those at many other public schools, the Headmaster, Roy Chapman, felt that the trend away from boarding, the doubtful future of government-funded assisted places, and the declining numbers of service families who receive help with school fees, all continued to make the admission of girls essential to the survival of Malvern as a public school. Indeed, he went even further by proposing and organizing the merger of Malvern with the neighbouring Ellerslie girls' school and a local boys' preparatory school. Eight full-time and a number of part-time teachers had to be dismissed; but by 1993 numbers, which had fallen to 600 in 1991, had risen to 700.

Fully co-educational schools now include, as well as Malvern and Marlborough, Bryanston, Christ's Hospital, Clifton, Denstone, Gresham's, Oakham, Oundle, Repton, Rossall, Leighton Park, Canford, Felsted, King's School, Canterbury, the Leys, Monkton Combe and Rugby. It was announced in March 1996 that Cheltenham also was to become fully co-educational. A majority of other independent schools have girls in their sixth forms. Apart from the Roman Catholic schools (though not Stonyhurst) only twelve of the better known public schools with boarders still accept boys only. In addition to Eton, Harrow, Radley and Winchester, these are Bedford, Sedbergh, Sherborne, Shrewsbury, St Paul's, Dulwich, Merchant Taylors' and Tonbridge. Only three of these schools – Eton, Harrow and Radley – have no girls and no day boys either.

The absence of girls at Radley has relieved the staff of certain responsibilities and problems which have plagued masters and mistresses at other schools and are seized upon so eagerly by the press. 'Marlborough, a Christian public school that put an under-age girl on the Pill' ran a headline in the *Mail on Sunday*, which revealed that the school doctor had authorized the handing over of oral contraceptives to nine girls in the school and that one of these girls had been expelled after being found 'in a state of undress' in her boy-friend's study.

Nor is it only the tabloids that seize upon such stories about public schools. An article in *The Times* headed 'Sex Rules at Public Schools' recounted the experience of girls who had been at Bedales and Stowe in the 1970s. The author of the article, Mary Ann Sieghart, who was herself at Bedales, described the recently published novel, *A Private Place* by Amanda Craig, as being 'based not so much loosely as chillingly tightly on our school then . . . The tales that made me go hot and cold as I read them, recognizing some of the characters and events involved, were those of sexual intimidation, verbal abuse and bullying.'

'Every time we walked across the quad,' Mary Ann Sieghart herself recalled, 'we had to run the gauntlet of groups of menacing boys lolling against the pillars and insulting us. Some of these were no innocent-looking schoolboys, but 17- or 18-year-olds who looked like grown men.'

The same kind of intimidation evidently occurred at Stowe where two of Ilona Dixon's friends 'became pregnant and had miscarriages. No teachers ever found out, of course, or any doctor.' At Stowe, Ilona Dixon eventually decided she could not face eating school meals because after helping herself to her food, she had 'to walk past table after table of jeering, taunting boys . . . I was in tears about every other day.'

At Marlborough in 1990 the sexual intimidation once took a more violent form when a sixth-form girl, in the words of an article in the *Spectator*, 'was set upon by a gang of boys two years younger who were watching a floodlit, unsupervised soccer game. The victim's upper clothing was torn off, some of it ripped, the sixth former was bruised, and all to a backdrop of raucous laughter from the many junior boys watching . . . Most of the boys covered up for one another. Only one was identified, who had been waving her torn bra around: he was suspended for one week.'

Public school headmasters interviewed by *The Times* after a boy and girl were asked to leave Charterhouse having been found 'in a sexually compromising situation' contended that the problem was a rare one but agreed that when it did arise the boys and girls involved would be asked to leave the school. Tom Wheare, Headmaster of Bryanston, for example, explained that 'if a boy and girl were discovered having sexual intercourse and the case was 100 per cent proved, they would be asked to leave.' 'It is made clear to them when they come here,' he said, 'and it is made clear to the parents if they ask, which they sometimes do. It is not something which happens often – I think three times in the past ten years.'

Yet 'attempts by co-educational public schools to present a picture of "normality" are certainly not borne out by my own conversational researches,' wrote the journalist, Rory Knight Bruce, an Old Stoic, in the *Spectator*.

> One Old Fettesian girl told me of a classmate who slept with 18 boys in one term, which even she thought was mildly excessive . . . What is certain is that teenage relationships in public schools are going to become more frequent. At present, schools are incapable of dealing with this, preferring to victimize occasional couples as a deterrent to others and reassurance to parents.

By the mid-1990s stories of sexual peccadilloes and bullying of girls by boys in co-educational schools had become rare. The public school system was adapting itself to the revolutionary change, although there were still those who strongly, indeed passionately, denied the benefits of co-education. When it was announced in 1995 that both Pangbourne and Eastbourne would become fully co-educational in September 1996 and Charles Bush, the Headmaster of Eastbourne, maintained in *The Times* that 'the trend to co-education is gathering momentum in line with changing parental attitudes and expectations', he was reprimanded by M.B. Fisher, the Deputy Sixth Form Master at Downside, who complained that Mr Bush left unanswered the question 'why the league tables unambiguously show that the highest attainment is to be found at single sex schools'. 'It is not good enough to talk about co-education as a "trend" which is gathering momentum and which "mirrors" society,' Fisher wrote. 'Education has suffered enough from this kind of language. It is not the job of a school to mirror society, nor is it the job of a headmaster to follow whatever trends happen to be gathering momentum. It is his job to decide what is educationally desirable. Co-education, on current evidence, is not.'

*

Commenting upon a play performed by Radley boys with girls of St Helen's, Abingdon, in 1971, Warden Silk said that that seemed just about the 'degree of "co-education" we want'; and throughout his time at Radley, apart from one or two masters' daughters in the Sixth Form, that kind of co-operation in plays and concerts with nearby girls' schools was as near to co-education as the school ever got.

> There are two main difficulties with co-education [the Warden wrote, explaining his point of view, the school's settled policy and the firm opinion

of nearly all the members of Council]. The first is one of principle – parents choose Radley knowing it to be a single-sex school and maybe even because of that fact . . . The high number of applications may reflect that it is a valid principle for many parents who specifically do not want co-education . . .

The second difficulty is one of numbers. Places are fully booked . . . and introducing girls would mean going back on promises already made . . . The number of girls would be very small, and a high ratio of boys to girls brings a number of problems, as many other public schools have discovered.

This is also the view of Silk's successor as Warden who was told before he was interviewed for the appointment that the Council – having given much thought to co-education and having consulted various bodies and individuals on the subject – had concluded that Radley should not become a co-educational school. Indeed, more than one candidate for the Wardenship was turned down when it became clear that they did not share the Council's views on the matter.

That there were positive advantages in single-sex education was proposed by Judy Goodland, Headmistress of Wycombe Abbey School, who asked:

What about the preponderance of single-sex schools at the top of the academic league tables? Is there not, after all, something to be said for teaching teenage boys and girls separately? I believe that there is. Scientific studies are gradually revealing different ways of learning, some more suited to one gender than the other. Boys in mixed classes frequently take more of the teacher's time and attention. Some teenagers have difficulty being assertive in mixed company. Certain subjects are too often seen as male or female preserves, and peer pressure inhibits free choice of those most suitable for different individuals.

Concentration can lapse because of the desire to show off in front of the opposite sex. The different rates at which boys and girls achieve maturity can lead to problems in working harmoniously together . . .

Co-education is far too widely established for it to be displaced in the majority of schools. To suggest that single-sex education does not deserve to be equally valued is to base one's case on arguments that are no longer relevant.

Warden Silk thought that if Radley were a day school, co-education might be a better proposition. 'There is,' he wrote, 'no disputing the benefit and enrichment which girls would bring, particularly to the academic life of the school, nor indeed the fact that some Radleians' views on girls are superficial because almost the only contact with members of the opposite sex in term-time is at parties and dances, which are very artificial situations.

'The conclusion, then, is that Radley is bound to be artificial to some extent, but that the difficulties of introducing co-education in a boarding situation outweigh the advantages to be gained.'

The well-chaperoned dances which senior boys were taken to at Wycombe Abbey and elsewhere were certainly 'very artificial situations'. So, indeed, were the dances which girls from Downe House came to at Radley.

At some boarding schools, such dances sometimes got out of hand, usually because of over-drinking.

'Bug' (the Head) said after prayers that the end of term dance was off because last Saturday the party that went off to —— had 'disgraced the school'. They'd kissed in the dance, taken girls out into the grounds . . . cheeked the mistresses.

At a dance at Stowe in the mid-1970s a sixth-form boy was 'caught making love to a girl on the putting-green of the first tee by the Headmaster's wife who was "walking her dog" (a useful policing ploy). He was immediately expelled, much to the anger of the school who placed a master's car on the chapel altar steps and . . . refused to sing for a week.'

After some misbehaviour at a Radley dance during the Warden's first year, care was taken that it did not occur again. When girls from Downe House and St Mary's came to a dance in 1969 they were asked to arrive at five o'clock for 'a series of papers and group discussions before buffet supper in the Bryans Room and a dance in the Wilson Library'. Boys attending the leavers' dance at the end of the summer term were later issued with a list of rules to ensure they did not overstep the bounds of propriety: they were warned not to drink too much, not to smoke at all, not to take girls to their studies. It was difficult to ensure that all the rules were obeyed and masters in charge were much relieved when the last dance was over and all had been conducted without mishap.

35

An Outstanding Educationist

'One of Britain's strongest schools.'

OWARDS THE END of his twenty-three years at Radley, a period eight years longer than the Council had originally intended, Dennis Silk could look back upon what was certainly the longest and arguably the most successful Wardenship in the school's history. Not many years before, Radley was rarely spoken of in the same breath as the old schools examined by the Clarendon Commission. Indeed, it was not difficult to find parents of boys at preparatory schools who had scarcely heard of it or confused it with Repton. By 1989, however, a guide to good schools serialized in the *Daily Telegraph* described it as 'one of Britain's strongest schools'. It was 'deservedly successful, a place that stretches pupils, is efficiently run, gets results and does an all-round job of education, via discipline'. It was 'rare to find a dissatisfied parent', A level results were 'consistently high'; it was 'a strongly sporting' school with 'rowing cups galore' and it 'rarely lost at hockey'. The boys were 'relaxed – despite tight discipline – and civilized, self-confident and purposeful'. The staff and their wives were 'incredibly committed'. As at Eton where two out of three potential Etonians – whose names are often put down by their parents at birth – were eventually struck off the provisional list, there were at

Radley waiting lists stretching to the end of the century and well beyond.*

Due credit for this enthusiastic report was given to the Warden, 'an outstanding educationist . . . much respected and liked by other heads, staff, boys and parents'. The Warden himself gave due credit to his wife, to his friend and Bursar, M.M. Jones, who was to leave the school with him, and to the school's Council with whom he had always worked closely. Like Jock Burnett, the members of this Council were far more deeply concerned with the welfare of the school, and much more capable of caring for it, than the noble Trustees such as the 7th Duke of Marlborough whose offspring and not too distant relations the Founder would so dearly have liked to have had as Radley boys. Among the members of the Council in the 1970s, 1980s and 1990s were distinguished lawyers and academics, civil servants and bankers, chartered accountants and businessmen, two field marshals (Sir Geoffrey Baker and Lord Bramall) and a racehorse trainer (I.A. Balding). Some were Old Radleians: among these – as well as Sir William Oliver's successor, David Rae Smith, Chairman from 1976 to 1992 (when he was followed by an excellent successor, Michael Melluish), and John Pattisson, Vice-Chairman from 1992 – were T.B. Langton, Deputy Chairman of Lloyds in 1973–4; Sir Patrick Nairne; Michael Martin, a gifted fund raiser and expert in insurance who, when it became known that A.K. Boyd was living in penury on a minute pension, worked extremely hard to help him and all other retired masters who might be similarly placed; E.G. Nugee, distinguished lawyer and senior member of the Radley dynasty; C.G. Clarke, G.N.V. Jenkins, S.W.B. Whitworth, T.I. Perkins and Michael Hodgson. Others had experience

---

*At that time Radley, which had approximately three boys registered for each place, charged a £10 fee for registration. Most public schools charged £25; some, Gresham's included, charged £45, others (such as Eton and Haileybury) £35, and some (Oundle and Charterhouse among them) £50. At Radley places are offered on a first-come, first-served basis and final acceptance forms are sent out to all those who can be accommodated at the school three years before they are due to arrive. The return of this form in Warden Silk's time, together with the fee, which was then £75, guaranteed a place, subject to the candidate's passing Common Entrance. This was, and still is, a qualifying examination, not a competitive one. Every candidate reaching the pass mark of 55 per cent (including 55 per cent in both English and mathematics) is accepted. Today there is also what is known as a Warden's List which offers a limited number of places to boys who are not on the waiting list but who, it is considered, have qualities which will 'enrich the life of the school'.

of other schools – Bramall of Eton, Baker of Wellington, Balding of Marlborough – but all, as Paul Crowson, himself a member for a time, observed, gave the benefit of their experience and wisdom freely 'but not without stress to packed diaries and to reserves of emotional energy . . . If these talented people gave similar service, as part-time directors on the boards of great corporations, they would receive generous fees . . . All contrive to cover their generosity with the air of men for whom this work is their pleasure.'

Following the example set by Frank Fisher at Wellington, and at the instigation of Sir William Oliver, Silk took to inviting the members of Council to spend a night at Radley during the Easter term, later extended to the summer. They stayed in various houses about the school, listened to masters giving talks about their several departments, went to small dinner parties with members of Common Room, walked around the grounds to get the feeling of the place, the *genius loci* so vital to an understanding of the spirit of Radley. The Council dinner in the summer term, so the Warden thought, was 'the best evening of the year'; the Council itself the 'best club' to which he had ever belonged.

Above all, the Warden gave credit for Radley's success to the teaching staff, so many of whom he had appointed personally, and, in particular, to his Sub-Wardens – to Paul Crowson, 'a lovely man', always ready to come forward to support him in trying times and to fade into the background when things were going well, to the eccentric and amusing David Goldsmith, to Anthony Hudson, shrewd, clever and discriminating, who became Headmaster of Pangbourne, and to the worldly-wise Alan Dowding, one of Silk's oldest friends who was Sub-Warden for two years before handing over to the 'shambolic', 'overweight', 'most civilized' Hamish Aird, a well-read and 'wonderful teacher of English', the 'best liked of all' Silk's Sub-Wardens.

Most of Warden Silk's assistant masters were teachers of exceptional talent and industry. Indeed, it was essentially required of them to be industrious: there were those who complained they were driven too hard.* They were also expected to share the Warden's belief, as one of

---

*It cannot be said that they were adequately rewarded at this time for this hard and dedicated work. The basic salary of a Social Tutor in 1968 was no more than £1,000 a year. A Radley master who went as Headmaster to another public school in 1973 was paid a starting salary there of £5,000 a year which was more than Dennis Silk was being paid after five years as Warden of Radley. By 1991, however, masters'

them put it, that 'the competition of sport is tough and represents a good preparation for life'. The Warden himself suggested to a conference of preparatory school head teachers that 'hard and serious games' could introduce boys to the hard situations in life which they would later have to experience and to 'disappointment and failure without much risk of damage being done'.

There could be no doubt that a kind of competitive 'bloodism' lingered on at Radley: a boy academically gifted but no good at games, while not necessarily derided, was known as a 'veg'. A Tutor, Peter Stuart, who introduced into his Social the same sort of marks of respect for scholarly as for athletic attainments was regarded by the enthusiastic games players as highly eccentric.

There could also be no doubt that the Warden was a traditionalist both in social and religious matters. He continued, term after term, to insist upon the boys' neat appearance, clean finger-nails and good manners; a devout man himself, he spurned all suggestions that the rule of compulsory Chapel attendance five days a week, and the High Anglican services, should be relaxed; he strongly supported the continued wearing of gowns for lessons, meals and Chapel and for all formal occasions; he held firmly to his view that single-sex education was much to be preferred to co-education; and he lamented, as a man from a poor family, the regard for personal possessions that was so

---

salaries had much increased. By then they ranged from £11,149 a year for a newly appointed inexperienced master living in Common Room, and provided with free board and lodging during term time and for up to two weeks in the holidays, to £27,585 for a master with thirty-five years' experience and living in his own accommodation. There were 'special responsibility allowances' of, for instance, £1,760 for the heads of various departments, £1,500 for the careers master and £770 for the master in charge of the paperback bookshop. By new scales introduced in 1994 assistant masters start at £14,197 a year, with full board in Common Room. With annual increments, they may eventually earn almost £30,000 a year. Teaching staff with special responsibilities earn between £20,000 and nearly £32,000 a year, and Social Tutors between £25,000 and £35,000 a year.

All teaching staff are expected to live in College for the better performance of their duties but for those not living in College a supplement of £2,625 is paid. Expense allowances are paid for assistant masters, Sub-Tutors and Social Tutors.

In 1994 the headmaster of a good public school might expect to earn between £60,000 and £65,000 a year, though some earn more, certainly more than most university professors. A classroom teacher in a state school could expect rather more than £11,000 in the first year and eventually just over £20,000 a year. More than forty heads of higher education institutions earn more than £100,000 a year.

distressing a feature of the modern world. He deeply regretted that schools in Britain were 'beset with young people who had done too much too soon', and was shocked to discover that one of his sixteen-year-old pupils had blithely informed a national newspaper that he was sleeping with his girl-friend in the holidays with the full consent of his parents.

Some of the boys in the school condemned the Warden for being old-fashioned; but nearly all parents welcomed his stand. Many, indeed, obviously expected Radley to give their sons that sense of moral responsibility, the culture and spirituality so clearly lacking in their own homes, and to turn out the 'rounded Radley Renaissance man', well-mannered, self-confident and urbane, rather than the fact-filled product of a Gradgrind's classroom.* Although Radleians who had their eyes set on a profitable rather than a rounded life were common enough, the Warden could take credit at the end of his career at Radley for having done his utmost to deserve the trust reposed in him. Finally, having held the appointment for a longer period than any of his predecessors, Silk retired as Warden in 1991.†

---

*A large proportion of parents were, and still are, bankers, lawyers, accountants or employed in various capacities in the City as well as in advertising, broadcasting, the entertainments industry and the racing world. Most live in London and the Home Counties. The tables in Appendix 4 show that the provenance of Radleians, unlike that of the pupils of many other schools, has changed little in the past fifty-odd years.

†Since 1994 he has been Chairman of the Test and County Cricket Board. He was appointed CBE in 1995.

36

Radical Approaches

1991–1996

'The greatest inheritance of any of my predecessors.'

'WHAT WERE YOUR ambitions when you first came to Radley?' the editor of *The Radleian* asked Dennis Silk's successor soon after he had taken up his appointment. His answer to this question revealed ideas for the future of the school more far-reaching and revolutionary than had been brought to it by any Warden since William Sewell.

Formulator of these ambitious plans was Richard Martin Morgan, fifty-one years old, a man of most varied interests and numerous enthusiasms, ranging from art and music, English literature and the poetry and history of the First World War, to cricket, golf, Rugby fives, rackets, politics and the stock market. His father was a distinguished Queen's Counsel and County Court judge of Welsh descent and Morgan himself, after leaving Sherborne, had read law at Caius College, Cambridge, and later, for a year, English at York University. He had come to Radley as an assistant master in 1963 and was immediately recognized as a remarkably good teacher, particularly of less able boys who required patient encouragement. Six years later he became a Social Tutor; and in 1978 was appointed David Ashcroft's successor as Headmaster of Cheltenham at the age of thirty-eight, having married ten years before the stepdaughter of the Rt. Revd Launcelot Fleming, a former Bishop of Norwich, Margaret Agutter, with whom he has three daughters and who, as skilful and attentive a hostess as her predecessor, was to do much at Radley to bring the village and the school closer together.

At Cheltenham Morgan soon made his mark as a headmaster who, while respecting tradition, was eagerly responsive to new ideas as well as one determined to impose a firm discipline upon the boys and to follow Thomas Arnold's celebrated example in ridding the school of its undesirable chaff. In a mass expulsion, which many headmasters of maintained schools would have dearly liked to have been able to emulate, he rid Cheltenham of no fewer than thirty-two boys in his first two years there. 'They were yobs,' he was quoted as saying, 'and I think the job of public schools is to fight yobbishness to the death.' He also eased out of the school a number of masters who, he felt, were no longer able to give of their best, so that by the time he left almost three quarters of the teaching staff which he had inherited had departed. 'What does Lord Hanson do when he moves into a bad outfit?' he explained. 'He puts in new management within six months. Unfortunately, you can't do it that quickly in a school, but I did end up with a staff whose average age, at 33, was a lot younger than it had been.'*

Before long the results were apparent: when he arrived at Cheltenham the proportion of boys achieving A and B grades was only 23 per cent. So, with the agreement of staff he determined on a goal of 40 per cent within four years. In the event a figure of 46 per cent was reached. So he raised the target to 50 per cent. 'Last year [1990] we managed 56 per cent,' he reported. 'So I upped it again to 60 per cent for the benefit of my successor, poor chap.'

Morgan left a school which, according to its most recent historian, had begun 'to be talked about as it had not been since the 1920s'. The years of his headmastership had been one of 'high activity'. 'Everything was undertaken at full stretch – some would have said that we tried to achieve too much, though it was always Richard Morgan's philosophy that, given the right incentive, everyone could achieve more than they thought they could.'

At Radley, Morgan's ambitions went far beyond the raising of targets in examination results, significant though the rise in the percentages of Grades A and B was to be.

---

*The average age of the staff at Radley in 1994 was 37. This compared with 40 at Malvern, Oundle, Uppingham and Sedbergh, 39 at Sherborne and Harrow, 38 at Marlborough and Wellington, 35 at Stowe, 34 at Cheltenham and 33 at Bradfield.

As he had found at Cheltenham, there were immediate problems to face with some unruly boys: three sixteen-year-old fifth formers were expelled for driving around Oxford in a car borrowed from the mother of one of them; not long afterwards ten sixth-form boys, aged seventeen and eighteen, were expelled after having admitted to smoking cannabis. The fathers of five of them, rich and successful men, took counsel's opinion as to whether he was within his rights to punish the boys in this way. It was, he says, 'unquestionably the worst time' he has ever had in his career.

*

As a boarding school in the country, drugs have been less of a problem at Radley than at schools which take day boys or are situated in the middle of towns. There are, however, few public schools which, like Radley, are now wholly boys' boarding schools and all of these have at some time had to deal with boys taking soft drugs such as cannabis.

It is naturally not a subject to which school historians devote much attention, nor one which most school authorities wish to see made a matter of public discussion. John Rae who became Head Master of Westminster in 1970, and who, in 1993, described the drug problem in schools as 'growing more acute', wrote in his memoirs, 'In all but one of the conversations I had before moving to Westminster [the exception being an interview with the boy who edited the school magazine] – with John Carleton [Rae's predecessor], with the Dean and other governors, with senior members of the staff – no one mentioned the word "drugs" . . . Drugs, indeed, were seldom discussed at private meetings of the Headmasters' Conference and it was unthinkable that they should appear on the agenda of the public Annual General Meeting.' Yet, as Rae soon discovered, 'the use of cannabis was so widespread at Westminster that the drug was sold openly in Little Dean's Yard and across the tables in College Hall.'

When he perceived the extent of drug taking in the school Rae realized that 'doing nothing was no longer an option'. Yet he could hardly expel or rusticate all the boys involved, over a hundred of them, though he was tempted to threaten to do so, 'if only to shake the masters and governors out of their complacency'. What made him angry was 'not the behaviour of the boys but the cowardice of the adults'.

Shortly after his first half-term, John Rae discovered that a fifteen-year-old boy had been distributing cannabis in College Hall at tea-time. He immediately expelled him. Soon, other cases came to light; a second boy was expelled, four others rusticated and, at a special school assembly, the rest warned that those who brought drugs into the school for sale would be expelled and those in possession of them rusticated.

After this experience of drugs in his first term Rae wanted to earn the reputation for taking a hard line. His aim was to 'get rid of Westminster's reputation for permissiveness, particularly on the question of drugs' – a reputation which had induced several parents, who had registered their sons for Westminster, to send them elsewhere. But he also wanted to retain the school's 'reputation for being more mature than the country boarding schools in its handling of the wild oats of adolescence'. To a large extent he succeeded. His ultimate decision to expel any pupil involved in drug taking in any way, either as user or supplier, kept the problem under control though it did not cure it.

Rae's experiences at Westminster were by no means unique. Although most schools were able to deal with the problem of drugs without undue publicity, there were those which were not. Roger Ellis, who became Master of Marlborough in 1972 and who felt obliged to expel more boys for drug taking in his first eighteen months than in the whole of his subsequent career, was unable to escape the attentions of an ever-curious press; nor was Rossall; nor was Canford from which boys were expelled in 1991 after expulsions had been reported from Wellington; and nor was Whitgift whose headmaster accused parents themselves of using illegal drugs after he was strongly condemned in 1994 for expelling ten pupils and suspending fifteen more in what was described as 'one of the biggest crackdowns on drugs by any public school'. Later on that year the parents of boys at Whitgift began a test case for damages against the school, claiming that their expulsion breached natural justice. By March 1996, however, no papers had been served on the Whitgift Foundation.

In that year also pupils at Ampleforth were arrested for alleged drug offences and released on police bail; the next day the Headmaster, Father Leo Chamberlain, was obliged to suspend other pupils; within a few weeks sixth-form boys at Winchester were sent home for smoking cannabis; and six months later four boys at Radley were expelled for taking drugs including cannabis and Ecstasy. Not long after that it was Eton's turn to be in the news when that school was reported in the press as being 'rocked by another drugs scandal'.

Towards the end of 1994 it was revealed that some public schools were introducing urine tests after a national study had concluded that the number of fifteen-year-old schoolboys experimenting with drugs had trebled in the last five years. 'More than a dozen top fee-paying schools', including Marlborough, Stowe and Haileybury, were reported in the *Sunday Times* as being prepared to use urine testing, although four years before Dr David Jewell, Master of Haileybury and then Chairman of the Headmasters' Conference, had been quoted in the *Spectator* as describing random drug testing in schools as 'a deplorable practice'.

In June 1995, after newspapers had reported that within the previous two months boys had been expelled from Eton, Millfield, Pangbourne, Uppingham, Wellington and Westminster, it was announced that 'leading independent schools are holding a national investigation of drug taking as an alarming series of expulsions highlights the problem among their pupils'. The Headmaster of Sevenoaks was said to have abandoned automatic expulsion and, with the approval of parents, introduced a system of urine testing. Instead of being expelled pupils found with illegal drugs were to be suspended and allowed back into the school once they and their parents agreed to the tests. 'Only if they subsequently test positive are they expelled.'

At the Headmasters' Conference in October that year guidelines were presented which took this softer line on cannabis, proposing that, contrary to government advice, not all pupils caught smoking the drug would be reported to the police. Pupils suspected of taking drugs would have to take urine tests at school; those whose tests proved positive would have to submit to regular testing and would be expelled for a second offence.

At Radley the Warden has no doubt that Dr Rae's forceful and unequivocal approach is the right one; and boys in his care found taking drugs will be automatically expelled. 'If you touch drugs,' they are warned, 'you go.' This was the policy he adopted when he went as Headmaster to Cheltenham in 1978; it was not an uncommon one then; now it is much rarer. The problem is, he thinks, 'the most horrible one any headmaster has to face', particularly in 'the youth culture of the mid-1990s'. 'In the holidays heaven knows what happens,' he says, 'I'm just intent upon keeping Radley totally drug free.' The Warden's stand is supported by the school's Council.

*

With his strong approach to discipline established at Radley with the expulsion of miscreants and troublemakers, the Warden could once

more turn his thoughts to the ambitious plans which he had been for-
mulating ever since the possibility of becoming Warden had opened up
for him. He well recognized the importance of the challenge being
offered to him.

Radley had a higher reputation in 1991 than it had had at the time of
any previous Warden's appointment; it was also financially stable. His
inheritance, Morgan recognized, was the 'greatest without a shadow
of doubt' of any enjoyed by his predecessors. David Rae Smith,
Chairman of the Council, said to Morgan, 'Whatever you do, don't
waste the chance'; while Dennis Silk pressed upon him 'two pieces of
advice': 'Make sure you are there [which towards the end of his
Wardenship Silk could not always be] and recognize that there must
be a lot of changes' which Silk might have made himself but which he
preferred to leave his successor to do in his own way.

Morgan was determined not to waste the chance, nor to shirk the
responsibility of making changes. He began with two advantages: he
was the first Warden since Ferguson to have been a headmaster before,
and he had enough self-confidence to feel he could, if he were lucky,
'get away with' carrying out the plans he had in mind 'quicker than
anyone else'.

His most immediate task was to reform Common Room which he
perceived to be 'a bit staid, a bit bachelor, and a bit too self-indulgent,
especially in alcohol'.

Eager to tackle the problem, Morgan set about the task without
delay, warning the members of Common Room, in his first address to
them, that 'the boys come first'. 'I don't think,' he later confessed, 'that
they quite understood the implications of that.' They soon did so,
however: unsuitable staff were weeded out with as much determination as the Warden had displayed at Cheltenham. It was all most
'painful and unpleasant', both for him and for those who, he felt, had
to suffer for the sake of the school; and the process was not completed
until 1996.

The Warden comforted himself with the words of the school's
remarkably effective Chaplain, David Coulton, 'If you make all the
nasty decisions within the first five years you might enjoy the last
four.' Characterized by what a member of Council has described as a
tendency 'to rush into things with too much enthusiasm', the Warden
was, of course, unable at first, in pursuit of his reforms, to enjoy the
full support of Common Room, several of whose members, even those
whose confidence that they were doing well was supported by

examination results, were now worried about the tenure of their appointments. But by the beginning of 1996, with much help from the Sub-Warden, Hamish Aird, relations between Warden and Common Room were, in the words of a member of Council, 'coming right'. Certainly there were then in Common Room a number of dons who justified the Warden's description of it as 'truly formidable'. Among them were Andrew Reekes, the Director of Studies, 'unquestionably the best Director of Studies in England', David Fielding, James Wesson and Richard Greed.

*

The Warden's ambitious plans for Radley were reported in *The Times* a bare two weeks after he had taken up his appointment. They were no less than to turn Radley into 'the first truly European public school'. He proposed that in the near future 'anybody visiting Radley [would] hear French spoken as much as English throughout the school'. As many lessons as possible would be taught in French and he expected the school to be 'fully bilingual, inside and outside the classroom, by 1994'. French was to be the main language used, but Spanish and German were also to be spoken, and most of the seventy or so teaching staff, including the Warden himself, were to take crash language courses. 'Mr Morgan said that he believed Radley would lead the way for all English public schools to return to their original purpose of educating people to work abroad. "This time, however, we will not be training them to run the Empire but to work in Europe and the wider world," he said. "Radleians will be true Europeans."'

A year later, when he spoke to the editor of *The Radleian*, the details of the plan had had to be modified, much to the relief of Radley dons who, having become accustomed to being much envied on visits to other schools, were now liable to be ridiculed – as they still occasionally are – by such remarks as 'Have you started teaching Greek in French yet?' But the original concept remained and remains an essential theme of the Warden's philosophy. It was accepted that it was not practicable to teach lessons in French – and it had never been supposed that such practical subjects as mathematics and physics would ever be taught in a language other than English – nor could the entire Common Room be expected to devote what little spare time they had to learning foreign languages. Yet it was still hoped that, in due course, all boys would be fluent in at least one modern language and, in the meantime, some members of Common Room were 'trying to learn French'.

'I suspect that in time Common Room will be bilingual,' the Warden said, 'and I certainly hope that, although lessons won't be taught in another language, in a year or so you'll hear quite a lot of French spoken around the school naturally . . . The objective is very simple: that everybody feels European as well as feeling British.'

Efforts have been made to achieve this objective. The Sixth Form have completed a two-year course in a modern language ever since 1991; while the world beyond Europe has not been neglected: the study of Mandarin has been introduced and an Oriental Summer School, attended by seventy students from the Far East, was held at Radley in 1996. All boys, in addition to their A levels, have been expected to take an exam in a modern language which they have studied for five years. It cannot be said, however, that the initiative has been a success. Some boys decline to give up valuable time from their A levels to study for this exam; others make little attempt to pass it; the results are deeply disappointing. However, there has been a growing awareness of Continental problems and affairs, while the standard of work in the Languages Department has certainly improved appreciably.

Numerous visits have been made by different groups of boys to foreign countries, both within and outside Europe, from which pupils have come on exchange visits to Radley; and the school has organized congresses of European schoolchildren at which there have been debates and discussions on themes of mutual interest. In 1993, having won a national debating contest, Radley represented Great Britain in a meeting of the European Youth Parliament on the Continent; in March 1994 the Parliament met at Radley; and in October 1994 a Radley delegation attended the European Youth Congress in Italy.

While concerned to give boys at Radley a deeper understanding of their extra-national future as well as the kind of education and training which would help them not only to obtain university places but would also be of assistance to them beyond university – when they will compete in the search for satisfactory employment – the Warden was also anxious that boys should be concerned with the wider world while still at school. He recognized that Radley's splendid and extensive site was one of its great strengths but he saw it, too, as a potential weakness in that 'people might be thinking internally, looking inward' when the aim should be to broaden their outlook on life and society, 'to get Radleians' minds outside Radley'.

With this end in view, in 1992 he instigated compulsory community service for all boys except the Upper Sixth, believing 'an ability to understand and be sensitive to the life styles and needs of those in less favourable circumstances' was an 'essential part of a boy's education'. So boys, not always willingly, gave up a fortnight or so of their holidays to work with the police or the fire service, in hospitals, homes for the elderly or in special schools for handicapped children. In one characteristic venture a party of boys went to teach children in Romania; in another, less characteristic and highly adventurous, boys on an expedition to Nepal combined trekking in the mountains with community service in schools and hospitals.* Several parents were initially opposed to the compulsory nature of Radley's community service, often because of the difficulties of arranging it, but have now come round to accepting it as a valuable part of their sons' education, though by no means all boys take part in it.

Boys were encouraged, as they had been in the past, to broaden their outlook in other ways, to attend lectures, to go to the theatre and the opera, to read newspapers, academic journals and books on subjects beyond their set texts. Scientists were advised to read novels, boys on the arts side books of popular science. At the same time masters were encouraged to discuss openly with boys such matters as religion and sex, alcohol, smoking and drugs, the difficulties of adolescence.

Most of these concerns and endeavours were outside the experience of the typical Radleian of earlier generations whose imaginations had not been encouraged to wander too far from the classroom, the playing field and the *locus in quo* of such activities, musical, theatrical and otherwise, as were undertaken in those parts of the school assigned to them. Yet, beside the new endeavours, the traditional pursuits continued as before. Music still plays a large part in the life of a school in which almost every other boy learns a musical instrument and, while the Warden, towards the end of 1995, lamented the fact that there was 'no orchestra worth speaking of', he was pleased to report in his letter to Old Radleians at that time that the Chapel Choir, under the direction of Nigel Wilby, had begun to sing 'with much greater confidence' and that 'as a result, congregational singing had improved dramatically'.

He was also pleased to report a marked improvement in the production of plays. In earlier years he had regretted what he perceived as a

---

*There have been several subsequent expeditions organized by G.L. Treglown whose services to Radley have extended far beyond the teaching of chemistry. Boys have gone to North Cape as well as to Kenya, and to Iceland and north-east Greenland where research was carried out for the Wild Life Trust.

decline in drama at Radley, the school's major productions being in no sense as entertaining or moving as similar performances at, for instance, Uppingham and Shrewsbury. They were, indeed, in his opinion, 'inward-looking and self-indulgent'. Even though performances as diverse as *Jesus Christ Superstar*, *The Caretaker* and *One Flew over the Cuckoo's Nest* (also performed at the Edinburgh Festival) had been staged at Radley and had met with the warm approval of less demanding critics, it was not until Simon Barlass's production of Ionesco's *La Cantatrice Chauve* in French that the Warden felt able to pronounce unqualified praise and hope for similar performances in the future, a hope realized by an outstanding production in 1996 of *Macbeth* with the Convent, Abingdon.

Social plays are performed with all the enthusiasm of earlier years and the Haddon Cup, instituted 'to promote drama in the lower school', is eagerly contended for. The Art Department, under the direction of Ian Ellis, a worthy successor to the inspirational artist, Charles Mussett, and the innovative Paul Kilsby,* continues to flourish and, as the illustrations in *The Radleian* and exhibitions in the Sewell Centre gallery testify, consistently produces work of a far higher standard than had been achieved in the 1930s and 1940s. Boys working on scientific and engineering projects also produce some remarkable work such as, for example, the exhibits displayed in the electronics exhibition in July 1994 and what was described in the *Oxford Mail* as 'a three-wheeled two-horse car' which won a major prize in a national competition in October of that year. Boys working under the supervision of Max Horsey also won awards in 1996 in the national Young Electronics Designer Awards.

As in the past a large variety of societies exists and new ones are formed from year to year, from a Beekeeping Society and a Clay Pigeon Society to societies devoted to mountaineering, judo, philosophy, bridge, natural history and film making. Yet the demands of exams have severely limited the numbers of members of these societies, and many have disintegrated altogether. There were half as many active ones in 1996 as there had been in 1990.

Chapel, which the Warden manifestly enjoys, remains an essential

---

*Under Paul Kilsby, a controversial figure at Radley, the Art Department became 'avant garde and somewhat introverted'. Kilsby was 'an excellent teacher', in the words of one of his colleagues, 'but he was weak on discipline and the department was not as Silk or his successor wanted'. Past students, however, speak highly of him.

part of school life; and, thanks to the ingenuity of the architect, Tony Platt, and the skilful management of the Bursar, Richard Beauchamp, who have realigned the seating, the whole school can now be accommodated in the building upon which £300,000 has recently been spent on new lighting throughout, amongst other improvements, and on carvings, finials and mouldings made out of plastic resin practically indistinguishable from the oak originals. Services are compulsory on five evenings a week and on Sundays there is a family service with dons' wives attending as well as their children.* In October 1994 the office of Compline was sung in Chapel with the full Sarum Rite in Latin which, it was believed, 'had not been sung in this country for several centuries'. A common enough opinion of Chapel at Radley was expressed by a boy who observed recently, 'skipping Chapel is one of the ultimate cardinal sins ... It is pretty harmless in itself, though, and a lot of people actually admit to quite enjoying it. There is a thriving Christian community at Radley, seen weekly at the buzzing Christian Forum meetings ... Probably the best thing about Chapel is the opportunity to sing really loudly.'

While time was found, as it had been under previous Wardens, for lectures on all manner of subjects from the Normandy campaign to British portraiture, for meetings of the school's ever proliferating societies and for such events as a Management Skills Conference, the school maintains its reputation for academic excellence, well over 90 per cent of boys going on to universities despite the tendency in some of them to discriminate against independent school applicants, the subject of complaint to vice-chancellors by some headmasters in 1995. Virtually every boy who wishes to do so finds a place on some course of further education.

The high position to which Radley has risen academically is reflected in *The Times*'s controversial league tables which, in 1993, showed Radley as seventh in the eighteen Rugby Group schools, and in 1994 as higher than all comparable schools other than Westminster, Eton, Winchester, St Paul's, the Perse School and Harrow. In that year

---

*Chapel, or Meeting in the case of Quaker foundations, is still compulsory at nearly all leading independent schools (a notable exception being St Paul's) although the occasions upon which attendance is required have been much reduced of late. Allowances are made for pupils of non-Christian faiths. At Clifton, for example, there are thirty-five Jews with their own synagogue. There is no chapel at Bedales, but attendance at Sunday evening 'Jaw' is compulsory for all boarders.

Radley was fifth in a table showing the proportion of boys gaining Grade As; and in 1995, in a table listing the first fifty boys' independent schools with boarders, Radley was again fifth with Winchester, St Paul's, Westminster and Eton once more in the first four places. In March 1996, in a table printed in the *Daily Telegraph* of independent schools entering forty-five or more candidates for A levels and showing the percentages of subject entries graded A or B, of the eighteen Rugby Group schools, Radley was second to Winchester. In a table published in *The Times* in November that year, Radley was shown as having overtaken Winchester (as well as Eton).

The publication of these tables in newspapers angered many headmasters, not only of those schools which came towards the bottom of the lists. David Summerscale, Head Master of Westminster, protested to the editor of the *Daily Telegraph*: 'I wonder if you realize what a disservice you do to so many schools by conducting a league table of this kind? . . . [It] can only generate the wrong kind of competitiveness amongst schools, increase parental perturbation and uncertainty and overlook the excellence which so many schools achieve both in and out of the classroom with less gifted candidates.'

Richard Morgan made a similar point in a letter to *The Times*:

A-level results are important, as all candidates, their parents and schools know. But their importance can be exaggerated by the league tables.

Last year I interviewed two candidates for a post. Both had A levels that would have done credit to any league table, both had excellent degrees, both were set to gain their doctorates. Both were exceedingly dull . . .

The key question facing the schools is whether we can help our pupils to lead fulfilled adult lives. For the majority, that will almost certainly mean gaining a good job in an international job market.

And this means looking after the wholeness of every person and will include the development of qualities such as vitality and motivation as well as skills such as language and technology.

A levels may tell but half the story, if that.

However, as the Warden wrote later, 'If there are going to be tables, then we should do well in them.' Radley has certainly done so.

The year after the Warden's letter to *The Times* was written, the newspaper's Education Correspondent reported that 'teachers' organizations and local government groups were united in their criticism of the publication of examination data . . . Critics argued that schools near the foot of the league tables would be damaged if the background and educational standards of entrants were not taken into consideration.' However 'Ministers shrugged off the criticism and hailed the Government's largest post-war publishing venture as a revolution in parental choice . . . The Education Department's switch-board was jammed by parents wanting copies of the tables.'

> Those who condemn the publication of any raw data [the *Independent* told its readers] are almost invariably the providers of the service, in this case education, rather than the consumers (or their parents). The providers of education have a vested interest in mystifying their clients. In the case of the examination tables, the condemnation often carries unpleasant over-tones of class prejudice. For example, the National Association of Schoolmasters/Union of Women Teachers said yesterday: 'They [the league tables] do nothing but confirm the obvious, that children in the gin-and-tonic belt do better than those from poorer areas.' Apart from its inherent snobbery, this remark is objectionable on a more fundamental ground: it is simply wrong. The tables indicate that some working-class schools do outstandingly well in terms of examination results, and some schools in leafy suburbia do rather badly.

When Westminster came top of the tables in 1992, David Summerscale told *The Times* that he was 'absolutely delighted' with the published results. 'With probably 70 Oxbridge places and a big improvement in the number of top grades, it is the best we have ever done . . . But we do not want to say we are better than anyone else. There are schools doing their job in harder circumstances just as well.'

The Times defended its publication of the tables by explaining that its intention was 'not to label schools as good, better and best but to measure their relative academic importance'. By this criterion the 'rankings confirmed the supremacy of independent schools at A level . . . The pass rate of independent schools [which filled all the top forty places] was almost 92 per cent, compared with less than 80 per cent overall. As in the state system, single-sex schools dominated the top places for 1992. Westminster, with a co-educational sixth form, was the only one to break the monopoly.'*

---

*It might have been added that girls' independent schools did particularly well: in 1993 they occupied the top seven places, St Paul's Girls' School (with 83 candidates) obtaining 87.4 per cent passes at Grade A as compared with 74.5 per cent at Winchester (with 136 candidates).

37

'The New Direction'

'To instil in each Radleian a quest for knowledge.'

R ADLEY'S REPUTATION AS a 'games school', which had led to
Oscar Wilde's son being sent there, was at this time more justified than it had been in 1899. Having won all their eleven
school matches in 1990, the First XV lost only one in 1991 (to
Wellington) and four in 1992. In 1995, after a shaky start, the First XV
had another successful season, beating successively Wellington,
Sherborne, Harrow and Rugby. The next year the XV won every
match. The Hockey XI lost only three of their twelve matches in 1992,
five of their fourteen in 1993 and five of their eleven in 1994.

The Cricket First XI was undefeated in 1991, lost but one school
match in 1992, one in 1993 and but one again in 1994, a year which saw
decisive victories over Winchester and Wellington and, in the trophy
named after Warden Silk, over Shrewsbury and Eton. Robin Martin-
Jenkins, the captain, who played for the England under-seventeen
team and then for the public schools against MCC at Lord's, showed
himself to be an exceptionally gifted player. In 1995 the First XI, probably the best since Dexter's of 1953–4, won all their school matches.

The first cross-country teams were undefeated in three successive
years. In athletics Radley beat fourteen other schools in 1993, and in
1994 the javelin and long jump records were both broken. The golf
team won all their matches in 1994, having previously twice won the
West of England Public Schools Championship.

In 1993 the First Tennis VI won all their ten matches (neither the Second nor Third teams were defeated that year) and lost only one match in 1994.

The school's polo team won the Schools Polo Challenge Trophy in 1994, beating Wellington, Bloxham and Millfield who had disposed of Eton in the first round, and the following year they won the competition for the second time, while the sailing team won both the Midlands and the North Area Championships. The 1994–5 rackets season was one of the most successful of the past decade; and two national trophies were won in the public schools' championship at Queens'.

The rowing results were not so gratifying. A new young coach had been brought to the school in 1991 but, while the Warden gave the Boat Club great support – far more so than either of his immediate predecessors – the appointment was not a success and five unsettled years ensued.

As in Dennis Silk's time, however, as much pleasure was taken in the number of boys rowing and playing games as in the matches and races they won. For instance, no fewer than fifteen teams represented the school at cricket, from the First XI to the Midgets' Fifth XI; while the tennis club turned out more teams than any other school in the country.

Gratified as he had good reason to feel by these sporting successes, the Warden was concerned, as previous wardens of Radley and headmasters of other public schools had felt concerned in the past, that the striving for athletic achievement might interfere with the maintenance of academic progress and aesthetic development, that 'bloodism' might once again become a menace to the school's true purposes; and in recent times increased efforts have been made to give academic success greater status within Radley as well as to improve the boys' ability to communicate and articulate fluently and coherently.

An editorial in the 1994 *Radleian* posed the problem that Radley had to face:

At present we are hearing much about the new 'change of direction'. The change in emphasis that is the Warden's plan appears to be an 'academization' of the school at the expense of the importance of sport, which had been steadily becoming more influential in previous years. This influence perhaps was most visible in the manner in which the Captain of Rugby would frequently appear as Senior Prefect while many of the school prefects were among his team-mates . . . It is still the case that some pupils are held in high regard simply for their sporting prowess rather than for any other merit.

The leader writer went on to discuss the new 'academic priority' and its 'flagship' the proposed central library, a facility 'many years overdue', designed to encourage students towards a sense of individual responsibility, to enable them to seek information for themselves away from the classroom and 'to instil in each Radleian a quest for knowledge'.* In the 1995 *Radleian* also the leader writer took up this theme and expressed the hope that the new library would stimulate a 'sense of individual responsibility'. Certainly the Warden and the recently appointed Director of Studies were already working hard to promote the 'New Direction' in which the library was intended to play a vital part.

---

*The New Library, now built in School, was one of a number of developments at Radley initiated in 1995. The estimated cost of these improvements was £4.5 million, £2.5 million being set aside for a new academic building to replace all temporary classrooms, the remaining £1 million being the object of an appeal which was chaired by Michael Martin and which had already raised £600,000 by March 1996. Other improvements proposed were the refurbishment of the ground floor of the House, the reconstruction of the Old Gym and the construction of a second astro-turf pitch in the middle of the Athletics Track. Already by the end of 1995 more money had been spent on general improvements in the preceding two years than in any other similar period in the school's recent history.

38

Threats and Debts

'The public school system is in a very precarious situation.'

THROUGHOUT THE CENTURY the merits of the public school system have been intermittently called into question and the very survival of such schools held to be in doubt. Between the wars a falling birth rate, a heavily taxed middle class, a large reduction in the number of fathers in the services, and a growing reluctance to send children away to school had so severely reduced admissions to several schools that they were forced to face the prospect of bankruptcy. It was suggested in the House of Commons towards the beginning of the Second World War that before long nearly all of them would have to be given financial assistance to avoid closure; and Sir Cyril Norwood, President of St John's College, Oxford, and a former Master of Marlborough and Headmaster of Harrow, proposed the appointment of a Royal Commission to devise means whereby they could be incorporated into the state system.

As the war got under way there were renewed demands that public schools be abolished altogether or that means be found to open them to all boys, regardless of their parents' financial standing. 'The public school system is in a very precarious situation,' wrote Edward C. Mack in his *Public Schools and British Opinion since 1860*, published in 1941.

For the first time in public school history the real danger, a financial one, is from a source beyond the control of either conservatives or radicals . . . But

339

provided that complete ruin does not overwhelm England, the public schools may yet be saved, despite the hatred of their enemies and the disastrous state of their finances . . . The most likely solution – if there is to be one at all – would be one in which the public schools would take state money and accept state interference in order to bring into their ranks the best element of the working class, would reform in the direction of liberal and working-class aims, and yet would remain at least semi-independent boarding schools.

The prognostications of those who foresaw either the demise or the wholesale transformation of the public school system were not, however, to be realized. The Fleming Report on the public schools in 1944 merely recommended that they should accept a quarter of their pupils from the state sector, a proposal which was never implemented, while R.A. Butler's Education Act of the same year left the private sector outside and separate from the state system, subject only to inspection and approval by the Ministry of Education. The post-war Labour Government, led by the Old Haileyburian, Clement Attlee, aware that the general public was more concerned about employment, housing and health than about education, left public schools alone. As the French social historian François Bédarida wrote in his *La Société Anglaise 1851–1975*:

Labour's achievement was a remarkably comprehensive series of measures which had the effect of fixing the shape of British society for years ahead. Some sort of timidity, however, inhibited Labour from laying hands on two institutions, the public schools and the City of London, thus leaving intact two keystones of bourgeois capitalist society, educational separation and big business.

In 1966, after another Labour election victory, a Public Schools Commission was appointed under the chairmanship of Sir John Newsom; but the Commission was essentially intended to fulfil an election promise rather than to formulate policy. Described by the Headmaster of Charterhouse, Oliver Van Oss, as a 'rather muffled flop' which had had 'a uniformly bad press', and by Lord Annan, a member of the Commission, as 'a complete waste of time', the Commission's report was shelved.

So the public schools were free to go on just as before, 'faithful to their traditions and leaving their educational principles unchanged', lording it, as Bédarida put it, 'with imperturbable ease at the summit of the educational system, surviving unshaken all the nation's crises and any outward signs of democratization imposed upon them'.

In 1973, however, the Shadow Education Minister, Roy Hattersley, a sturdy and steadfast critic of the public schools, announced at a conference of preparatory school headmasters that they must be in no doubt of Labour's 'serious intention to reduce and eventually to abolish private education in this country'. Yet when Labour came to power the following year and Roy Hattersley became Minister of State in the Foreign and Commonwealth Office, discussions about the removal of public schools' taxation benefits as registered charities came to nothing. After years of debate, it was announced in March 1992 that the Labour Party had 'removed a key threat to the future of independent schools by softening its line over their charitable status'. At that time over a thousand schools were registered as charities and it was claimed that if their status was changed, fees would have to be raised by 30 per cent and many would be forced to close.

As it was, many schools were owed thousands of pounds in unpaid fees: one was believed to be owed almost £250,000. 'We are facing a problem of bad debts for the first time in our history,' a headmaster reported. 'It is a very hard-hearted headmaster who sends a boy away at the start of term . . . but the time has come when I may have to.' In 1993 Taunton School felt obliged to tell parents that debt collectors would have to be called in if outstanding fees were not paid; in 1995 the authorities at Dean Close School were driven to withhold A level results from two pupils whose parents owed the school £25,000; and at Eton reminders have to be sent to about 10 per cent of parents who fail to pay their bills. At the same time many excellent schools, like Cheltenham, have had to reduce their staff: Ampleforth, for example, was obliged to make six staff redundant in 1991 partly because of falling numbers which were largely attributed to parents wishing to have children educated nearer home.

The demand for boarding places at public schools had been falling for a long time. The Independent Schools Information Service announced in May 1992 that the number of boarders had dropped appreciably for the first time in a decade; in 1993 there was a further drop of over 6 per cent (5,000 in all) and in 1994 yet another fall of over 5 per cent. In that year the total number of boys boarding at independent schools was 60,165 compared with 81,488 in 1985. Martin Vander Weyer, writing in the *Spectator* in September 1993, explained:

In the past, boarding schools were not so much chosen as predestined, sons following fathers . . . Nowadays, mothers tend to control the decision, and the children themselves are often allowed a vote: surveys show that in almost one in five cases the child has had the final say . . .

The result is that many public-school parents no longer want to send their children away, and especially not to the sort of remote, uncomfortable, undistinguished academies they may themselves have endured. Of my own middle-class friends with small children, virtually all are determined to avoid state schools if they possibly can, but only one (an army officer) is determined that his sons should follow precisely in his footsteps. A few others admit to day-dreaming about Eton or Radley.

Sons still follow fathers to Radley more frequently than they do at nearly all other public schools. In 1995, of the 616 boys at the school, 75 were the sons of Old Radleians. The proportion was considerably higher a decade or so ago, one reason being that the standard of entry, while not having gone up, had been enforced so that the less academically gifted sons of Old Radleians who might have been accepted in the 1970s and early 1980s would not now be offered places if they failed to pass the entrance examination. At Eton the number of boys who are the sons of Old Etonians has dropped from about two thirds to approximately one third in the past generation or so. At Harrow the percentage of boys who are the sons of Old Harrovians is 25; thirty years ago it was 35.*

The fall in the numbers of boarders in schools was greeted with widespread approval in the press. It was not a question of money, journalists contended: the Old Harrovian, Duke of Westminster, one of the richest men in England, had chosen to send his children to a day

---

*The number of pupils of some other representative schools in 1995 who are or were the sons or daughters of Old Boys are shown in the table below, the total number of pupils in the school being given in brackets:

Radley	(616)	75	Stonyhurst	(400)	23
Rugby	(700)	c. 70	Dauntsey's	(620)	20
Tonbridge	(660)	46	The Leys	(420)	15
Malvern	(638)	42	Rossall	(420)	12
Sedbergh	(342)	41	Denstone	(302)	10
Fettes	(377)	35	Epsom	(652)	10
Repton	(570)	33	Giggleswick	(301)	7
Glenalmond	(280)	30	Pangbourne	(345)	7
Canford	(504)	27	Ellesmere	(290)	4

school. It reflected a change of attitude. One of those who agreed that the change was for the better wrote in the *Sunday Times* in 1993 of 'a pillar of British life' having 'entered terminal decline', and castigated the 'unthinking reflex of parents seeking the same sort of social initiation for their offspring which they had had'. 'Boarding school, of course, was never about anything so crass as examination success or intellectual superiority. Its whole ethos was geared to what was euphemistically known as "well-roundedness": turning out good chaps who knew how to play the game. It was about not getting things out of proportion, not taking ideas too seriously. It concerned itself with certain virtues, the most fundamental being loyalty and a reverence for friendship ("team spirit").'

A somewhat ambiguous leader in *The Times*, commenting upon the foundation of a support group for Boarding School Survivors, established by a London psychotherapist – incidentally an Old Radleian – to help those who consider themselves 'seriously damaged by the supposed benefits of an expensive education', reminded its readers that from the Renaissance onwards, foreign visitors have remarked on 'the strange native custom of sending ordinary well-behaved children away from home as soon as possible, originally to court or the household of the local magnate, and then to the public schools . . . They usually conclude that the English prefer their animals to their children.'*

Those with experience of boarding spoke up to defend the system. A boarder at Cheltenham Ladies' College, in a letter to *The Times*, which might equally well have come from a boarder in a boys' single-sex school, found it 'hard to believe that learning to be independent, tolerant, patient and considerate, as one must when living in a close-knit community, can be disregarded as "character building". We learn to develop our strengths, both academic and personal, so that ultimately we can benefit the societies in which we live after we leave school . . . Obviously restrictions are imposed on boarders, but these are for our safety and are sometimes fewer than those imposed on us at home . . . The amount of freedom we are allowed increases as we progress within the school.'

Other advocates of the system, including the Headmasters of

---

*A survey of 5,000 parents with children at boarding schools published in 1995 indicated that two thirds of them felt uncomfortable or guilty about parting with them. Others maintained that sending children away to school was an archaic and cruel practice.

Oundle, Repton and Ardingly, questioned the proposition that the philosophy of boarding rested on physical privation and alienation from the family as a means of character-building. 'It would hardly still attract nearly 100,000 pupils if it did. Parents support boarding education because they value the opportunities and facilities offered by a full programme of activities.'

The Chairman of the Boarding Schools Association, Ian Small, Headmaster of Bootham School, York, further emphasized the benefits and indeed, the pleasures of a boarding education:

> Boys and girls in boarding schools have, in most cases nowadays, chosen the boarding option themselves, with the support and encouragement of their parents, of course. They know what they will gain: a sense of worth in a community, a sense of self-confidence and independence, a true sense of participation and being valued, a wealth of enjoyment . . . In my school we offer over 90 different activities each week . . . a busy life, an ability to take charge of their own destinies . . . an ability to shoulder responsibility . . .
>
> I do not think I am making out too idealistic a case for the boarding experience. These are feelings that the pupils themselves have expressed. They also have said that they feel that boarding has enriched the relationship they have with their parents.

Such sentiments have recently been expressed by other headmasters and their pupils.

39

Survival

'The future of independent education is assured.'

FOR ALL THE disparagement that public schools have to face from enemies beyond the gates and from disputatious critics within, they still contrive to provide a very large proportion of the leading men in the country's service and in its political, legal, ecclesiastical and academic élites. In the mid-1960s well over half of all admirals, generals and air chief marshals, of physicians and surgeons at London's teaching hospitals, of Church of England bishops and of judges and Queen's Counsels had been to public school. So had most heads of colleges and professors in English universities. Out of twenty members of Harold Macmillan's Cabinet in 1963, all but three had been at Headmasters' Conference schools, nine of them, including Macmillan himself, at Eton. Two were at Harrow (Keith Joseph and William Deedes), two at Marlborough (Henry Brooke and R.A. Butler), one at Fettes (Macleod), one at Merchant Taylors' (Maudling), one at Oundle (Frederick Erroll) and one (Enoch Powell) at King Edward's, Birmingham.

This ascendancy of men educated at independent schools has been largely maintained in the national life, though not so noticeably in the Anglican Church and in politics. In the Church of England in 1995, only eight of the twenty-three bishops of the older dioceses attended a public school (all five Roman Catholic archbishops did so); and of the twenty-three members of John Major's Cabinet no more than

345

twelve had attended an independent school with boarders. These were Michael Heseltine (Shrewsbury), Malcolm Rifkind (George Watson's College, Edinburgh), John Gummer (King's School, Rochester), Peter Lilley (Dulwich), William Waldegrave (Eton), Ian Lang (Rugby), Sir Patrick Mayhew (Tonbridge), Stephen Dorrell (Uppingham), Lord Cranborne (Eton), Sir George Young (Eton), Douglas Hogg (Eton) and Roger Freeman (Whitgift).

Politics and the Church apart, however, British public schools, in the words of Jeremy Paxman in his *Friends in High Places: Who Rules Britain?* (1990), are 'doing very nicely thank you . . . their status un-diminished'.

> Over forty years after the legislation which opened secondary education to all [Paxman added], the public schools account for seven out of nine of the army's top generals, two thirds of the external directors of the Bank of England, thirty-three of the thirty-nine top English judges, all the ambas-sadors in the fifteen most important overseas missions, seventy-eight of the Queen's eighty-four lord lieutenants . . . Even the bold, thrusting entrepreneurs who have become such folk heroes have failed to cast aside old money: of the two hundred richest people in Britain, thirty-five were educated at a single school, Eton.

The position is much the same today. For every Alan Sugar there is a John Aspinall (Rugby) or a Nigel Broackes or Richard Branson (both Stowe). At the end of 1995, to take a few appointments at random, the Chiefs of the General Staff, the Naval Staff and the Air Staff had all attended well-known public schools; so had nine of the twelve Lords of Appeal in Ordinary – one of them, Lord Jauncey of Tullicettle, was an Old Radleian; the remaining three had been educated either in South Africa or Scotland. The Chairman of the BBC was at Rugby; the man shortly to be his successor was at Sedbergh; the chairmen of both the Arts Council and the British Council were at Eton; so was the Principal Private Secretary at the Foreign and Commonwealth Office whose counterpart in the Prime Minister's Office was at Harrow. The Governor of the Bank of England was at Dulwich, the Director-General of the Secret Intelligence Service at Sherborne, the Secretary of the Cabinet and Head of the Home Civil Service at Harrow, the Head of the Diplomatic Service at Magdalen College School, the Master of the Rolls at Sedbergh.

Yet even the most successful of public schools, with no dearth of applications for places, have had to recognize that parents are far more critical than they used to be and far more capable of assessing value for money.* And the schools themselves have to compete with each other for pupils. Increasingly lavish brochures have to be prepared – some, like Rossall, have videos – a number advertise their benefits in news-papers; others have appointed press officers or public relations con-sultants; many eagerly seek pupils from overseas.† Such efforts have been largely successful.

Although the numbers of boarders in independent schools are falling year by year, the total number of pupils being educated in these schools has remained fairly constant. It was clear that despite the steep increase in fees in a period of recession, parents were prepared to make sacrifices for the sake of small classes, a wide curriculum, sporting and leisure facilities and strong discipline. In 1992 the Independent Schools Information Service recorded a drop in the number of pupils of a mere 0.2 per cent after eight successive years of increase had been recorded in 1991. In 1994 the numbers still remained close to 600,000, and the Secretary of the Headmasters' Conference, Vivian Anthony, who emphasized the importance of the individual attention, often given out of class, to pupils in independent schools, particularly in boarding schools, felt confident that 'the future of independent education [was] assured'. After all, the capital cost to the state of taking over inde-pendent schools was estimated in 1985 at more than £1,500 million, while over £1.2 billion a year is saved for the nation by parents choos-ing such schools. The fees of foreign pupils are estimated to be worth £175 million to the country in foreign currency.

---

*The advertised fees at leading public schools, in fact, vary very little. Of the eighteen schools in the Rugby Group only two charge fees for boarders of less than £12,000 a year. These are Monkton Combe (£11,685) and Repton (£11,604). Two charge more than £13,000 – Winchester (£13,290) and Harrow (£13,425). Radley's fees (£12,300) are slightly less than the average of the remaining fourteen schools. Eton's are £12,888, Westminster's £12,900.

†In 1996 there were about 18,000 pupils from overseas at independent schools in Britain. At Eton there were 93, 20 of them from Hong Kong and 15 from the United States. At Fettes there were 152 in a school population of 486. Of these 43 came from Hong Kong, 20 from Bulgaria, 8 from Germany, 7 from Russia and lesser numbers from a total of 37 countries. At Haileybury in 1986 there were 103 pupils from overseas (22 from Hong Kong), in a school population of 672, as compared with 17 in 1886 (11 of these from India) when the total number of boys in the school was 500. At Gordonstoun 28 per cent of pupils come from abroad from 29 countries. At Harrow, where there were 780 pupils in 1996, 118 were foreign nationals: 28 came from the Far East, 21 from the United States and 32 from various European countries.

40

Past, Present and Future

'It should never be forgotten that Sewell and Singleton founded Radley to be different from other public schools.'

S ATISFACTORY AS RADLEY'S academic status was in the early 1990s, its general reputation had never been higher. In a list of what it described as 'the best independent schools' in the country in 1993, the *Sunday Times* referred to its 'excellent' academic standards, its 'very strong' music department, its 'exceptional' sports facilities. In 1994 – when Radley was again listed by the *Sunday Times* as one of the best independent schools in England – mention was again made of its high academic standards, as well as its 'fine design centre', its sporting achievements, its stress on European languages, its strong music department and its staff–pupil ratio of 1:10. Of the seventeen other schools in the Rugby Group only six – Charterhouse, Harrow, Oundle, Rugby, Shrewsbury and Winchester – were featured in the *Sunday Times*'s list.

In 1995 Radley appeared for the third year running in the *Sunday Times*'s list, the same six schools again being the only others of the Rugby Group to be mentioned. The latest edition of the best of the guides to independent schools, *The Good Schools Guide*, edited by Amanda Alka and Sarah Drummond, also speaks very highly of the school, while commenting that it 'still feels very slightly inward-looking', a fault which the Warden – 'famously outspoken which upsets some parents – appears to be addressing with a will'. According

348

to another schools guide, *The Equitable Schools Book*, Radley 'is one of the most successful of boarding schools for boys and has first-class facilities of all kinds'. A former National Director of the Independent Schools Information Service has expressed the opinion that Radley is now 'one of the four top public schools in the country'.

A Headmasters' Conference report, following an inspection of Radley in April 1995, confirmed the findings of other independent assessments.

> Radley [the HMC report affirmed] is running well and is led by a strong chairman and a vigorous and determined Warden with a clear vision of the College's future needs . . . The academic standards are high . . . The dons are energetic and their dedication is impressive . . . There is an obvious and pleasing rapport between pupils and dons . . . The less highly academic achieve well in this caring ambience . . . Pupils are well groomed and their behaviour is exemplary . . . A willingness by many to serve in the local community and through the new Community Action Programme is impressive . . . The College has a very pleasant atmosphere . . . There is a strong demand for places, and parents are generally happy with the College's philosophy . . .
>
> The College was founded to reform and civilize schooling, placing religious observance and Christian values at the centre of the community . . . The College is following the founder's intentions remarkably closely.

One of the inspectors was so impressed by the school that, having inspected thirty-four others in her professional career, she asked for an entry form for her own son.

*

A visitor to Radley in William Sewell's time thought the boys were 'a superior lot – very – and looked v. happy'. 'Some men object to Radley that it will turn out finicky and effeminate,' he added. 'Whether such will be the case has to be proved. At present the men who come up to Oxford are v. like others.' So, indeed, they have remained. People claim that there are certain recognizable characteristics in Old Etonians as there are, so it is said, in Wykehamists; but there do not appear to be typical Old Radleians, although a liking for each others' company has been observed as a not uncommon trait: the travel writer, Eric Newby, when taken prisoner in Italy during the war, was approached by a fellow officer who pointed out to him a group of other prisoners in close consultation. '"Do you know," this officer said in a voice filled with awe, "this place is filled with people from Radley. It's quite unbelievable but they've formed an Old Radleian Society and they all sit around talking about when they were at school together. There they are. Over there." And sure enough seated on the ground in a corner of the compound there was a ragged little band of Old Radleians, talking about the past.'

Most Old Radleians, as has been observed often enough, are inclined to lead happy and generally fulfilled lives. Professional and other mal-practices are extremely rare. They are for the most part pleasant, like-able men, noted for that kindliness, generosity of spirit and those good manners which visitors to the school have remarked upon generation after generation into our own day. On a return visit to Radley in 1993, Canon Lunt, the Old Etonian former Chief Master of King Edward's School, Birmingham, who sent his own son, Paul, the BBC broad-caster, to Radley, was much impresssed by these pleasant manners. 'Boys smiled at strangers,' he wrote, 'opened doors for them, were pre-pared to enter into conversation: it is a wonderful feature of Radley. I have not met it so beautifully done anywhere else.'

New boys ('stigs') are now informed of this tradition of good manners before entering the school. In a booklet issued for their guid-ance they are advised, under the heading 'Some Tips from Previous New Boys', 'Courtesy *works wonders*. But arrogance will make you very unpopular very quickly. Keep a low profile when you first arrive.'

The politeness and easy manners of Old Radleians was noted as the one common attribute of their kind by the Revd L.R. Phelps, the gregarious Provost of Oriel College in the 1920s who, bestowing upon them a somewhat ambivalent compliment, once remarked, 'I always like to have Radleians here – for dinner parties, you understand.'*

It has often been contended that with this well-mannered sociabil-ity went a lack of competitiveness, of that ambitious striving for success and determination to get to the top of the tree which A.K. Boyd identified as being characteristic of Radleians in the 1930s. It is to be noted, however, that their names now appear far more frequently

---

*It is said that, for rather different reasons, Sir Desmond Morton, the intelligence officer who became Churchill's personal assistant in 1940, liked to recruit for intelligence work Radleians, together with Marlburians and Wykehamists, preferring them to men who had been to Harrow, Westminster, Rugby and his own old school, Eton.

in *Who's Who* than the names of Old Radleians have done in the past. At Appendix 5 is a table, compiled two generations after that drawn up by Boyd, from which it will be seen that, for its size, Radley then produced – and continues to produce – more men considered worthy of inclusion in *Who's Who* than all but a few other schools in the country.

When shown these figures a man who had been a master at Radley for many years commented that, while they certainly did credit to the school, they did not present a full picture, that there were qualities to consider in Old Radleians other than worldly success: 'You may have noticed, for instance, that Oriel College enjoyed a pre-eminence in Oxford college rowing from about 1965. This was the achievement of three Oriel College captains of rowing, all *Third* Eight men from Radley. Consider the pastoral service of these three as they mobilized into the Boat Club lonely freshmen, many of whom, nowadays, will not have been away from home before. Surely they have a worth as eminent as the one or two who get Blues.'*

The Warden often asks prospective parents why they are considering Radley for their sons. The mothers, he says, often reply that the Radleians they have known have been so 'very nice' or that 'we like young men who have been to Radley more than those who have been to other schools.' There is a charm about so many of them, an ease of manner and kindliness of temperament which, the Warden conceded, 'people find attractive'. But the best Radleians, he goes on to say, have 'always been quite steely and competitive under that charm of manner . . . I am trying to harden up the steel without losing that great tradition.' The modern Radleian, he insists, must 'strive not for the ordinary but the extraordinary . . . The key is to give every boy confidence in himself. That confidence stems from doing worthwhile things. As Thoreau wrote, "Not failure, but low aim, is crime."'

A century and a half ago when Radley was founded with such high hopes of becoming, in William Sewell's words, 'an ideal and influential creation', there had seemed little enough chance that the school would survive, let alone that it would flourish. Its growth has not been an easy one; but the ideals of its founders, like Radley's *genius loci* to which so

---

*The captain of the Christ Church First Eight which finally toppled Oriel as Head of the River in 1985 was John Pattisson's son, W.T. Pattisson, who also never rose above the Third Eight at Radley and similarly devoted himself to college rowing at Oxford.

many who have lived here have felt ineluctably drawn, have survived into our own day. 'It should never be forgotten,' the present Warden has said, 'that Sewell and Singleton founded Radley to be different from other public schools. Amongst other ideas, radical in their time, there was to be that emphasis on the individual boy which stemmed from a close relationship with his dons. The hallmark of Radley has been warmth, and that warmth and generosity which, in spite of the changes of 150 years, have remained special and distinctive. That is as it should be and will remain so.'

APPENDIX 1
Who's Who Entries, 1926

The following table, compiled by A.K. Boyd, shows the number of old boys of public schools, per thousand entries, in the 1926 *Who's Who*.

Eton	57
Harrow	19
Winchester	15
Rugby	13
Wellington	12
Clifton	10
Marlborough	10
Charterhouse	9
Cheltenham	9
St Paul's	9
Haileybury	7
Westminster	7
Uppingham	6
Dulwich	5
Manchester Grammar School	5
Merchant Taylors'	5
Malvern	4
Repton	4
Sherborne	4
Shrewsbury	4
Christ's Hospital	3
Radley	3
Rossall	3
Tonbridge	3
Bradfield	2
City of London	2
King's, Canterbury	2
Mill Hill	2
Lancing	1
Oundle	1

APPENDIX 2

University Admissions, 1993–5

Of the 110 Radleians to leave the school in 1993, 99 went on to university; a further 8 who failed to find places made further attempts. Only one boy went straight into employment; the fate of the last two is unknown. In all, places were obtained at 27 universities. The universities which accepted two or more candidates were as follows:

Edinburgh	12	Durham	5
Cambridge	10	Oxford Brookes	5
London	10	Exeter	4
Bristol	8	Birmingham	3
Newcastle	7	Manchester	3
Oxford	7	West of England	2

In 1994 90 per cent of leavers went on to degree courses, 19 per cent of these to Oxford or Cambridge. The number of places won at Oxford and Cambridge during the years 1988–95 are as follows:

1988	34	1992	17
1989	30	1993	17
1990	26	1994	19
1991	19	1995	23

The number of candidates for places at these two universities has been steadily falling: in 1988 there were 60 candidates, in 1995 36. But whereas 56.6 per cent obtained places or offers in 1988, in 1995 61.1 per cent did so.

In all, in 1995 107 Radleians entered higher education. After Oxford and Cambridge the universities which accepted most candidates from Radley were Newcastle (14), Bristol (11), Edinburgh (9), Durham (5), Exeter (4).

APPENDIX 3

Subsequent Occupations

The subsequent occupations of Old Radleians who entered the school in 1930 and 1945 (the 1945 figures are given in brackets, the total of new boys in 1930 being 73 and in 1945, 97) were: Army, 12 (4); family and other businesses, 12 (10); insurance, 7 (6); the law, 6 (7); the consular and colonial services, 6 (1); medicine, 5 (5); engineering, 5 (7); architecture, 4 (1); accountancy, 4 (3); tea or rubber planting, 2 (1); farming, 2 (9); schoolmastering, 2 (4); chemists, 2 (0); the church, 1 (1); journalism, 1 (0); RAF, 1 (0); advertising, 1 (1); stockbroking, 1 (1); art, 1 (1).

Occupations for the post-war intake which were not pursued by any of the 1930 boys are banking, (1); marine biology, (1); hotel management, (1); brewing, (2); Royal Navy, (2); airline pilot, (1); surveying and estate management, (4).

From a study made of the occupations of Old Radleians who left the school in the years 1955, 1965, 1975 and 1985 it appears that 35 became lawyers, 31 went into industry or business, 27 joined the Army (as opposed to 5 who went into the Royal Navy and one into the RAF), 23 became medical pratitioners, 17 accountants, 16 farmers, 15 went into banking and the same number into surveying; 5 became architects. The next most commonly pursued careers were teaching (14), insurance (11), stockbroking (8), engineering (8) and the stage (8).

Of those who left Wellington in the years between 1949 and 1968 – and whose occupations are known – most (636) are listed in the College registers as being in business or commerce, rather more than joined the armed forces, police or merchant navy (569). The next most commonly pursued careers are given as scientists and engineers (224), accountancy (192), farming, forestry, planters, ranchers etc. (157), law (119), education (103), doctors, dentists and veterinary surgeons (96), artists, musicians, actors, authors (72), surveying and architecture (64).

The figures can be compared with those given in a survey made of the occupations – so far as they can be discovered – of Old Etonians who left the school in the years 1967–89. The most commonly pursued careers are given as:

Bankers/financial services	389
Officers in armed services	380
Accountants	369
Lawyers	279
Industrial executives/trainee managers	196
Land agents/surveyors	195
Insurance brokers/underwriters	146
Journalists/publishers	118
Stock Exchange	117
Medical practitioners	82
Entertainment/films	75

Engineers	74
Farmers	71
Schoolmasters/lecturers	66
Advertising/public relations	57
Fine arts/antiques	53
Management/business consultants	49
Retail managers/trainees	45
International trade: import/export	42
Wine merchants	35
Architects/town planners	35
Computer technologists/programmers	34
Musicians	34
Civil and Diplomatic Service	31
Shipping/ship broking	25
Commodity brokers	23
Property developers	20
Community workers	18
Racehorse trainers	15
Actors/theatre directors	14
Interior designers/decorators	14
Priests	11
Political research assistants	11
Artists	9
Photographers	9

Few, if indeed any, schools record such a variety of occupations pursued by former pupils as Eton does. Five years after leaving the school Old Etonians were employed, for instance, as police officer, jockey, carpenter, fireman, lorry driver, missionary, scrap metal merchant, explorer, psychotherapist, stained glass window designer, racing driver, clerk, fashion designer, ghillie, customs officer, flower seller, sculptor, football coach, bell ringer, biochemist and motor-cycle courier.

APPENDIX 4

Provenance of Pupils, 1938/1993

In 1938, of the 401 boys in the school, about two thirds came from London, the Home Counties, southern and south-eastern England, the precise figures being as follows:

Home counties, southern and south-eastern England	208
London	44
The West Country	52
The Midlands	12
The North	42
East Anglia	9
Wales	7
Northern Ireland	2
Scotland	1
Abroad	24

As in 1938, so in 1993, when the numbers in the school had risen to 613, two thirds of the boys came from London, the Home Counties, southern and south-eastern England, 156 of them from Berkshire, Buckinghamshire and Oxfordshire. Proportionately the figures for the rest of the country remained much the same except for a rise in the number of boys living abroad and in Scotland:

Home counties, southern and south-eastern England	301
London	102
The West Country	84
The Midlands	26
The North	19
East Anglia	19
Scotland	11
Wales	4
Northern Ireland	2
Channel Islands	2
Abroad	43

At Eton also most boys come from London (95) and the Home Counties and southern England (419). The proportions of those who came from elsewhere in Britain are again similar to the Radley figures:

The West Country	134
The Midlands	27
The North	41

357

East Anglia	60
Scotland	31
Wales	12
Isle of Man	1
Channel Islands	7

Harrow has traditionally drawn pupils from London and its immediate environs. About one third lived there in the 1880s; about half do so now.

Most independent schools now draw their pupils from a much more circumscribed area than they did in the past, largely no doubt because visits, exeats and half-terms, not important considerations in earlier days, are more easily arranged when schools are close at hand. At Haileybury, for example, in 1886, of the 483 boys living in the British Isles only 18 lived in Hertfordshire; in 1986, 285 of the school's pupils lived in that one county alone. At Bryanston in 1936, when there were 265 boys in the school, only 6 lived in Dorset; now 26 pupils out of 440 do so. The overwhelming majority of the September 1995 intake at the King's School, Canterbury, came from Kent, London and the Home Counties; the remainder (about one fifth) came from abroad, with a single exception. At Westminster 94 per cent of the pupils live in London and the Home Counties. At Denstone only 3 per cent of pupils live south of Birmingham; at Giggleswick less than 30 out of 318; and at Sedbergh no more than 23 out of 342. At Gresham's over 80 per cent of pupils live in the eastern counties.

The record of public schools in Scotland is rather different. At Gordonstoun, for example, 30 per cent of pupils come from England, Wales and Northern Ireland, 42 per cent from Scotland, the rest from overseas (8 per cent of them from Germany).

APPENDIX 5
Who's Who Entries, 1986

Like Boyd's table (see Appendix 1) the table below is based on *Who's Who* entries but, since *Who's Who* is now a far bigger reference work than it was in Boyd's day, the number of entries examined in the volume published sixty years after that used by him was much larger.

The schools listed are the 60 Headmasters' Conference Schools outside London (plus Fettes, Glenalmond, Loretto and Gordonstoun) which take boarders and which appear ten times or more in the 15,000 or so entries examined.

School	Number of pupils in 1956	Number of entries in Who's Who, 1986
1. Eton	1,180	896
2. Winchester	521	277
3. Rugby	720	260
4. Marlborough	782	194
5. Harrow	730	192
6. Wellington	678	190
7. Charterhouse	640	149
8. Stowe	560	123
9. Shrewsbury	530	104
10. Haileybury	550	94
11. Clifton	650	86
12. Christ's Hospital	834	85
13. Sherborne	464	84
14. Oundle	650	82
15. Radley	446	80
16. Cheltenham	450	77
17. Ampleforth	567	71
18. Uppingham	550	69
19. Repton	471	68
20. Sedbergh	410	65
21. Malvern	562	64
22. Bedford	962	63
23. Tonbridge	500	63
24. Fettes	440	62
25. Bradfield	385	57
26. Lancing	408	52
27. Epsom	500	50
28. St Edward's	482	42

29. Blundell's	400	41
30. The Leys	300	40
31. Berkhamsted	755	39
32. Eastbourne	410	39
33. Gresham's	348	38
34. Bryanston	400	37
35. Stonyhurst	310	35
36. Felsted	462	34
37. King's School, Canterbury	685	32
38. Brighton	350	30
39. Rossall	524	29
40. Leighton Park	230	27
41. Loretto	240	26
42. Glenalmond	400	25
43. Pangbourne	370	24
44. Bromsgrove	330	23
45. Cranleigh	422	23
46. Aldenham	360	21
47. Bedales	420	21
48. Canford	408	21
49. Perse School	550	21
50. Bootham	233	20
51. Gordonstoun	412	20
52. Taunton	769	20
53. Monkton Combe	315	17
54. St John's, Leatherhead	333	17
55. Cranbrook	240	15
56. Wrekin	380	15
57. Ardingly	490	14
58. Rydal	280	13
59. Trent	212	12
60. Ellesmere	334	11
61. Oakham	322	11
62. Dean Close	380	10
63. Denstone	312	10
64. Framlingham	500	10

The figures for schools in London are

Westminster	360	126
St Paul's	616	115
Merchant Taylors'	700	81
Dulwich	1,300	74
Mill Hill	400	58
Highgate	640	52
Whitgift	775	49

City of London	800	43
Latymer Upper	1,100	37
King's College School	630	34
Haberdashers' Aske's	1,700	29

BIBLIOGRAPHY

PRIMARY SOURCES

The Radley College Archives contain numerous documents, manuscript letters, reminiscences and diaries relating to the school's history, and to those who have lived and worked here, as well as books, periodicals, prints and photographs, files on Old Radleians, records of societies and clubs, reports and minutes of meetings and committees, punishment books, and confidential memoranda. The following is but a list of some of those items which I have found most useful: The Reminiscences of Dr William Sewell; the Journal of the Revd Robert Corbet Singleton; 'Notes and Remarks on Mr Singleton's Journal', Samuel Harvey Reynolds; the Recollections of the Revd Arthur Sewell; the Diary of the Revd William Wood; Memorandum of Mrs Emma Wood; the Diary of the Revd George Wharton; the letters of J.A. Godley, Lord Kilbracken, the Talbot family, Norman Whatley, C.E. Cotter, F.E. Stone and Francis Storrs; the diaries of M.A.A. Blake and John Ashby Rolls; and the reminiscences of Ernest Bryans, C.E.J. Freer, Canon W.H. Ferguson, Mrs A.A.M. Gardiner, Stephen and Agnes Paton, Christopher St J. Ellis, Kenneth Brookman, Robin Miller, the Revd John Livingstone, Alex Bowlby, Richard Blencowe, and Patrick Mullins.

D.J.V. Hamilton-Miller, 'The Feud: The Internal Disturbances which took place at Radley during the Lent Term of 1918'; 'The Autobiography of the Revd A.C. Nugee'; 'An O.R. Looks at Radley' [the paper read to the D.S.C. by A.K. Boyd, 13 July 1933]; Norman Whatley's comments on and amendments to A.K. Boyd's *History*; V. Hope's comments on and amendments to Boyd's *History*; J.C.V. Wilkes, 'Confessions of a Lotus Eater'; J.C.V. Wilkes, 'Rambling Reminiscences of Radley, 1937–1954'; J.C.V. Wilkes, 'Eastbourne and Radley, 1940–1945'; Robert Cyril Storrs, 'Eastbourne College in Exile'; 'Eastbourne at Radley, 1940–1945' [the reminiscences of Old Eastbournians and members of Eastbourne's staff]; Paul Crowson, 'Three Just Men: Radley College, 1947–1974'; Paul Crowson, 'A Postscript to "Three Just Men": Radley College, 1974"'; David Rae Smith, 'Some Notes about the Radley College Council'.

SECONDARY SOURCES

Adamson, J.W., *English Education 1798–1902* (1930)
Ainger, Arthur Campbell, *Eton Sixty Years Ago* (1917)
Allom, V.M., *Ex Oriente Salus: A Centenary History of Eastbourne College* (1967)
Annan, Noel, *Roxburgh of Stowe: The Life of J.F. Roxburgh and his Influence on Public Schools* (1965)
Argent, Nigel, *Ardingly College 1939–1990* (1991)

Bibliography

Atha, Amanda, see *Good Schools Guide*

Badley, J.H., *Bedales* (1923)

Baker, Derek, *Partnership in Excellence: The Leys School, Cambridge, 1875–1975* (1975)

Bamford, T.W., *The Rise of the Public School* (1976)

——*Thomas Arnold* (1960)

Barber, John, *The Story of Oakham School* (1983)

Barnard, H.C., *A History of English Education from 1760* (1970)

Barnett, Correlli, *The Collapse of British Power* (1972)

Bédarida, François, *A Social History of England, 1851–1975* (1976)

Beddoes, V.R.M., *A Memoir of the Revd George Wharton: Precentor of St Peter's College, Radley* (1931)

Bentley, James, *Dare to be Wise: A History of the Manchester Grammar School* (1991)

Betjeman, John, *Summoned by Bells* (1960)

Birt, Dom Henry Norbert, *The History of Downside School* (1902)

Blackie, John, *Bradfield, 1850–1975* (1976)

Blumenau, Ralph, *A History of Malvern College, 1865–1965* (1965)

Blunden, Edmund, *Christ's Hospital* (1928)

Bourne, Jeremy, *Seventy Years at Bromsgrove School* (1993)

Boyd, A.K., *The History of Radley College, 1847–1947* (1948)

Bradby, Henry Christopher, *Rugby* (1906)

Bradstreet, John, *Repton Sketches* (1928)

Brenan, Gerald, *Personal Record 1820–1972* (1974)

Brereton, Henry, *Gordonstoun: Ancient Estate and Modern School* (1968)

Briggs, Asa, 'Thomas Hughes and the Public Schools' in *Victorian People* (1956)

Brown, Sidney K., *Bootham School* (1973)

Brown, S.W., *Leighton Park: A History of the School* (1952)

Bryans, Ernest, *A History of St Peter's College, Radley, being a Continuation of the Revd T.D. Raikes's 'Fifty Years of Radley'* (1925)

Butler, Samuel, *Life and Letters of Dr Samuel Butler* (2 vols., 1896)

Card, Tim, *Eton Renewed: A History from 1860 to the Present Day* (1994)

Carleton, John D., *Westminster School* (1965)

Chandos, John, *Boys Together: English Public Schools 1800–1864* (1984)

Cherniavsky, M.T. (with A.E. Money), *Looking at Radley: An Architectural and Historical Survey of the Earlier Buildings* (1981)

Clark, Kenneth, *Another Part of the Wood* (1974)

Clarke, A.W., *Jasper Tristram* (1899)

Clarke, Henry Lowther & W.N. Weech, *History of Sedbergh School, 1525–1925* (1925)

Coleman, Richard (ed.), *Leighton Park: The First Hundred Years* (1990)

Connolly, Cyril, *Enemies of Promise* (1938)

Coulton, G.G., *A Victorian Schoolmaster: Henry Hart of Sedbergh* (1923)

Cowie, Leonard & Evelyn, *That One Idea: Nathaniel Woodard and His Schools* (1991)

Craig, Patricia (ed.), *The Oxford Book of Schooldays* (1994)

Craze, M.R., *A History of Felsted School 1564–1947* (1955)

Croom Johnson, R.P., *The Origin of Stowe School* (1953)

Dancy, J.C., *The Public Schools and the Future* (1963)

Danziger, Danny (ed.), *Eton Voices* (1988)

Bibliography

Darwin, Bernard, *The English Public School* (1929)

Devlin, Tim & Hywel Williams, *Old School Ties* (1992)

Dilke, Christopher, *Dr Moberly's Mint-Mark: A Study of Winchester College* (1965)

Douglas-Smith, A.E., *The City of London School* (1937)

Drummond, Sarah, see *Good Schools Guide*

Eason, R.E., *1902–1978: A Tapestry of Facts and Memories* (1979)

Edwards, D., *A History of the King's School, Canterbury* (1957)

Equitable Schools Book, ed. Klaus Boehm & Jenny Lees-Spalding (1994)

Evers, C.R., *Rugby* (1939)

Field, John, *The King's Nurseries: The Story of Westminster School* (1987)

Firth, J. d'E., *Winchester College* (1949)

Fisher, G.W., *Annals of Shrewsbury School* (1899)

Flower, Raymond, *Oundle and the English Public School* (1989)

Fox, A.D., *Follow Up! The Story of a Commonplace Harrovian* (n.d.)

Fraser, George Macdonald (ed.), *The World of the Public School* (1977)

Furness, W. (ed.), *Centenary History of Rossall School* (1945)

Gardner, Brian, *The Public Schools* (1973)

Gathorne-Hardy, Jonathan, *The Public School Phenomenon* (1977)

Gaunt, H.C.A., *Two Exiles: Being a Record of the Adventures of Malvern College During the War* (1946)

Good Schools Guide, ed. Amanda Atha & Sarah Drummond

Goodrich, Harold S., *Thomas Field, D.D. A Memoir* (1907)

Goulay, A.B., *A History of Sherborne School* (1951)

Graham, Edward, *The Harrow Life of Montagu Butler* (1920)

Graves, Robert, *Goodbye to All That* (1929)

Greene, Graham (ed.), *The Old School* (1934)

Hall, P.A., *Fifty Years of Ellesmere* (1934)

Handford, Basil, *Lancing College: History and Memoirs* (1986)

Harries, Gillian E.B., see *Independent Schools Year Book*

Harrow School Register, 1885–1949, ed. James W. Moir (1951)

Harrow School Register, 1971, ed. L.J. Verney (1971)

Harvey, A.D., 'A.W. Clarke's *Jasper Tristram* and Autobiography', *London Magazine*, June/July 1994, 76–81

Heeney, Brian, *Mission to the Middle Classes: The Woodard Schools, 1848–1891* (1969)

Heffernan, Dorothy A., *Sir George Bowyer* (1983)

Heward, Christine, *Making a Man of Him: Parents and their Sons' Education at an English Public School 1929–50* (1988)

Hibbert, F.A., *Chapters in Denstone History* (1897)

Hickson, Alisdare, *The Poisoned Bowl: Sex, Repression and the Public School System* (1995)

Hill, R.D., *A History of St Edward's School, 1863–1963* (1962)

Hillier, Bevis, *Young Betjeman* (1988)

Hinde, Thomas, *Highgate School: A History* (1993)

——*Imps of Promise: A History of the King's School, Canterbury* (1990)

——*Paths of Progress: A History of Marlborough College* (1972)

Holden, W.H. (ed.), *The Charterhouse We Knew* (1950)

Holland, Vyvyan, *Son of Oscar Wilde* (1954)

Hollis, Christopher, *Eton* (1960)

Honey, J.R. de S., *Tom Brown's Universe: The Development of the Victorian Public School* (1977)

Hope, V., 'The Architect of Radley Hall', *Country Life*, 27 January 1950

Horne, Alistair, *A Bundle from Britain* (1993)

How, F.D., *Six Great Schoolmasters* (1904)

Howarth, T.E.B., *Culture, Anarchy and the Public Schools* (1969)

Icely, H.E.M., *Bromsgrove School through Four Centuries* (1953)

Independent Schools Year Book, 1994–5, ed. Gillian E.B. Harries

Inglis, Brian (ed.), *John Bull's Schooldays* (1961)

James, Lionel, *A Forgotten Genius: Sewell of St Columba's and Radley* (1945)

James, Norman G.B., *History of Mill Hill* (1909)

Jameson, E.M., *Charterhouse* (1937)

Jones, M.D.W., *Brighton College, 1845–1995* (1995)

Kalton, Graham, *The Public Schools: A Factual Survey* (1966)

Kilbracken, Lord, *The Reminiscences of Lord Kilbracken* (1931)

Kirk, K.E., *The Story of the Woodard Schools* (new edn. 1952)

Laborde, E.D., *Harrow School: Yesterday and Today* (1948)

Lace, A.F., *A Goodly Heritage* (1968)

Lambert, Royston & Spencer Millham, *The Hothouse Society: An Exploration of Boarding School Life through the Boys' and Girls' own Writing* (1968)

——& John Hipkin & Susan Stagg, *New Wine in Old Bottles? Studies in Integration within the Public Schools* (1968)

Latymer, Lord, *Chances and Changes* (1931)

Leach, A.F., *History of Bradfield College* (1900)

——*A History of Winchester College* (1899)

Leach, Colin, *A School at Shrewsbury: The Four Foundations* (1990)

Leys School Handbook and Directory (20th edn.), ed. M.F. Howard & G.C. Houghton (1991)

Linnell, C.L.S., *History and Register of Gresham's School, 1555–1954*

Lowerson, John, *Sport and the English Middle Classes, 1870–1914* (1993)

Lyte, H.C. Maxwell, *A History of Eton* (4th edn. 1911)

McConnell, J.D.R., *Eton, How it works* (1967)

Macdonald, Alec, *A Short History of Repton* (1929)

Mack, Edward C., *Public Schools and British Opinion, 1780–1860* (1938)

——*Public Schools and British Opinion since 1860* (1941)

Mais, S.P.B., *Caper Sauce* (1952)

Malvern College Register (3rd Supplement, 1977), ed. M.A. Staniforth (1977)

Mangan, J.A., *Athleticism in Victorian and Edwardian Public Schools* (1981)

Marlborough College Register, 1843–1952, ed. L. Warwick James (1952)

Marlow, Louis, *The Puppets' Dallying* (1905)

——*Swan's Milk* (1934)

Matthews, Bryan, *By God's Grace: A History of Uppingham School* (1984)

Mead, A.H., *A Miraculous Draft of Fishes* (1990)

Money, A.E., see s.v. Cherniavsky

Money, John, *The Impresario* (1959)

Morgan, M.C., *Bryanston, 1928–78* (1978)
——*Cheltenham College: The First Hundred Years* (1968)
Motion, Andrew, *The Pale Companion* (1989)
Muir, T.E., *Stonyhurst College, 1593–1993* (1992)
Newsome, David, *A History of Wellington College, 1859–1959* (1959)
——*Goodliness and Good Learning* (1961)
Ogilvie, R.M., *Latin and Greek: A History of the Influence of the Classics on English Life from 1600 to 1918* (1964)
Ogilvie, Vivian, *The English Public School* (1957)
Oldham, J. Basil, *Headmasters of Shrewsbury School, 1552–1952* (1952)
——*A History of Shrewsbury School, 1552–1952* (1952)
Olive, Geo. W., *A School's Adventure* (1951)
Oliver, William, *Rough Notes and Reminiscences* (1879)
Ollard, Richard, *An English Education: A Perspective of Eton* (1982)
Orchard, Barry, *A Look at the Head and the Fifty: A History of Tonbridge School* (n.d.)
Parkin, G.R., *Edward Thring: Life and Letters* (1898)
Paston, J. Lewis, *The English Public Schools* (1905)
Paxman, Jeremy, *Friends in High Places: Who Runs Britain?* (1990)
Pearce, Tim, *Then and Now: An Anniversary Celebration of Cheltenham College, 1841–1991* (1991)
Percival, Alicia C., *The Origins of the Headmasters' Conference* (1969)
——*Very Superior Men: Some Early Public-School Headmasters and their Achievements* (1973)
Percy, F.H.G., *Whitgift School: A History* (1972)
Perkin, Harold, *The Rise of Professional Society: England since 1880* (1989)
Perry, R., *Ardingly 1858–1946: A History of the School* (1951)
Peterson, A.D.C., *A Hundred Years of Education* (1952)
Public Schools from Within: A Collection of Essays written chiefly by Schoolmasters (1906)
Quick, Anthony, *Charterhouse: A History of the School* (1990)
Quigly, Isabel, *The Heirs of Tom Brown: The English School Story* (1984)
Rae, John, *Delusions of Grandeur: A Headmaster's Life, 1966–86* (1993)
——*The Public School Revolution: Britain's Independent Schools, 1964–79* (1980)
Raikes, T.D., *Sicut Columbae: Fifty Years of St Peter's College, Radley* (1897)
Rathbone, Michael, *Canford School, 1923–1983* (1983)
Rawnsley, H.D., *Edward Thring, Teacher and Poet* (1889)
Rodgers, John, *The Old Public Schools of England* (1938)
Rubinstein, W.D., *Capitalism, Culture and Decline in Britain, 1750–1990* (1993)
——'Education and the Social Origins of British Elites, 1880–1970', *Past and Present* (No. 112), 163–207
——*Men of Property: The Very Wealthy in Britain since the Industrial Revolution* (1981)
——*Wealth and Inequality in Britain* (1986)
——(ed.), *Wealth and the Wealthy in the Modern World* (1980)
Sabben-Clare, J.P., *Winchester College* (1981)
St Peter's College, Radley Register, 1847–1962, ed. R.W. Robertson (1965)
St Quintin, G., *The History of Glenalmond* (1956)

Bibliography

Salmon, Michael, *Epsom College: The First 125 Years* (1980)

Sampson, Anthony, *The Essential Anatomy of Britain: Democracy in Crisis* (1992)

Scott, Michael, *A Modern Tom Brown's Schooldays* (1937)

Sergeaunt, John & Ernest Hockliffe, *A History of Bedford School* (1925)

Sewell, William, *Journal of a Residence at St Columba's* (2nd edn. 1848)

——*Sermons for Boys preached in the Chapel of St Peter's College, Radley* (1859)

——*A Speech at the Dinner of Old Radleians by the Founder, William Sewell* (1873)

——*A Year's Sermons to Boys preached in the Chapel of St Peter's College, Radley* (1854)

Simon, Brian & Ian Bradley (eds.), *The Victorian Public School* (1975)

Simpson, J.R. Hope, *Rugby Since Arnold: A History of Rugby School from 1842* (1967)

Skrine, J.H., *A Memory of Edward Thring* (1889)

Smith, Brian S., *A History of Bloxham School* (1978)

Snow, G., *The Public School in a New Age* (1959)

Stanley, Arthur Penrhyn, *Life and Correspondence of Dr Arnold* (1844)

Stewart, Frank, *Loretto One-Fifty: The Story of Loretto School from 1827 to 1977* (1981)

Strong, Douglas [D.B. Cancellor], *Young England* (1919)

Tanner, Lawrence F., *Westminster School: A History* (1934)

Thomas, Imogen, *Haileybury, 1806–1987* (1987)

Thornton, P.M., *Harrow School and its Surroundings* (1885)

Tod, Alexander Hay, *Charterhouse* (1900)

Trott, Anthony, *No Place for Fop or Idler: The Story of King Edward's School, Birmingham* (1992)

Turner, E.S., *Boys will be Boys* (new edn. 1957)

Vachell, H.A., *The Hill: A Romance of Friendship* (1905)

Wake, Roy & Pennie Denton, *Bedales School: The First Hundred Years* (1993)

Wakeford, John, *The Cloistered Elite: A Sociological Analysis of the English Public Boarding School* (1969)

Walker, W.G., *History of the Oundle Schools* (1956)

Walters, D.J., *Bromsgrove in Exile* (1971)

Waugh, Alec, *Public School Life* (1922)

Webb, Barry, 'Radley: A View from Inside', *Listener*, 27 March 1980

Wells, H.G., *The Story of a Great Schoolmaster* (1924)

West, J.M., *Shrewsbury* (1937)

Wheen, Francis, *Tom Driberg: His Life and Indiscretions* (1990)

Whitehouse, J.H. (ed.), *The English Public School: A Symposium* (1919)

Whitridge, Arnold, *Dr Arnold of Rugby* (1929)

Wiener, Martin J., *English Culture and the Decline of the Industrial Spirit, 1850–1980* (1981)

Wilkins, Harold T., *Great English Schools* (1925)

Wilmot, E.P.E., *Charterhouse Old and New* (1895)

Wilson, John, *Public Schools and Private Practice* (1962)

Winchester College, 1836–1909: A Register, ed. J.B. Wainewright (1907)

Winterbottom, Derek, *Clifton after Perceval: A Public School in the Twentieth Century* (1990)

Woodgate, W.B., *Reminiscences of an Old Sportsman* (1909)

Bibliography

Woodruff, C.E. & H.J. Cape, *Schola Regia Cantuariensis: A History of . . . the King's School* (1908)

Worsley, T.C., *Barbarians and Philistines: Democracy and the Public Schools* (1940)

Wright, Donald (ed.), *Walter Hamilton: A Portrait* (1992)

Wymer, N.G., *Dr Arnold of Rugby* (1953)

Index

The Radley Wardenships are entered in chronological, not alphabetical, order.